CW01668603

Old Houses and Cottages of Kent

By the same author

WINDMILLS OF ENGLAND
ENGLISH FARMHOUSES
THE ENGLISH COUNTRY COTTAGE
TIMBER-FRAMED BUILDINGS OF ENGLAND

Old Houses and Cottages of Kent

R.J. BROWN

ROBERT HALE · LONDON

© *R.J. Brown 1994*
First published in Great Britain 1994

ISBN 0 7090 4342 2

Robert Hale Limited
Clerkenwell House
Clerkenwell Green
London EC1R 0HT

The right of R.J. Brown
to be identified as author of this work has been asserted
by him in accordance with the Copyright, Designs and
Patents Act 1988

2 4 6 8 10 9 7 5 3 1

Photoset in Plantin by
Derek Doyle & Associates, Mold, Clwyd
Printed in Great Britain by
St Edmundsbury Press, Bury St Edmunds, Suffolk
Bound by WBC Limited, Bridgend, Mid-Glamorgan.

Contents

Illustrations

Acknowledgements

In the preparation of this book I am greatly indebted to all the writers mentioned in the Bibliography, whose research over numerous years has made the task possible. In particular I would like to acknowledge the help given to me by John Newman's two volumes in *The Buildings of England* series – *North East and East Kent* and *West Kent and the Weald* – in guiding me to the numerous houses of interest within the county. In addition I would like to acknowledge the help given by the numerous articles by E.W. Parkin, S.E. Rigold and Eric Swain published in the county magazine *Archaeologia Cantiana* and elsewhere. Three other books have in particular helped me: first Eric Swain's book *William Twopeny in Kent*, which includes a collection of drawings by William Twopeny from the first half of the nineteenth century, next Kenneth Gravett's *Timber and Brick Building in Kent*, which includes part of the J. Fremlyn Streatfeild Collection, a collection of over a hundred drawings by various artists from the second half of the nineteenth century, and thirdly Davie and Dawber's *Old Cottages and Farmhouses in Kent and Sussex*, published in 1906 with photographs taken at the turn of the century. Many of the houses illustrated in these three books have been included in my book and it is of interest to compare them.

I would also like to express my sincere appreciation of the courtesy, assistance and interest shown to me by the owners of the houses I have visited, recorded and included within this book. I would point out that the majority of these houses are privately owned and not open to the public, and I would request that their owners' privacy be observed. The majority of the houses can be viewed from the public highway.

Finally, I would like to thank my wife for her continuing encouragement and assistance through the years and in particular for correcting and typing the draft; and also my sons David and Peter from whose photographs the drawings were made.

R.J.B.

Glossary

ARCADE. The structural members – posts and braces – which form the lateral division between the main span and its aisles.

ARCADE-PLATE. A horizontal member supported by the arcade-posts, tying them together and carrying the feet of the rafters of both the main and aisle roofs.

ARCADE-POST. A vertical member, forming part of the arcade and supporting the arcade-plate.

ARCHITRAVE. The lowest member of an entablature, often adopted as a moulding around an opening in a wall such as a door, window, etc.

BALUSTER. A vertical member supporting the handrail.

BARGEBOARD. A timber board, sometimes carved, fixed at the gable end and following the slope of the roof to mask the ends of the horizontal roof timbers.

BATTEN. A small strip of wood used horizontally to hang or attach tiles, slates, etc.

BOLECTION MOULDING. A raised moulding of bold outline of double curvature.

BOND. The regular arrangement of bricks or stones in order to avoid a continuous vertical joint and so increasing the strength of the wall.

BOSS. A projecting ornament, either square or round, covering the intersection of the ribs in a panelled ceiling or roof.

BRACE. A diagonal timber, either straight or curved, to strengthen framework.

CAMES. Grooved bars of lead for joining small pieces of glass into a larger sheet.

CAP, CAPITAL. The ornamental expanded top of a post or pillar designed to receive an arched superstructure as in a crown-post.

CASEMENT. A window, of either metal or wood, which is hinged on one side, so opening inwards or outwards.

CATSLIDE ROOF. A roof having the main slope extending uninterruptedly over an extension.

CHAMFER. A splay, usually forty-five degrees, formed when the arris is cut away.

CLADDING. A material which covers the external face of the building but is not structural.

CLOSER. A small brick – a half-header – used to complete the bonding pattern at the return of the wall or at a jamb.

COLLAR, COLLAR BEAM. A horizontal timber placed above wall-plate level, spanning between and tying together a pair of rafters.

CONSOLE. A decorative bracket, usually in the form of an 'S'.

CORBEL. A projection of stone or timber from the face of the wall for the support of a superincumbent weight.

COVE. A concave surface set at an angle, generally between vertical and horizontal surfaces.

CROSS-WING. A range at the end of and set at right angles to the main range of a house.

CUSP. The projecting points separating the foils in tracery.

DAMP-PROOF COURSE. A horizontal layer of impervious material inserted in a wall to prevent rising damp.

DENTILS. Small projecting rectangular blocks giving a tooth-like appearance, used as a decoration on cornices.

DIAPER. An all-over pattern of diamond, square or lozenge shapes generally used in brickwork and formed with bricks of two colours.

DORMER. A window projecting vertically from a sloping roof and having a roof of its own.

EAVES. The horizontal overhang of a roof projecting beyond the face of a wall.

ENTABLATURE. In Classical architecture the horizontal part, generally consisting of architrave, frieze and cornice supported on columns or pilasters.

FASCIA. A horizontal board to conceal the ends of floor joists in jetty construction and the ends of rafters etc. at roof level.

FENESTRATION. The arrangement of windows on the elevation of the external wall.

FIELDED PANEL. A panel with recessed and bevelled margins.

FOILED. In Gothic architecture, cut into circles which may be grouped together in threes (trefoiled), fours (quatrefoiled), fives (cinquefoiled), etc.

GABLE. The vertical triangular wall at the end of the roof; also applies to the wall at the end of a ridged roof.

GALLETING. The use of pebbles or chips of stone inserted into the mortar courses generally for decoration but sometimes, when the mortar joints are large, for strength.

GAUGE. The part of a roofing-slate or tile which is exposed to view.

HEADER. A brick or stone so laid that only its end appears on the wall-face.

HERRINGBONE. Stones, bricks or tiles laid diagonally and sloping in opposite directions to form a zigzag pattern.

HIP. The sloping external intersection of two inclined roof surfaces.

HOOD-MOULD. A projecting moulding over a door, window or other opening.

INGLENOOK. The area under a large chimney or firehood.

JAMB. The vertical side of an opening for a door or window in a wall.

JETTY. The projection of an upper floor beyond the storey below on a timber-framed house.

JOIST. One of several horizontal parallel timbers laid between walls or beams to carry flooring.

JOWL. The enlarged head of a timber post to carry a tie-beam.

KEYSTONE. The central stone of an arch.

KNEELER. A corbel stone at the bottom of a gable parapet or coping.

LATH. A thin, narrow strip of wood used to provide a backing for plaster.

LIGHT. The vertical opening of a window framed by mullions and/or jambs.

LINTEL. A horizontal timber, stone or concrete beam spanning an opening.

MORTAR. The material used in bedding, jointing and pointing one brick or stone with another.

MORTISE. A socket cut in a piece of wood to receive a tenon.

MULLION. A vertical structural member subdividing a window.

NEWEL STAIR. A spiral stair with steps framed into a central vertical post.

NOGGING. Brick used in the filling of panels between timber studwork.

OUTSHUT. An extension of a building under a lean-to roof.

OVOLO MOULDING. A moulding of Classical origin forming a quarter-round or semi-ellipse in section.

PEDIMENT. A gable of low pitch, straight sided or curved above a door, window, etc.

PILASTER. A shallow pier attached to the wall, usually having a base, shaft and capital to comply with one of the Classical orders.

PLATBAND. A horizontal plain projecting band of masonry or brickwork as distinct from a moulded string course.

PLINTH. The projecting base of a wall, often with a splayed top.

POINTING. The exposed face of a joint of brickwork or stonework which is smoothed with the point of a trowel.

PURLIN. In roof construction, a longitudinal horizontal timber supporting the common rafters.

QUOIN. Dressed stones or distinctive brickwork at the external angle of a wall.

RAFTER. One of several inclined timbers supporting the roof covering.

RANDOM. Not laid in courses.

RENDERING. Cement or lime-plaster covering to the external face of a wall.

REVEAL. The side wall of an opening or recess which is at right angles to the face of the main wall.

RIDGE. The apex of a roof, the ridge-piece being the horizontal longitudinal timber supporting the tops of the rafters.

RISER. Of a staircase, the vertical member of a step.

RUBBLE. Unsquared and undressed stone.

SASH. A glazed wooden window which slides up and down by means of a pulley.

SHUTTERS. Timber boards between which semi-liquid material can be poured for building a wall.

SOFFIT. The underside of a lintel, beam or arch.

SOLAR. The principal chamber, usually at the upper end of the hall, in a medieval house.

SPANDREL. The space between the curved or shaped head of an opening and a rectangular outer frame; the space between the curved brace and a tie-beam.

SPERE. A wall usually at the lower end of the open hall and projecting from one or both sides of the hall to screen the entrances.

SPERE-TRUSS. A roof truss, with below the tie-beam two speres leaving a wide central opening into the hall from the screens passage.

STOP. The feature at the end of a moulding or chamfer to transfer the member to a square section.

STRAPWORK. Flat interlaced decoration derived from strips of cut leather, popular in the Tudor period.

STRETCHER. A brick or stone so laid that only its long side appears on the wall-face.

STRING. Of a staircase, the raking side-member carrying the treads and risers. The treads and risers are housed in the closed string; in the open string the string is cut to the profile of the treads and risers.

STRING-COURSE. A projecting horizontal band or moulding on the external face of a wall.

STRUT. In roof construction, a vertical or diagonal timber which does not support a longitudinal member.

STUDS. The vertical members of a timber-faced house between the main posts.

SWAG. An ornamental festoon of foliage etc. which is fastened up at both ends and hangs down in the centre.

TENON. The end of a piece of wood reduced in width in order to fit into a mortise of another piece of wood, thus making a joint.

TIE-BEAM. In roof construction, the main horizontal timber of a truss joining together the feet of the principal rafters at the wall-plate.

TORCHING. The filling-in with lime-and-hair mortar of the uneven space between the underside of tiles or slates on an unboarded or unfelted roof.

TRACERY. The decorative pattern at the head of a Gothic window or opening, generally formed by the interlacing extension of the mullions.

TRANSOM. A horizontal structural member subdividing a window.

TREAD. Of a staircase, the horizontal member of a step.

TRUSS. A rigid framework spanning the building used to support the ridge, purlins, etc. that carries the common rafters.

UNDERBUILT. A wall added beneath a jetty.

VALLEY. The sloping internal junction of two inclined roof surfaces.

VENETIAN WINDOW. A window with three openings, the centre one arched and wider than the others.

WALL-PLATE. A horizontal timber member at the top of the wall to receive the ends of the rafters, tie-beams, etc.

WINDBRACE. A timber member, often curved and set diagonally between the principal rafters and the side purlins to increase resistance to wind pressure and stiffen the roof structure longitudinally.

WINDER STAIR. A stair turning continuously.

YOKE. A short horizontal timber joining the rafters together near the apex of the roof, often supporting a ridge.

Introduction

Apart from Greater London, Kent possesses more historic buildings than any other county in England. Of the 25,000 or so historic buildings in the county, about two-thirds have been classified as of architectural or historical importance. A large proportion of these buildings are relatively small houses built for former farmers, merchants and traders.

This book is about these smaller houses for, although many of the fine country houses have been fully described in articles and architectural books, little has been written concerning the majority of houses within the county. It is, however, these houses, built by local craftsmen from local materials, which reflect the nature of the county and the living conditions of the inhabitants brought about by the economic and social background of the area. Unlike the big houses, these smaller houses were not designed by architects. Some of the larger houses, for instance Penshurst Place, Knole and Ightham Mote, have been included, for they all started life, although on a grander scale, with the traditional medieval concept of an open hall flanked at one end by a solar wing and at the other by the service wing and only in later years enlarged to their present size. The period covered by the book extends from the thirteenth century until the middle of the nineteenth century, when the mass production of building materials coupled with the development of a more reliable transport system – canals and railways – enabled the distribution of these materials to most parts of the county and so eventually severely curtailed the use of local materials, thus influencing local styles.

1

Geology and Materials

The use of local materials in Kent can clearly be seen in so many of the old houses and cottages, their variety clearly reflecting the somewhat complex geology of the county.

Apart from the Tertiary and Pleistocene clays and sands which extend across most of north Kent from Cliffe Marshes on the Thames Estuary to Sandwich Bay (including the Isle of Sheppey but excluding parts of the Isle of Thanet), Kent belongs entirely to the Cretaceous period. This period lasted for some 70 million years, from about 135 million years to about 65 million years ago. These Cretaceous rocks were deposited in water; the rocks of the High Weald, known as the Hastings Beds, were deposited in a large internal lake. This period was followed by the so-called Upper Cretaceous period, when the whole region was again flooded, this time by the sea, with the succeeding deposits being the rocks of the Lower Greensand, the Gault, the Upper Greensand and the Chalk.

Building Stones

The building stones of Kent are from three of these strata – the sandstones of the Hastings Bed, the Lower Greensand and the Chalk of the North Downs – which run in approximately parallel bands eastwards across the county.

The largest of these bands is the Chalk of the North Downs, which stretches from Surrey eastwards, passing north of the towns of Sevenoaks, Maidstone and Ashford, to the cliffs of Dover and the South Foreland, with an outlier in the Isle of Thanet culminating in the North Foreland. Unlike similar chalk areas in the country, chalk was not widely used as a building stone in Kent, because it was generally too porous, although in some areas, particularly at the foot of the Downs, it can be found. In Kent its primary use was for quoins, which can be seen on a number of Norman churches, and for bonding flint walls; it is sometimes found in the construction of medieval vault

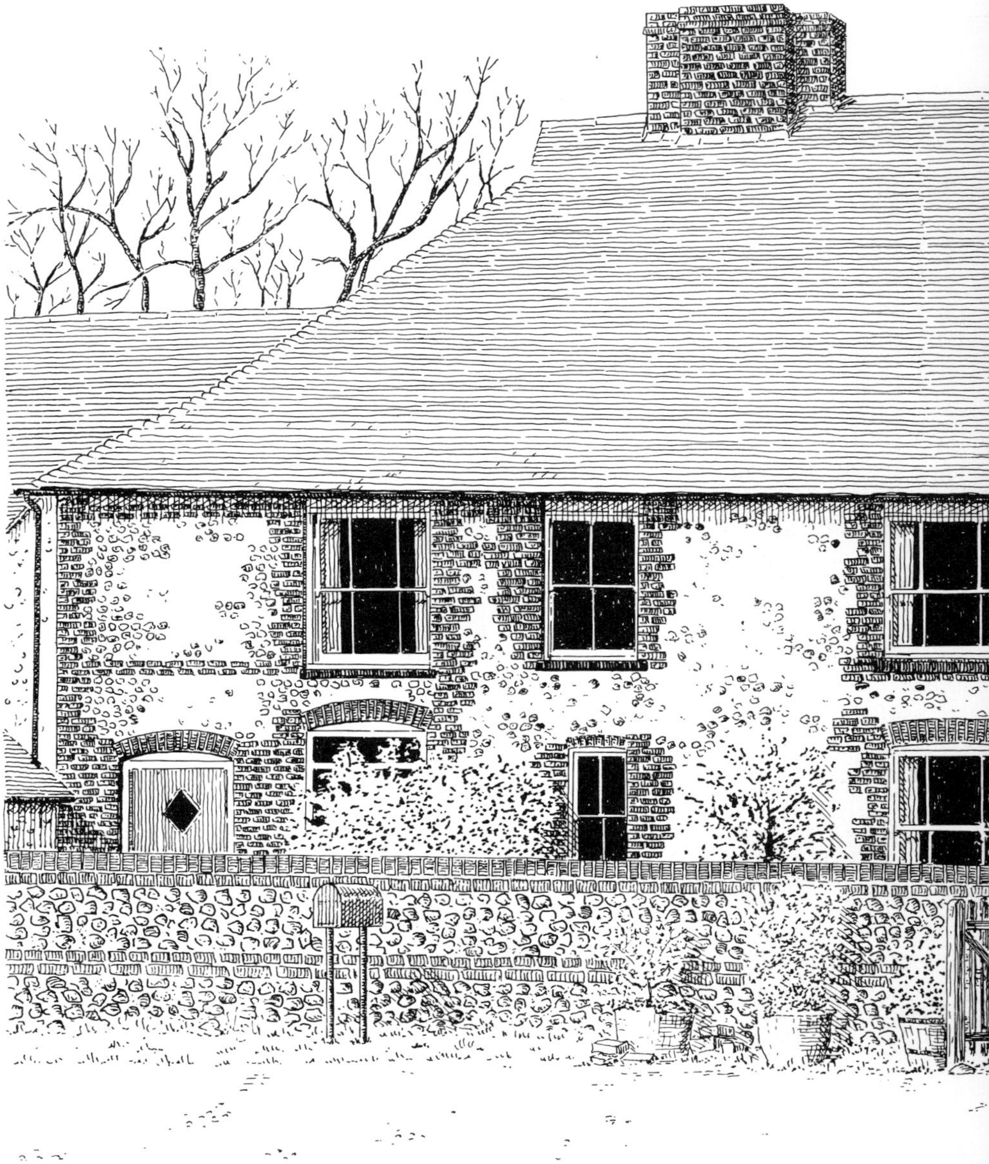

1. Hoad Farm, Acrise. Built in the fourteenth century and attached to a thirteenth-century first floor hall house.

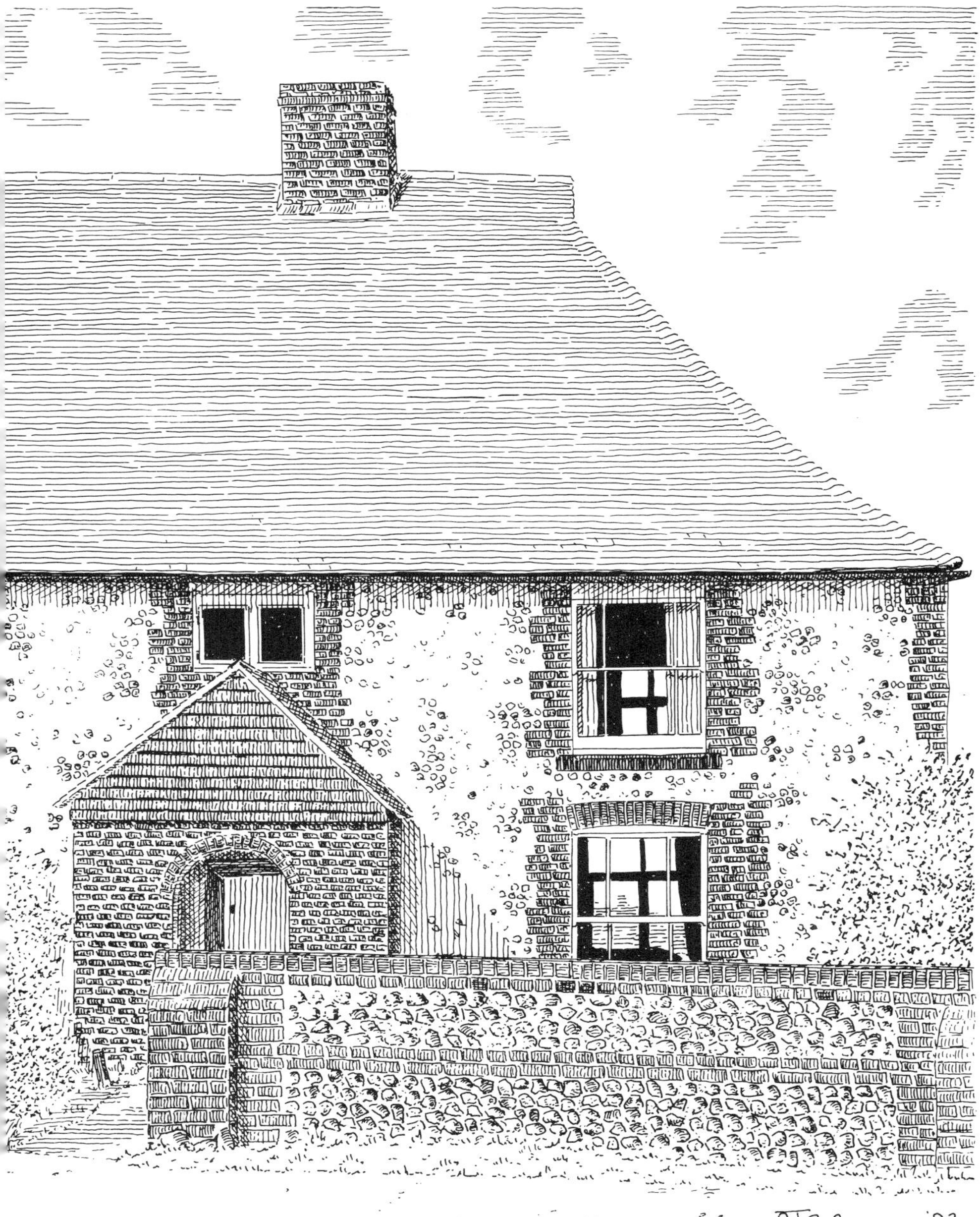
RJBROWN '93

work as for instance at Temple Manor, Strood, because of the ease with which it could be worked. The stone used was often tufa, a light, porous stone found where springs issuing from the chalk deposited a calcareous rock. Pugged chalk (crushed chalk mixed with water and rammed between timber shutters), frequently employed in parts of the downs of Hampshire, Dorset and Wiltshire, was an art not practised in Kent.

Lime was an important by-product of Kentish chalk. Obtained from the chalky Downs, it was the basic ingredient in mortar, rendering plaster and in more modern times cement, the making of which requires one part of clay to three parts of pure chalk.

The real importance of chalk in Kent was as a source of flints. Flints which are to be found in the upper layers of the Chalk formation are irregular-shaped modules of silica, extremely hard and virtually indestructible. It is this quality that has made flint an important building material since Roman times and even before; during the Saxon and Norman periods it became of paramount importance and has continued to be used in all subsequent periods. Flint has always been in great demand in the coastal towns, where the salt in the atmosphere can easily eat away at brick and other kinds of stone.

Flint is therefore to be found today in the older parts of such places as Margate, Ramsgate, Sandwich, Deal, Dover and Folkestone. There are many examples of its use in medieval houses surviving today. Southfleet Rectory is one; another is Hoad Farm, Acrise (*1*). The Old Rectory, Ickham, Copton Manor, Sheldwich, Nurstead Court and Temple Manor are others, all of which are of thirteenth- or fourteenth-century date.

Flint cottages and houses can also be found in a number of villages at the foot of the North Downs. One such village is Shoreham, where flint and brick are used in what can only be described as a local vernacular. One cottage of note in the village, beside the lychgate, has the flints banded vertically with red bricks, rather than the more customary method of horizontal bands.

One of the advantages of using flints is that they require no quarrying for they are there for the gathering, from the fields or from the beaches below the chalk cliffs. They vary considerably in size, anything from a few inches to even twelve inches across. Knapped flints – that is, flints cut to expose the core built into the wall with the split face exposed, can be seen on some Kent buildings. The walls of the fourteenth-century Nurstead Court are of knapped work, while the fifteenth-century gatehouse to Dent-de-Lion at Garlinge has flints laid in alternate bands with bricks. Flints were on occasions knapped and squared, a refinement that can be seen on a number of Georgian houses, for instance Jossingblock Farm, East Longdon, of early

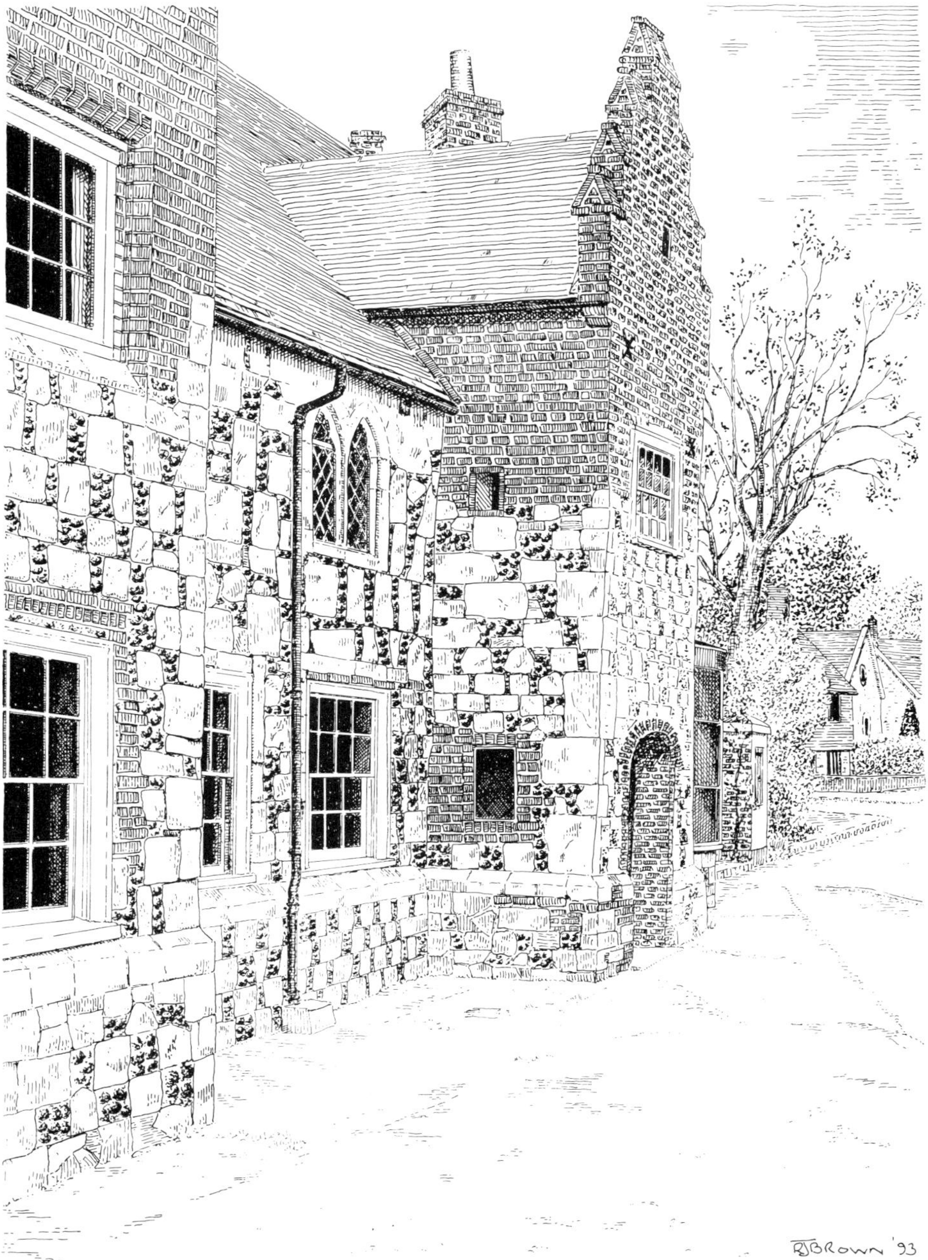

2. Old Stone House, Wickhambreux. A medieval store house raised in the brickwork in the sixteenth century.

eighteenth-century date. Because of the difficulty in building quoins and jambs, these were generally constructed of brick or stone. Occasionally stone can be found in combination with flints made into a chequer pattern as at the Old Stone House at Wickhambreux (*2*) formerly the Old Post Office, and also at the Barbican, the former toll-gate at Sandwich. However, the practice is not as common as in East Anglia or Wiltshire.

In the coastal areas water-worn flints from the beach are to be found laid in level courses, often with brick quoins, window and door surrounds, eaves, verges and lacing courses, but their use is not as popular as it is along the north Norfolk coast. In the old village of St Peter's and Reading Street, which has now been amalgamated with the hamlet of Broadstairs to form the present-day Broadstairs, there are a number of flint houses, some with shaped and pedimented gables edged with brick; one is dated 1710. Often, however, the flints were used in what Alec Clifton-Taylor has described as 'a rather uninviting hodge-podge'. One example is Pellicane House, Sandwich, a house formerly known as Flint House and St Peter's Rectory. John Newman in *The Buildings of England: North East and East Kent* queries whether the building is basically medieval, but it is in fact a fifteenth-century timber-framed house refronted in the seventeenth century in small flints and brickwork interspersed with pieces of Caen stone and Kentish rag; it was much altered in the eighteenth and again in the nineteenth century.

Running parallel to the chalk hills and forming the northern limit of the Weald are the Hythe Beds of the Lower Greensand belt which yields Kentish rag, the best known and most extensively used stone in the county. The chief quarries were in the neighbourhood of Maidstone – at Allington, Boughton Monchelsea and other places where the Hythe Beds are near the surface, for instance near Hythe and Sandgate. The quarries at Allington not only provided material for the castle, but are thought to have supplied the stone for the Tower of London and before that the Roman walls of London, while Boughton quarries were the most prolific source of ragstone in Kent in medieval times.

Kentish rag is a limestone, grey in colour, of coarse texture, hard and brittle. It is difficult to work and so most of the building is uncoursed, of irregular-shaped blocks, producing a wall incapable of being bonded. Castles such as Rochester and Allington, large houses such as Knole, numerous churches, as well as many smaller houses were built of this stone. Of the smaller houses many are of medieval date, for instance Old Soar at Plaxtol, built towards the end of the thirteenth century.

A house of some importance is Boughton Place, Boughton

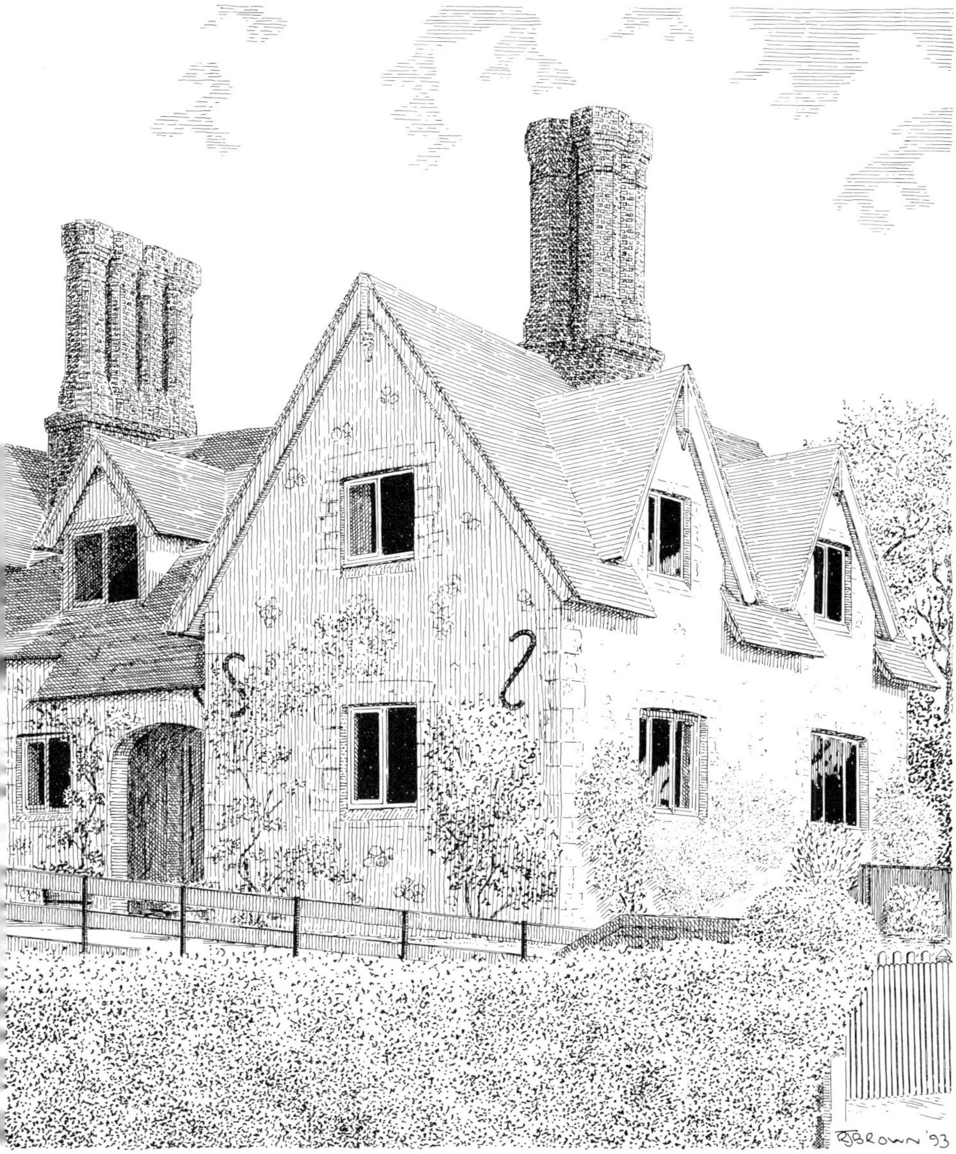

3. Pair of ragstone estate cottages at Linton.

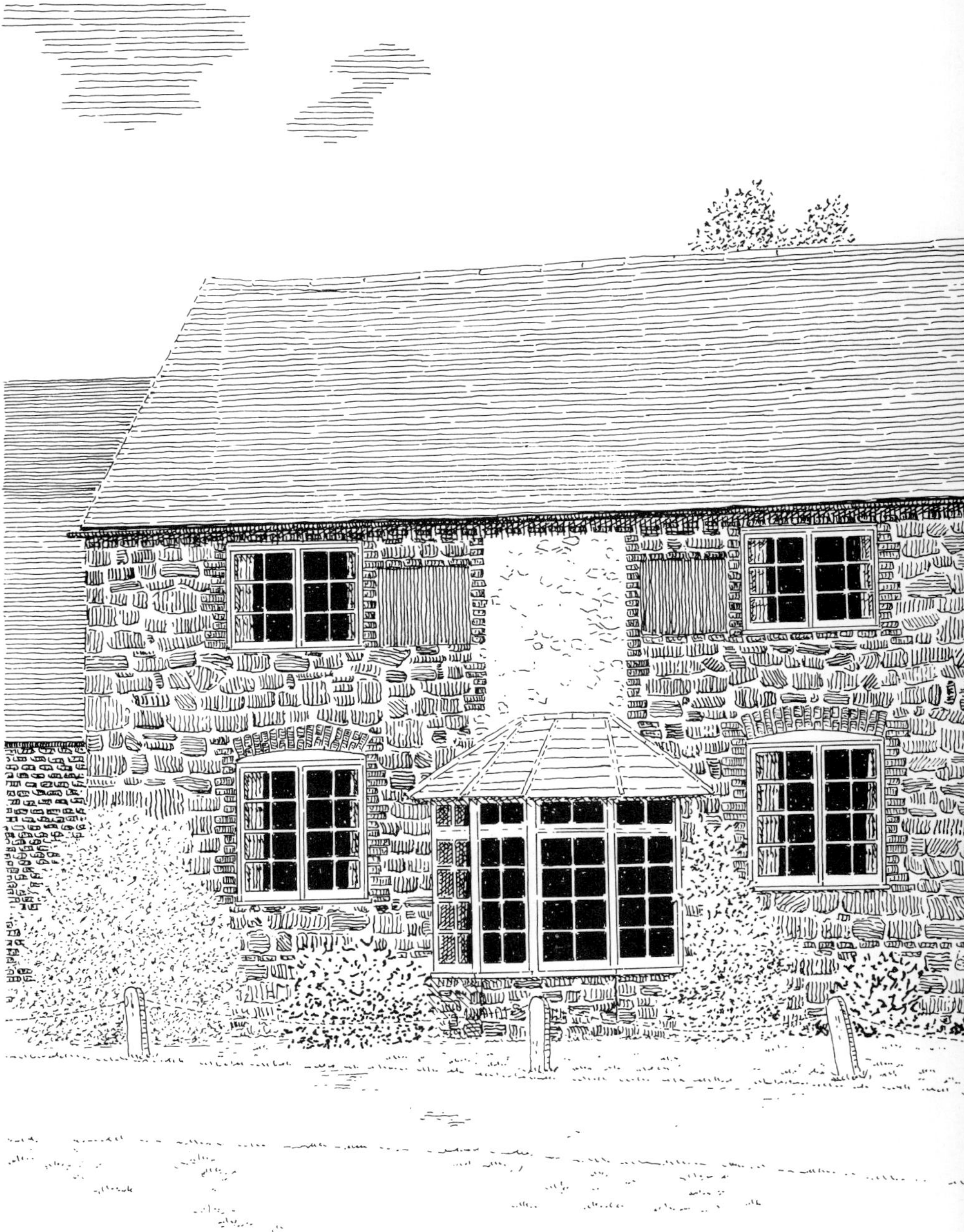

4. Carstone cottages at Trottiscliffe.

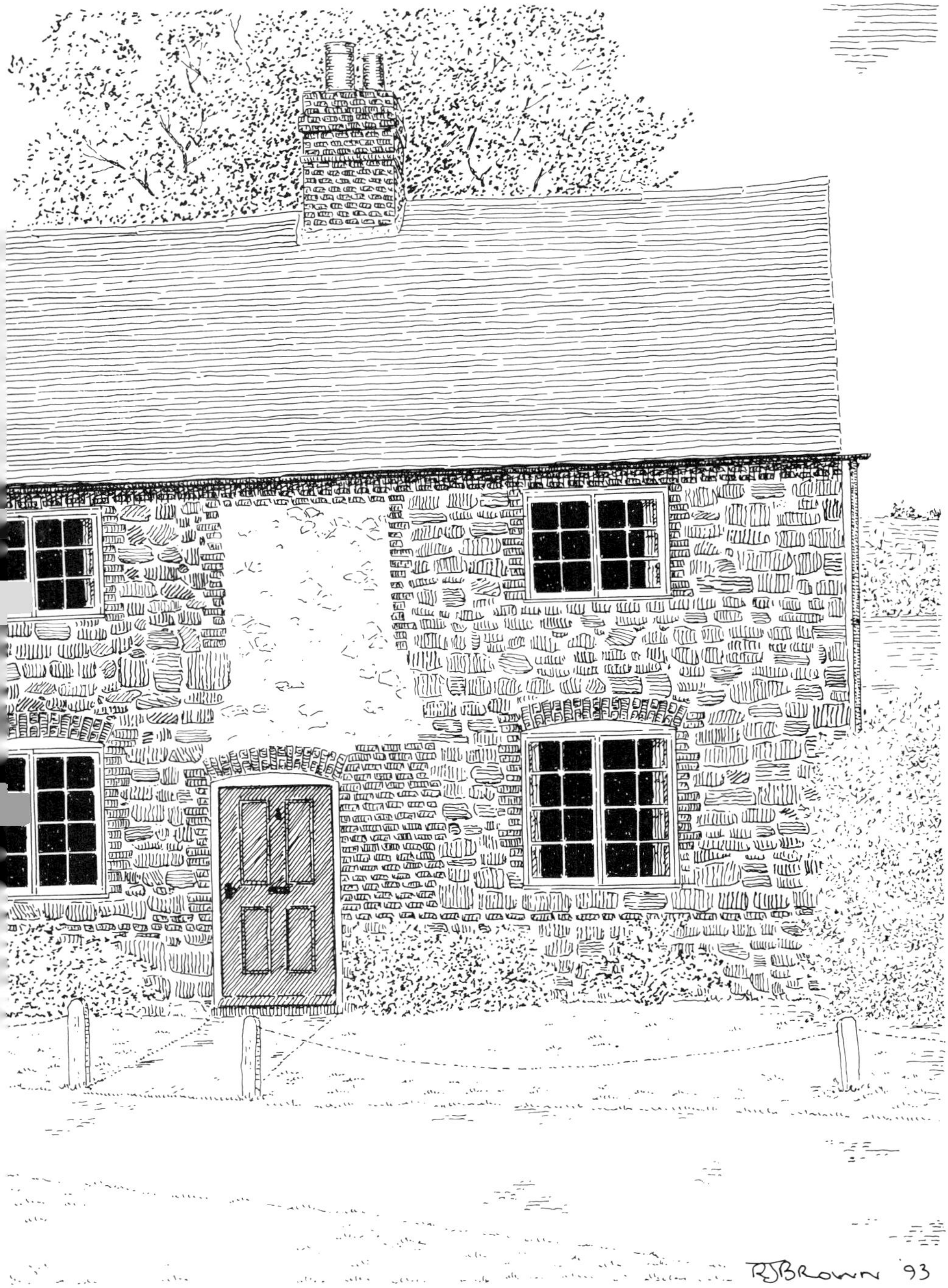
RJBROWN '93

Malherbe, built between 1520 and 1530. What is left is only one wing of the original house, later extended in around 1553 to the south in ragstone and to the north with late sixteenth-century brickwork complete with chimney and stepped gables. Another house of some importance is Boughton Monchelsea Place, built about 1567–75 on a courtyard plan. All that now remains is the east range; the south range was largely rebuilt around 1819.

In Georgian times the use of ragstone declined, although houses of the period can be found here and there and are best seen in the villages to the east and south of Maidstone. At Greatness to the north of Sevenoaks is a terrace of ten cottages built around 1765 for the workers of the nearby Novailles lace factory. The use of ragstone was revived in Victorian times, when it became a fashionable and favourite building stone for churches, especially in the London area. It also began to be used again for houses and cottages. The estate village at Linton is constructed of ragstone, the cottages being built in pairs under a tiled roof with large octagonal brick chimney stacks (*3*).

On the Greensand ridge to the west of Maidstone is to be found a narrow belt of a dark brown ironstone known as Carstone. Its use is perhaps more common in Surrey than in Kent, but it is used in the construction of cottages, particularly around the village of Trottiscliffe. A good example is a group of cottages (*4*) near the church, dated 1758. The stone can also be found at nearby Wrotham Heath and at St Mary's Platt. The joints of these ironstone cottages frequently had small chips of stone pushed into them to form a decorative feature known as galleting.

The finest of the building stones of Kent are the Wealden sandstones from the Hastings Beds, unrivalled for their texture and colour. They play a more significant role in neighbouring East Sussex than in Kent but occur in many places in the south-west fringe of the county along the Kent–Sussex border, particularly in and around Tunbridge Wells, and here and there they outcrop to form curious formations such as the High Rocks at Tunbridge Wells. The stone often proved durable, as in the gatehouse at Tonbridge Castle. Penshurst Place and Somerhill, a Jacobean mansion, are pleasantly streaked with iron-ore of a deep orange-brown hue. This stone was used in 1784–5 by Robert Adam in the construction of Brasted Place, near Sevenoaks. Another stone of the same type as the more famous Reigate stone was quarried from the Upper Greensand at Ightham and along the western end of the Kentish stretch of the North Downs.

Some of these sandstones are sufficiently fissile to yield roofing slates. These heavy stone slabs, known generally as Horsham slate (the principal quarry being at Horsham) are less evident in Kent than in Surrey and Sussex, although around Tunbridge Wells, where they were also once quarried, they may well have been more extensively used before tiling became common. Certainly in the last hundred years or so many have disappeared. An example is a house at Stanford's End, near Edenbridge (5), illustrated in Kenneth Gravett's book *Timber and Brick Building in Kent* (pl. 4); Howard Gaye's drawing of 1881 shows a stone-flag roof, but it is now tiled. The stone flags were nailed and fixed with oak pegs hooked over the roofing battens and laid with diminishing courses, that is, with the largest at the eaves and the smallest at the ridge. Because of their size, often at the eaves being some four feet wide and two or three inches thick, stone flags were, in general, used only for simple gabled roofs laid in the main to a pitch of around forty-five degrees.

Bricks

Between the stone-producing strata are three further strata – the clays of the Weald, the Gault and the Tertiary – which have over the centuries produced the bricks and tiles for which Kent is so rightly famous. The predominant impression left by the buildings of Kent is of the rich, glowing reds of their bricks and tiles.

Kentish bricks and brickwork are without doubt some of the finest to be seen in the country. The materials from the three geological strata are quite different. The finest of all come from the brown and blue clays of the Weald, along the south-west portion of the county from Hythe to Edenbridge. Here the presence of iron in the clay produces those glorious red bricks of Wealden Kent. Further north, from the Gault, a belt of stiff, bluish clay overlying the Lower Greensand, come the so-called white bricks, although they are more of a pale yellow. These are to be found mainly to the north of Maidstone along the Medway valley, where the lime content of the clay is sufficient to override the reddening influence of iron. The brick-making clays of north Kent are from the alluvion clays, which produce not only some good red bricks but also bricks of a yellowish-brown colour. Pale yellow bricks were also a speciality of the Isle of Thanet. Made from mud rather than brick clay, they can best be seen in Sandwich – Manwood Court, built about 1580, and the top of Fisher Gate of 1571 are two examples. Brown bricks of various shades, a feature of eighteenth-century brickwork in Kent, could be achieved by the addition of lime and a little iron.

The colour of bricks was not only obtained from the impurities in clay, such as iron and lime, but also by the process of firing. Changes in colour could be achieved by increasing the heat, and so the bricks exposed to the greatest heat emerged the darkest; white bricks could therefore be turned brown and red bricks could be turned various shades of purple. Changes in colour could also be obtained by the use

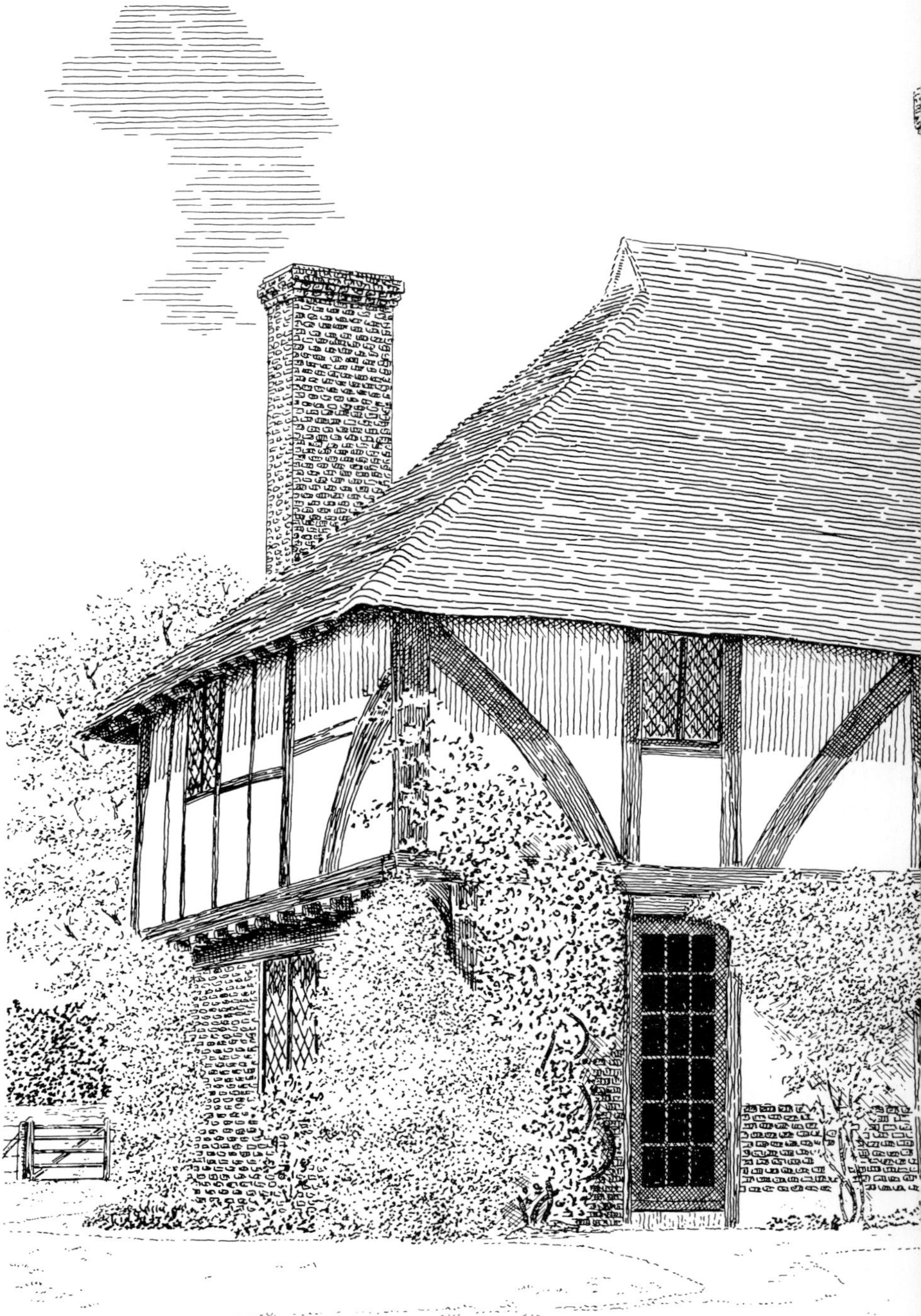

5. End-jetted house at Stanford's End, near Edenbridge.

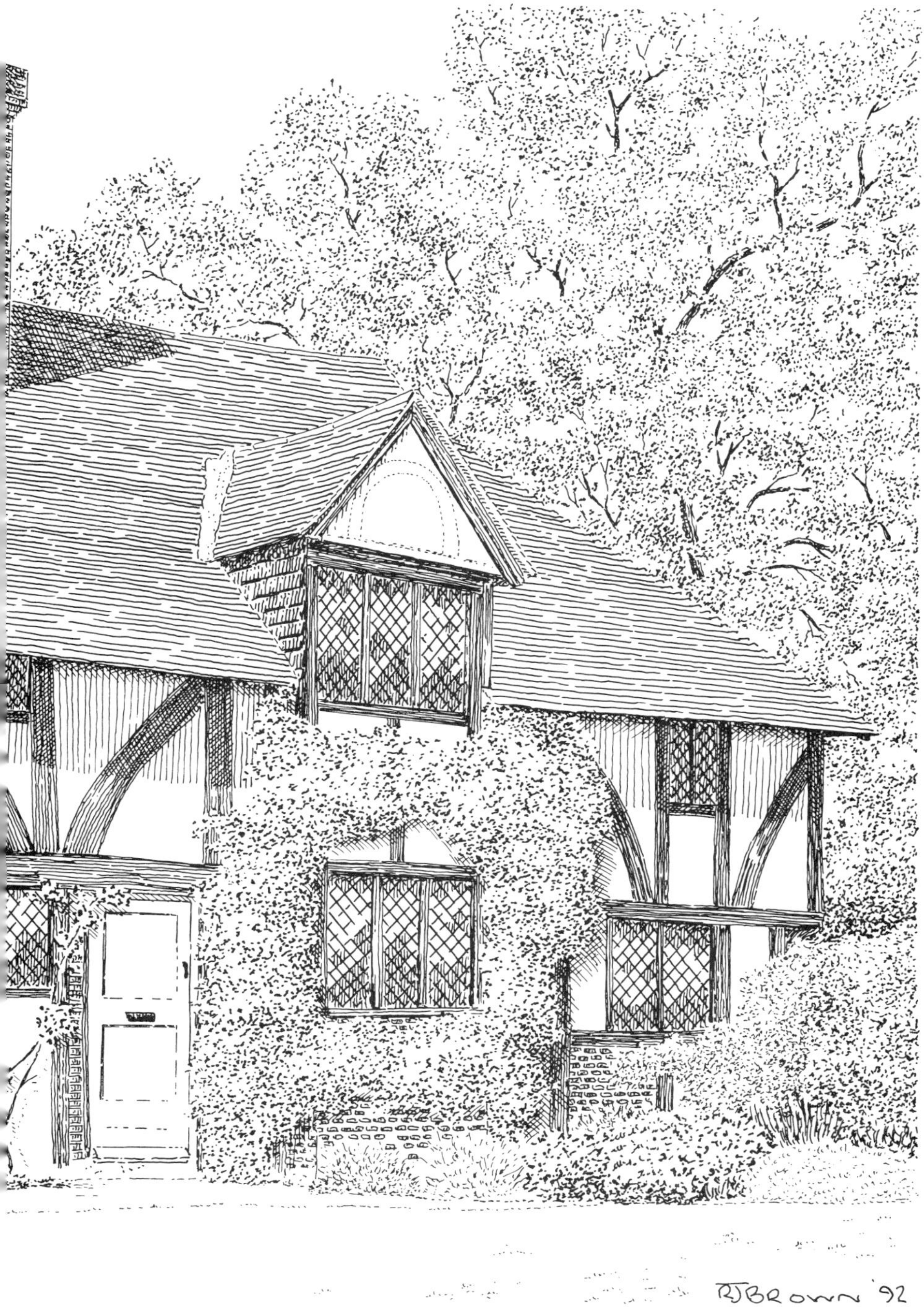
RJBROWN '92

of different fuels. Flared headers for instance, used in diaper work, were obtained by burning furze with the ends of bricks so placed that they were in contact with the flames.

Tiles

Perhaps even more memorable than Kentish brickwork is Kentish tilework. No other county, not even Sussex, can rival Kent in its employment of tiles of the highest quality. The steeply pitched roofs of the Weald give even the smallest house a dignity which few other roofs can give; they are frequently carried down over an outshut to the rear or side, often to within a few feet of the ground, to form what is known as a catslide. Tiles were first produced here by the Romans and by the fourteenth century the Benedictine monks of Battle Abbey were having tiles manufactured at Wye, near Ashford, while the Cistercian Order at Boxley Abbey also had its own tile yard. These two places are on the Gault belt but the Tertiary and Wealden clays also produced tiles of equal quality. Early roof tiles varied greatly in both size and manufacture and it was not until 1477 that an attempt was made to standardize the size – 10½ × 6¼ × ⅝ inches – and manufacture. Whether the statute had much influence is doubtful, for in Kent tiles continued to measure 9 × 6 inches. In 1725 the sizes laid down in 1477 were reaffirmed.

In Kent nearly all roofs are covered with plain tiles – double-lap tiles in which there is a double thickness of tile over the entire roof, each tile overlapping two others, leaving only about four inches exposed. They are laid in regular courses, not overlapping their neighbours in the same course. Early plain tiles were known as 'peg tiles', because the tiles had two holes near the top in which were driven small pegs, generally of oak but sometimes of hazel, willow or elder. The tiles were then hooked over riven oak laths fixed to the rafters. Later in the nineteenth century, nibs were provided on each tile to hook over the softwood battens with every fifth course or, when the pitch was above fifty degrees, every third course nailed.

Plain tiles are usually laid to a pitch of forty-five degrees or more, and in medieval Kent a pitch of between fifty and sixty degrees was generally employed. This is visually most pleasing, giving the vast sweep of tiling so characteristic of many of the houses. The tiles were at one time bedded on hay, straw or moss but later, to weatherproof completely the roof, tiles would usually be torched – pointed in lime-hair mortar on the underside. Today, all tiled roofs have a felt underlay fixed to the rafters beneath the tile battens.

Peg tiles were handmade with an exaggerated camber in both their length and breadth, and this, coupled with a slight variation in size, texture and shape, gives an aesthetic appearance with shades of light

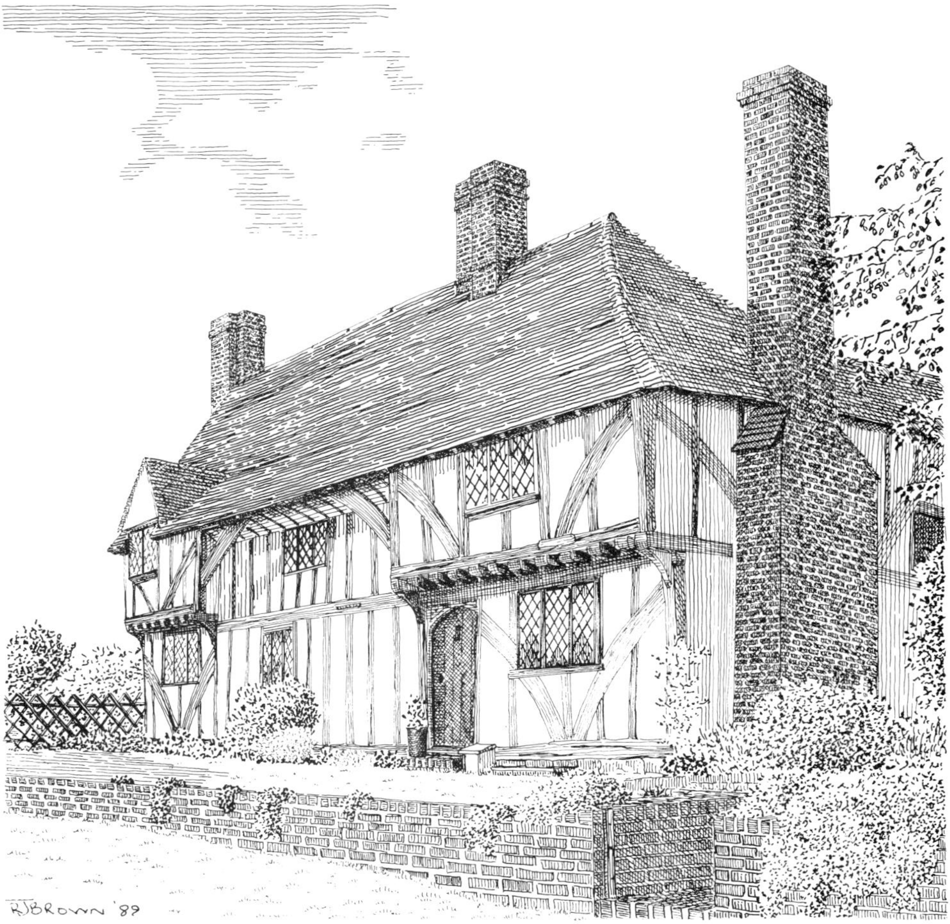

6. High Birch, Upper Bush, Cuxton, a well restored Wealden house.

and shadow that few Victorian or modern roofs of machine-made tiles can match. These undulations may not be due entirely to the irregularity of the tiles, but also to the sagging battens and rafters or the settlement of the walls.

Early roofs in Kent were generally fully hipped, as in the yeomen's hall houses (6, 7), or half-hipped. Half-hipped roofs provided a part-gable at the end of the house into which could be fitted a window to light the roof space, for dormer windows are not a traditional feature of Kent houses. Characteristic of many old Kentish houses is the gablet at each end of the ridge; it is thought that the original purpose for this was to allow the smoke from the open hall to escape.

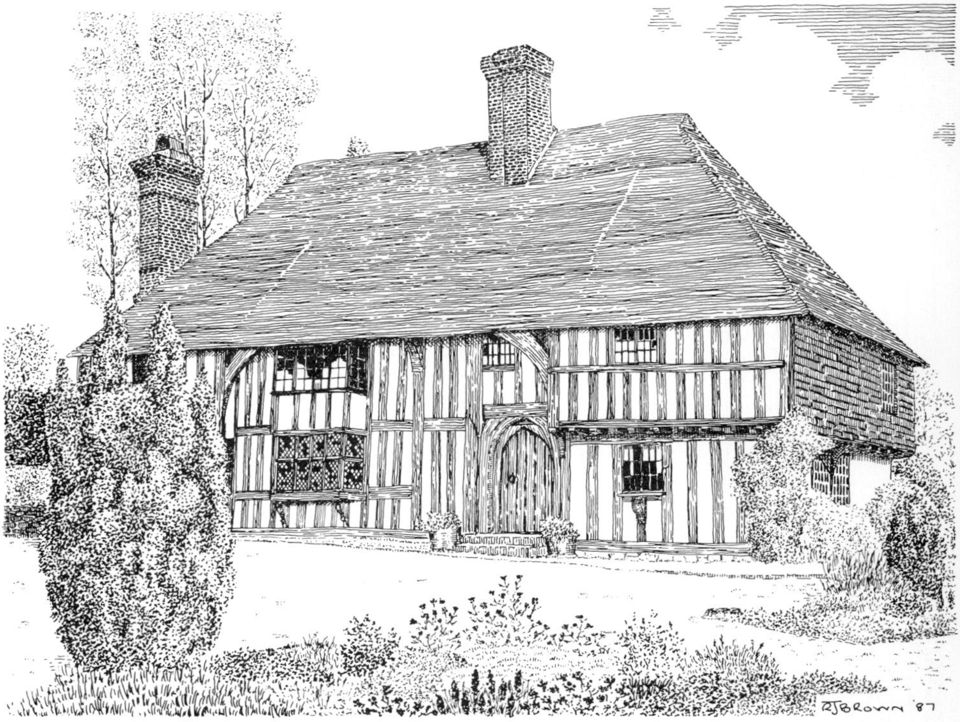

7. Link Farm, Egerton. A fifteenth-century hall house described as one of the finest Wealden houses.

The hips in Kent were generally finished to bonnet hip tiles, which added further charm to the overall appearance of the roofs. Later, roofs were generally gabled but in some instances houses have both a gabled and hipped or half-hipped ends. This is particularly true of some of the smaller houses of the Weald (*8*).

Clay pantiles, first imported from Holland in the seventeenth century, became a popular roof-covering in eastern England from Essex northwards to Northumberland and spreading westwards into the adjacent counties. For some reason they never gained popularity in the south-east and in Kent, apart from in isolated areas, plain tiles remained the general roof-covering material. One area where a sprinkling of pantiled roofs can be found is in Sandwich, presumably because of its connections with Holland – it is said that at the end of the century more Flemish immigrants than Englishmen lived in Sandwich – but even here the majority of roofs are covered with handmade plain tiles.

The production of bricks and tiles for roofing is only part of the

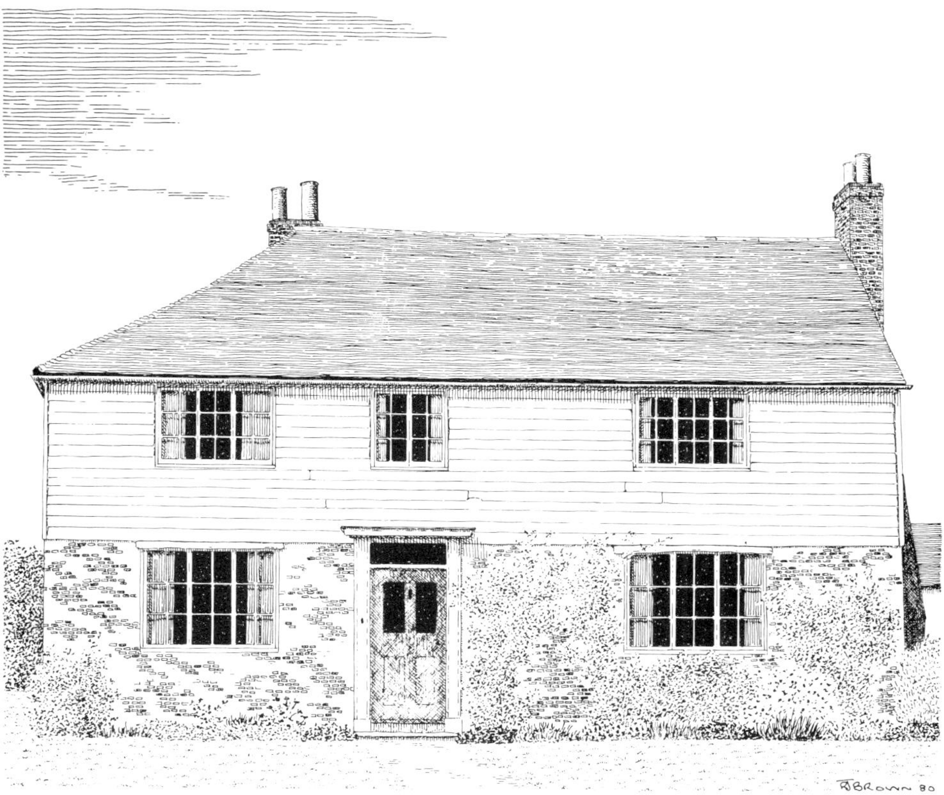

8. Maytham Farm, Rolvenden.

story, for such was the quality of Kent's clays that they were widely used from the latter part of the seventeenth century onwards for the manufacture of tiles for tile-hanging (*9*). The clays of the Weald produced the beautiful, rich terracotta tiles so admired today which over the years have mellowed but still retain their glowing red. Each tile varies slightly in colour, shape and texture from its neighbour, giving an overall appearance of great charm. Because these tiles were hung vertically, lichens, mosses and dirt do not adhere to the surface as they often do on roof tiles, and so they tend to hold their rich colour much better than roofing tiles. Alec Clifton-Taylor in his book *The Pattern of English Building* gives the perfect description: 'a good tile-hung wall is a creation of infinite subtlety, an agglomeration of shallow and slightly irregular convexities, seemingly held in place, under the right conditions of light by a fine mesh of shadow.'

The tiles for tile-hanging in Kent are for the most part plain. Their

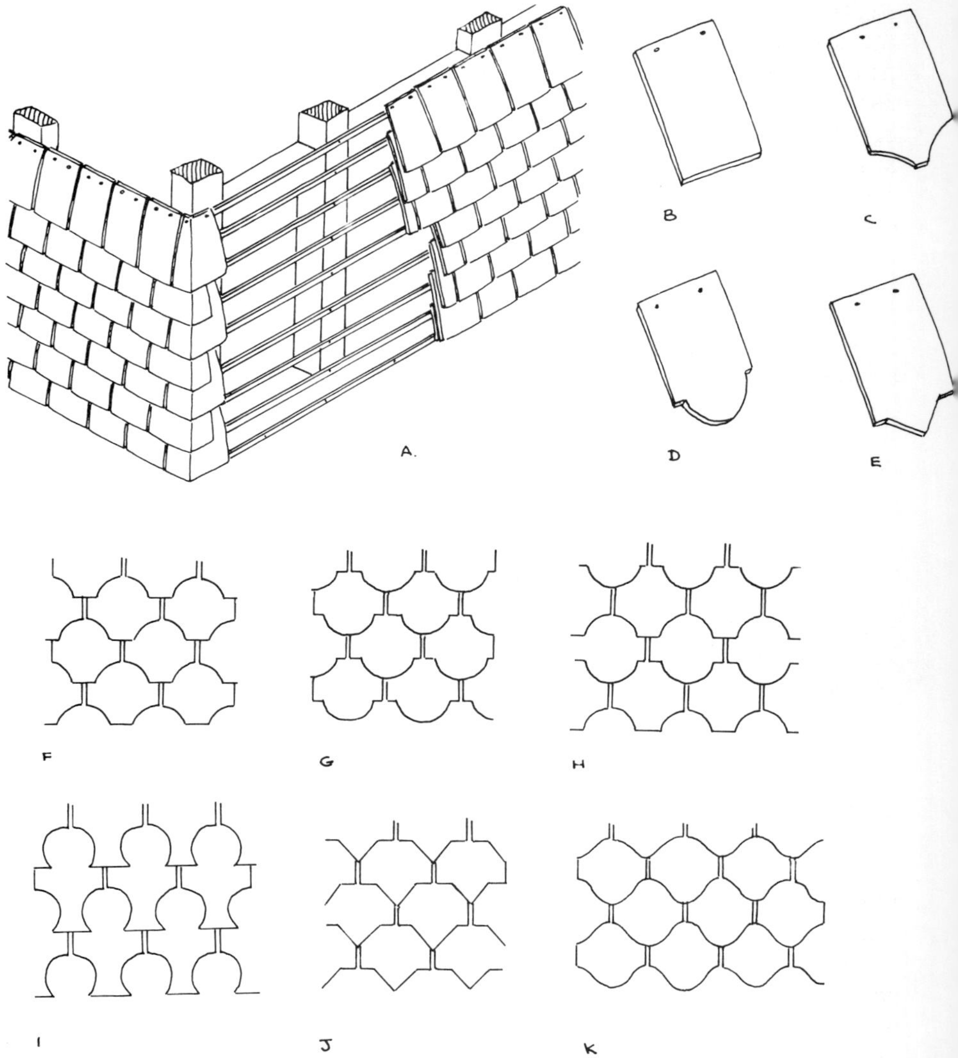

9. Tile-hanging. A. isometric view showing plain tiles hung on laths; B. plain tile; C. Hammerhead tile; D. Fish scale tile; E. Arrowhead tile; F, G, H, I, J and K various tile patterns.

slightly cambered face and irregular shape are all that is needed to give the cladding an attractive overall appearance and this is particularly true of the Weald. Pattern tile-hanging is by no means rare; a method used at one time was, prior to firing, to dab the surface with the bristles of a stiff brush, producing a rough surface which weathered more quickly than plain tiles: plain and brushed tiles could thus be arranged to form a pattern. Another method was to use tiles of different colours obtained by increasing the heat so that red tiles exposed to the greatest heat in the kiln turned to various shades of purples and could therefore be arranged in patterns. These two methods of obtaining a pattern are today rare and by far the commonest method is to use patterned tiles, of which there are considerable variations in design. Most of these patterned tiles were machine-made in the Victorian period and were not so popular in Kent as in the neighbouring counties of Surrey and East Sussex. The decorative tiles could be used in an all-over pattern or, more commonly, they were used in combination with plain tiles; rows of patterned tiles either alternated with rows of plain tiles, or were arranged in diamond-shaped panels set within plain tiles.

These tiles were manufactured in the same way as roof tiles although they were sometimes slightly thinner, and so in Kent generally measure nine by six inches. They were hung on oak, hazel or willow pegs to riven oak laths which were, in turn, fixed to the timber frame in such a way as to give a triple lap, each tile covering two others. To make the tiling permanently waterproof the upper ends were often bedded in lime-hair mortar. Corners always presented the tiler with a problem, and to overcome this he used either specially shaped tiles or, more commonly, a stout vertical timber batten with the tiles butting up to it. Very occasionally the vertical joints would be filled with mortar but generally these were left open, which gives a much more attractive appearance.

The use of tile-hanging was not only restricted to timber-framed structures; sometimes tiles were used on brick walls. In some instances they were fixed to horizontal laths, either directly to the face of the brickwork or to additional vertical timber battens fixed to the brickwork to support the laths. In other cases the tiles would be pegged or later nailed directly into the joints of the brickwork.

Kent had another use for the excellent clays found within the county, in the manufacture of brick tiles, commonly referred to as mathematical tiles (*10*). These tiles were produced, like the Kentish bricks, in various colours – red ones in Canterbury, Tenterden and Hythe, yellow at Belmont near Faversham and dun-coloured at Chevening. While these local tiles were generally used, so-called 'white' tiles became fashionable and were also employed in larger

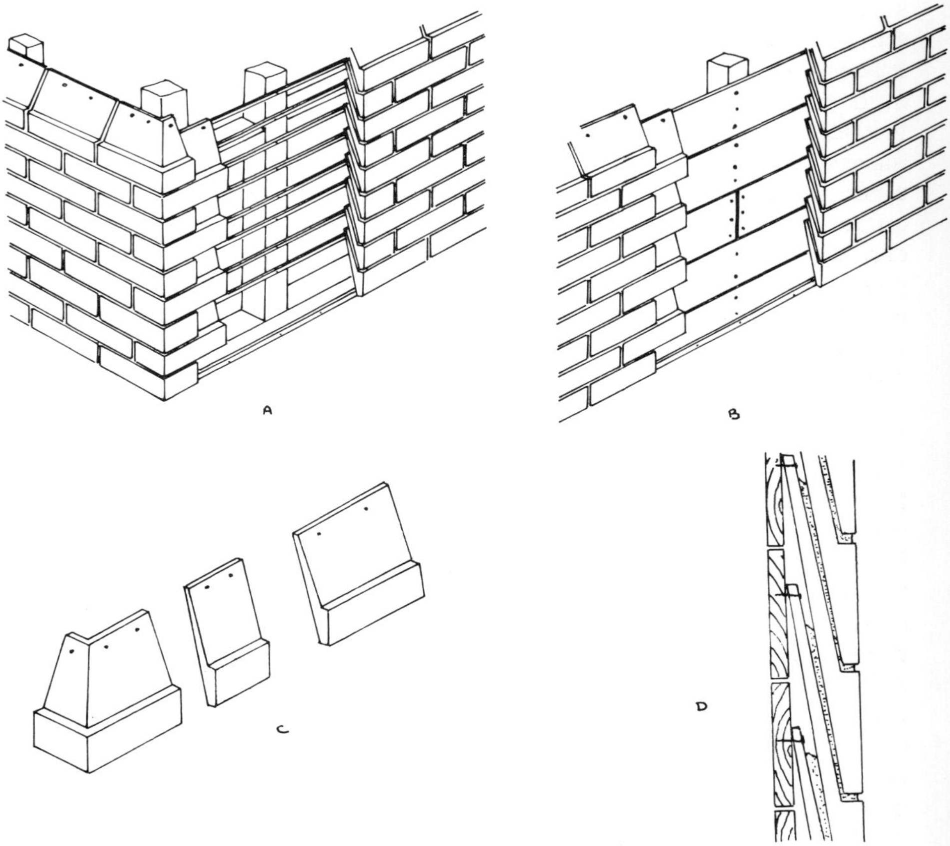

10. Mathematical tile cladding. A. isometric view with tiles fixed to battens; B. isometric view with tiles fixed to boarding; C. typical mathematical tiles; D. section showing method of bedding.

houses. One such house is Cocksditch, Faversham, where white tiles were employed to the front, with the red tiles to the flank walls. The date of this house is 1780, but the two brick pavilions are later additions of about 1795. Mathematical tiles had the same face dimension as bricks and were fixed to the face of old timber-framed or brick buildings. When well constructed, walls clad with these tiles are almost indistinguishable from those constructed of brick which they were intended to resemble. Yet this illusion of brickwork is often dispelled by a number of tell-tale features: the lack of arches over windows and doors, the widespread use of header bond instead of the more usual Flemish bond, the necessity of setting the windows and door frames forward in line with the face of the wall or the use of a timber fillet around the opening to hide the ends of the tiles are all signs of the use of these tiles. Despite these features, it is at the external corners that the true construction is most frequently revealed, for generally the use of these tiles was restricted to the main elevation, with the side and rear walls covered with tiles or weatherboarding. In these cases it was common to use a softwood batten fixed vertically to hide the joint between the two. Even when two adjacent sides of a building were clad with these tiles, vertical softwood battens were still used at the corners, for although special corner tiles were manufactured towards the end of the eighteenth century, these were for some reason rarely used in Kent. Possibly the best way of dealing with the problem was the use of rusticated timber blocks, painted to represent stone quoins as at 19–21 High Street, Tenterden.

When mathematical tiles were first introduced is unknown, but it is evident that they appeared before the introduction of the Brick Tax in 1784 – the earliest acceptable date for their use being 1716 at Nunwell House, Isle of Wight, with the earliest dated tile being 1724 at Westcott, Surrey. The majority appear to date from between 1770 and 1810. The avoidance of the Brick Tax is often put forward as a reason for their popularity in the eighteenth and nineteenth centuries but this, however, is not strictly correct, for these tiles were also taxed in 1784. However, unlike the tax on bricks which increased twice after 1794, the tax on mathematical tiles remained unchanged. Furthermore, the tax on tiles ceased in 1833 while that on bricks continued until its abolition in 1850. So, although taxed, they were undoubtedly cheaper than bricks, being easier to fix. Moreover, they were a practical solution when modernizing a building, whether built in timber or brick, to give it the desired Georgian look without the cost of either cladding or rebuilding in brick.

Timber

The most important building material throughout the medieval period and beyond was timber. Oak was the timber predominantly used in construction, for its strength and durability were unrivalled. Kent was fortunate in that oak trees flourished in most parts of the county, except for parts of the chalk downs and some coastal areas, and this is especially true of the Weald where the heavy clays produced the soil needed for their growth. The Weald (the word is derived from the Anglo-Saxon for wooded country), was once covered by the vast forests of Anderida and so plentiful was oak that in the Sussex Weald it was referred to as the 'Sussex weed'. There is some evidence that sweet chestnut and to a lesser extent elm was also used in timber-framing, but its use appears to have been limited. By the eighteenth and nineteenth centuries, the forests had been severely depleted, not only for house building but also for the making of charcoal for the iron forges, for Kent was the centre of the iron industry, and it became increasingly necessary to use imported softwood from the Baltic and Scandinavia. These softwoods, although easier to work than the traditional English hardwoods, were inferior in their structural capabilities. These timbers were used during the eighteenth and nineteenth centuries in the construction of houses and cottages clad with weatherboarding or tiles.

Generally the oak was not seasoned; its peculiar nature and the large scantlings required made it impracticable to dry out each baulk before use, and so the wood was used as soon as possible after it had been felled, being left to season in position. This probably explains the sag, warp and twist of many old buildings. Even when oak has been fixed in a building for centuries, it will warp and twist, as if new, when cut up and used again. When oaks were plentiful the heart of the timber was used; later, with the depletion of the country's oak trees, builders were forced to economize not only in the size of the scantlings used but also in the quality of timber.

This constraint probably explains the lack of uniformity of studs sometimes observed in late sixteenth-century houses, and the use of rafters, particularly in cottages, where the bark has been left on.

Considering the limited and crude tools available to the early carpenters, the skill with which they wielded them was remarkable. The oaks were felled with a narrow axe, although if the tree was large it was usually first cut around with a broad axe before the narrow axe was used on the heart-wood. The larger trees were split into baulks by means of an axe and iron wedges, and they were cut into suitable lengths by a cross-cut saw, called a 'twart-saw'. This was a two-handled saw managed by two men. For the principal timbers (the posts, wall-plate and bressummers) these baulks were simply shaped by means of the broad axe and finally trimmed with the adze – an attractive feature on the timbers of many old houses today. For the smaller timbers (the studs, rafters, joists and floorboards) it was necessary to cut the baulks along their length to the required scantling. This was undertaken with a pit-saw worked by two men, one below and one above, with the baulk of timber being set over a pit. Two types of pit-saw were in common use: one, the great pit-saw, was similar in shape to the twart-saw but was longer with larger teeth set to facilitate cutting along the fibres of the timber; the other, the framed pit-saw, comprised a narrow blade fixed in the centre of a large rectangular frame designed to keep the blade taut; its principal use was for cutting boards.

With the timbers so prepared, it was necessary to cut the joints. These joints were either mortise and tenon, half-lap or scarf. The mortise and tenon was the most important and was the basis of all traditional framing. The tenons were cut with a hand-saw – a one-handled tool with a scimitar-like cutting edge – while the mortises were formed either with a chisel and mallet or with a series of holes bored by an auger, with the remaining wood being chopped away with a twibill. Scarf joints were used to join two beams together to form one continuous member – mainly purlins, wall-plates and sill-beams. These often occurred near a main post, and unlike the mortise and tenon joints, there were many different forms. Half-lap joints, although an important element in early medieval forms of construction, were later used in relatively few positions in timber-framed buildings, being almost entirely restricted to the joint between the collars and rafters in roof construction and in cruck construction to the joints between the blades and the tie-beam and collar.

Extensive research undertaken by C.A. Hewett during the last twenty years or so has established that joints used in the construction of timber-framed buildings are an important criteria in dating a building. Half-lap joints, as previously mentioned, were important in medieval times, for relatively few mortise and tenon joints were used during this period; many of the subsidiary members such as scissor braces were inserted after the main frame had been assembled, and so a lapped joint was essential. These joints were either notched or dovetailed, open or secret, and were generally superseded by the beginning of the fourteenth century when the use of long braces declined. More importantly as an aid to dating are the scarfed joints, of which there have been many varieties over the centuries (*11*). The earliest are of the splayed variety and are almost certainly of thirteenth- and fourteenth-century date. These were followed by various types of edge-halved scarf joints used from the fifteenth to the early seventeenth centuries, and finally by face-halved scarf joints. There are other types of scarf joints, such as the bridle, but these are less common than the three major types.

Another important joint is the complex joint between the post, wall-plate and tie-beam known as the tie-beam lap-dovetailed joint (*12*). The tie-beam is secured to the wall-plate by a dovetailed joint, generally of a lap-dovetailed type, although sometimes of the bare-faced variety, that is with a shoulder to one side only. In some instances the lap-dovetailed joint would open up due to the strain, showing a gap, and to overcome this the shoulder of the joint was sometimes entrant or housed. The post is secured to both the tie-beam and the wall-plate with a mortise and tenon joint. To enable the joint to be undertaken satisfactorily, the maximum amount of timber was required and thereby the maximum rigidity in the joint could be achieved. This thickening out of the post is known as the 'jowl', and

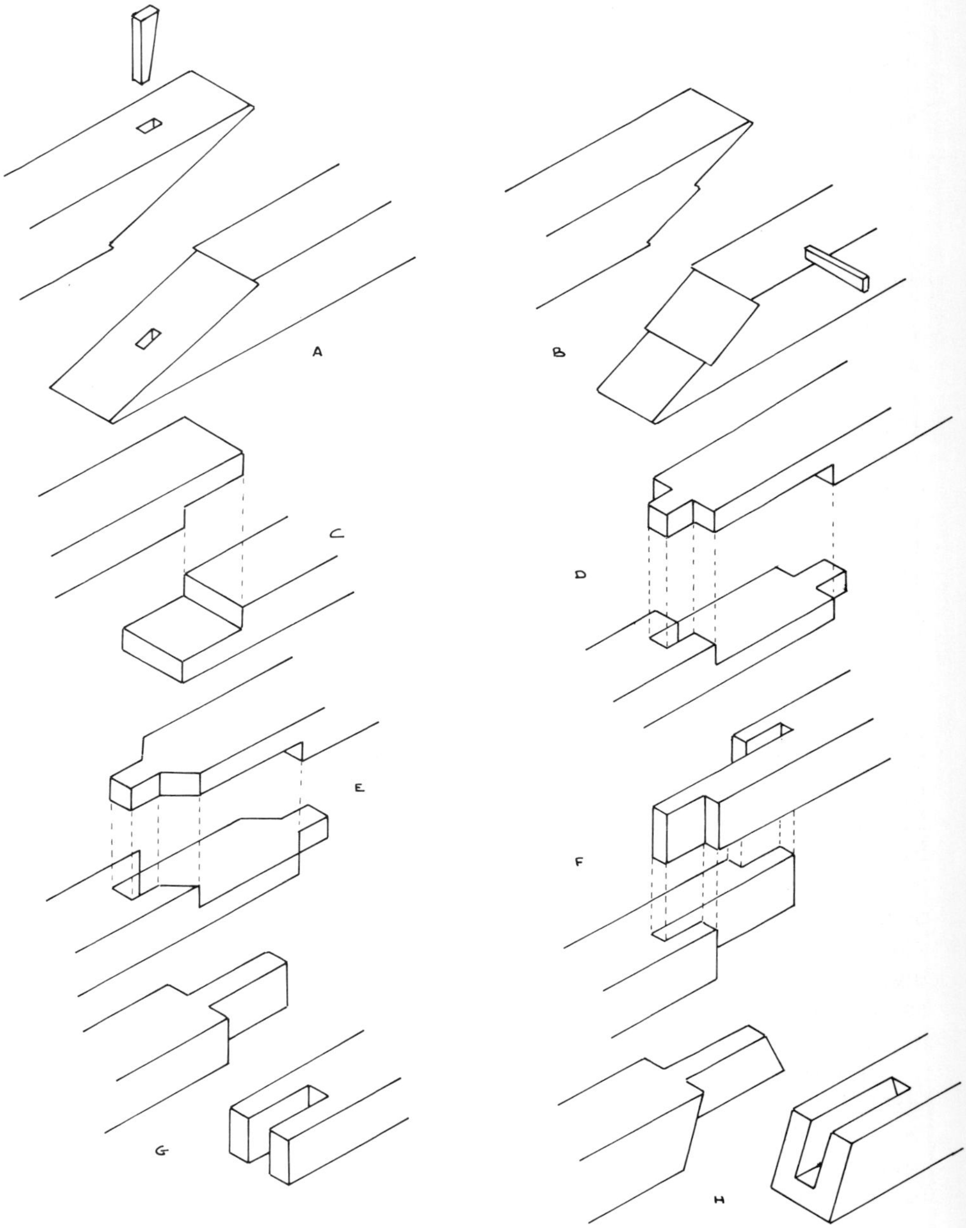

11. Scarf joints. A. and B. splayed and tabled; C. lapped; D. edge-halved; E. edge-halved with sallied shoulders; F. faced halved; G. and H. bridled.

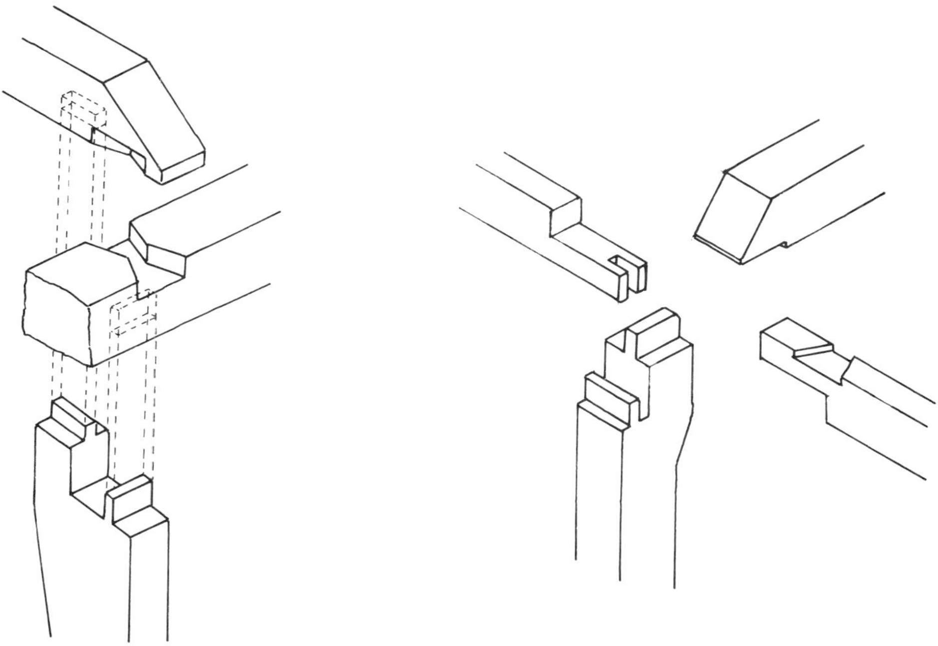

12. Tie-beam lap-dovetail joints.

though associated with the reversal of the trunk, that is root uppermost, thus using the expanded growth of the tree's root, it has like many other techniques undergone numerous changes. First used in the thirteenth century, the jowl finally declined in the sixteenth and seventeenth centuries, when it became highly decorative but structurally poor. Also in the seventeenth century long, swelling jowls were used before generally being dispensed with altogether in the eighteenth century. The tie-beam lap-dovetailed joint was a very satisfactory joint and was used from the thirteenth until the nineteenth century with little variation.

All of this work was carried out at the carpenter's workshop or yard – the 'framynplace' – the timbers being framed on the ground and the components incised at the joints for assembling on site. These carpenters' numerals were based on a system of Roman numerals; although not strictly Latin they were simple and effective (*13*). In Tudor times they were cut with a tool used for cutting straight lines, called a 'scribe', but later in Jacobean times, when the marks were smaller, they were cut with a gouge or chisel. The system was based on various combinations of I, V and X with the Roman IV becoming IIII and IX becoming VIIII. This was necessary because on site the timbers could become inverted, with IV being misread as VI and IX being read as XI. Other variations were that Vs were often cut upside down, and one cross-cut sufficed when both X and V were used together, or when two or more Xs were used. To assist in locating the various timbers to different parts of the building, carpenters' marks were added to the Roman numerals. These were a series of circles and segments made with the use of a 'scribing compass', each mark denoting particular section of the dwelling, such as the front, the rear, the sides, the floors, the roof trusses and so on. This enabled the timbers to be sorted easily prior to erection.

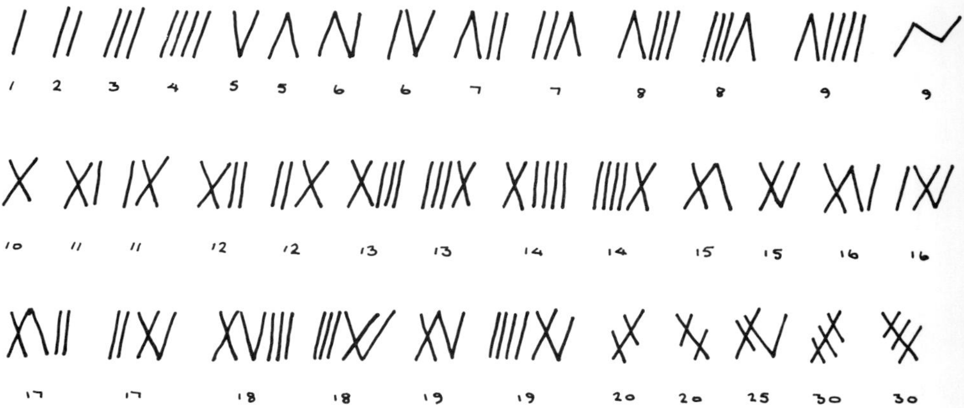

13. Medieval carpenters' numerals.

Once framed at the yard, the timbers were dismantled and transported to site and re-erected. The joints were in addition secured with heart-of-oak pegs, often referred to in medieval times as 'trashnails', which were driven into holes already bored by an auger at the yard, and left slightly projecting. Iron bolts, screws and nails were rarely used, for iron was then too precious to be employed. Moreover, had they been used the acid in the unseasoned oak would have soon corroded them and although the dipping of bolts and nails was practised, the expense involved restricted this to work of great importance. The use of galvanized iron was unknown before the eighteenth century. It is not known whether the carpenters of the period were aware of the effect of unseasoned oak on untreated iron, but heart-of-oak pegs tightly fitted would have been equally as effective as untreated bolts, and more so than nails. So strong were these pegged joints that in 1530 John Palsgrave wrote: 'I shall pynne it so faste with pynnes of yron and of wodde that it shall laste as longe as the tymber selfe.' There is evidence that from the eighteenth century

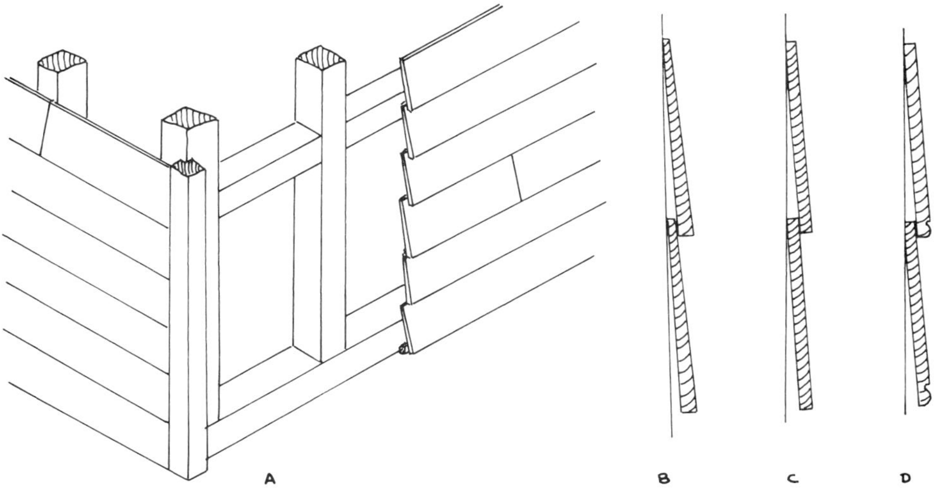

14. Weatherboard cladding. A. isometric view of boards fixed to studwork; B. feather-edge boarding; C. square-edged boarding; D. beaded-edged boarding.

onwards nails began to be used, but by then softwood was in frequent use and even if oak was used, the scantlings would have been small and easily seasoned. There is also evidence that the timbers were not at first permanently fixed during erection. Joseph Moxon in *Mechanik Exercises*, produced between 1677 and 1679, states that plenty of play was left for the easy insertion of the summer and other beams, with the sills and posts not immediately pegged together but temporarily held by means of long, tapering wooden pins, shaped rather like tent-pegs, called 'hook-pins'. These could not be driven in too far and consequently could be easily loosened and withdrawn.

The other use of timber in Kent was not for structural purposes but for cladding. Weatherboarding (*14*), sometimes referred to as clapboarding, is indigenous to the South-east and in particular to Kent, occurring in the Weald of Kent more frequently than anywhere else in the entire country. Early weatherboarding was of oak or elm pegged to the timber frame and left untreated, but what is seen today dates mainly from the eighteenth or nineteenth centuries and is of softwood. The boards, lapped and fixed horizontally to the timber frame, are usually chamfered or beaded along their lower edge and are nearly always painted white or cream, unlike in parts of Essex where they are often blackened (*15*).

Oak in the form of cleft-oak shingles was also used as a roofing material and could at one time be seen on many of the church steeples

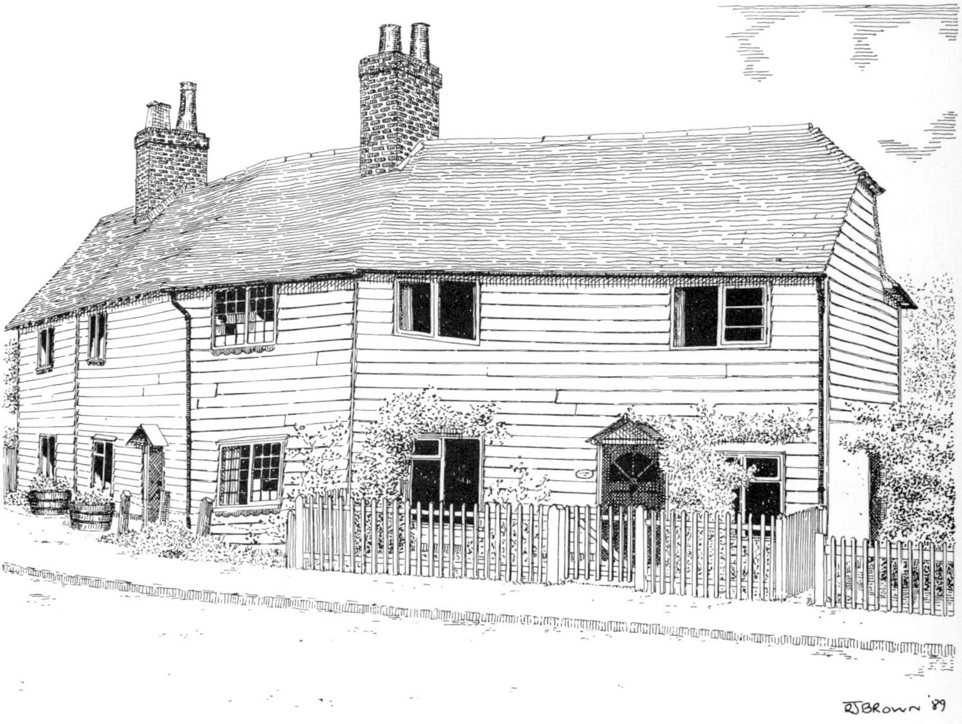

15. Weatherboarded cottages at Rolvenden.

of the Weald. Shingles were also used on some of the more important houses in the county; Parker, in his *Domestic Architecture of the Middle Ages*, mentions that at the hall at Ightham Mote part of the original covering of oak shingles existed beneath the later roof. Oak shingles have to be replaced every hundred years or so and for reasons of economy shingles of Canadian cedar are often used instead. Only on the octagonal turrets of the towers of Sissinghurst Castle can Wealden oak shingle still be found, and these date only from 1958.

Thatch

Thatch was undoubtedly once a more familiar roofing material in Kent than is evident today, but even so it is unlikely that it was ever as popular in Kent as it was in many other parts of the country, for such was the excellence and availability of tiles that their use was widespread even on relatively small houses. The steep pitch to be seen on many of the houses is suitable for either thatch or tile and it is now impossible to say to what extent thatch was used, for over the last three centuries much must have been replaced. Yet even some of the

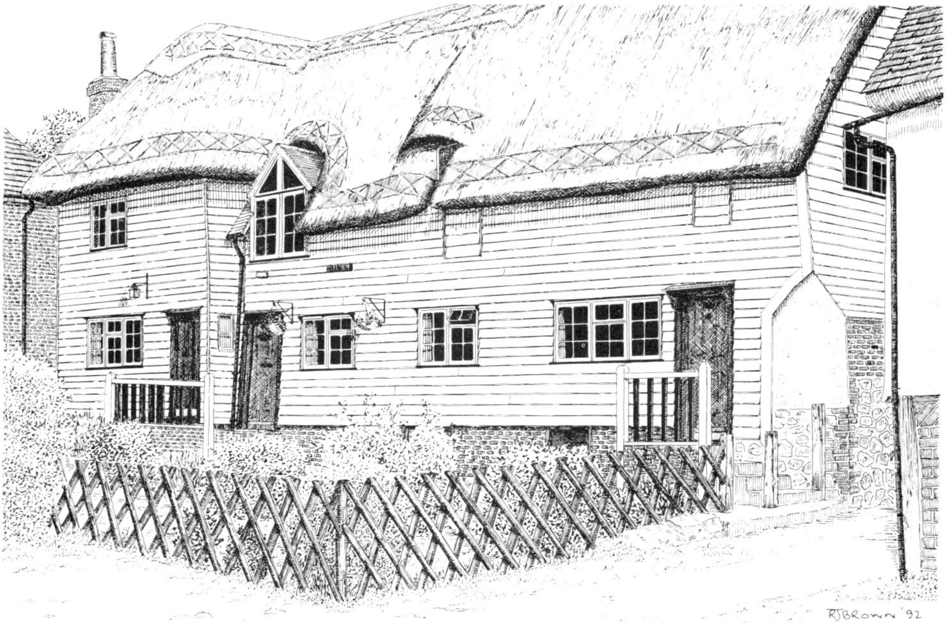

16. Randall Cottages, Yalding.

houses that are today thatched are the direct result of the agricultural depression that followed the Napoleonic Wars, for several still have sprockets or at least the peg-holes of earlier side-sprockets used to carry out the tiles beyond the eaves, an arrangement unnecessary when using thatch.

Thatch in the county is not now common. In the Weald it is indeed rare – the Thatched House at Smarden is one of the few examples – and even elsewhere to find a thatched roof is something of an event. There is a pair of cottages known as Randall Cottages at Yalding (*16*), and another, a mile or so away, at Little Benover – Thatchers (*17*) – which are typical examples. Perhaps the majority of these thatched cottages are to be found to the east of the county, for example: Goodnestone (Old Post Office) Staple (Summerfield Cottage and Gander Court Farm) and Petham (Dormer Cottage).

To summarize, the regional style for domestic buildings in the county prior to the nineteenth century is timber-framed, often with exposed timber, but frequently with the timbers completely or partially covered with plaster, tiles, weatherboarding or even faced with brickwork. Intermingled with these houses are houses of local mellow bricks, built in increasing numbers from the middle of the sixteenth

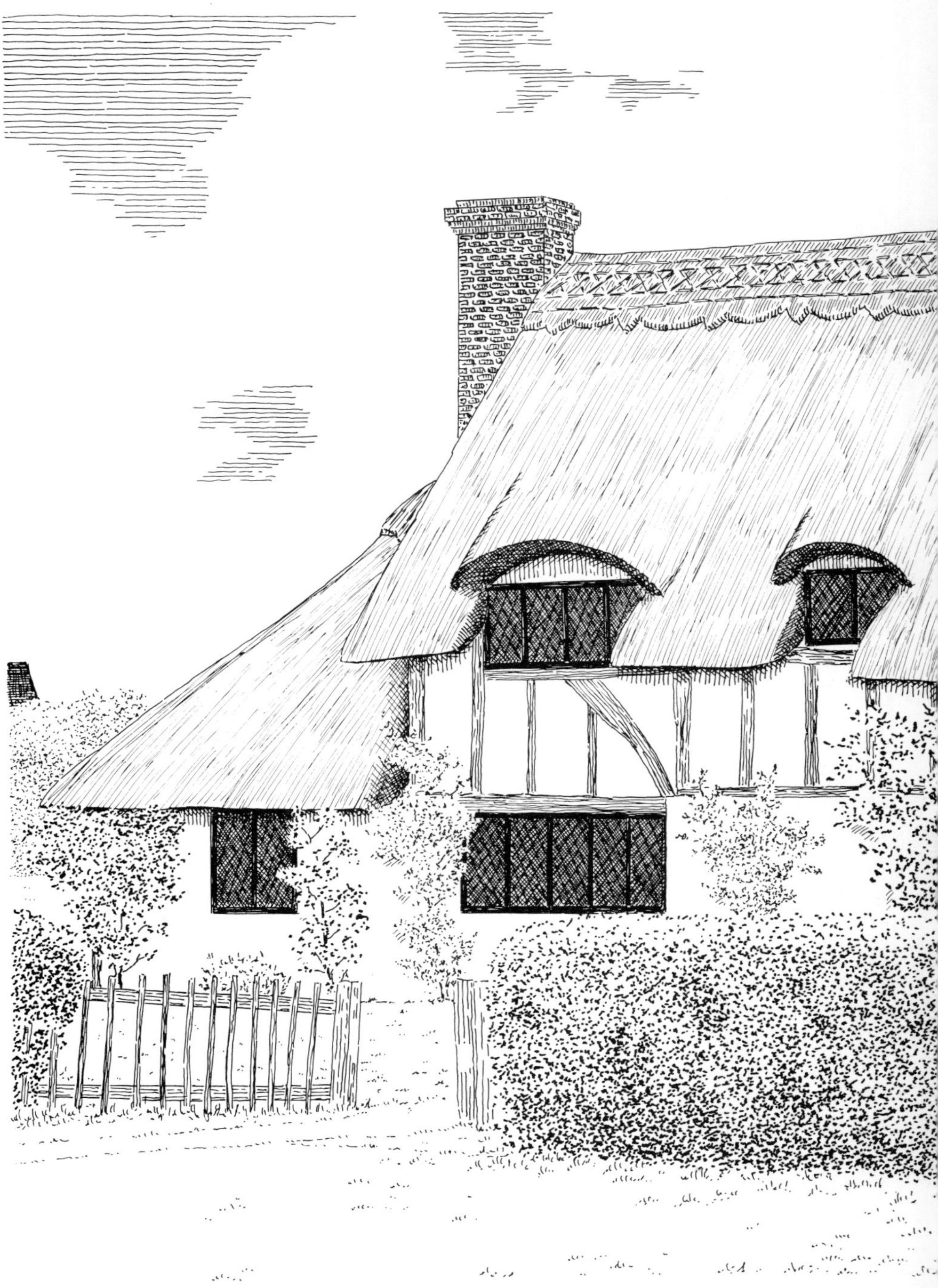

17. Thatchers, Little Benover.

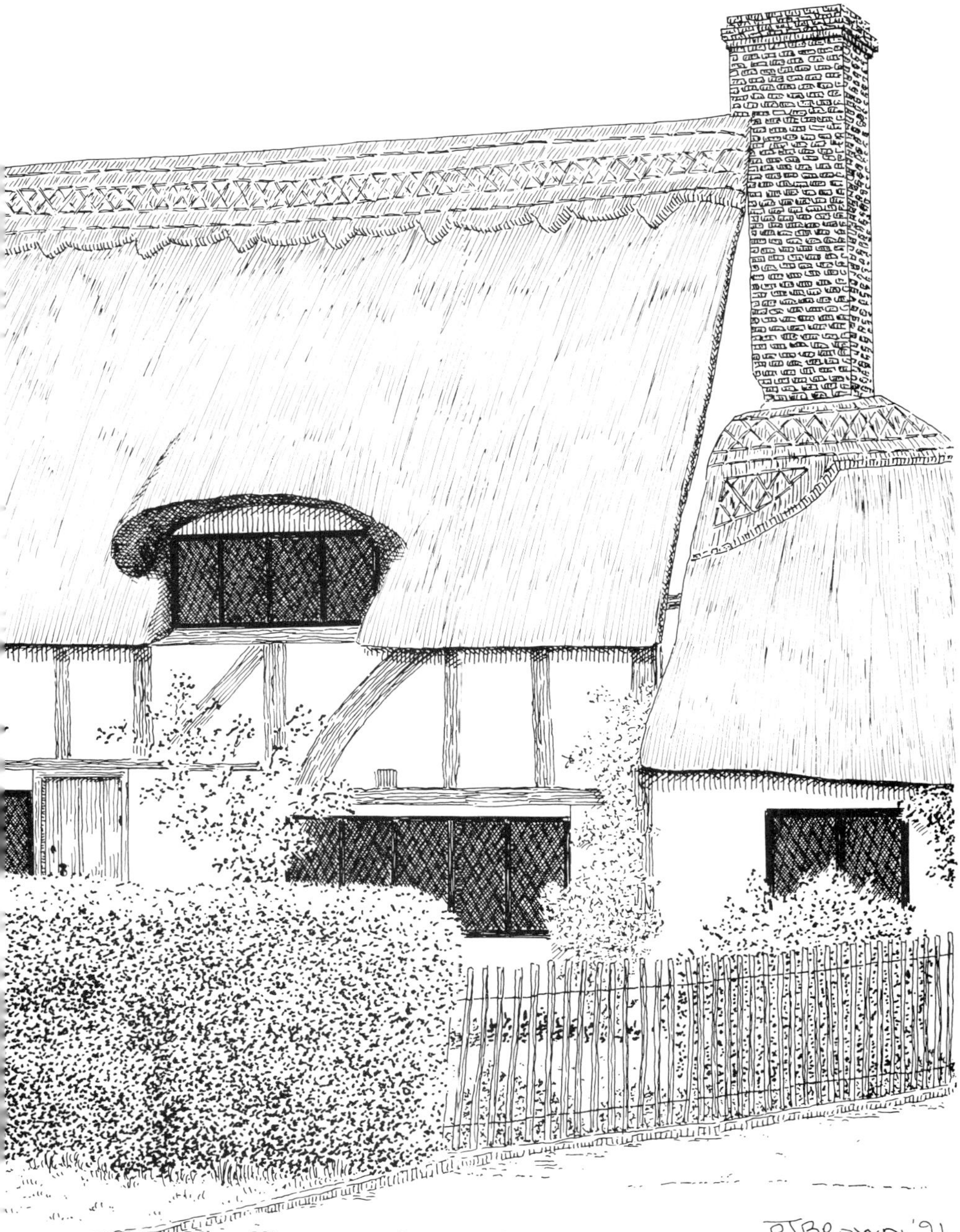
RJ BROWN '91

century onward, particularly in East Kent. Stone, although playing an important part in medieval times, has little significance in the overall picture of Kent housing. Plain tiles are the predominant roofing material although thatch, now somewhat rare, obviously had a more important role than is evident today. Welsh slate, imported in large quantities throughout the country in the nineteenth century, has perhaps less influence in Kent than in any other county; certainly in rural areas it is rare and even in towns it is less likely to be found than elsewhere in the country.

Unlike counties such as Gloucestershire or Northamptonshire, where the oolite limestone made it possible to evolve a regional style, in Kent such is the diversity of materials found within its boundaries that there is often no conformity of practice either in the same area or at any one period. Therefore we find houses built of timber alongside houses built of brick, all of the same period. Often there is a fascinating blend of stone and brick or stone and timber or a combination of stone, timber and brick, as at Ightham Mote.

2

Historical and Economical Background

Few counties have such an abundance of old houses as Kent; so many in fact that John Newman states that 'wherever one goes in Kent ... a view free of buildings can hardly be had.' It is not difficult to account for this when the county's early history and geographical position are taken into consideration.

Kent's position between London and the Continent has always been an important aspect and must, in part, explain its constant prosperity throughout the centuries. It has always been the gateway of England and the shortest route between London and the Continent. This is why three Norman castles – at Dover, Canterbury and Rochester – were stationed at strategic points on the line of the Roman Watling Road. It is why it became the county in which the metropolitan cathedral of England was established and hence the chain of houses which the various archbishops of Canterbury founded – Charing, Maidstone, Wrotham, Otford and Knole.

Not only was Kent the gateway of England, but it also became the garden of England. Agriculture has always played an important part in the prosperity of the county, for Kent has always been renowned for the good quality of its farming; unlike many counties there is very little non-productive land – no moors, no mountains, no heath lands, no vast tracks of salt marshes. Throughout the centuries travellers have noted the prosperity of the countryside. Thomas Baskerville, a Berkshire man, travelling to Dover after the Reformation, described Kent as one of the best cultivated counties in England. In 1823 William Cobbett, surveying the land from a hill near Hollingbourne, remarked:

> This is what the people of Kent call the *Garden of Eden*. It is a district of meadows, corn fields, hop-gardens and orchards of apples, pears, cherries and filberts with very little if any land which cannot, with propriety, be called good. There are plantations of chestnut and of ash

frequently occurring; and as these are cut when long enough to make poles for hops, they are at all times objects of great beauty.

Unlike most of medieval England where subsistence farming was general, in Kent, even from early times, the land was divided into numerous small manors with crops produced to sell. The main crops were wheat, oats and barley (used mostly for brewing), with peas and beans also being common crops, partly for human consumption and partly as fodder for large numbers of cattle. Christ Church Priory, with its vast estates throughout much of the county, sold its surplus food, generally to London or for export through Sandwich. It concentrated its flocks of sheep on the Romney Marshes or on Thanet, selling their wool to Italian merchants based in Sandwich.

Most of the present villages in north and east Kent are among the 300 Kentish manors mentioned in the Domesday Book, while most of those of the Weald were established in the twelfth and thirteenth centuries as the woodland was cleared. So at the time of the Norman Conquest only the fringes of the Weald had been brought into cultivation. The area was of heavy clay soil which was difficult to work, densely wooded and generally regarded as inaccessible. As the population expanded, freemen colonized the area, establishing small clearings in the wood. These areas, known as assarts, were individually owned. They became permanent, the piecemeal settlements producing not nucleated villages as in the manors owned by the monasteries, but hamlets of three or four houses, or isolated farmsteads linked by a network of lanes that still enmesh the Weald.

The Saxon words *hurst* meaning a knoll, especially a wooded knoll, and *den* meaning a wooded swine-pasture clearly show the early incursions of settlements into the Wealden forest, to which such names as Goudhurst, Hawkhurst, Sandhurst, Lamberhurst, Smarden, Bethersden and Rolvenden are almost completely restricted. Some show ownership of these clearings by people often originating many miles away, for instance, Tenterden, the *den* for the men of Thanet.

With much of the land privately owned or leased, often in small lots, the typical Kentish farmer was free to introduce new crops and methods as he pleased, not only for consumption by himself and his family but also to sell. Hops were introduced from the Low Countries during the fifteenth century. By around 1600 hop-gardens of one or two acres were being planted alongside other crops by many farmers. By the end of the seventeenth century one-third of England's hops were being produced in Kent, while some twenty years later Defoe found that Canterbury's prosperity depended no longer on the textile industry but on hops. Fruit too was another crop grown commercially. Richard Harrys, fruiterer to Henry VIII, obtained in 1533 105 acres of land at Teynham and there planted from 'beyond the seas the sweet cherry, the temperate pippin, and the golden Reinette'. His house Newgardens stood at Teynham until a few years ago. Like hops, fruit orchards were small, some two or three acres, with the trees planted twenty feet or more apart so that the ground between could be used as pasture. In 1576 William Lambarde, in his *Perambulation of Kent* (the earliest history of any county ever written), observed:

> As for orchards of aples and gardeins of cheries, and those of the most exquisite and delicious kindes that can be, no part of the Realme hath them, either in such quantitie and number, or with such arte and industrie set and planted ...

Defoe found the cherry orchards around Maidstone, which supplied London by boat, the largest in England. As well as in the Weald, orchards were to be found in particularly large numbers between Gillingham and Faversham. Celia Fiennes, in the late seventeenth century, remarked on the cherry orchards around Gravesend which ran down to the Thames and produced fruit for the London market. Wheat also came from this area of north Kent as well as from the Downs, while barley came from east Kent and Thanet as it had done centuries before, when Christ Church Priory owned the land. The wheat and barley from north and east Kent supplied much of London's needs, leading to Kent being called the granary of the capital.

The Flemish immigrants who settled in and around Sandwich introduced market gardening to the area. The Flemish were the market gardeners of Europe: at first they grew carrots and cabbages and later peas, onions, parsnips, asparagus and flowers, again mainly for the London market. Root crops, such as turnips, as well as sainfoin and clover, were also introduced in an attempt to restore fertility into the soil. Cattle were bred and fattened on the Weald and in north Kent and the Isle of Thanet for sale at Tenterden and Maidstone markets. Pigs had been kept on the wooded pastures of the Weald since before the Conquest – we have seen that place-names ending in *den* mean a woodland swine-pasture – and this continued throughout the fifteenth and sixteenth centuries. Sheep and cattle were kept on the open pastures of Romney Marshes and on the Downs, supplying wool for the weaving industry which grew up in the Weald as well as being fattened for market.

The prosperity which agriculture generated is reflected in the houses that the farmers built. Kent was famous for its yeoman class, whether free or tenant, rather than for any other group. From the beginning of the fifteenth century onwards their houses appear in great numbers throughout the county, at first built of timber but later more frequently of brick. The size of the houses as well as the yeomen's incomes varied greatly. Some, and this is especially true of those holdings in the Weald, farmed only five or ten acres; others might hold a hundred acres or more. Their income might be as low as £20 a year or more than £200. One important advantage whether their holding was large or small was that, as 40-shilling freeholders, they were entitled to vote for members of Parliament.

Many of the farmers were no more than husbandmen or smallholders with a limited amount of land, who worked for larger landowners at certain times of the year, such as ploughing or harvest times, to supplement their own incomes. Some were rich enough to live in the style of a yeoman farmer, but others were little better off than labourers. The country craftsmen and tradesmen such as blacksmiths, wheelwrights, carpenters and shopkeepers lived very much as the husbandmen, often supplementing the income from their trade with earnings either from their own land or by working on someone else's land. Most appeared to have had a chamber called a drinkhouse or milk-chamber and from the variety of wooden vessels found – tubs, churns, pails, milk bowls – many must have had a few cows to milk. The houses or cottages of the craftsmen or tradesmen would normally have been situated within the village, while the husbandmen would live on their holdings.

The largest class would have been labourers. The number varied greatly: in the Weald the proportion was only about a third of the population, undoubtedly because there still remained many small farmers, while in the corn-growing areas to the north and east of the county, which had larger farms, the proportion of labourers was much greater. Labourers were either resident or non-resident. Resident labourers lived in. Often they were domestic servants, but in some instances the term applied to farm-workers employed for a particular period. The majority would be non-resident labourers, married men, employed either on a full-time basis, or more likely by 'the piece', or contracted for a particular job – shearing, hedging, ploughing. The wages of Kentish labourers were regarded as among the highest in England but still they often had to have two jobs. By the coast, for instance, they often worked on the fishing-boats as well as the land.

The labourers' cottages were often small, usually no more than two or three rooms. In much of Kent they would have been built of timber, poorly constructed, and would have been long since swept away. There were some that survived until the twentieth century. One cottage recorded before its demolition in the 1960s was St Mary's Grove, a late medieval cottage at Tilmanstone which had two rooms, a

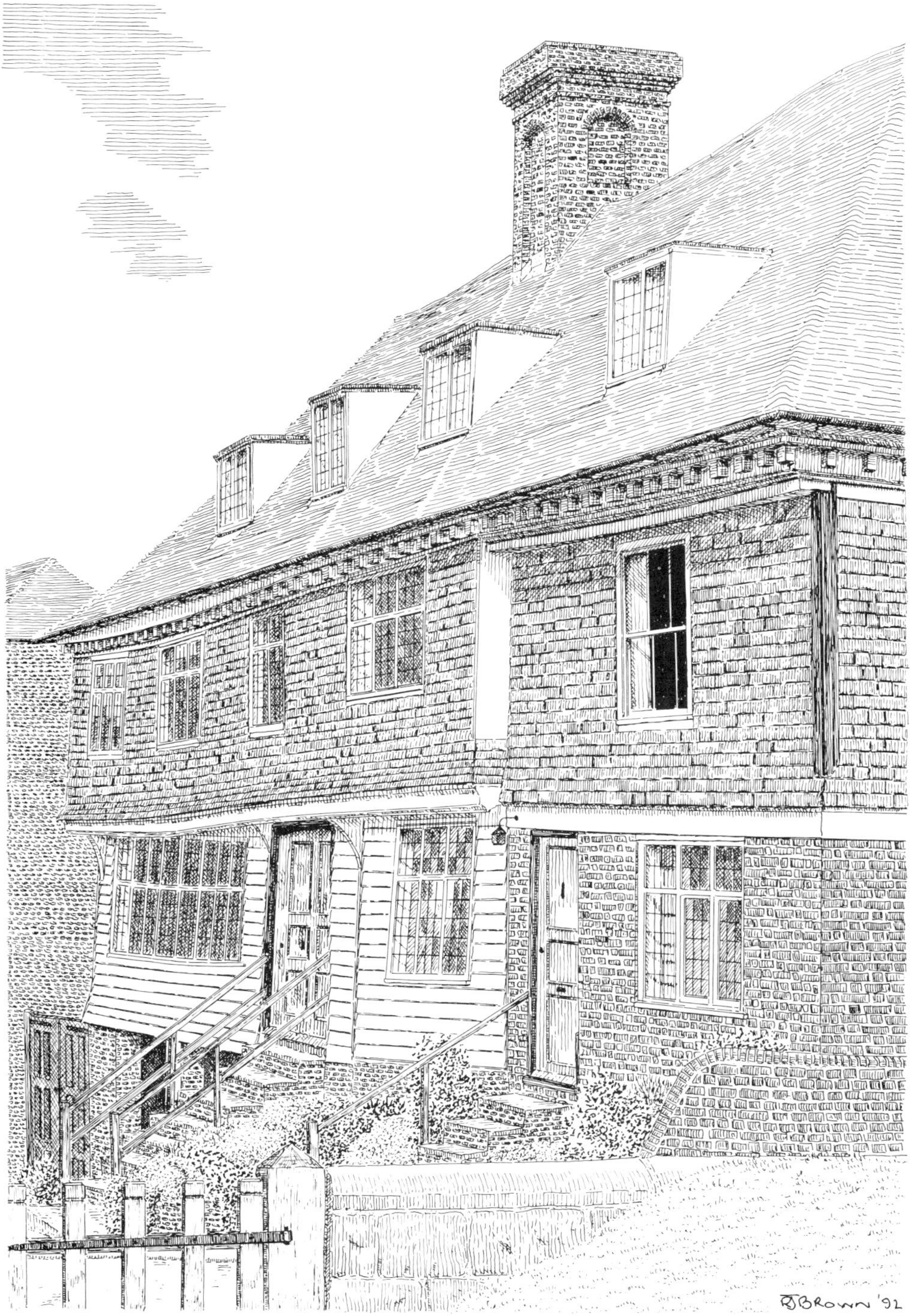

18. Church House, Goudhurst. A former master weaver's house.

hall and a service room both open to the roof. Cottages with such accommodation must at one time have been common. John Bevill, a labourer from Thanet who died in 1624, lived in such a house. It consisted of a hall simply furnished with a table and a bench, two chairs and two cupboards, with a chamber to one end containing two beds and four chests for linen. Because there was no other room, in the hall there was an axe, a shovel and two suckles, while the chamber contained a kneading-trough and two small pans. In many cases labourers would have lived in houses formerly belonging to yeoman farmers, or tradesmen who when having their new 'modern' houses built would subdivide the old house into cottages. An example of this is to be found at Hale Street, East Peckham, where a Wealden house has been divided into three cottages. There are numerous examples of similar houses throughout the county. Purpose-built terraces of cottages did not begin to appear until around the middle of the eighteenth century, to cope with the spectacular rise in the population in the second half of the eighteenth century.

1815 saw the end of the Napoleonic Wars and with it a dramatic drop in the living standards of much of the population. The county, which had during the eighteenth century been one of increasing prosperity and the home of prosperous yeoman farmers, was by 1822 being described as the most depressed county in England. During the war the farmers enjoyed high prices for their produce, in particular their corn; after the war prices fell. The population continued to rise. Between 1801 and 1831 Kent's population increased by 56 per cent. Labour became cheap: many people were unemployed and even more under-employed, forcing large numbers to rely on payments out of the parish poor rates. Such was the demand on this poor relief that there are reports that some farmers could not pay their rents and rates and were forced to sell. The situation was further aggravated by the increased competition from Australasia and the New World, especially in the second half of the nineteenth century. Workhouses became established in the parishes. These were seldom purpose-built, but were existing houses adapted for this use. One such house is Chessenden, Smarden, a house originally built in 1462 and the finest Wealden house in the parish. Another is Church House, Goudhurst (*18*), formerly the house of a master weaver, which became a tenement for the poor.

The depressed state of farming resulted in few new houses being built. Cottages to house the ever-increasing number of poor, often built of softwood and clad with weatherboarding, are to be seen in many of the villages of Kent, especially the Weald. Church Row, Plaxtol (*19*), is one picturesque group, probably built about 1850. Outside the Weald these cottages were often built of brick.

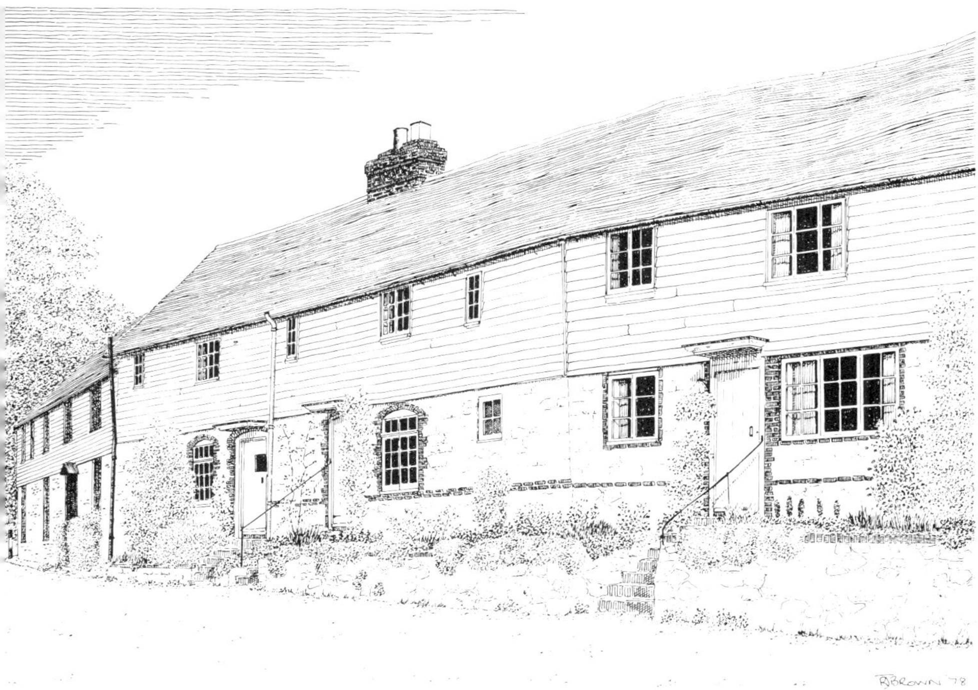

19. Church Row, Plaxtol. Cottages built of ragstone and weather-boarding, probably around 1850.

Accommodation would be small – at best no more than four rooms – at a time when the size of farmhouses was still increasing.

Agriculture was not the only industry which brought early prosperity to the county and therefore encouraged the building of houses. As early as the beginning of the fourteenth century Edward III introduced the weaving industry into the neighbourhood of Cranbrook, when he persuaded Flemish cloth-workers to emigrate to England, making Cranbrook one of the largest and wealthiest towns in Kent. From Cranbrook the industry spread throughout the Weald and to places as far afield as Maidstone and Tonbridge. Wool, although not of the finest quality, was readily available from the many flocks of sheep in the county, especially on Romney marshes, and fuller's earth, essential for getting out the grease from the newly woven cloth, was available at two or three places, in particular from deposits between Boxley and Maidstone. At Smarden, another Wealden cloth-town, there is Fullers Farm, a fifteenth-century end-jettied house where fuller's earth was probably found.

For some two hundred years cloth-making brought prosperity to

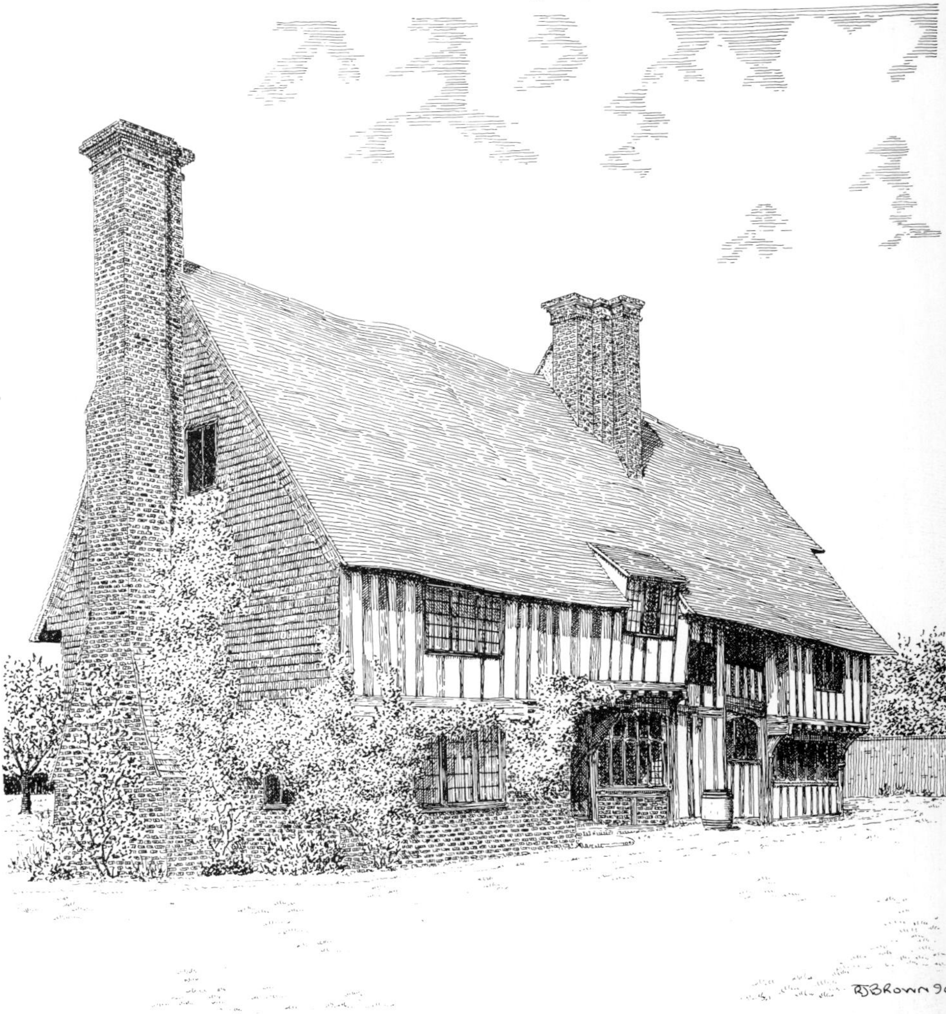

20. Old Cloth Hall, Smarden. A fifteenth-century house at one time owned by a cloth merchant.

the Weald, as can be seen from the many master clothiers' houses built in and around the villages. Clothiers were rich men and the industry employed hundreds of people. In the various processes of manufacture to produce one piece of cloth – between thirty and thirty-five yards in length – as many as thirty or forty men, women and children were engaged. Cranbrook has several early timber-framed wool-cloth halls in the main street of the town, while outside in the hamlet of Wilsley Green is Old Wilsley, a large timber-framed

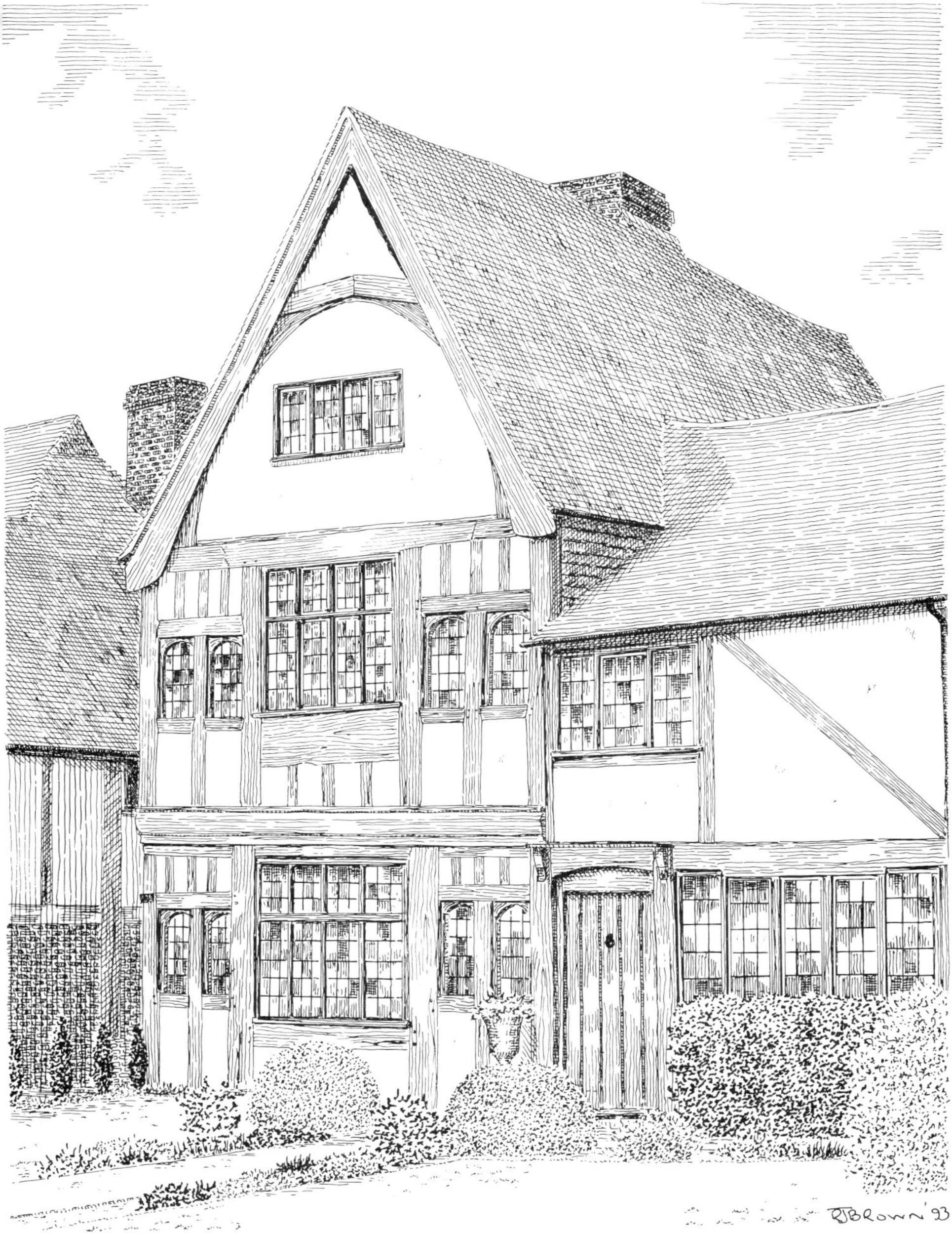

21. Shakespeare House, Headcorn. A former clothier's house built in the sixteenth century.

house probably built by one of the master weavers in the fifteenth century and certainly owned by John Weston, a flourishing clothier in the seventeenth century. Goudhurst, which had its beginnings at the time of the Norman Conquest as a hilltop clearing in the surrounding forest, also prospered from the broad cloth produced by the Flemish weavers who settled there in the fourteenth century from Cranbrook. Church House, on the north side of the main road, is a sixteenth-century master weaver's house and cloth hall. Close by is a terrace of cottages known as Weavers Cottages which probably provided accommodation for the Flemish workers. Although these houses were small, the carding of the wool to get rid of the tangles and the spinning were carried out in the workpeople's own houses, usually by the women. Weaving required looms and space in which to set them up, so this part of the operation was carried out elsewhere, usually in the master clothier's house, often in an attic running the length of the building. At Church House weaving was probably carried out in the lower room, which until the beginning of the twentieth century still contained two looms. Even by 1725 when the industry was in decline there were over twenty looms in Goudhurst, each employing eighteen women as well as several men. The Old Cloth Hall at Biddenden is another fine timber-framed clothier's hall obviously occupied by clothworkers; workshops were built during the sixteenth century and enlarged at various times, with the east gable, dated 1672, being the final addition. At Smarden, close by the church, is Old Cloth Hall (*20*), originally built in the fifteenth century as a farmhouse belonging to the church but later acquired by a cloth merchant, Tomas Yates, who used it as his residence and warehouse for wool woven in the village. To the north end of the house is a pulley for hauling the bales of wool to storerooms; the access gained by two external doors, the lower of which is reached by a permanent ladder, can still be seen today. Also in the village is the Dragon House, a house originally built by a family of Flemish weavers in 1331, where the former first-floor weaving-room still has its original loading-door and window visible from the interior. Another clothier's house, found in Headcorn along the north side of the High Street, is Shakespeare House (*21*). Within the steeply pitched roof is a storeroom with an external door.

By the later part of the seventeenth century the Kentish cloth industry was in decline and during the eighteenth century it ceased, unable to compete with the woollen industries of Yorkshire and the West of England. Many of the former clothiers' and weavers' houses found other uses. Old Cloth Hall, Smarden, was converted back to a farmhouse, known as Tuck Farm, until it was restored in the 1940s. The Dragon House became a shop, while Church House, Goudhurst, became barracks for soldiers during the Napoleonic Wars, tenements for the poor, an eighteenth-century coffee tavern, an annexe for the Star and Eagle, a temperance hall, a reading-room and library before becoming a residence.

The other important industry of Kent was also situated in the Weald – iron-making. The Weald provided all the raw materials necessary for the manufacture of iron: iron-ore in the form of ironstone, fuel in the form of wood or charcoal and power in the form of streams which could be dammed into ponds to provide sufficient water-force to work a wheel. The large, almost natural-looking ponds are scattered throughout the Weald, still known as 'hammer' ponds, or like the ones near Cowden and Horsmonden, 'furnace' ponds. The industry was certainly old, for in the Roman period the brown and ochre-coloured stone in the Cranbrook-Tunbridge Wells area had been smelted for iron. The industry was certainly in operation in around 1300 when there was reference to the smelting of iron at Tudeley. By the second half of the sixteenth century there were eight furnaces in the Weald. Fifty years or so later, by the end of Queen Elizabeth I's reign, at around the time that the Wealden iron industry reached its zenith, ironworks existed at Cowden, Ashurst, Tonbridge, Brenchley, Horsmonden, Lamberhurst, Goudhurst, Cranbrook, Hawkhurst and Biddenden. William Camden, the Elizabethan historian, found that towards the end of the sixteenth century the Weald was full of mills 'beating with hammer on the iron', filling the neighbourhood both day and night with continuous noise. In some cases the works were relatively small, employing only a few men, but others employed many more. Early in the seventeenth century an ironmaster by the name of Browne, at Brenchley, employed 200 men, thought not necessarily all at the same works.

Just as the woollen industry made rich men of the clothiers, the iron industry created great wealth for the ironmasters as well as employment for many men. Some ironmasters founded families of note. Crippenden, a delightful old house near Cowden, was the home of the Tichbornes, having been built in 1607 by Richard Tichborne, who had a foundry in the parish. The Streatfeilds of Chiddingstone Castle are also descended from an ironmaster, Richard Streatfeild, who is commemorated by a cast-iron slab in Chiddingstone Church.

The former widespread manufacture of iron in the Weald is still evident from the names that still survive. There is Furnace Farm, close to the Sussex border at Cowden. At Lamberhurst there is the Furnace Mill, a former mill connected to the iron industry which finally closed down in 1765 before being converted to a corn mill. At Goudhurst there is another Furnace Farm together with a Forge Farm and a house called Three Chimneys. On the road between Sissinghurst and Biddenden is Hammer Mill Farm. In many parts place-names also reveal the presence of the former industry – Hammer Stream, Hammer Dyke, Furnace Hill, Hammer Wood are all to be found in the area between Tonbridge, Lamberhurst and Biddenden.

By the end of the seventeenth century the Wealden iron industry was in ruins. It could not compete with those areas of northern England where better ore was to be found or could be imported from abroad; even more important, where coal was readily available it was, of course, better than wood for smelting the ore. The collapse of the industry had its economic effect on the area.

There were two other industries introduced into Kent as a result of the immigration of foreign workmen towards the end of the sixteenth century. They were not as important as the cloth and iron industries, but had significant influence locally. One town to prosper from these immigrants was Sandwich, when in 1561 the government invited Flemish protestant refugees to settle there. They brought with them the art of making serge cloth known as 'says and bays'. These refugees like later Dutch settlers, left their mark on the town and in the surrounding countryside.

Another textile industry introduced into Canterbury by French protestant refugees was silk-making. The Huguenots developed into a flourishing and very prosperous community during the seventeenth century and their numbers were swelled with a further influx of refugees after restrictions were imposed on the protestants in France in 1685. Around this time it is said that there were about 2,000 people engaged in the silk industry, some 1,300 immigrants and 700 English, and so almost a third of the families in the city must have been associated with the industry. Early in the eighteenth century, with the import of woven silks from the Far East, the industry collapsed suddenly and completely.

Of the other industries within the county two were started by foreigners: linen thread and paper-making. Linen thread was made at Maidstone in the seventeenth century and exported around the world. The industry declined and finally disappeared during the eighteenth century. Paper-making was introduced by a German at Dartford in 1558. It proved so successful that soon 600 men were employed. Later, during the seventeenth century, the industry grew with the arrival of French refugees who started two further paper mills at Aylesford and Canterbury. Shipbuilding, including the refitting of ships, was carried out at Chatham and Deptford, together with the smaller dockyards at Woolwich and Sheerness. The timber for building and repairing ships was obtained from the Weald. There was also a small shipbuilding yard at Faversham which also had a gunpowder mill that remained in operation until the twentieth century.

All these industries – cloth, iron, silk, linen thread, paper, shipbuilding and gunpowder – were introduced to supply a demand that was more than local. From the fourteenth to the eighteenth centuries they brought wealth into the county and with this wealth houses of all types were built, from large houses for the owners to cottages for their workers. Nevertheless, these industries were on a small scale, employing only a minority of the total workforce. The industry which employed most workers, either directly or indirectly, remained agriculture.

Another reason for the large number of small houses within the county was undoubtedly that large tracts of land were formerly owned by the ecclesiastical establishment. Some twenty years after the Norman Conquest the Church owned around a half of the cultivated land in Kent. The archbishop owned Sandwich, the most important port at this time, and twenty-five manors elsewhere in the county including Otford, Wrotham, Charing and Maidstone. Most of east Kent, including much of the Isle of Thanet, belonged to the two great abbeys at Canterbury – Christ Church Priory, which owned thirty-four manors in Kent and twenty-two others elsewhere, and St Augustine's Abbey. Other large ecclesiastical landowners were the Bishop of Rochester, the Canons of St Martin's at Dover, which owned about 4,000 acres of land, and Battle Abbey, which owned the royal Saxon manor of Wye with rights over much of the Weald. These estates consisted of a number of manors scattered throughout Kent; only the Constable of England, Hugo de Montfort, had holdings more or less in one block in the area of Dover, Folkestone and his castle at Saltwood. Some of these scattered manors were administered by the ecclesiastical establishments through a bailiff who would live at the 'Court Lodge' – the usual name in Kent for the administrative centre of an ecclesiastical manor. In other estates the manors were too distant to serve as a demesne and tenants in free socage became established.

Several natural calamities early in the fourteenth century changed the structure of society. Famine and the Black Death reached England in 1348 and destroyed a third of the population of Kent, especially west Kent, and further visitations in 1361 and 1369 depleted it still further. The immediate result, due to the heavy mortality, was an acute shortage of labour to work the land. In the last decade of the fourteenth century this shortage of labour was responsible for far-reaching changes. The ecclesiastical and manorial estates previously farmed by direct labour under bailiffs or serjeants were all leased out for money rents. The advantage of this, as far as the landowner was concerned, was that the demesne was continuously occupied without fragmentation, it could be maintained and improved and rents were paid promptly without arrears. By 1396 this system was established everywhere on the estates of Christ Church Priory and, by about 1450, on all the archbishop's estates. Both landowners and tenants contributed to the upkeep of the land and buildings, with up to 20 per cent of the annual rents being allowed to the tenants for repairs.

Following the Dissolution the land owned by the two great ecclesiastical establishments at Canterbury, Christ Church and St Augustine's, and land owned by other abbeys, monasteries and priories was all transferred to the Crown. Some two-thirds of the land held was immediately transferred to other ecclesiastically bodies (the Archbishop of Canterbury, and the Deans and Chapters of Canterbury and Rochester). About a tenth was retained by the Crown, although within a generation almost all had been sold or given away, while the remainder was given or sold to private individuals, resulting in a further break-up of the estates.

Large estates with a resident landlord emerged and this had an effect on many of the villages. As in medieval times when men of wealth acquired great estates, for instance Penshurst Place, successful bankers, merchants and politicians acquired country estates, and this was particularly true in west Kent and those areas closest to the capital. In many instances this resulted in resources from outside the agricultural economy of Kent being injected into the county. In most cases the villages benefited, the old houses being replaced with ones designed to a similar pattern to give the uniform appearance so familiar in estate villages.

One such village is Pluckley, with a collection of red-brick cottages set at all angles around the forecourt of the Black Horse Inn. These cottages are of the nineteenth century and each has windows of one, two, three and four brick arched lights painted white, often under a depressed relieving arch. These so-called 'Dering lucky windows' were the concept of Sir Edward Cholmeley Dering, who thought they brought luck and had them fitted not only to the village houses, but also to his own house (sadly partially burnt down in 1952) and in all the buildings on his estate. These lucky double arched windows can also be seen on some of the houses at Little Chart (*22*) which forms part of the Dering estate. At Great Chart, the Tokes family used red brick and shaped gables, reflecting the architecture of their home Godington, for their nineteenth-century estate buildings. Red brick was also used for the estate cottages at Chevening, which forms one side of the village street opposite the church. Here the emphasis is on moulded brickwork, mostly English bond.

At Penshurst and Leigh one of the most notable Victorian architects, George Devey, was engaged. Devey trained as a water-colourist under J.S. Cotman and also J.D. Harding and it was

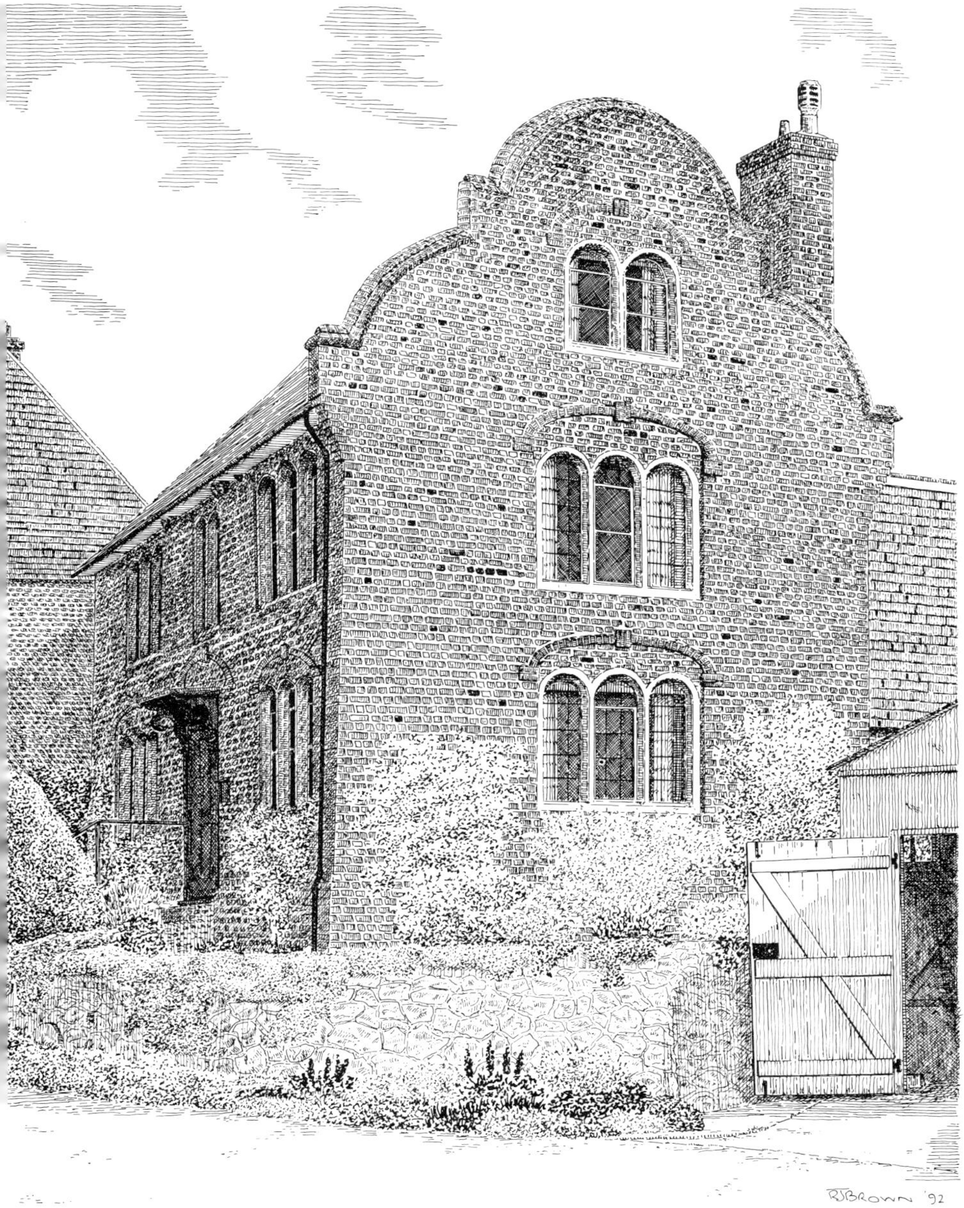

22. Seventeenth-century house at Little Chart with Dering 'lucky' windows.

obviously this training which gave him his feeling for picturesque grouping which is so evident at Penshurst. In 1850 Lord de L'Isle commissioned Devey for the restoration of Penshurst Place and the building of the estate cottages. He added the cottages to the sixteenth-century ones by the churchyard to form Leicester Square. Built in the Tudor style, stone below, timber above, jettied and rendered, they form the perfect group. This traditional style was continued at Leigh by Devey and later Sir Ernest George. The work was commissioned by Samuel Morley MP, a textile manufacturer with works in London and also in the Nottingham areas, who had purchased Hall Place in 1870; he had it demolished and rebuilt in the Tudor style to Devey's design.

Not all landowners had a beneficial effect on their villages. In some instances the extensions to the great house and the enlargement of parks meant that the villages themselves were swept away, leaving only the church, within the park, as no more than a private chapel to serve the squire and his family. One example of this is Knowton, where the church interior is still arranged as a family chapel. Only the church and Waldershare Park, a Queen Anne mansion, survives at Waldershare and here even the church was declared redundant in 1981. At Eastwell the situation is even worse. Eastwell Park, an eighteenth-century mansion belonging to the Earls of Winchelsea, has been demolished, leaving only the more recent gatehouse built about 1845. The church too collapsed in 1951 and has since become a ruin, for it did not justify rebuilding as nobody lived nearby. The deer park has become farmland, the only relic of the former village being Lake House, a thirteenth-century first-floor hall house which stands near the church at the edge of the park's artificial lake. This house too is derelict.

Probably the most important influence on housing development was the pattern of land-tenure, not farming. The Midland open-field system, common in the Midlands and elsewhere in the country, of large, open fields surrounding a nucleated village, was never common in medieval Kent, although some cases are known, for example in east Kent and around Wrotham. Even in Saxon times the villeins of Kent were already virtually tenant farmers, for at the time of Domesday it is recorded that they owned 78 per cent of all ploughs. Instead the pattern was generally one of houses grouped together in small hamlets or of isolated farmhouses each linked to relatively small but privately owned lots. In Kent, therefore, farmhouses remained for centuries on the same site, being slowly changed, enlarged or adapted to meet the changing needs of the times and of the family. This gradual change brought with it continuity rather than the major upheaval which the enclosure movements of the eighteenth and first half of the nineteenth century brought to many parts of the country, in particular the Midlands, where new, isolated Georgian farmhouses were constructed, with the old farmhouses in the village street being turned into cottages. In Kent, some farms were enlarged at the expense of small owners, and properties so acquired were incorporated within the larger farms. When this happened the old farmhouse was often split into cottages while others were enlarged and modernized.

The system of inheritance in Kent was what is known as 'gravelkind'. In most other places in the country, when the Normans conquered England they imposed their own system of inheritance whereby an estate was inherited by the eldest son, a system known as primogeniture, but in Kent the people managed to retain their own peculiar system in which the estate was divided equally between all the sons unless otherwise directed by a will. The Norman custom naturally tended to increase the power and wealth of the landed families but the older Saxon custom, although apparently fairer to all members of the family, tended to provide a wide distribution of possessions and consequently the equalization of families and the creation of small independent farms.

In practice, the property was not always physically divided but might be leased, with the income divided between the heirs, or one of the heirs might buy out the other heirs, thus keeping the property intact. In other cases, not only the land but also the dwelling was divided, sometimes into two but often into three.

The traditional story of the means by which the Kentish people forced William the Conqueror to respect their ancient customs is quaintly told by William Lambarde, in his *Perambulation of Kent*. After the overthrow of Harold on the battlefield, Stigand, Archbishop of Canterbury, and Egelsine, the Abbot of St Augustine's, were placed at the head of the Kentish people, who had met at Swanscombe. Lambarde relates:

> This done, eache man gotte him a greene bough in his hand, and bare it over his head, in such sort, as when the Duke approached, he was much amazed therewith, thinking at the first, that it had been some miraculous wood, that moved towards him: but they as soone as hee came within hearing, caste away their boughes from them, and at the sounde of a trumpet bewraied their weapons, and withall dispatched towards him a messenger which spake unto him in this manner. 'The commons of Kent (most noble Duke) are readie to offer thee, eyther peace or warre, at thine own choyce and election: peace with their faithful obedience, if thou will permit them to enjoy their ancient liberties: warre, and that most deadly, if thou deny it to them.'
>
> Now when the Duke heard this, and considered that the daunger of deniall was great, and that the thing desired was nut smal, he forthwith,

> more wisely than willingly, yealded to their request: And by this meane both he received Dover Castle and the Country to obedience and they only of all England (as shall hereafter appeare) obtained for ever theyr accustomed priviledges.

There can be no doubt that the existence of the gravelkind preserved for the people of Kent their rights and privileges. The Kentish inheritance system restricted the accumulation of a large estate and so a large proportion of the population held their lands subject only to a fixed rent; as their wealth grew, rents became merely nominal, and a strong yeoman class became established at an early date. Their substantial if not wealthy conditions are well described in the following lines from an old song:

> A squire of Wales, a knight of Cales,
> And a laird of the North Countrie;
> A yeoman of Kent, with half a year's rent,
> Will buy them out all three.

This wealth is reflected in the number of medieval and post-medieval houses which are still to be found within the county.

3

Medieval Houses

Whatever the material used in medieval houses, the one feature that was common to all was the hall. It could be on either the ground floor or the first floor but it was always the largest room in the house, and originally perhaps the only one. It was divided into two, with the owner, his family, his guests situated at the upper end and his servants or retainers at the lower end. The hall was where they all dined, slept and lived when indoors and where the manorial court was held. In the twelfth century the hall was often a separate building but gradually other buildings, with separately roofed wings, were added. Over the years they became incorporated under one roof to form, by the fourteenth century, the characteristic medieval plan. These additional rooms, whether detached or not, were known by the Anglo-Saxon name 'bower', the only word available until supplemented by the word 'chamber' in Norman times; the latter term could be applied to both ground-floor or first-floor rooms.

The medieval ground-floor hall house developed from the barn-like structure of Saxon times. The method of heating the hall was the central hearth and so a hall with a lofty roof for the smoke to escape was essential. At the lower end of the hall, the house became extended to provide the service rooms: a buttery for drinks and a pantry for bread and table utensils. Sometimes between these two doors was another doorway leading to the kitchen, which up until the fifteenth century was an independent structure as a precaution against possible fire. Over the service room was the solar used by the owner and his family as a private room. This was a superior room matching the open hall in its splendour, open to the roof with moulded timber members. The word solar means no more than an upper part of the house which is supported on beams. This room above the service rooms was seldom heated but in the larger stone houses from the late eleventh century onwards, wall chimneys were used. Access to the room above was obtained from one of the rooms below or in a few cases directly from the screens passage via a third door.

Later the solar over the service room became inconvenient, for it was situated at the opposite end of the hall to the high table, and so a solar was provided at the upper end with a storeroom beneath. From the often rough and rude square ceiling joists in nearly all early medieval houses it is clear that this was not regarded as a room of any importance. The architectural details bestowed on the hall were not carried into the other ground-floor rooms; the ceiling joists and underside of the floor boards received nothing more than a coat of whitewash. In superior houses, from the end of the fourteenth century onwards, the storeroom became a 'withdrawing room' for the female members of the family and a secluded room for conversation and entertainment. For the first time the word 'parlour' for a room in a house occurred, taken from the place set aside for the reception of visitors in a medieval monastery. Among ordinary folk this ground-floor room, usually referred to as the chamber, became the principal bedroom and remained so in many households until the seventeenth century; it was never thought of as a parlour. The preference for most people remained for ground-floor living, using the upper floor only for storage. The main entrance into the house was at the lower end of the hall, separated by a timber screen – hence the name screens passage.

In Kent this layout, the open hall flanked at one end by the solar block and at the other end by the service block, can be found in all types of houses, from the largest to the smallest. The characteristic layout was both convenient and compact, with the most important aspect architecturally being the asymmetrical layout.

In the earlier Middle Ages the Normans introduced the first-floor hall house with the hall placed at first-floor level. These first-floor halls were more defensible, being raised on a stone basement or undercroft, which was often vaulted. The basic plan was simple: on the first floor was the hall, usually of two bays, with generally a single-bay solar at one end, both open to the roof. Access to the hall was obtained by means of a door reached by an external staircase. The hall was heated by a fireplace located on either the rear or side wall, but the solar was rarely heated. The undercroft was usually an open space with an external door and small windows for ventilation and was used for storage or as servants' quarters. In early stone buildings the rooms beneath the upper floors were vaulted. Three main types of vaulting are to be found: the barrel vault, semicircular in the twelfth century, developing into the pointed form in the thirteenth century; the groined vault, formed by the intersection of two barrel vaults; and the ribbed vault, where the weak groin intersection was strengthened by stone arches, with the four compartments forming a quadripartite

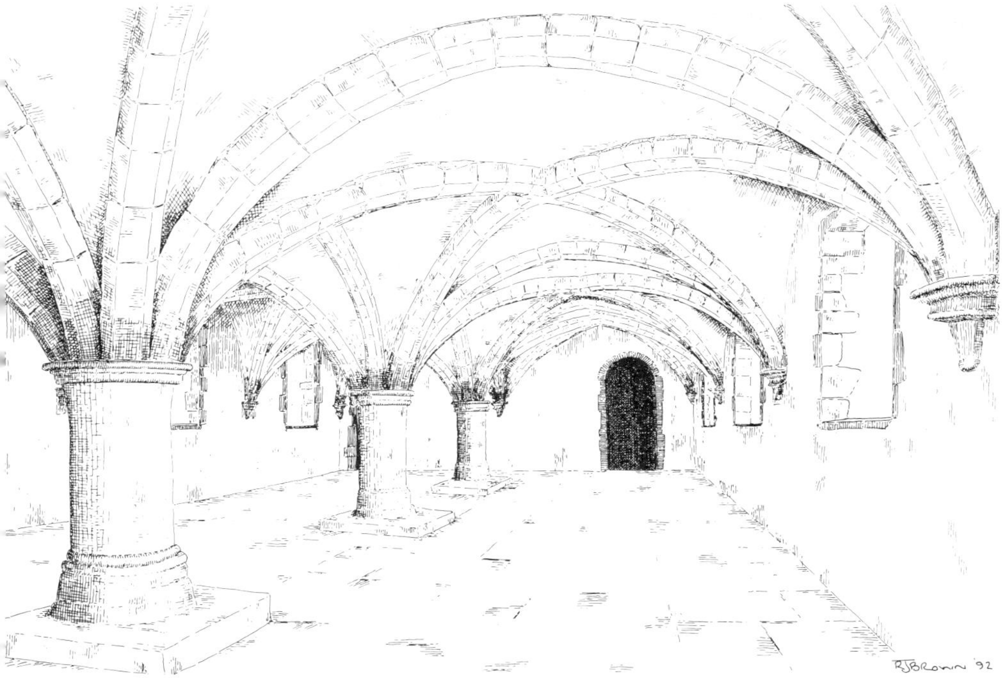

23. Undercroft, Nettlestead Place, from an old photograph.

bay. One of the finest examples of a vaulted undercroft is to be found at Nettlestead Place (*23*); it is all that remains of the thirteenth-century house. The undercroft is of four bays divided into two aisles supported by short round piers, with quadripartite vaults with chamfered ribs.

The open hall was divided into the upper and lower ends, the social division marked by the central open truss. The upper end was occupied by the family and contained the high table and bench, possibly on a raised dais. This bench was usually fixed, being no more than a long, narrow plank some eleven inches wide and two feet high. In some cases the peg-holes for the support of these benches can be found. The partition between the hall and parlour was usually formed with vertical oak boards, with a moulded beam to the head above the bench which in Kent was often crenellated. Even in the smallest of houses this division between the upper and lower ends is noticeable, with the superior architectural detailing not only in the upper end but also those areas in the lower end which were visible from the upper end.

Features of the Medieval House

GROUND FLOORS

The ground floor in all but the largest medieval houses belonging to the nobility (Penshurst Place still retains its original fourteenth-century tiled floor) would have been little more than compacted earth, strewn with rushes or straw, treated perhaps with ox-blood and ashes. This created a surface sufficiently bound to prevent dusting and wear and which could be polished. In those areas where chalk was available, this was used. Chalk lumps, rammed and sealed with sour milk and lightly tempered produced, it seems, a durable floor. Chalk was used at the Old Hall, Sundridge, where the original floor of hard-trodden chalk was discovered under a later brick floor when this was taken up in the restoration work carried out in 1926. It is known that this is the original floor, for set in the chalk was the original old hearth, a circle of fire-worn stones. The durability of a chalk floor can be seen at the Clergy House, Alfriston, Sussex. During renovations of the building in 1977 a new rammed chalk floor was laid – four inches of chalk lumps sealed with thirty gallons of sour milk – which is standing up well to the thousands of feet that have since walked over it. Where available, lime was added to earth floors.

FIREPLACES AND CENTRAL HEARTHS

Few medieval houses possessed chimneys, although there are examples known in the stone-built Norman first-floor hall houses. At Luddesdown Court (*24*) there is a perfectly preserved example. The hooded fireplace is a rare example to survive from the thirteenth century, thought to date from around 1250. Here the simple carved jamb-shafts with bracketed tops support a joggle-jointed stone lintel with a moulded projection above. Between the random-coursed walls to the recess itself can be seen brick-tile coursing, another feature of the period. Although the ground-floor hall in stone-built houses generally retained the open hearth, on occasions the solar at first-floor level had a fireplace built against the wall. The remains of one jamb of the fireplace can still be seen at Old Soar, Plaxtol, and at Copton Manor to the north of Sheldwich the upper room of the solar block also appears to have had a fireplace.

As we have seen, the hall floor would in most cases have been of compacted earth or chalk, apart from a hearth formed by a rough square or circle of flat stones about four feet across set flush with the floor. Usually referred to as the central hearth, it was not usually central but towards the upper end of the hall towards the parlour. The reason for this was probably two-fold: firstly, the fire could not be placed directly under or close to the tie-beam supporting the

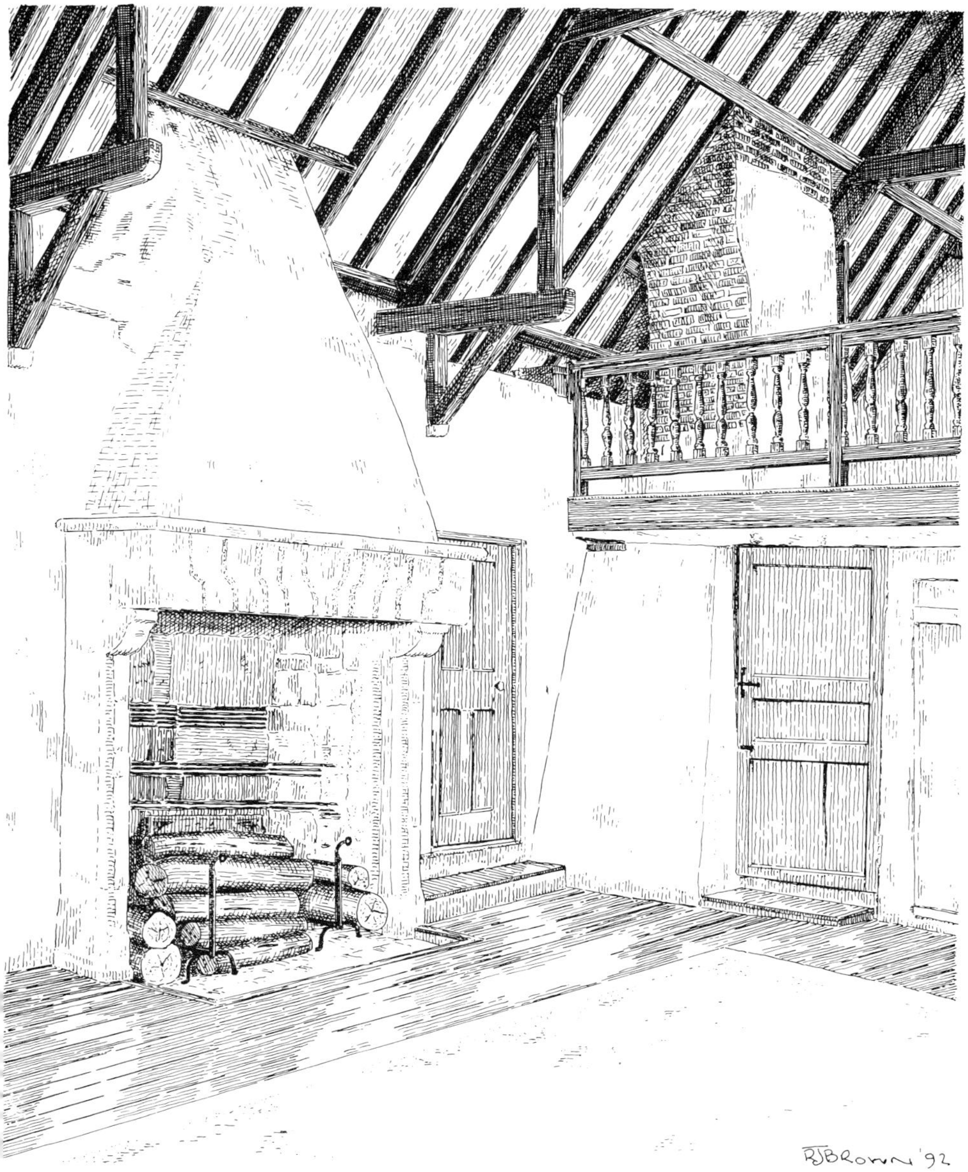

24. Fireplace, Luddesdown Court dating from around 1250.

crown-post; secondly, it was positioned nearer the high table. It is interesting that the central truss is not generally central either: it is invariably a little nearer the service end.

Today we have to rely mainly on museums for an authentic picture of the early domestic central hearth. In the Weald and Downland Open Air Museum at Singleton two examples of former Kent houses have been reconstructed, showing what an old hearth was like. When the reservoir at Bough Beech, near Tonbridge, was constructed in the late 1960s, two houses were saved for re-erection at the then newly formed open-air museum. Winkhurst Farmhouse was one, and shows an example of the open central hearth in the open hall; here a cauldron is suspended by a chain from a great beam above the fire, representing a simple method of cooking common in the fourteenth century. The other house was Bayleaf Farmhouse, of later date than Winkhurst, which shows a typical fifteenth-century central hearth with a stone hearth set in the earth floor.

Kent also has one very fine example of fourteenth-century central hearth, although it is not typical of what the ordinary householder would have used. This splendid hearth is to be found at Penshurst Place (*25*), in the open hall, and has a massive double trestle of wrought iron to take the burning logs, with each upright embossed with the Sidney family's coat of arms. Firedogs of this type, known as

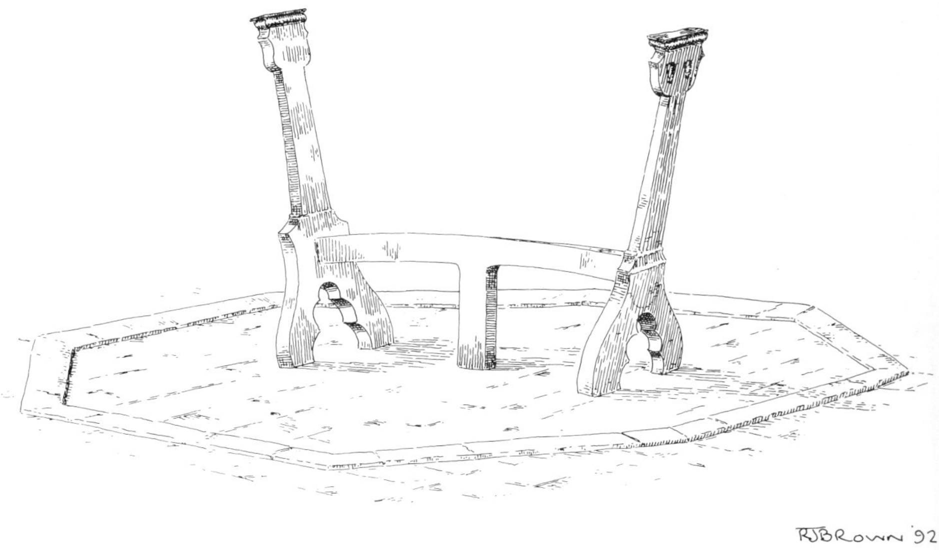

25. Central hearth, Penshurst Place showing the double andiron on which the logs burnt.

'andirons', are of great antiquity: these probably date from the second half of the sixteenth century, when the Sidneys arrived at Penshurst. The hearth itself is octagonal, about eight feet across and formed of brick paviors, level with the floor and surrounded by a low curb.

The smoke from the open fire would escape as best it could, and the soot-coated rafters found in old houses are a clear indication of a former open hall with an open fire. In some medieval roofs there is evidence of a louvre or smoke outlet above the hearth; in others the small gablets at both ends of the ridge were used as smoke outlets. In this case the partition between the open hall and the end-bays would not extend to the full height of the hall, and a triangular space between the partition collar and rafters could be formed. To prevent smoke entering the room below, a plaster lining was laid over the collars, thus completely sealing the room beneath. However, in many cases the partitions between the hall and the service and solar ends were full height to the ridge, to exclude smoke from the sleeping-quarters. In such halls other methods must have been used for removing the smoke. When Durlock Grange, Minster-in-Thanet, a house built in around 1414, was being demolished in1960, Mr E.W. Parkin discovered a number of tiles with a hump or raised part in the centre which had a deposit of soot on the underside. When laid alternately with flat tiles they acted as small vents and were clearly used to let the smoke escape. Since this discovery similar tiles have been found in other houses. An example can be seen on the roof of a detached medieval brew-house at Minster Abbey, which has a number of these tiles spaced out at even intervals.

In many cases, however, it seems likely that no actual method of extracting smoke was incorporated into the house. Medieval tiles were extremely irregular, and it is probable that as long as the tiles were not torched, the smoke could readily escape. This is borne out at Bayleaf Farm, where the service end was torched with straw and the later solar end in clay but the hall itself was untreated. Houses with thatched roofs, however, provided more of a problem, for smoke would have had difficulty penetrating the thatch, and here a small vent of some sort appears to have been usual. Some old illustrations show a flap which could be opened or closed by means of a string.

ROOFS

The earliest ground-floor halls were aisled, like a church, with two or occasionally one row of timber posts or stone pillars to support the 'arcade-plate', a longitudinal beam running the full length of the hall. The arcade-plate supported the common rafters which ran from the ridge to the arcade-plates and from the arcade-plates to the wall-plate of the external walls. To increase rigidity a tie-beam was introduced,

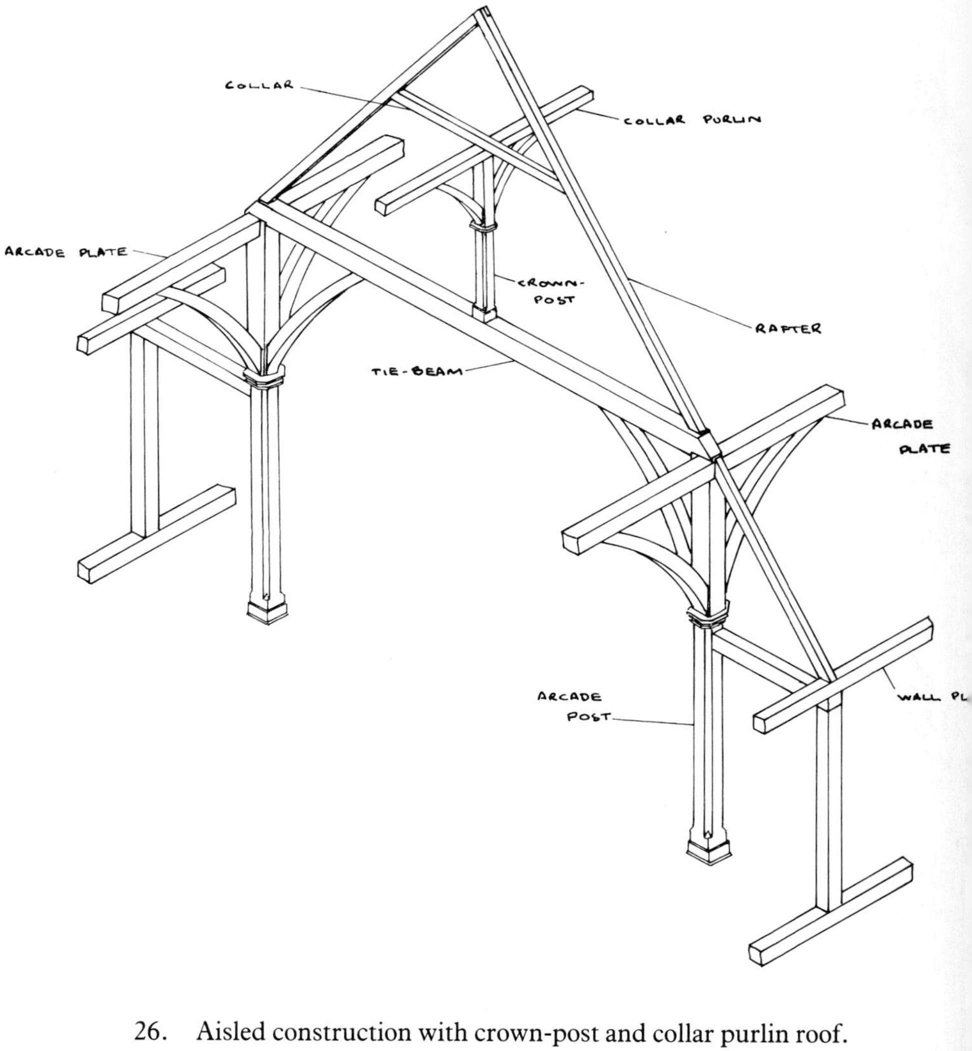

26. Aisled construction with crown-post and collar purlin roof.

spanning the hall and sitting on top of the arcade-plate above the post into which the principal rafters were framed. The rafters were further strengthened by a collar at high level. Further stability was achieved by the introduction of braces between the arcade-posts and the tie-beam, and between the arcade-post and the arcade-plate.

Early aisled roofs were of a single-framed collar rafter roof which used only rafters, with each pair pegged at the apex and tied together with a collar. This type of roof can be found at Cogan's House, Canterbury, and a merchant's house at West Street, New Romney. To

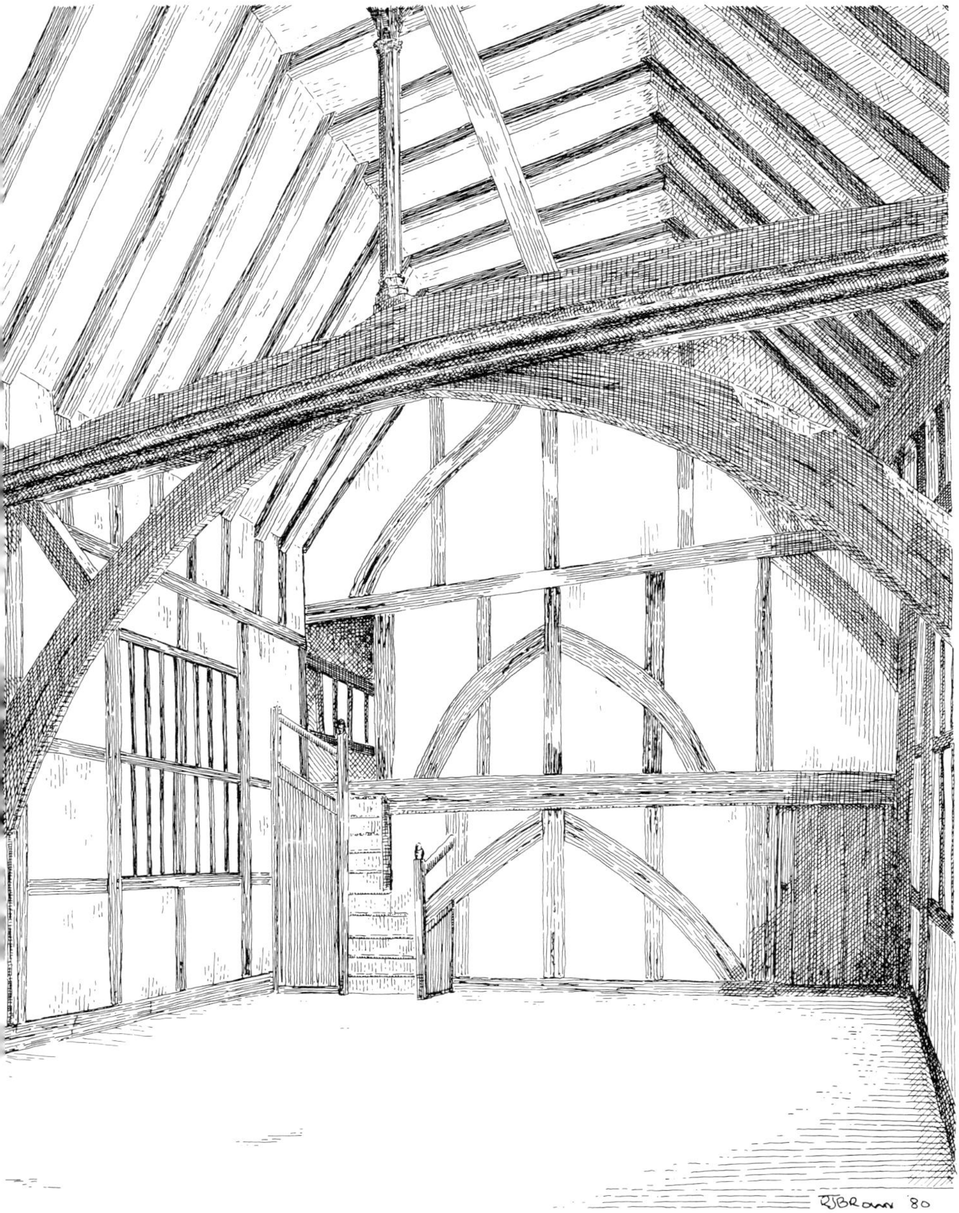

27. Open hall, Wardes, Otham showing the arched brace central boss.

increase the stability of the roof, which had no longitudinal members apart from roof battens, a system of passing bracings was introduced. This was used at Cogan's House and unique in Kent, being akin to the early aisled buildings of Essex and Suffolk. Later aisled halls had a crown-post roof in which a longitudinal plate, known as the collar purlin, was placed under the collar, transferring much of the roof's weight by means of crown-posts positioned in the centre of the tie-beams. The tie-beam was not fixed to the collar purlins and the stability of the roof relied on friction between the two. These crown-posts themselves required braces between the post and collar to

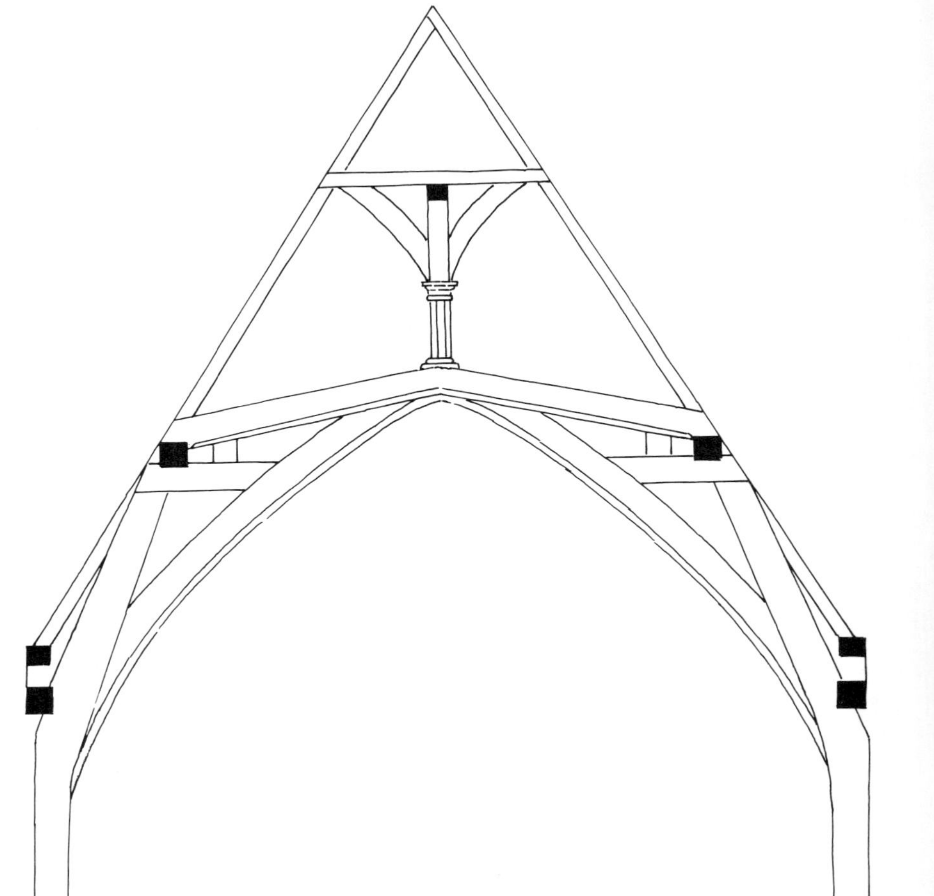

28. Base cruck construction, based on Hamden, Smarden after S.E. Rigold.

prevent lateral movement, and usually additional braces were provided between the crown-post and the collar purlin. The crown-posts were set at regular intervals along the length of the roof framed into the tie-beam at the bottom and to the collar purlin at the top.

There are houses that predate the crown-post type roof but which are not of aisled construction. One such house is Copton Manor where the open hall, the two-storey solar block and a third block, the bailiff's quarters, all have roofs of scissor-brace construction. The third block originally had tie-beams at eaves level, but these have now been cut. The roof at the Deanery, Chartham, comprising paired rafters and two sets of straight collar beams, is known to have been built in 1303.

Although aisling provided a greater floor area to the hall, the arcade posts caused an obstruction and from the beginning of the fourteenth century other methods were devised to overcome this problem, yet still maintain the overall overspan. On larger domestic houses large arch-braces to support the tie-beam were used to span the hall. These occur in the stone-built Ightham Mote and Battel Hall; at the timber-framed Yaldham Manor, Wrotham; Wardes, Otham (*27*); and at the Old Rectory, Horsmonden, which also has curved windbraces. A variant of the arch-braced truss, recorded by R.T. Mason at Walnut Tree Cottage at East Sutton, is the extended arch-brace. Mr Mason believes that as it is the only example so far recorded it is likely to be an *ad hoc* device – a spontaneous and unique invention. Structurally it is not sound, for excessive stress is transferred to the joint at the apex where the braces met the collar, resulting in the failure of the joint by the breaking of the wooden pegs. Mr Mason noted that this is what happened at Walnut Tree Cottage and that the truss only remains stable on the strength of the other members of the truss. The medieval hammer-beam roof so favoured in East Anglia for church roofs and occasionally found in dwellings is virtually unknown in Kent.

Another method widely used in most parts of England, with the exception of East Anglia, is the base-cruck, which enables the arcade plate to be supported from the external wall (*28*). Only three examples of base-cruck construction have yet been discovered in Kent, namely Hamden, Smarden; Burnt Oak, Benover, near Yalding; and Barnes Place, East Peckham. No true crucks have been found in Kent. Crucks at first-floor level, however, are widely scattered throughout the county. They are to be found in association with jetties rising from the jetty-sill to the plate under the pitched roof and are to be seen at Burnt Oak, Benover, at Frogholt Cottage, Newington-next-Hythe, at the fourteenth-century Barton Cottage, Kennington, at Upstreet Cottages, Etchinghill, near Lyminge, a former open-hall house of about 1500 date, and at a house at Staple.

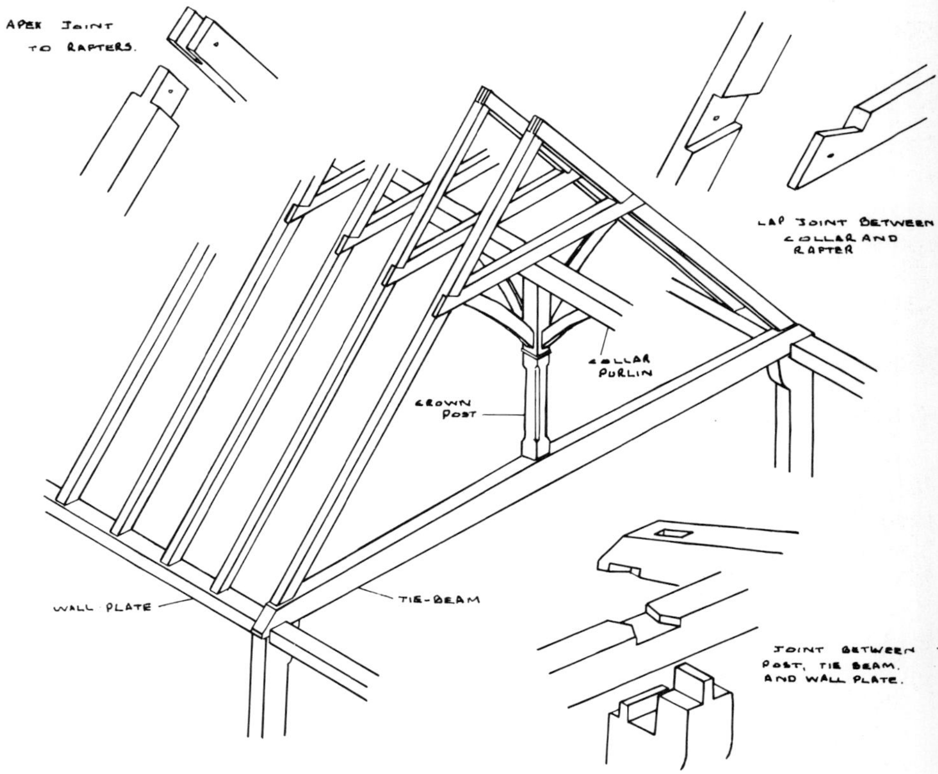

29. Crown-post roof construction.

However, the most widely used form of roof construction in the medieval houses of Kent is without doubt the crown-post roof (*29*). This roof type was well established in church roofs during the first half of the thirteenth century but the first known examples in domestic buildings are not before the second half of the century – Old Deanery, Salisbury and Manor Farm, Bourn, Cambridgeshire. In Kent the earliest is of late thirteenth-century date – Old Soar, Plaxtol, of about 1290 (*30*) – but by the beginning of the fourteenth century the crown-post roof had become firmly established on all the important houses. The earliest datable example is to be found at Court Lodge, Great Chart, which is known to have been built in 1313. Another early crown-post roof can be seen at Court Lodge, Fawkham. By the fifteenth century crown-post roofs had become almost universally adopted in domestic houses in Kent.

Because so many of these roofs were built in a relatively small area, over a fairly limited period, for people of more or less the same social

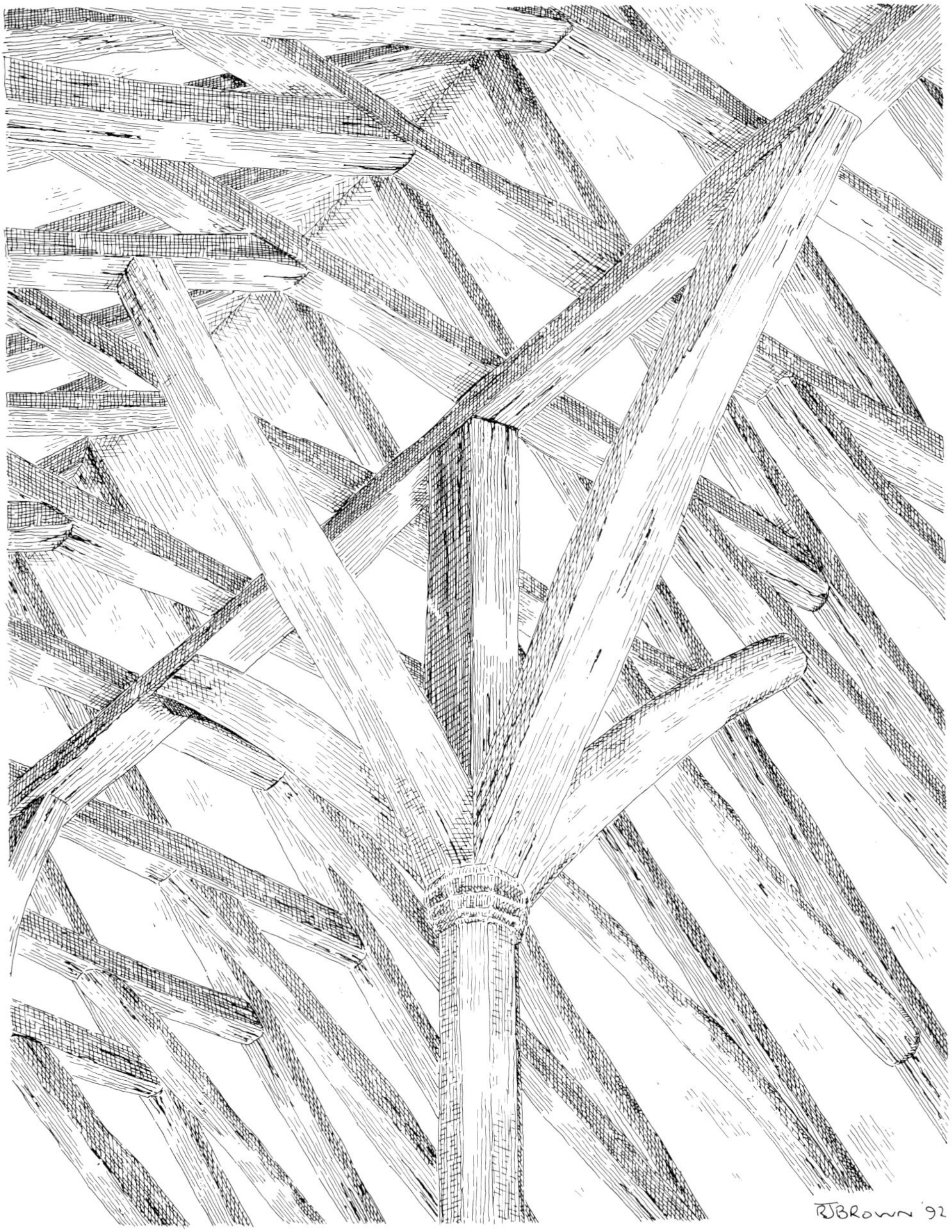

30. Crown-post roof, Old Soar, Plaxtol. Built around 1290.

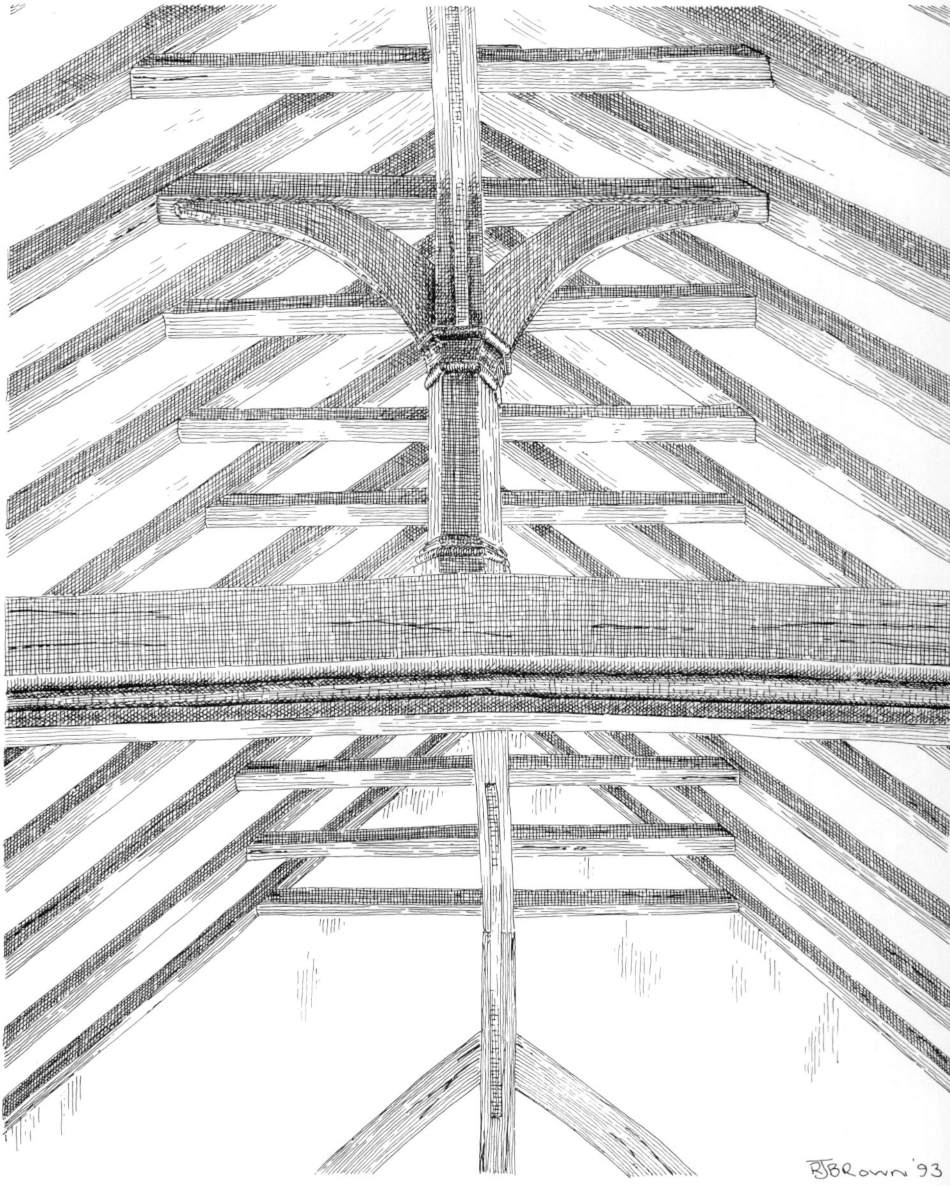

31. Crown-post roof, Yeoman's House, Sole Street, Cobham.

standing, the design was fairly standard. Basically, the crown-post, especially that to the open hall, was slender, some five or six inches square with a height of between five and six feet from the tie-beam to the collar. The shaft was generally octagonal or with chamfered edges, with a moulded base and cap, but at Stoneacre, Otham, the shafts are of a moulded cruciform section. The cap was set at some two-thirds of its height. Immediately above the cap sprung the curved braces to the collar and the collar purlin. A typical example is to be found at Yeoman's House at Sole Street, near Cobham (*31*). Needless to say, there were many variations to the basic form and these are generally associated with the bracing; apart from the usual method of four-way bracing at the head, there are crown-posts which have only longitudinal bracing to the collar purlin at the head, and there are some which in addition to the longitudinal bracing at the head also have downward braces at the foot to the tie-beam; another type has no braces at the head and is only braced at the foot to the tie-beam; the last type has no bracing whatsoever. The braces at Old Soar are straight and support not the collar but the rafters. The other variation is the length of the crown-post itself. Although five to six feet is the most common, they can vary from as little as three to four feet as at Nurstead Court to some seven feet or more, as at Headcorn Manor and Wardes.

Efforts have been made to date crown-posts by the length of the crown-post and the length of the bracing, on the assumption that short shafts and long braces are early and that long shafts and short braces are later (*32*). Clearly, from the evidence of Nurstead Court and Wardes this is not the case. It must be said that many late crown-posts do have long shafts and short brackets but the main factor appears to be rather the span, slope and collar height than anything else. The crown-post roof prevailed unchallenged until the time of the Reformation when it was replaced by side-purlin roofs entering Kent from the west.

UPPER FLOORS

The upper floors of medieval Kent houses, except those stone houses with an undercroft below, would have been of oak joists and boarded construction. There is clear evidence that floorboards were not always fixed. They were often inserted by the tenant and, like glass for windows, not infrequently included in an inventory along with furniture and often described as being 'loose and movable'.

Few original boarded floors still survive within the county; uneven wear is the characteristic feature of those that survive, with the softer parts being worn away and the rays standing proud. However, most have now been replaced. The early boards would have been either

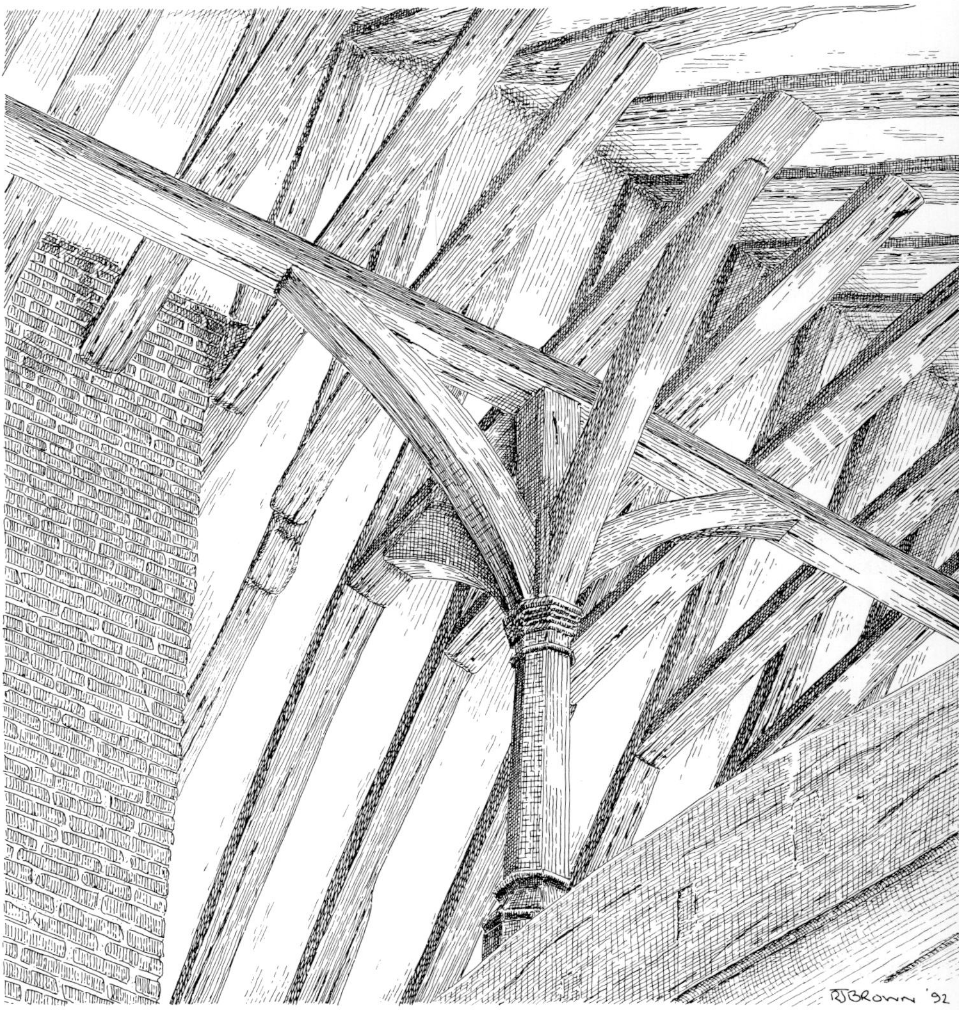

32. Crown-post roof, 'The Wealden Hall', Larkfield.

clefted or pit-sawn, the length obtained largely depending on the quality of the timber and the method used; clefted boards were generally shorter – often only a few feet long – and rarely of any great width. Pit-sawn boards could be obtained by three methods: the log could be quartered and then cut obliquely across the medullary rays at a very acute angle, finally being adzed to produce boards of a similar thickness; alternatively the log could be squared to the right width and then cut up to produce boards of the same width, usually about twelve inches wide; more commonly the logs would be simply slabbed, producing boards of varying widths between one and three feet. This method was most commonly used for, unlike the other two methods, there was very little waste. When the upper floor of Durlock Grange was inserted into the open hall this method was used, with the boards being all sawn from one oak tree. Mr Parkin discovered that the widest board was in the centre and measured no less than 22½ inches; the boards then diminishing in width on either side: 19½, 14, 12 inches and so on.

In the early days of closely spaced joists the boards ran parallel to them, either fitting in rebates with the joists forming part of the floor or more commonly laid over them. Later, when the joists were set wider apart, the floorboards were laid at right angles to and not parallel with them, thus helping to distribute the weight. This was even true in those houses jettied on two adjacent faces: the joists would meet the dragon-beam at the angle, and the boards would be mitred above the beam. This type of flooring enabled boards of varying widths to be used. At Durlock Grange the original boards were discovered beneath the floorboards. These were of random widths, one inch thick and lap-jointed, with the outer boards rebated into the bressummers at front and back. Few, if any boards, would span the whole room and the carpenter's main aim would be to fill in the area and produce a sound floor with the boards available. These boards varied not only in width but also in thickness. To overcome this, if the boards were too thick, the underside would be hewn away with an adze, or if the boards were too thin, the joist would be packed.

CEILINGS

In the medieval house it was usual to leave the joists and beams of the upper floors exposed to view from beneath and the boarding upon them formed the ceiling of the room below. With the open hall the upper floors would only be over the parlour and perhaps over the service room as well. In these rooms the beams would rarely be moulded. In fact the rude, square joists of the parlour ceiling in particular are a common feature of the medieval house. This can clearly be seen at Wardes, Otham. When boards were used, and this was always so in Kent, they would be left exposed and at best whitewashed. It was not until the sixteenth century that plaster was used between the joists. There is evidence that when the boards were left exposed, the boards and sometimes the joists as well were often decorated with painted designs. It is unlikely that any of these now exist in Kent, for most of the old medieval boards would have been replaced but examples exist in other parts of the country – in Edinburgh and Durham for instance, where they probably date from the late sixteenth or seventeenth centuries. There is also evidence that on rare occasions in the fifteenth century very thin timber board were used to line the underside of the joists. Joseph Gwilt in his *Encyclopaedia of Architecture* quotes an example of this type of ceiling in a house at Wingham and states that it was usually distempered.

STAIRS

Although the first-floor hall houses of the thirteenth century had an external staircase, when the ground-floor open hall was adopted, with its two-storeyed solar and service bays at either end, internal stairs became essential. These early medieval stairs were either a simple ladder or at best the more elaborate companion-way – a straight flight with the steps formed of triangular oak blocks with the first five or six set vertically, one above the other. Evidence of these steep companion-ways is sometimes to be found in the layout of the ceiling joists, where an almost square but small stair-trap or opening has been infilled with later timbers.

Later, stairs consisting of steps formed of baulks of solid timber triangular in section were introduced and continued to be built through much of the sixteenth century in ordinary houses. Straight flights, with or without winders, dog-legs and newel stairs, were all constructed with these solid steps. Of these the most common was the straight flight, in which the solid steps were pegged to two inclined bearers and usually set at an angle of forty-five degrees, were the most common. These solid steps still survive here and there, one of the best examples being at Olde House, formerly Old Bell Farm, Harrietsham.

Newel stairs (tapered treads rising around a central post) were preferred in some houses, particularly small ones, for they occupied less space. The solid steps were housed at one end to the newel post – circular or octagonal in cross-section – which went from floor to ceiling or on occasions for the full height of the house, and at the other end to the studs and wall-posts. Winders incorporated in straight flights at the top or bottom, to reverse the stairs direction, were also constructed in the same way as newel stairs. Surviving examples of newel stairs with solid timber steps are rare, but evidence of their former existence can sometimes be seen in the irregular mortises in studs and plates, which represent the outer fixing of the treads.

In the open-hall house with both a solar and service wing two stairs were required. The flight in the lower end would usually be incorporated within one of the service rooms. Occasionally in the large houses it would have a separate doorway leading from the screens passage, as at the Old Cloth Hall, Smarden, Headcorn Manor and Pattenden, Goudhurst. At the upper end access to the stairs would be either from the hall or from the parlour. When it was from the hall, the dais would be protected from the stairs by a screen. Usually the stairs were contained within the solar wing but occasionally they would be in the corner of the hall as at Wardes, Otham. The stairs would normally be enclosed in a framed compartment with a door at the bottom and top.

In medieval stone houses both straight and newel stairs were constructed of stone. Newel stairs were allied to the centuries-old spiral stairs of castles and church towers. A good example can be seen at Old Soar, where the inner end of each step forms a circular section of the newel. The stairway down from the solar has the first four steps in the solar itself, then continues within a semicircular turret. The door from the solar opens into a recess in the wall of the stairway, leaving it clear.

DOORS AND DOORWAYS

The two significant features of the medieval doorway, whether external or internal, were the fact that the doors had no frames – all doors were hung directly to the jambs, whether stone or timber – and the overall shape of the opening. The typical Norman doorway has a semicircular arch and although a fairly common occurrence in churches and castles, at the domestic level survival is rare. The two-centred arch of the Early English and later periods are far more common. The hood-mould is a characteristic feature of this period, with stop-moulded jambs.

An unusual door can be seen at Old Soar, Plaxtol (*33*); here the two-centred arch is depressed with a wide chamfer to the outer face.

Timber two-centred arches are more usual, formed of large baulks of timber. A fine example is to be seen at Link Farm, Egerton (*34*), constructed out of two massive baulks of oak set upside-down and hewn in such a way that enough was left to form half the arch of the doorway. So each half – the jamb, spandrel and arch – is formed out of a single timber. Other examples are to be found at Hawkenbury, Headcorn, Wardes, Otham, and the Thatched House, Smarden.

By 1425 these two-centred door-heads had begun to be replaced with four-centred arches, often with sunken tracery in the spandrels of the door-heads. Examples are common enough on the timber-framed

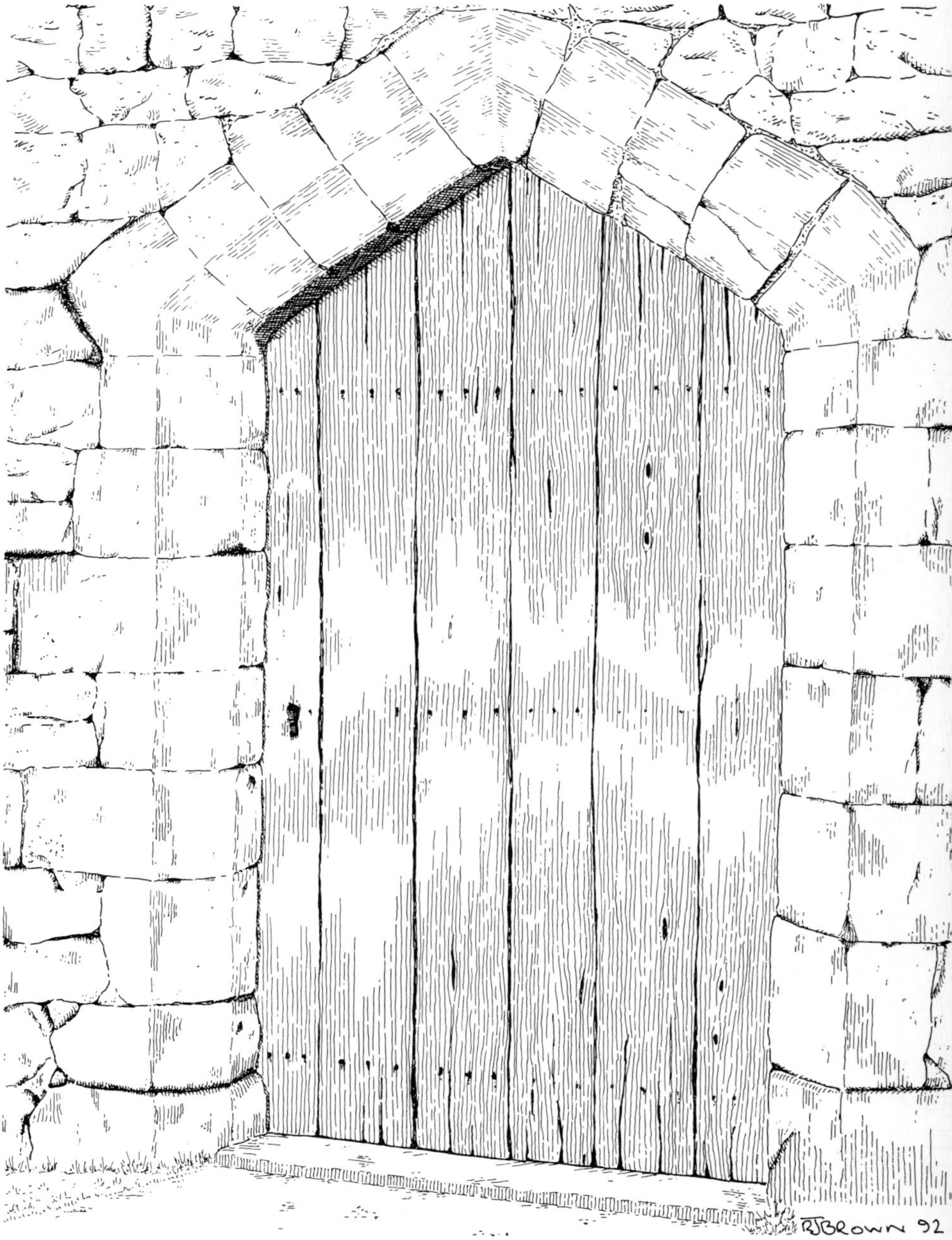

33. Old Soar, Plaxtol. Door to ground floor under-chapel.

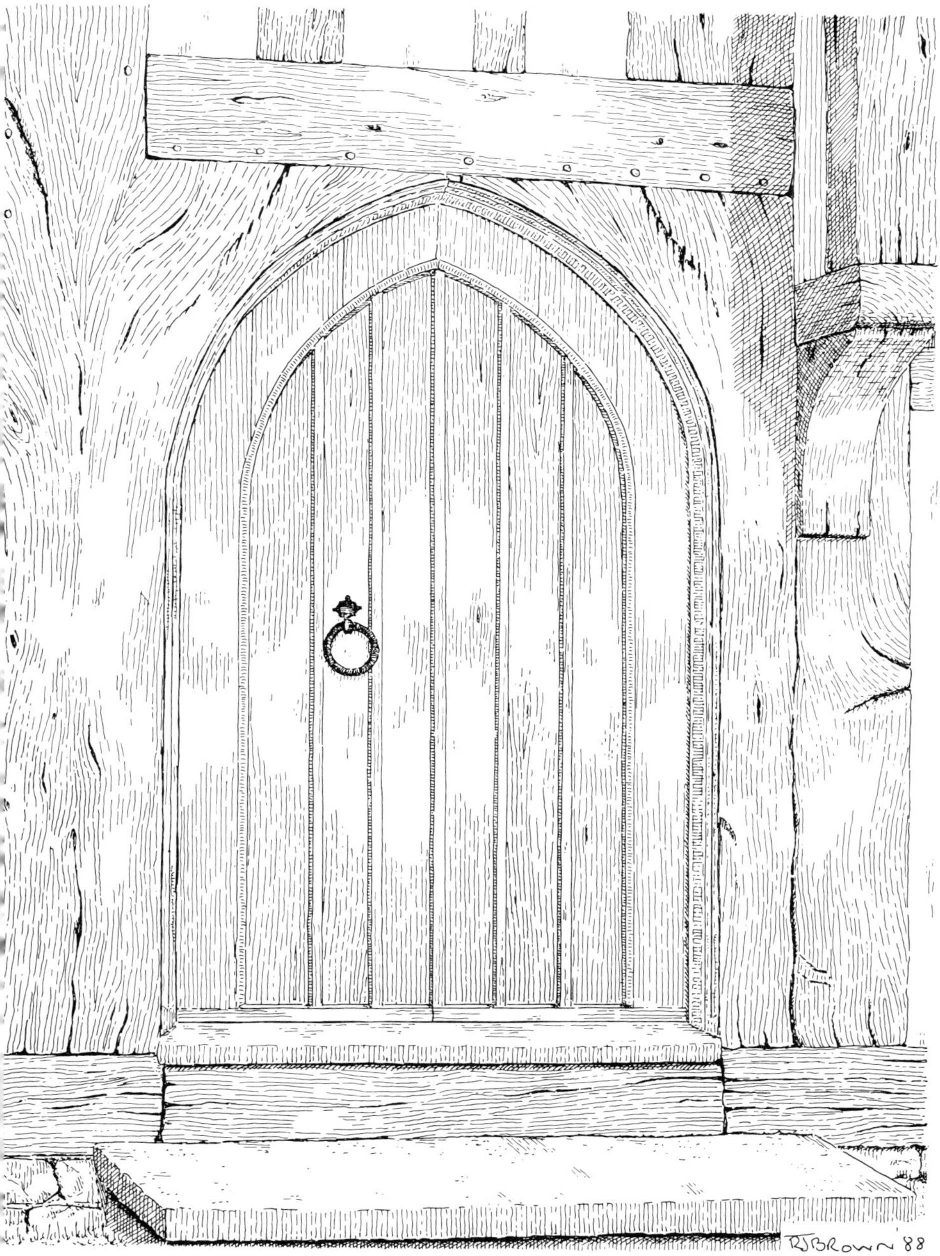

34. Link Farm, Egerton. External door to screens passage.

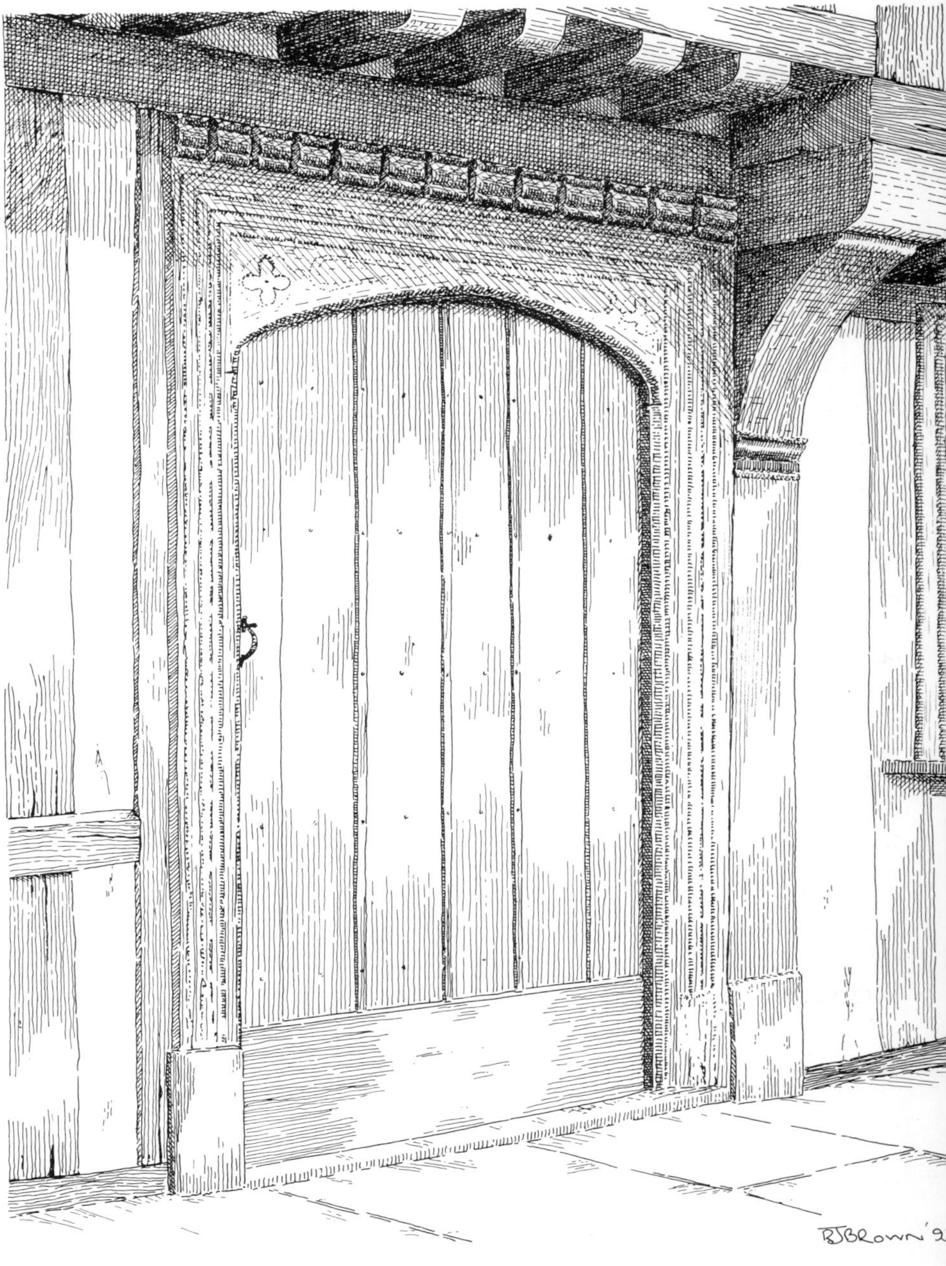

35. The Tudor Rose Café, Tenterden. Entrance door with crenellated moulding to doorway.

houses of the fifteenth and sixteenth centuries; crenellated moulding to the head was a characteristic decoration of the period in Kent and can be seen on the entrance doors to the Tudor Rose Café, Tenterden (*35*), Kite House, Monks Horton and the Olde House, Harrietsham. The moulded beam above the door leading to the service rooms often had this form of battlement cresting as can be seen as Synyards, Otham, Kite House, and the Yeoman's House at Sole Street.

The earliest doors were ledged ones, the simplest consisting of no more than vertical boards secured at the back with horizontal battens or ledges and, when the door was particularly wide, with additional diagonal braces to prevent the door from sagging. A stronger and more elaborate form was for the ledges to be replaced with a continuous series of horizontal boards. The vertical boards were either butt-jointed, half-lapped or occasionally tongued and grooved at each joint; each board was fixed to the ledges with either wooden pegs or nail studs with the gap between the boards covered with a moulded cover-strip.

WINDOWS

Windows in the medieval house were kept to a minimum, for they were unglazed even in superior houses; they remained so in all but the largest houses until the sixteenth century, when for the first time the use of glass became more widespread. Windows were therefore situated whenever possible on the east or north sides of the house, away from the prevailing winds. Oiled cloth, preferably linen, stiffened by a wooden lattice arranged in a diamond pattern and fitted to each opening, was a common substitute for glass, but oiled paper, the horn of cattle as well as lattices of wood, wickerwork and reeds were all employed to provide some protection.

In most cases these early unglazed windows were fitted with some form of battened wooden shutters (*36*) to afford some protection from the elements and to provide security. Hinged shutters, fitted either externally or internally, were frequently used on larger houses, especially on the large windows to the open hall, but on small windows and the windows of cottages sliding shutters fitted internally were commonly employed, obviating the necessity for expensive iron hinges. Although these days few original shutters remain (one exists although not in use at Bexon Manor, Bredgar), grooves into which the shutters fitted can be found; but as the whole complex was easily removed, often little evidence remains apart from nail- or peg-holes. Horizontal sliding shutters were the most widely used but vertical sliding shutters, perhaps of a slightly later date, were also employed. In Bayleaf Farmhouse vertical sliding shutters were provided in the solar wing of the house, which seems to have been added at a later

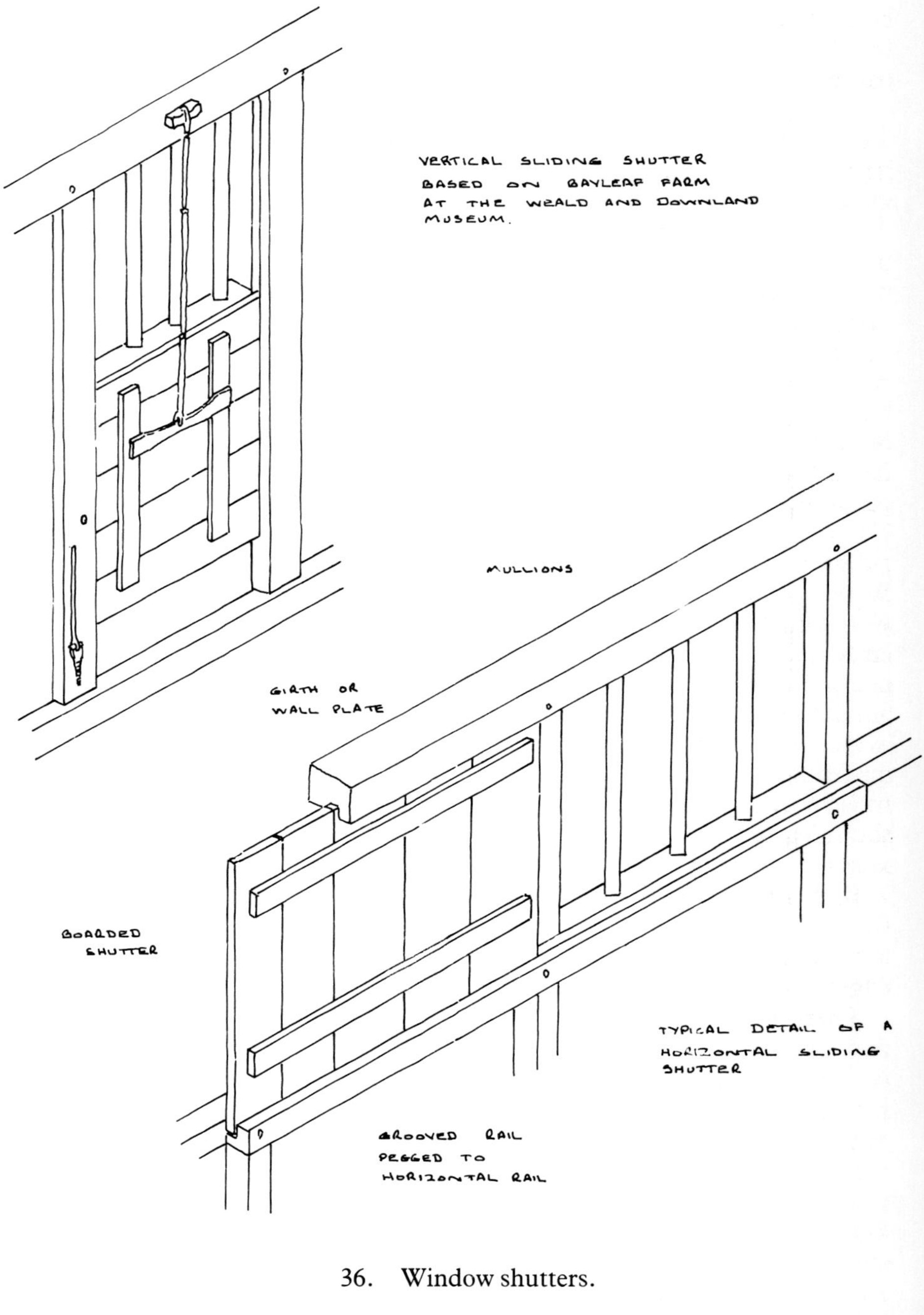

36. Window shutters.

date. Although shutters are generally associated with timber-framed buildings they were also widely used on stone buildings. Even the parish church of the early Middle Ages relied on shutters to close the small windows of the Saxon and Norman periods. At Ightham Mote the fourteenth-century east window of the hall retains the rebates for its timber shutters, while at Old Soar the east window of the solar has a pointed recess in the jamb for a shutter.

Although glass was manufactured in Normandy and other places on the Continent and imported into England, the amount was small and its use reserved for important houses. The process used on the Continent produced what is known as crown glass, in which the glass was blown into a disc or crown by the use of a glass-blower's pontil, the molten material at one end of the pontil being spun round and round in the palms of the hands with the bubble at the end flattened out by a wooden bat to produce a disc. The disc was always thicker towards the centre where the glass was attached to the pontil. The glass so produced was much favoured for its brilliant 'fire-finish'. However, in most houses which contained glazed windows and, although Kent was a wealthy county, this would have been very few, the glass would have been what was known as cylinder glass. This glass was blown into a cylindrical shape or 'muffs' which, after the ends had been cut and removed, was then split along its length, gradually opening up and flattening as it cooled. It produced a rough glass, often speckled and with a greenish tint.

Because of the manufacturing process of early glass the panes or quarries were by necessity small, rarely exceeding six inches by four inches. In order to make a light of reasonable size these quarries were set in lead cames which in turn were joined together to form a lattice known as a leaded light. Because of the expense of glass the quarries were diamond-shaped, although not the symmetrical diamond pattern we see today; more often than not the leading was made up irregularly, thus enabling even the smallest pieces to be used at the edges.

These lights were at first regarded as furniture rather than part of the structure of the building and there are medieval references to their removal. When fixed, the lights were stiffened by horizontal iron saddle-bars set inside the glazing and housed into the mullions and jambs, to which they were secured with lead tape or later with wire. When installed into an existing timber opening the lights were often nailed directly to the mullions and jambs of the previously unglazed window. The lights were therefore narrow, usually between six and eight inches wide.

Early Norman buildings have round-headed windows. These are of course rare, but at West Malling there is a two-storeyed stone building

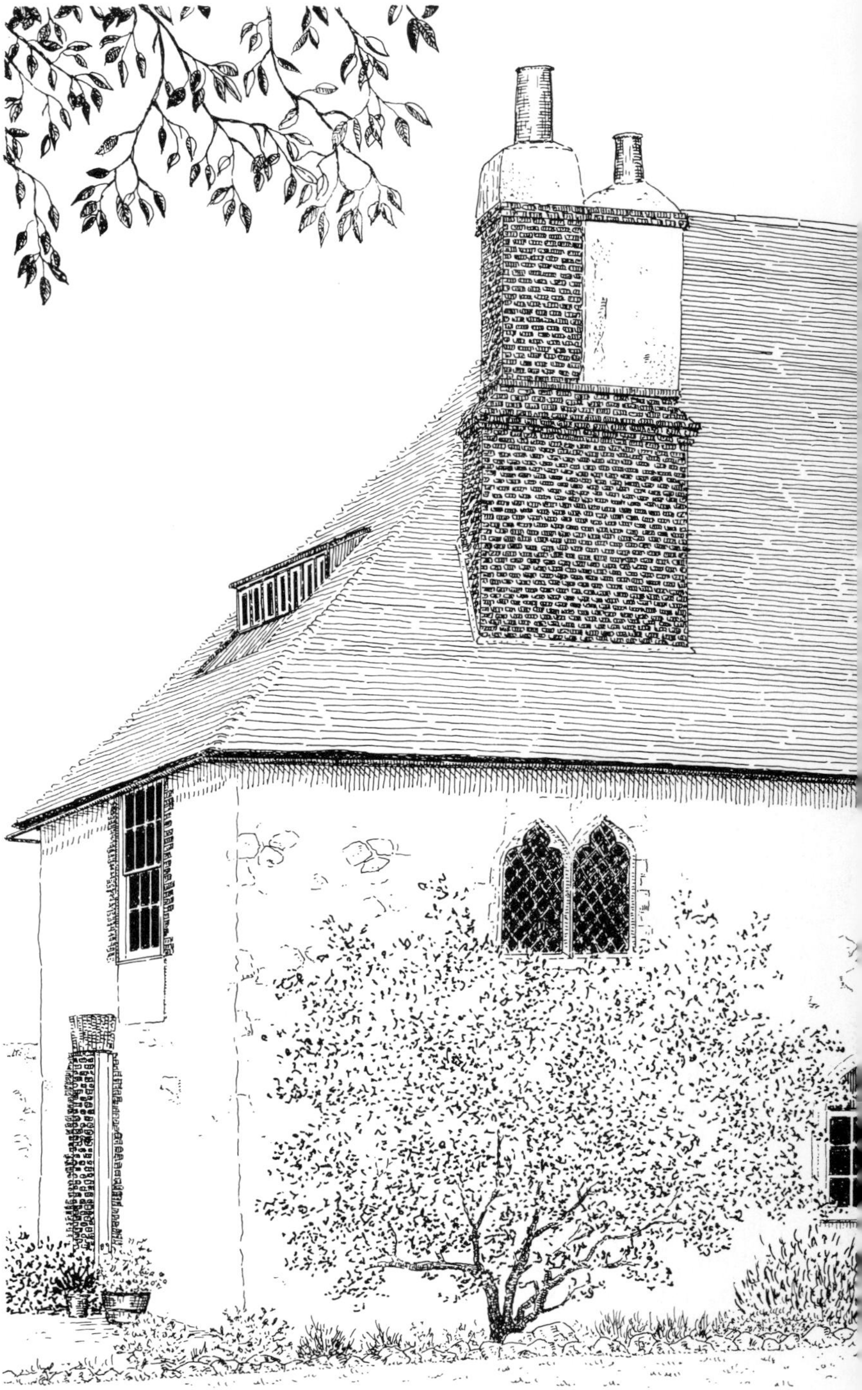

37. Court Lodge, Mersham, built about 1350 for Christ Church Priory.

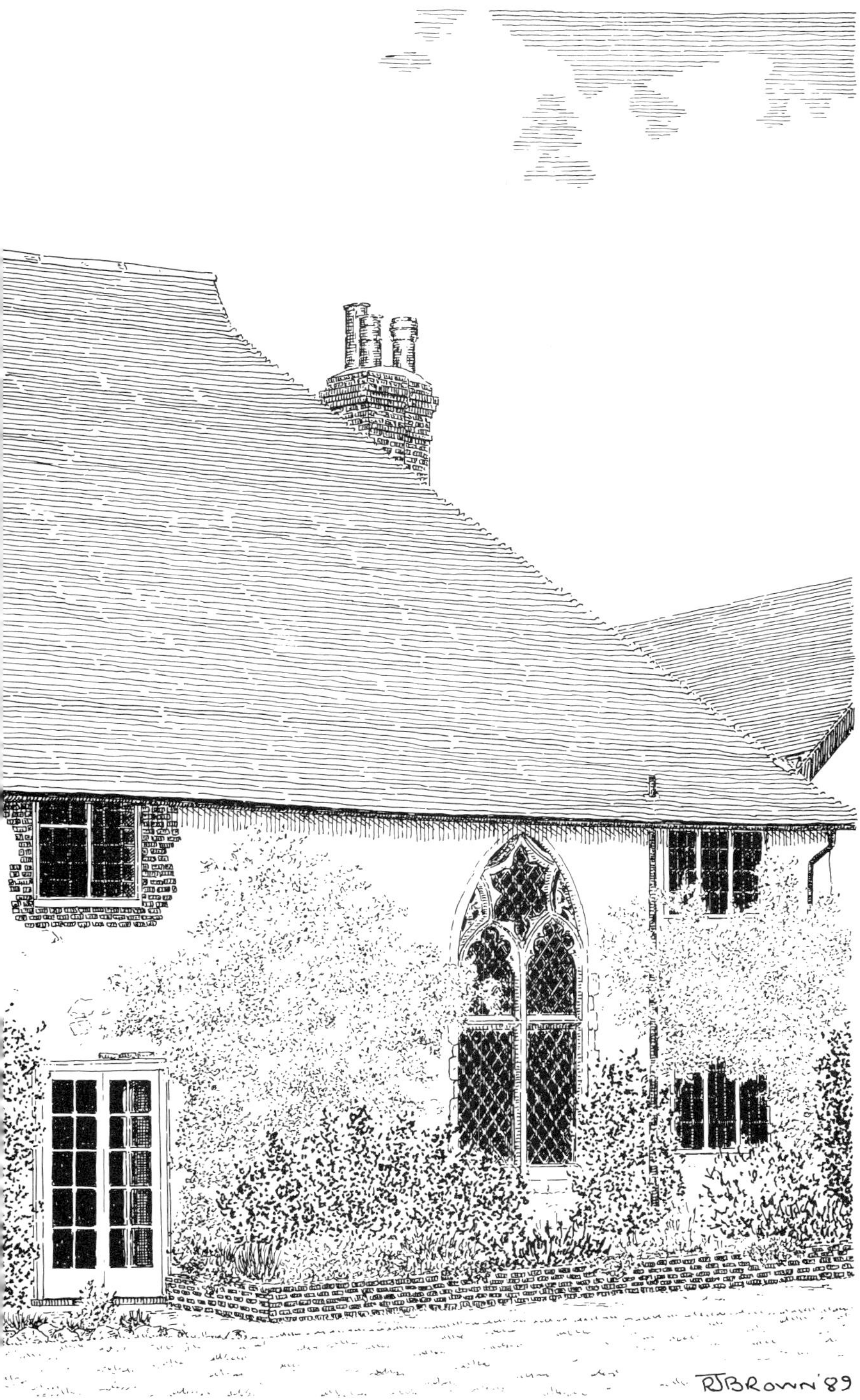
RJBROWN '89

in which can be seen typical Norman windows shafted with scalloped capitals and zigzagged arches which light the first-floor hall. During the thirteenth century there was a great variety. In domestic buildings some windows have rectangular openings or depressed-pointed arches, as at Old Soar; the solar of the same house also has a shoulder-lintel with splayed jambs and sills. But the majority would have had lancet windows – slender, pointed-arch openings. The earliest form of lancet windows have plate tracery, with decoratively shaped openings cut through the solid stone infilling. These are to be found only three times within the county, one example being at Squerries Lodge, Westerham, in what was possibly the window to the first-floor hall, and the other two at the Archbishop's Palace at Canterbury and the window of the nave at Stone Church. Other early windows are to be seen at Hoad Farm, Acrise, which has lancet windows to front and back of the thirteenth-century first-floor hall and at Old Rectory, Ickham, a house of slightly later date with two trefoiled lights at upper level. At Nurstead Court there remains only one of the original windows to the former hall; it was of two lights with trefoiled lights below the transom and at the apex a parted trefoil within a circle, but now has later casement windows inserted. At the fourteenth-century Court Lodge, Mersham (*37*), there are two windows of interest, one a large, renewed, two-light window with a transom and a concave-sided hexagon at the top to the hall, and the other a two-light window with ogee-trefoil to the former solar. At Old Rectory, Southfleet, although few original features remain visible from the outside, one can still see the head of a small window high on the west wall of the south wing, trefoiled with split cusps, while to the rear can be seen the mullioned and transomed hall window with sexfoiled ogees in the square head.

Original windows in medieval timber-framed buildings are rare and in most houses have been replaced by later window types. They were usually square-headed and situated at high level, either beneath the first-floor bressummer or at eaves level. The windows would have been unglazed, divided by plain square mullions set diagonally, about six inches or slightly wider apart, usually but not always subdivided vertically by a slender intermediate bar. However, as early glass lattices required no structural preparation other than the provision of vertical bars to which they could be tied, it is often difficult to decide if such a window was originally glazed or not. Where the window was covered with oiled cloth, a slightly different arrangement occurred. The window was fully framed as for an unglazed window but the square mullions were not set diagonally. Externally around each light was a rebate to which the cloth, probably stiffened with a diamond-patterned lattice, was fitted. The cloth was supported internally by a smaller intermediate vertical member similar to that used for unglazed windows.

Not all of these windows would have been plain, without any form of decoration. Those in important rooms of a timber-framed house of any significance had some form of tracery, often of Gothic design, in their heads. Although some of the important houses would have been glazed in the fifteenth century, the majority would not; the mullions would have been hollow-chamfered on each edge, with the tracery carved on the inside as well as the outside. Although most windows remained unglazed until the post-medieval period, it can be assumed that those in the hall of the later and grander Wealden house, for instance, may have been glazed. The tell-tale sign is that the tracery to the head would have been carved to the outside only, the inner face being flat with the glazing behind it. Such original traceried heads are indeed rare, but are still retained at the jettied ends of Yardhurst, at Great Chart (*38*). Sometimes the windows have been blocked in.

EXTERNAL DECORATIONS

Limewash was the traditional external finish to buildings and this really applied only to timber-framed buildings, for stone and brick were never decorated in medieval times. Unlike modern paints limewash was absorbed into the plaster, allowing it to breathe and dry out, an important factor if, as in most cases, no damp-proof course was provided. Traditionally limewash comprised two ingredients, quicklime and a water-repellent, usually tallow or linseed oil. Other material such as cow dung, size, animal glue and even egg yolks, milk and beer were added. Colour was obtained by the addition of various pigments, the most popular in medieval times being the dull reds, browns and yellows from oxides in clay. Limewash was therefore a cheap form of protection and although its application was a traditional craft, little skill was required in either its manufacture or application.

External timbers were also treated, for medieval manuscripts and paintings frequently show a contrast between the timbers and infill panels. It is known that in the South-east the oak face of the framing was limewashed over with the panels or at best left in its natural state to weather into a silvery hue. The blackening of the timbers seems to be a later rather than an early form of decoration, for a permanent black was not widely available until pitch and tar were manufactured from coal in the nineteenth century. However, there is evidence that at an earlier date timbers were treated to darken the frame, for there is reference to the use of bullock's blood, mixed with soot, rudd or red ochre to produce a rich, matt surface.

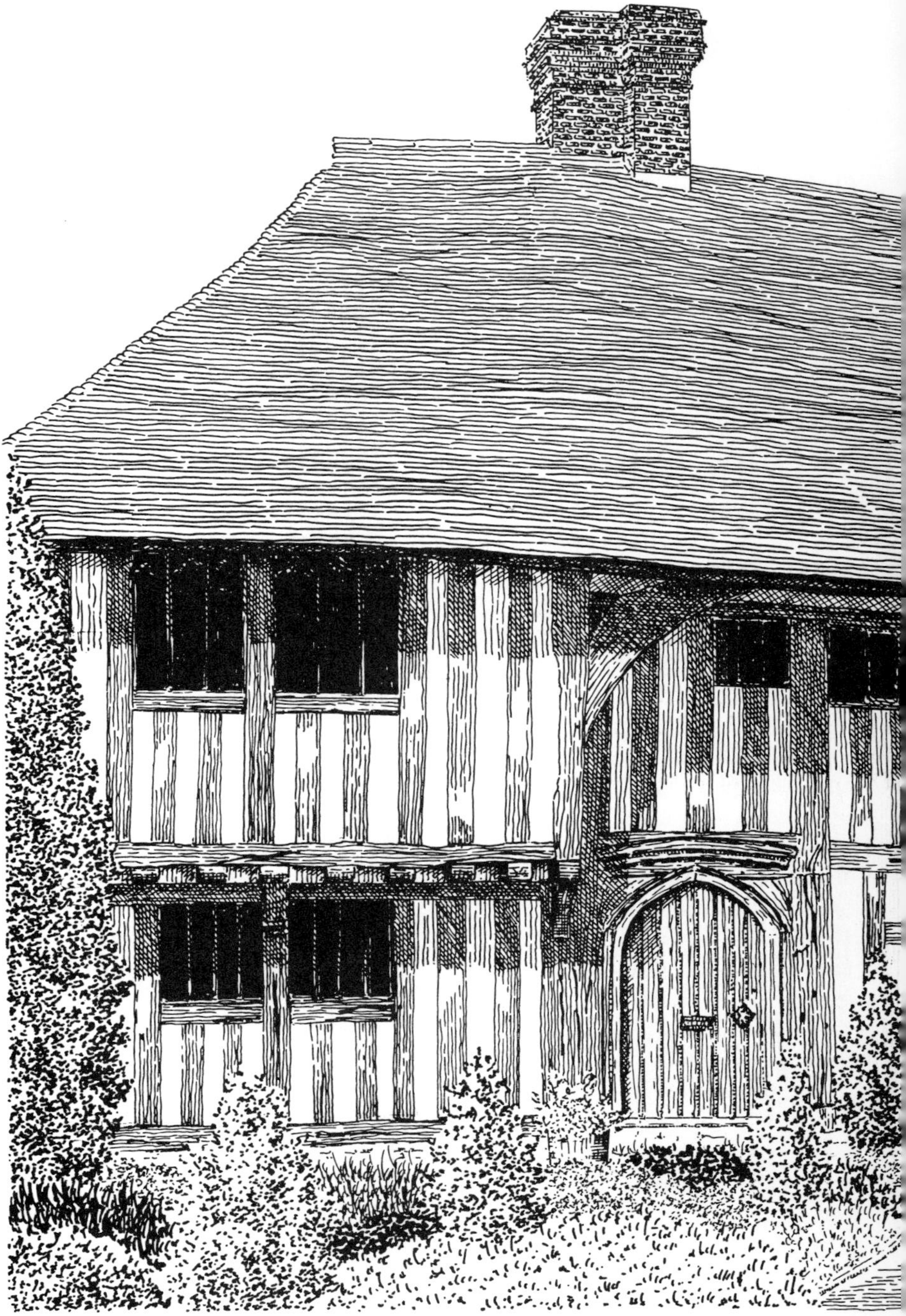

38. Yardhurst, Great Chart. Fine Wealden house which still retains its original tracied head to the windows and the jettied end.

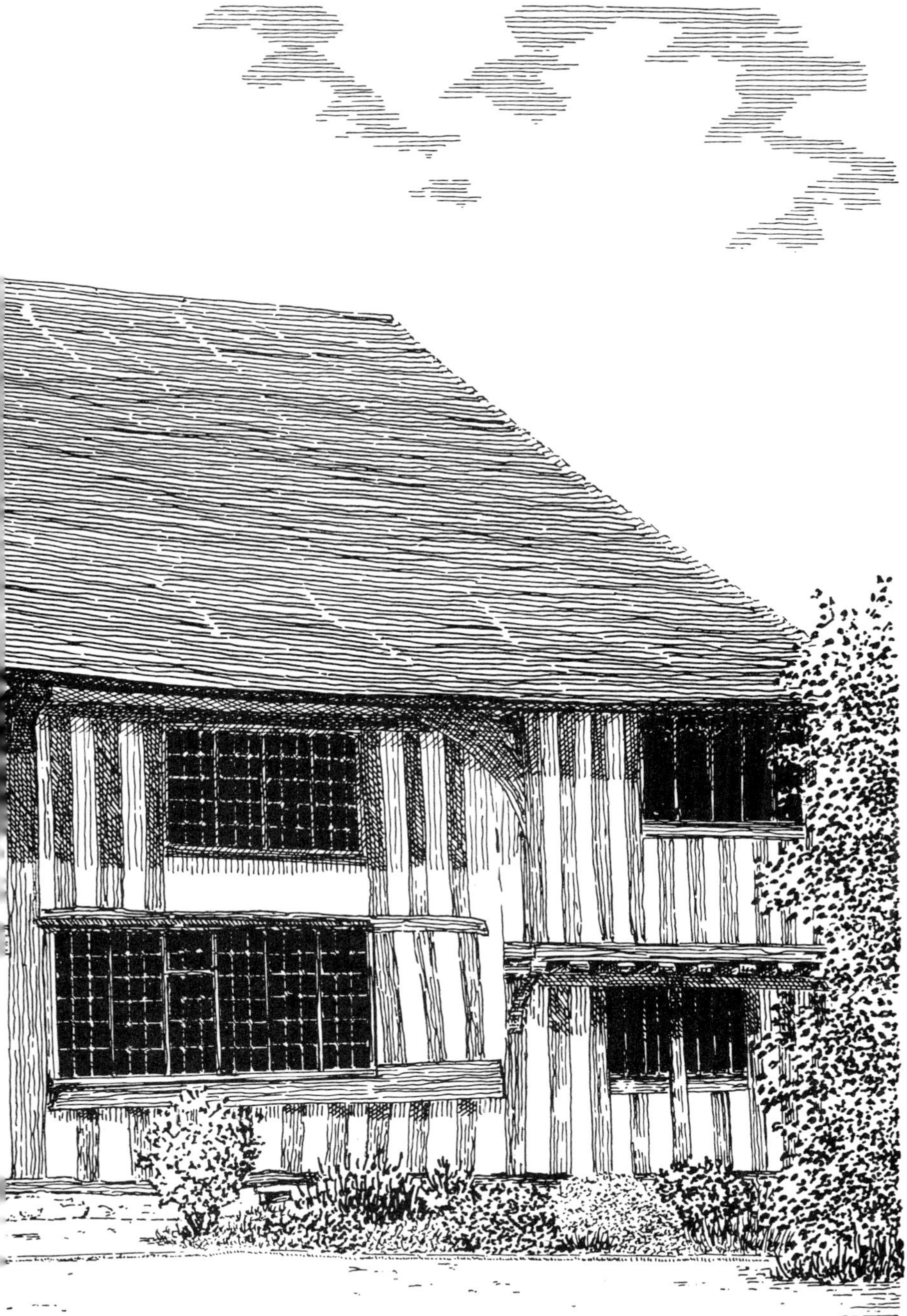
RJBROWN '87

INTERNAL DECORATIONS

Few houses, even the poorest, would have been without some form of decoration, even if this was confined to the mere chamfering of the main timbers. Usually quite lavish expenditure was made in the fabrication of the hall truss and its crown-post, which must have been the most striking feature of the medieval house. In some instances the wall-plate too would be moulded.

The 'dais-beam', the moulded beam which runs across the upper end of the hall at about head height, was of equal importance. Where money or rank permitted, oak panelling was inserted below this beam, so forming the partition between the hall and the parlour. This partition is subject to some variation of design; an early type has vertical boards overlapping one another. A partition of this type was recorded by E.W. Parkin when Durlock Grange was in the process of being demolished; it had been whitewashed so many times over the centuries that it looked like rough boards and was destroyed before its true value was realized. In some instances the boards were not merely overlapped but carefully tongued and grooved, producing two faces, one of overlapping boards and the other flush. The flush face was always the best side, for the smooth face presented an ideal surface on which to apply some form of painted decoration.

Another and much more common form of partition was the so-called plank-and-muntin partition, which consisted of vertical boards or planks housed into the edges of the muntins which in turn were framed into the underside of the moulded dais beam and the massive sill beam just above floor level. Any ornamentation was confined to the hall side, the parlour side being plain and often crude. The muntins were often only chamfered, but on better-class work they were sometimes moulded. The planks might be plain but they were often given a simplified type of linenfold pattern. At Synyards, Otham, the muntins are chamfered and the planks formed of triangular sections, while at Old Wilsley, near Cranbrook, the muntins are again chamfered and the planks ribbed. The partition often incorporated doorways to the parlour and sometimes to the staircase as well, and occasionally a fixed bench. When the chamfer or moulding stops some way from the floor, this implies the former presence of such a bench.

Where funds did not permit such a partition, a moulded dais beam might still be provided but the space below would be filled in with timber framing and wattle-and-daub. Sometimes the original oak partition has been removed and the opening filled in but with the dais beam remaining. In such a case the nature of the grooving on the underside of the beam will indicate if this has happened or not. Even on the poorest of homes the dais beam would generally be chamfered.

A similar moulded beam and partition can on occasions be found to the screens passage, with two or possibly three doorways leading into the service apartments. It has been noted that the decoration to the hall was confined not only to the upper end but also to those timbers visible from this end. However, in most cases decoration to this wall was restricted to a continuous moulded beam above the doors.

All these mouldings are naturally of great assistance in dating. The mouldings of the thirteenth and fourteenth centuries were often deeply undercut with the frequent use of three-quarter hollows, the heavy bowtells – with fillets – and even scroll mouldings. In the fifteenth century the mouldings changed to the larger quarter-hollow with bold rounds above and below, with the beam crenellated along its upper edge.

Wall panelling was first introduced into houses in the late fifteenth century, when it was referred to as 'sealing'. The earliest form of panelling was similar to that used in partitions and comprised little more than vertical oak boards with the edges either simply overlapping or tongued and grooved into each other – a form, according to N. Lloyd in his *A History of the English House*, found frequently in the houses of Kent.

Apart from panelling, walls often received some form of decoration. The plastering of internal stone walls to render the interior of the house less austere was being undertaken by the thirteenth century. These walls, previously left bare or at best simply whitewashed, were given a thin coat of plaster on to which patterns and scenes were painted. These wall-paintings can be seen in many churches in the county. Village churches such as the remarkable little early Norman church at Brook, Ashford, show that interiors were once completely covered with paintings. Another example is the church at Ulcombe, south-east of Maidstone, where amongst the remaining frescos is one of three old monks looking down at the altar. Very few examples of domestic wall-paintings have been discovered which can be said to date from before 1500. Despite this, decoration of some sort must have been widespread as there existed the Guild of Stainers as well as a Guild of Painters: the two amalgamated in 1504. One house in which these wall-paintings can be seen is Penshurst Place, for in the fourteenth-century hall, between the windows, are the faint outlines of figures, said to be men-at-arms.

In timber-framed houses, as early as the fourteenth century, there is evidence that the wattle-and-daub infilling between the studs was decorated with simple combed designs similar to those associated with pargetting in the seventeenth century. However, in most of the larger houses tapestries, often depicting religious scenes, were the most popular form of wall of decoration. During the fifteenth century the desire for some form of wall decoration penetrated down the social scale into the houses of the yeomen. This new form of ornamentation, a cheap substitute for tapestries, was a painted hanging of cloth or canvas.

SERVICES

In medieval Kent, as elsewhere in the country, such was the risk of fire that the kitchen was often detached from the main house. Few of the detached kitchens still survive, for frequently they were of flimsy construction and so over the years have disappeared; the kitchen became incorporated into the main house. In some houses a third doorway from the screens passage would lead to the kitchen. This can be seen at Penshurst Place, where the third door led via a passage to the kitchen, in this case attached to the service rooms. A few detached kitchens still survive; one, according to S.E. Rigold, is at Yorks Hill Farm, Ide Hill and another to the rear of Pierce House, Charing. Typically they measured about twenty feet square.

The garderobe (the medieval French euphemism for a privy) with its stone or wooden seat and a chute to a ground-level drain, was a feature of many medieval stone buildings (Old Soar, Plaxtol, Starkey Castle, Wouldham and Court Lodge, Great Chart) but there is evidence also of their former existence in timber-framed houses. When Bayleaf Farmhouse was reconstructed at the Weald and Downland Museum at Singleton, a first-floor external doorway was found in the solar bay with four mortises which supported a timber structure on the outside, indicating, it was concluded, the former existence of a garderobe. The reconstruction is conjecture but is based on the evidence available. Similar structures have been found elsewhere as, for instance, at Slaybrook, Sandling, a fifteenth-century Wealden house. Blocked doorways in the end rooms at first-floor level are sometimes to be found, as at Yardhurst, Great Chart, and these probably indicate the presence of a former garderobe. Again at Smallhythe Place there is a doorway in the back wall of a first-floor room and probably this too is the remains of a garderobe.

Stone Houses

There was never a medieval vernacular building tradition in stone in Kent for as we have seen, although by no means deficient in building stones, it was timber that was the predominant building material in the county in medieval times. There is nevertheless a wealth of medieval stone houses, many of which have been obscured by poor ashlar and the renewal of exterior detail. They range in size from the small, early twelfth-century house at West Malling to Boughton Place, Boughton Malherbe, built by Sir Edward Wotton in the third decade of the sixteenth century. Many of these buildings from the thirteenth and fourteenth centuries are the result of ecclesiastical patronage, for the preponderance of tenures by the great religious houses and spiritual lords in north and east Kent can only be rivalled in the Severn-Cotswold area of England.

First-floor halls were a feature of private houses in the twelfth and thirteenth centuries. They were Norman in origin and, apart from their occasional use in town houses, are manorial or religious in origin. These houses in Kent are generally unfortified, unlike those in the border counties of northern England. No complete medieval town house survives in the county but in Canterbury undercrofts of half a dozen twelfth- and thirteenth-century stone houses have survived, the most notable being at Boots the Chemist at the corner of Mercery Lane and the High Street, which is built on vaulted stone cellars, two deep, with an overall depth of some thirty feet. At Sandwich there are remains of merchants' houses, the best preserved being at 27 Strand Street, where there is part of a thirteenth-century stone house (dated by E.W. Parkin to about 1240) with the remains of an upper hall above a twin-bay vaulted undercroft. The walls and three first-floor windows of another thirteenth-century stone house has been discovered by Mr Parkin at 50 St Peter's Street, while behind 11 Strand Street are the remains of a small rectangular medieval flint building.

Outside the towns examples of these first-floor hall houses are to be found within defended sites. At Eynsford Castle excavations have established a characteristic stone hall house of 1125–50 date. The undercroft of the hall and solar remain with a forebuilding – a defensible stair approach – to the west side of the building. Chilham Castle, it appears, was built on part of an unfortified stone house of the eleventh century. Excavations in 1928 revealed a rectangular hall thirty feet by over nineteen feet wide. Thought to be a semi-fortified house of Norman origin are the ruined flint walls of Walmer Court, which is situated in the grounds adjoining the churchyard of St Mary Old Church in Church Street.

Less formidable are the houses at West Malling of twelfth-century date, Luddesdown Court, of early thirteenth-century date, the early fourteenth-century Lake House, Eastwell, and the two-storeyed so-called Master's House at Maidstone College, probably of late fourteenth-century date. The most interesting of these is Luddesdown Court. This manor house is built of flint and its round-headed entrance door seems to date it to around the beginning of the thirteenth century, although it may well be earlier; it claims to be the oldest house in England still in use. This claim is, of course, very doubtful. The aforementioned hooded fireplace to the first-floor hall is a later addition to the building, its weight being carried by corbelled brickwork from the wall of the room below. The house also had a bear-pit and a pigeon-loft. The lord of the manor here in 1346 was one of Edward III's officers when the King besieged Calais, and almost a century later the house belonged to Thomas de Montacute, seventh Earl of Salisbury.

All the previous examples of first-floor hall houses form part of a larger complex, but there are some complete free-standing chamber blocks which provided accommodation for upper-class households or else the relatively enclosed conditions for clerics. The main accommodation was the first-floor hall but in some cases the undercroft might have provided subordinate lodging. A very fine house of this type is Temple Manor, beside the Medway at Strood. This thirteenth-century flint-built house formed part of a larger manor house of the Knights Templar. It is remarkably complete, having been rescued by the then Ministry of Public Buildings and Works in 1961 and restored. The building has a three-bay vaulted undercroft, with the first-floor hall reached by an external staircase. The building, which dates from about 1240, is open to the public. There is another small but very complete hall-house of this type at Ickham, Old Rectory (*39*); built about 1280, it is the remaining part of the Prior of Christ Church's manor house. At Hoad Farm, Acrise, there is another excellent example of thirteenth-century date which forms part of a fourteenth-century flint-built house. Another example is at Squerries Lodge, Westerham, which incorporates the remains of a thirteenth-century stone house in its south-east corner.

By about 1300 the first-floor halls became obsolete in Kent and were superseded by ground-floor halls with roofs supported by aisle-posts, which were of Saxon origin. Ancient houses of this type are certainly known in north-west Germany, the original home of the Saxons, while in England they slowly evolved and continued to be built for several more centuries.

Aisled houses, with the exception of those in Yorkshire, are to be found mainly in the east of England. Sussex – the home of the South Saxons – has a number of them as do Essex (where the East Saxons lived), Suffolk, Cambridgeshire and Kent. The majority of these houses have timber-framed walls, but in Kent there are at least three examples in which the timber arcades have been enclosed with stone walls. The earliest of these is Cogan's House, in St Peter's Street, Canterbury, built about 1200, although little of its age is now apparent either externally or internally.

Nurstead Court, near Meopham (*40*), one of the most famous small medieval houses, is of early fourteenth-century date, probably around 1320. Unfortunately, when a new house was proposed, the existing

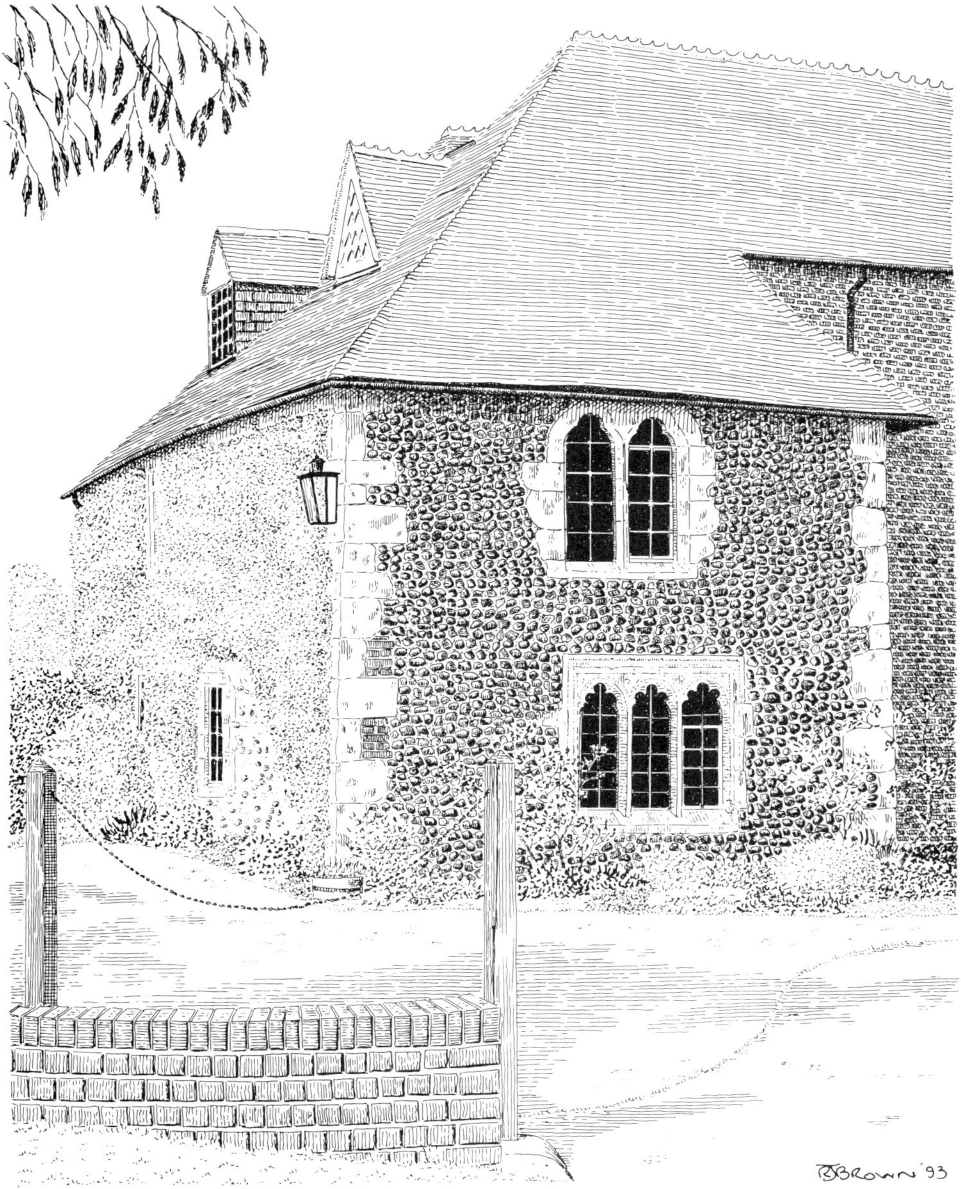

39. Old Rectory, Ickham. First floor hall house built around 1280.

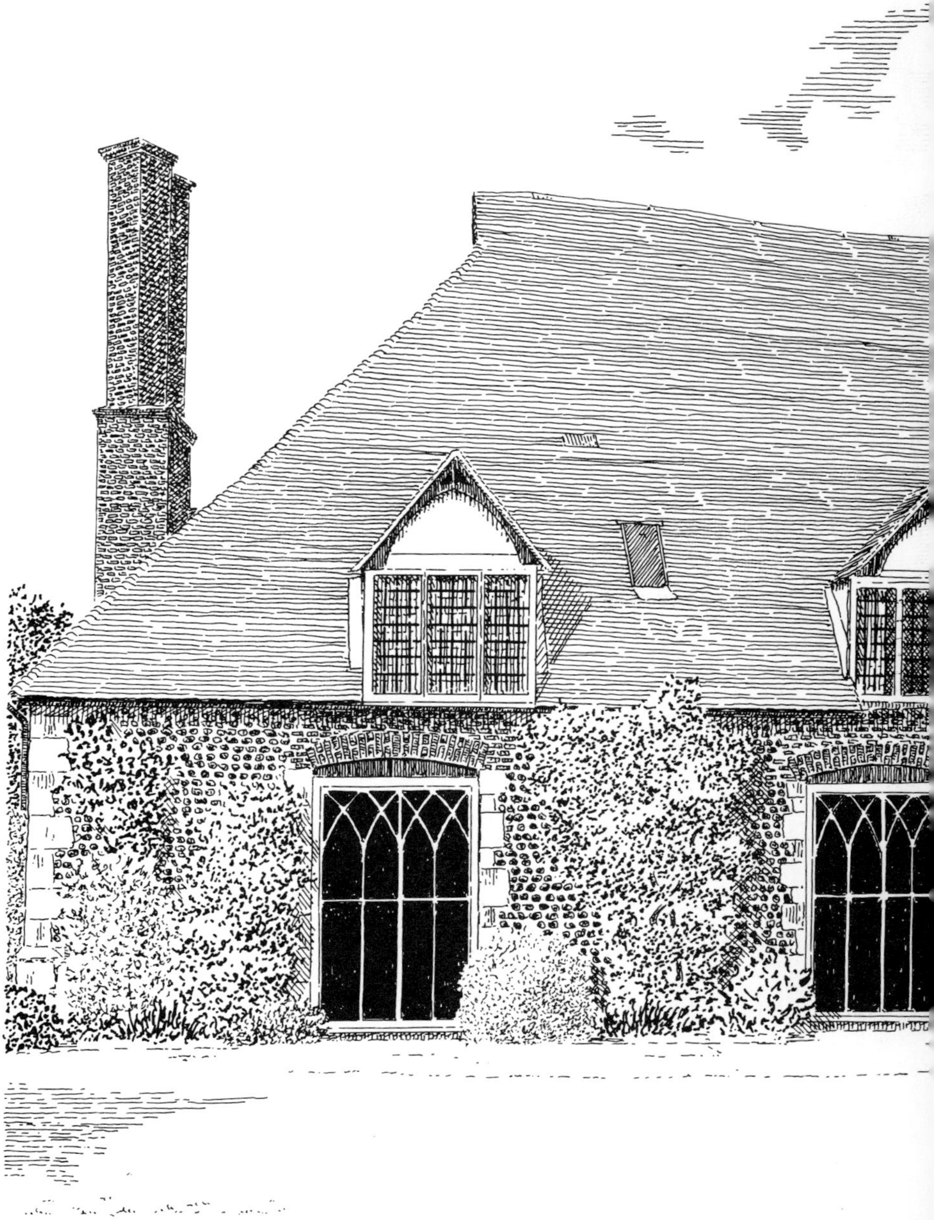

40. Nurstead Court, built around 1320.

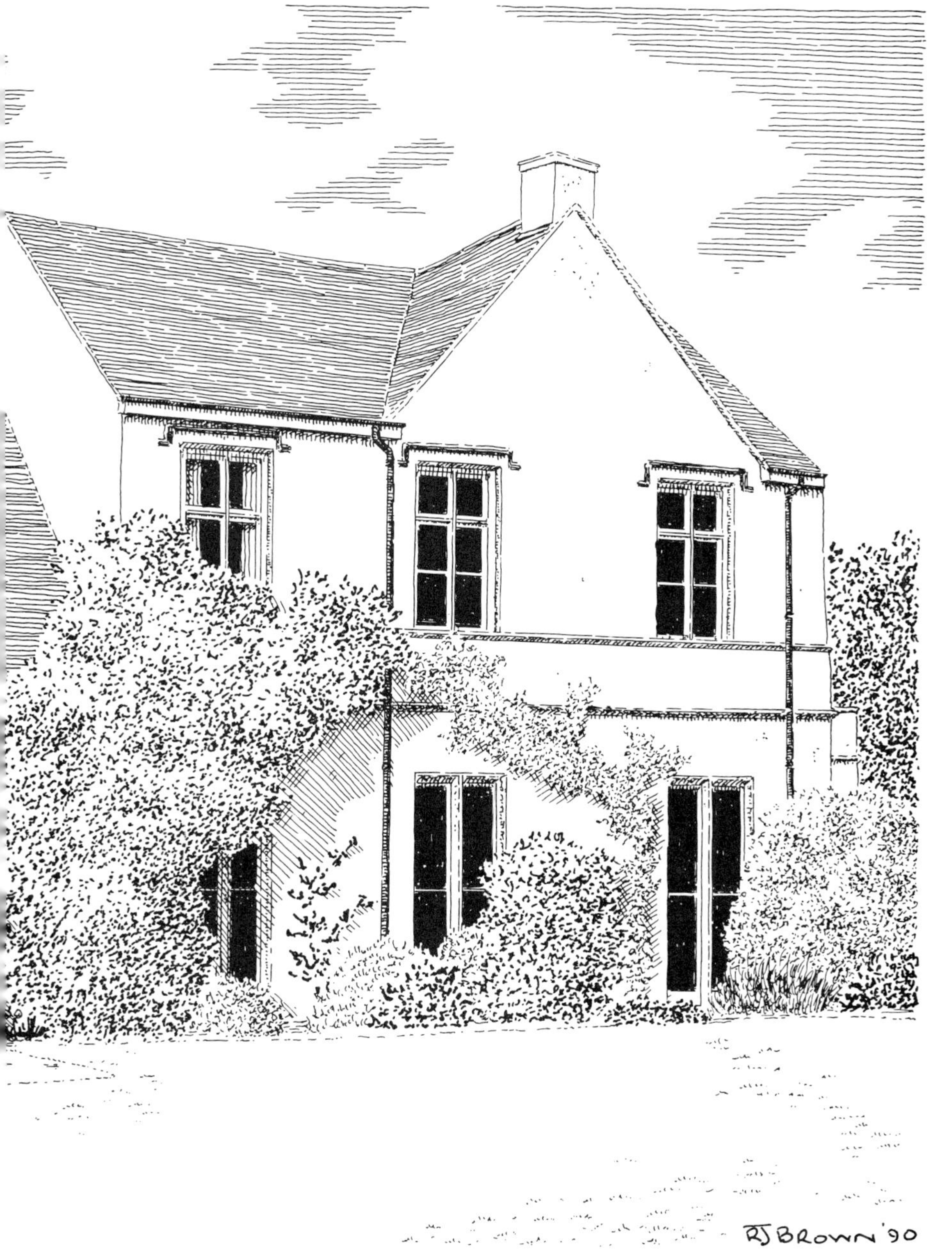
RJ BROWN '90

house was due to be demolished. The demolition, according to William Twopeny, began in 1825 a date confirmed by W.H. Ireland in his *History of the County of Kent* in 1830, but luckily the destruction was stayed and only the eastern portion was destroyed. The house was fully recorded before alterations occurred and had the characteristic medieval arrangement of a hall open to the roof flanked at one end with the service rooms, a two-storey solar bay at the other end, and a free-standing kitchen block. This is an early example of what was later to become the standardized house-plan which existed until the beginning of the sixteenth century. Within the stone walls the house was built entirely of timber, the circular aisle-posts being nineteen inches in diameter and supporting a richly moulded two-centred arch. Unlike Cogan's House, the roof has an early example of a crown-post with delicate detailing.

Cogan's House and Nurstead both had two aisles but a former merchant's house at New Romney – 3–4 West Street – had only one aisle to the rear. The external walls are again of stone, with a two-centred arched doorway leading into the house from the road. The original windows have been replaced with sash ones.

Although in Kent timber-framed aisled houses continued to be built, in stone houses the use of aisles to support the roof had been generally abandoned by the first quarter of the fourteenth century. Other roof types were developed to obtain an unimpeded hall and so developed the standard medieval house type of an open ground-floor hall flanked on either ends with the solar and service wings.

The grandest example of this house plan in the county and even perhaps in the country is Penshurst Place. Today one sees, as one approaches from the north, a building of mellow brick and stone but at its heart is the original stone house built in about 1341 by Sir John de Pulteney, a London draper's merchant who was four times Lord Mayor between 1331 and 1337. He was immensely wealthy: the house he built in London became, on his death, the residence of the Black Prince. He was also the founder of a chantry for three priests in St Paul's Cathedral; in the City church of St Laurence Pountney he established a college for a master, thirteen priests and four choristers and in Coventry a Carmelite friary. At Penshurst Place the entire screens passage arrangement survives and the hall itself, some sixty-two feet long and thirty-nine feet wide, remains almost intact including its central hearth, although the smoke louvre has disappeared. The great vaulted roof is formed of crown-posts on collar beams resting on moulded purlins with arch-braces down to the moulded wall-plates and large wooden figures. The tiled floor is also fourteenth century and in the west bay is the original dais. In the south-west corner a small doorway leads to the vaulted undercroft and a larger doorway leads up spacious stone steps to the solar itself, where a small squint enabled the lord or members of his family to observe the hall below. This solar is now the state dining-room. On the other side of the hall, beyond the screens passage, is the remaining part of the fourteenth-century house – the pantry and buttery. Between these two doorways is a third, larger than the others, which opens on to a passage which originally led into an octagonal kitchen which was demolished in about 1836. Above the single-storey pantry and buttery is another chamber – a room originally of some importance.

The house has been greatly enlarged throughout the centuries. In 1393 a second licence to fortify was granted in the name of Sir John Devereux. On his death the following near Penshurst passed on to his widow and later to her descendants. In 1430 the property was bought by John of Lancaster, Duke of Bedford and brother of Henry V and later Regent for the infant Henry VI. At this time the so-called Buckingham building was completed. In 1552 Penshurst was granted to Sir William Sidney in whose family it has remained. The screen to the hall was added at around this time and it is an interesting fact that the hall was still being used communally in the second half of the sixteenth century, exactly as Pulteney had used it two centuries before.

In 1456 Archbishop Bourchier bought the manor of Knole near Sevenoaks and after repairing the old manor house, enlarged it for his new palace. Although it is difficult to imagine that it was built with the same basic plan as Penshurst, the great hall has a quadrangle with a gate tower to the front and to the rear a back court. The solar leading off the hall developed into a state suite, culminating at the far south-eastern corner of the back court in a chapel. From the screens passage there are only two doorways, one leading into a vestibule from which is reached the vast kitchen which occupies the north side of the back court. It is so large that there are three fireplaces, one to the south and two to the north, dating from a time when most houses would have only one open fire. The house was further extended by Archbishop Bourchier's successors – Morton (1486–1500) and Warham (1503–52) – until Archbishop Cranmer was obliged to surrender it to Henry VIII. The vast scale of the building shows the enormous secular power of the Archbishop of Canterbury in the fifteenth and early sixteenth centuries. This is further emphasized by the fact that although Archbishop Warham acquired Knole, he built a second quadrangular palace between 1503 and 1518, of similar size to Knole, at nearby Otford. Little of that palace now remains.

There are remains of several other ecclesiastical palaces in the county. The most important is Charing Palace, which was owned by the Archbishop of Canterbury until acquired by Henry VIII. To the east are the sizeable stone ruins of the old first-floor manor house, dating from about 1300. The gatehouse probably dates from the time of Archbishop Stratford (1333–48), while the present farmhouse seen through this gatehouse is mainly of later material, built of flint and raised in brick to three storeys; it was probably built by Archbishop Morton. At Halling the ragstone walls to the north end of the churchyard are all that is left of the Bishop of Rochester's mid-thirteenth-century palace.

Penshurst Place, Knole, and the other episcopal palaces are not typical of the moderate-sized medieval stone-built houses of Kent and at the other end of the scale are the relatively small houses, usually of manorial status and often built by ecclesiastical institutes. The smallest of these houses had the same basic plan of the open hall with a solar bay at the upper end and service bay at the lower end, but all under an overall hipped roof. They were in effect stone versions of the timber-framed Wealden house for which Kent is so rightly famous. The early fourteenth-century part of Hoad Farm, Acrise, is one such example. The house is built of flint, and the blocked doorway in the north-west wall clearly indicates the position of the former screens passage; the head of a two-light window which lit the hall can still be seen. Another example is Court Lodge, Mersham (*37*), built about 1350 by the Benedictines of Christ Church Priory, Canterbury, with a big, steeply pitched hipped roof. It differs from the characteristic medieval house arrangement in that the solar was placed above the ground-floor service rooms. Close by Court Lodge is Evegate Manor, Smeeth, a large stone house with a big hipped roof built very similarly to Court Lodge and perhaps for Sir Edmund Pashley, who inherited the manor in 1341 and died in 1361. Court Lodge, Great Chart (*41*), is another stone house with the general arrangement of a ground-floor hall with solar and service ends, although the precise layout of these rooms has not yet been established. The house is remarkable in that it is known to have been built in 1313 and has a crown-post roof structure which is the earliest dated example in the county. The house is larger than the previous examples in that it has two stone extensions to the rear, the one to the north-east being a garderobe built at an angle to the main block. The south end of the front is a stone porch which is clearly original, for the moulded entrance is typical of about 1300. Little Buckland Cottage, at the bottom of Buckland Lane, Maidstone, is unusual in that it has a stone ground floor, and an upper floor which is mainly timber-framed, with a jetty at one of the short ends. The hollow-chamfered two-centred doorway and similar hollow-chamfered windows indicate a late fourteenth-century date.

These houses are relatively small, but there is another group in which the open hall is flanked either at one or both ends by

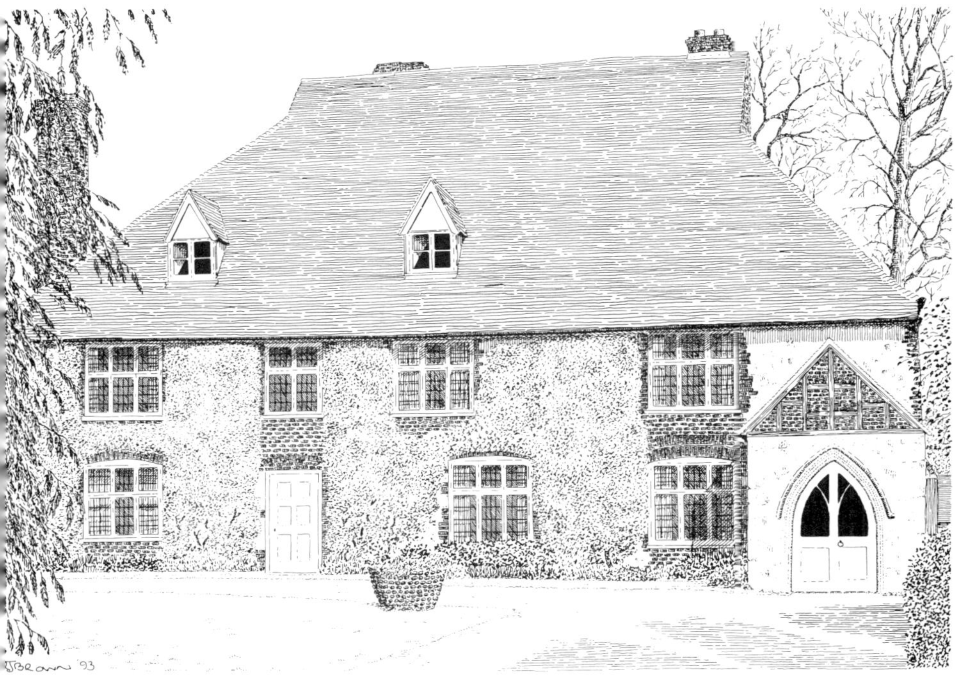

41. Court Lodge, Great Chart, built in 1313.

cross-wings roofed independently and transversely to the hall.

Copton Manor, Sheldwich, is a house of great antiquity based on the evidence of its three medieval roofs, for as previously stated, the scissor-braced form of construction preceded crown-post roofs, which we know were in use in Kent by the end of the thirteenth century. Certainly in documentary evidence Copton was named as early as 821, when the land was given to the Archbishop of Canterbury by King Cenwulf. Copton Court is mentioned again in the records of 1232 and also in the fourteenth century, when the lands still belonged to the archbishop. Externally there is now little evidence of its age, yet within the building remains the original medieval structure. This building comprised the open hall with a two-storey service bay to one end and at right angles to the hall a two-storey solar block. The third and smaller block adjoined the service bay and was occupied by the bailiff who looked after and ran the property when the owner was absent.

At Old Soar, Plaxtol, a house built around 1290, only the solar block or wing is complete; the original stone house, which was probably aisled, was replaced by the present eighteenth-century brick house. The solar block has a pointed, tunnel-vaulted undercroft with access to the first-floor solar by means of a newel staircase. At the eastern corner of the solar, towards the road, is a rectangular projection which is the chapel. At the northern corner a similar projection, and almost of equal size, is a garderobe. Both of these rooms have access from the solar. Old Soar was at one time the seat of the Culpeppers who later became the largest land-owning family in Kent and Sussex by the simple expedient, it has been stated, of kidnapping heiresses, whom they forcibly married. The solar end is open to the public but the house itself is not and so what survives of the original hall adjacent to the solar is not visible.

Similar, but with a narrower and more compacted hall and a generation or so later, is Battell Hall, Leeds. The walls of the hall, no longer open to the roof, still survive and to the northern end the solar on an undercroft, with a projecting garderobe wing. The solar was originally defensible, for the doorway leading to the staircase to the solar above has grooves for a portcullis. This doorway, situated to the north end of the east front, is now external but was originally internal. The service rooms to the south have been replaced by a seventeenth-century range. The hall still retains a stone roof-arch supported on crouching corbel figures. A feature of the house is the elaborate stone laver just inside the main door within which is a double-barrelled stone cistern with spouts in the shape of lions' heads.

Of similar age is the Old Rectory, Southfleet, probably built for Thomas of Alkham who was rector from 1323. The arrangement is the usual one: the open hall with cross-wings at either end, the one to the south being the solar, the other the service. The modernization of the building over the centuries has left few original external features to be seen.

Ightham Mote is another hall house, but now the original early fourteenth-century house has been integrated into a later stone and timber-framed courtyard house. It is without doubt the finest small medieval manor house in the county, in a perfect setting within its moat. The fourteenth-century house forms one side of the courtyard and faces one as one enters. The doorway to the hall has the characteristic features of the early fourteenth century with filleted rolled shafts, but it leads directly into the hall, not into the screens passage as was normal. The service end, to the right, originally contained the kitchen and buttery; to the left is the solar end. The hall itself is the finest room in Ightham Mote, still spanned by a central two-centred stone arch, with arches of timber of equal size at either end. At the upper end of the hall, beyond the dais, a doorway leads into the parlour, while another doorway leads into the undercroft of the first-floor chapel. The solar is timber-framed and appears to be sixteenth century.

Starkey Castle, Wouldham, is in no sense a castle and is now a farmhouse. Probably built about 1390, the hall is of two bays with corbelled buttresses carrying the timber two-centred arch. The service rooms were to the south under a transverse roof with a staircase projection on the west side leading to the floor above. The solar end has been demolished, together with the late fifteenth-century chapel built by Sir Humphrey Starkey. An appendage houses the garderobe wing with a privy pit like that at Old Soar, Plaxtol.

At Lympne Castle, where the defensive elements are clear enough, although it too can scarcely be called a castle, the nature of the additions provided a comfortable residence of the normal late medieval plan. The main range between the towers dates from about 1360, and the open hall is entered through the porch on the north side. The thirteenth-century square tower, the oldest part of the castle, formed the kitchen, with additional rooms on its southern side. The hall range continues to the west with a ground-floor parlour and a great chamber above.

There are several other buildings which incorporate parts of medieval stone houses into their present structure. It is possible that Crundale House, Crundale, originated as an early stone house, for there is a massive stone chimney breast which looks to be of Norman origin. Externally the house is part timber-framed with tile-hanging and part seventeenth-century brick, but E.W. Parkin has discovered that it was originally of aisled construction and he dates it to the early thirteenth century. Court Lodge, Horton Kirby, which to all outward appearances is a Regency building, has within its structure medieval, probably thirteenth-century, openings – an internal doorway and two square windows at first-floor level – in the south walls. At Eastry Court, a low flint building to the east of the present house is all that is left of a large medieval stone house that once belonged to Christ Church Priory. To the rear of Hawfield Farm, Chartham, is a rectangular two-storeyed flint building with a lancet low in the east wall, indicating a thirteenth-century date. The Old Stone House at Wickhambreux with its chequered walling of flint and stone is undoubtedly medieval in origin, as is the ground floor of Stourmouth Farm House, East Stourmouth.

Timber-framed Houses

The number of stone-built medieval buildings that survive in Kent is relatively small compared with those built of timber. Timber was the principal material used in the construction of small medieval houses in the county, yet despite the large number of late timber-framed houses, which survive in their thousands and can only be rivalled in number in certain areas of Essex and Suffolk, the number of really archaic examples is relatively few compared to these areas. Essex, for instance, has twelve or so, all timber-aisled houses and all of thirteenth- or fourteenth-century date, while the number in Kent can be counted on the fingers of one hand although more have been discovered in recent years. Unlike Essex and also Suffolk, Kent has a few houses incorporating base crucks, the most notable being Hamden, Smarden. These survivals, however, are enough to show that they were once common. It is clear that most of these old hall houses, earlier than, say, 1370, were all but exterminated in Kent by a great late medieval rebuilding, perhaps to be associated with a radical change in local agriculture.

The medieval timber-framed house of Kent was conservative both in plan and technique. As in Sussex the open hall remained in favour longer than in Essex and Suffolk. The houses were not, however, rustic; they were neat, robust, uniform and curiously egalitarian – for they were rarely humble yet never pretentious. Medieval open framing dominates the fourteenth and fifteenth centuries and lasts

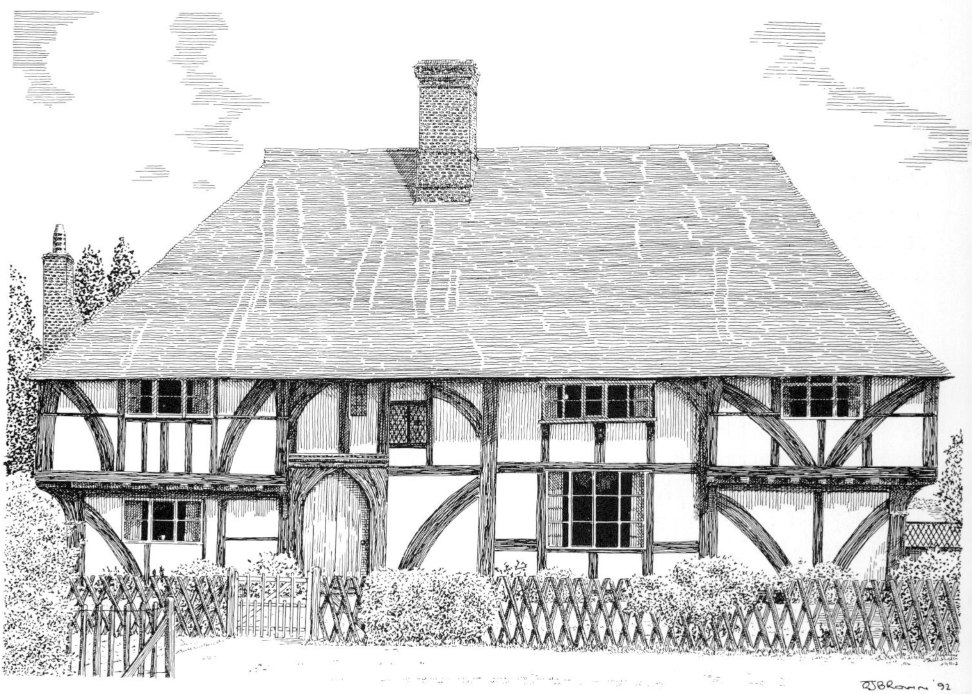

42. Hawkenbury Farm, Headcorn.

well into the sixteenth century, characterized by the tension brace running down from the post to the sill-plate or bressummer. So widespread is this framing in the county that it is known as 'Kentish framing', a typical example being Hawkenbury Farm, Headcorn (*42*). The alternative arch-brace form which was so popular in the West, that is with the brace rising from the post to the wall-plate or bressummer, never gained much favour in the county, although it can be found at the re-erected Winkhurst Farmhouse.

Ornamental medieval bracing is rare in the houses of Kent but an elaborate example survives at Rooting, Pluckley, where the cross-wing is all that remains of the original fourteenth-century house. The front of this cross-wing still retains its framing in almost its complete state – that is, above the ground floor which is now brick. The framing consists of two large semicircular braces to the first floor with 'S' bracing above. The manor is long established, for even in the Domesday Book, Rooting was already held by St Augustine's Abbey. Too distant to serve as a demesne, it was let to a family of tenants in free socage. Afterwards it passed to larger local landholders, the St Legers, and in 1570 the Derings of Surrenden Dering.

Close studding, in which the studs are storey-height and placed at intervals approximately equal to their own width, first appeared in the second quarter of the fifteenth century. Although the technique was accepted more slowly than in Essex and Suffolk, there are a few examples to which a date prior to 1450 can be attributed. Milton Court Lodge is of around 1440, while the hall at Wye College is a few years later, probably around 1445. Close studding began to gain popularity in around 1470 and came into general use after about 1480. Tension braces were still used, but in order not to affect the overall close-studded appearance they were of smaller depth than the studs,

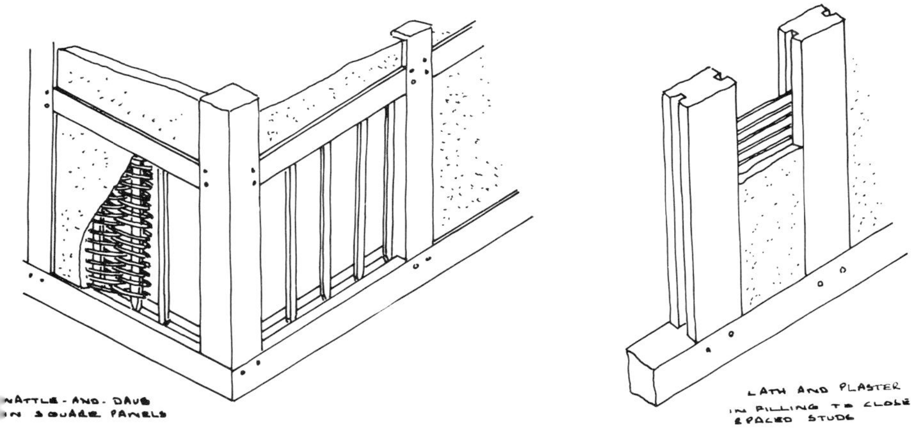

43. Wattle-and-daub.

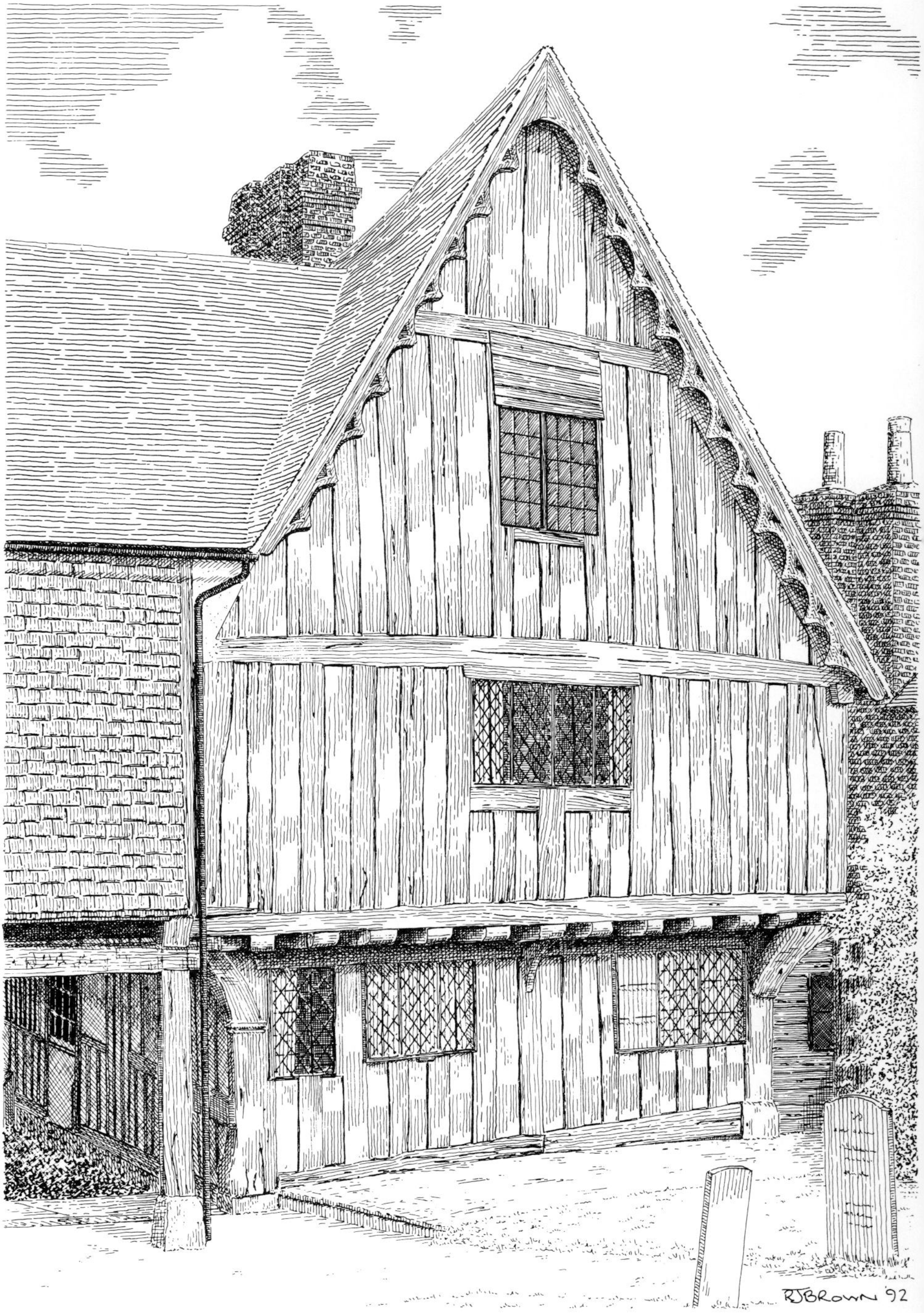

44. House next to the lychgate, Penshurst with oak boards between the studs.

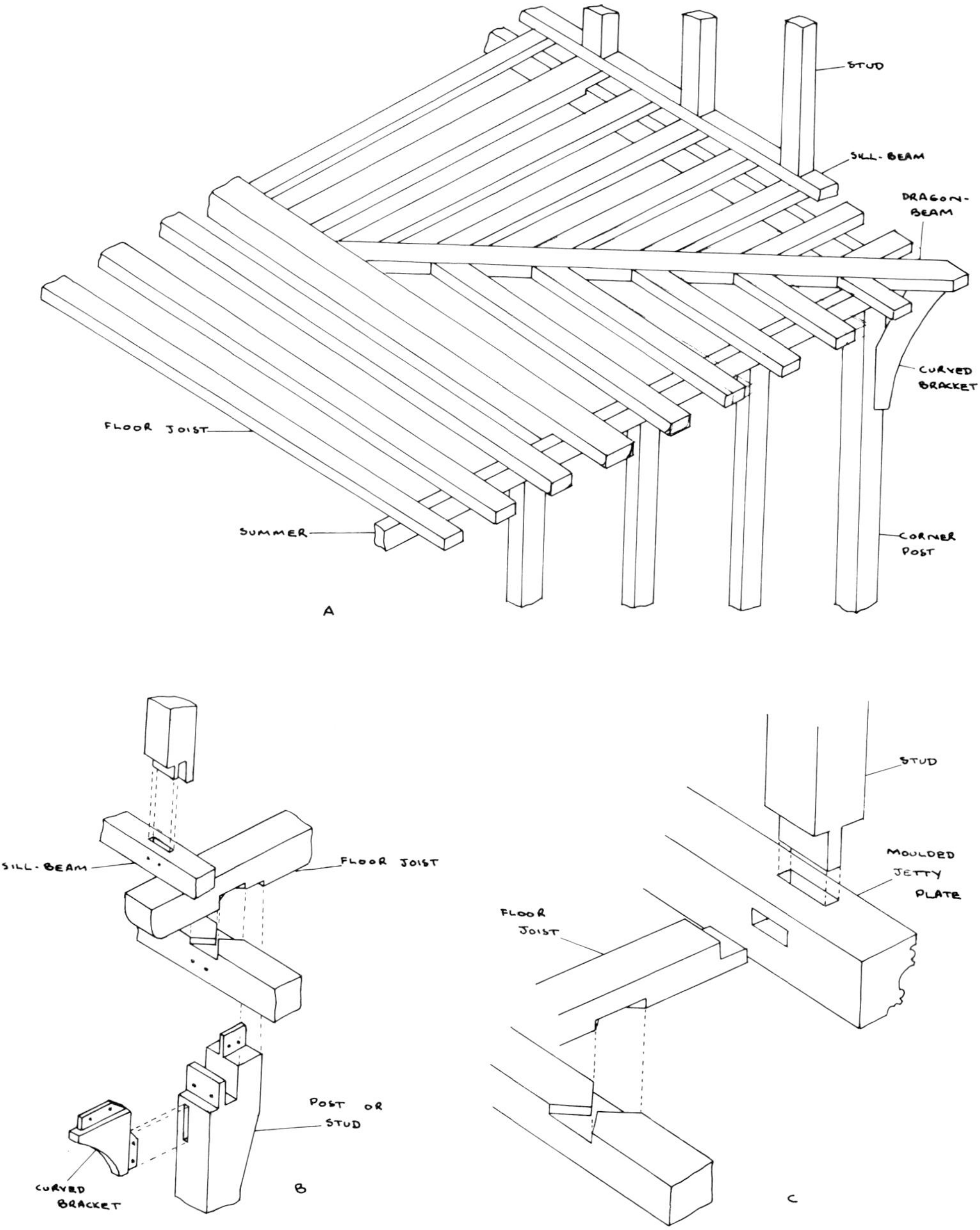

45. Jetty construction. A. general arrangement; B. joint between stud, summer, floor joist and sill-beam stud.

halved over the inside face of the intervening studs and concealed externally behind the wattle-and-daub.

The filling between the studs of the medieval house was wattle-and-daub (*43*). Where the panels were square it was normal to have vertical staves, usually of hazel, which were parted at one end and chisel-shaped at the other. Normally spaced around twelve inches apart, they were generally fitted into holes in the upper horizontal member and stud and then wedged into a groove in the lower one. Between these uprights, wattle – pliable wands, usually of unbarked hazel or ash sticks – were interwoven to form hurdle-like panels. In many of the early houses riven oak laths were used to form the wattle and since hazel wattling is of great antiquity, the difference between the two is one of quality, not age.

When the panels were narrow the uprights were omitted completely and instead of a woven panel, ash or hazel sticks or more commonly oak laths were fixed horizontally, wedged into grooves cut in the side of the studs.

Another method of filling the narrow space between the studs was by the insertion of oak planks. The method of construction would have to be different from that of wattle-and-daub, for whereas in the latter form of construction the infill would have been constructed after the erection of the timber frame, when oak planks were used it would have been necessary to fit them as the frame was erected. Today examples of this method of construction are rare, but Kent is fortunate to have one fine example which stands at the entrance to the churchyard at Penshurst (*44*).

One of the most pleasing features of medieval timber-framed houses in Kent, as in most counties, is jettying – the projection of an upper storey beyond the one below (*45*). The word jetty comes from the French *jeté*, which means something thrown out. Jettying can occur on one or more sides and even, as at the Tudor House in King Street, Margate, on all four sides.

In most cases the jettying was restricted to the first floor but where there was a second storey this too was often jettied like the floor below (*46*). An excellent example of this is 3 The Butchery, Sandwich. At Mercery Lane, Canterbury, at the corner with the High Street, is another example. Here the double jetties are to both sides; opposite and almost touching is another building (Boots) jettied and jettied again higher up, again on both sides. A second and even third jetty can be found on the many gable-fronted town houses to be found in such places as Canterbury and Faversham. In St Dunstan's Street, Canterbury, is a splendid range of such buildings, all half-timbered seventeenth-century houses, with thirteen gables in all with two overhangs, carved brackets and bay windows beneath them.

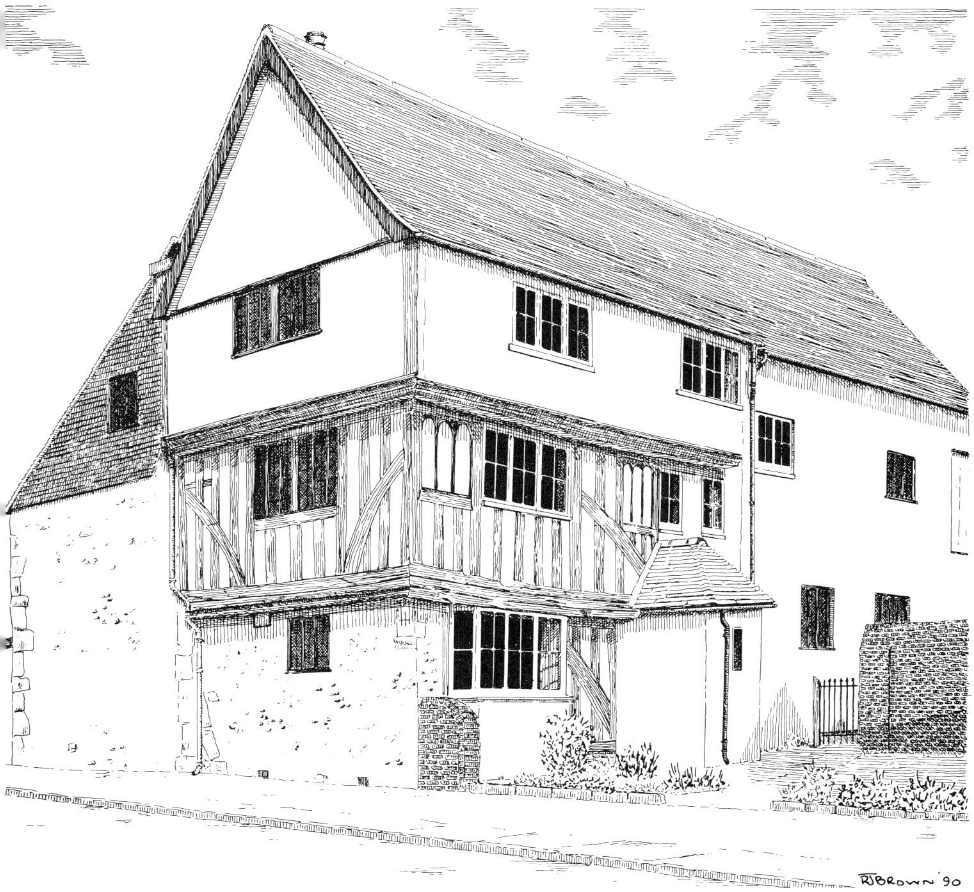

46. Arden's House, Faversham.

When jettying was restricted to one side only the construction was simple, for all that was required was for the floor joists to cantilever over the wall below and rest on the beam situated at the back of the overhang. When the overhang was on two adjacent sides, the process was more complicated. It was necessary to change the direction of the floor joists and to enable this to be undertaken one of the floor joists was replaced by a larger one to which was framed another horizontal beam, called the 'dragon-beam', which ran diagonally to the corner of the floor. Into this beam the ends of the floor joists were framed, each pair set at right angles, although often the last few were framed at a slight angle. Towards its end the dragon-beam was supported by a massive corner or 'dragon' post. In East Anglia these dragon-posts are frequently carved, but in Kent this is less common although they frequently received some form of decoration. In many cases the dragon-post was provided with a curved bracket to support the outer end of the dragon-beam. Often the post and bracket were cut from a single timber. To support the overhang along its length, additional curved brackets were sometimes provided, framed to the studs and floor joists.

Once the floor joists were in position, the framing to the next storey could continue with a bressummer laid along the ends of the floor joists. In some instances the projecting floor joists were left square but in the vast majority of cases the ends were shaped into a quarter-round and left exposed. In some instances the ends of the floor joists were framed into the back of the bressummer rather than supporting it from beneath, and this was a popular feature from the sixteenth century onwards. The bressummers were either moulded or richly carved.

An alternative method of concealing the ends of the floor joists, also popular in the sixteenth century, was to provide a fascia board. These fascias were rarely left without decoration in some form, either mouldings or some type of elaborate carving.

There has been much speculation as to why jetties were built. In 1254 Henry III much admired Continental examples and was possibly instrumental in their introduction into England. Tiptofts, Wimbish, Essex, is of thirteenth-century date and is thought to be the earliest example in England. But had they any practical purpose? Many theories have been put forward. One is that a jetty increased the floor area of the building – from 10 to 20 per cent per floor for an average two-foot projection – without increasing the land on which it sat. This was undoubtedly desirable in towns but not in the depths of the country where there was no shortage of land. This can be explained by the desire of country builders to follow the fashion of towns. However, jettying is nearly always to the front or end of the building which is visible to the public, and if the purpose was to increase the floor area it would have also been to the rear.

Another reason often given is the need to protect the building from damp. There were, of course, no gutters and downpipes in those days and on buildings without jetties much of the rainwater would on windy days pour off the roof and be blown back on to the face of the building. It is obvious that a building constructed of timber with wattle-and-daub infilling would deteriorate if incessantly soaked by rainwater, and jettied construction would certainly help to protect the wall beneath. Once again this theory is not plausible for as we have seen, jetties were normally provided to the 'public face' irrespective of the prevailing wind and rain.

The other reasons are structural. It has been suggested that jettying was used to overcome the problem of obtaining posts long enough to run the full height of the building, for with jetties it was only necessary to have posts of one-storey height. Certainly this alleviated the difficult joint of the three mortises from three directions at one point at the junction of the studs and floor joists with the bressummer. Once again the problem seems to have been overcome on those sides on which jettying was not employed, and they seem to be no less sound structurally than walls employing jetties. Another structural reason given is that the weight of the walls and roof transferred to the cantilevered end of the floor joists counteracted the possible mid-span deflection of these joists caused by the weight of furniture, particularly if the floor joists were placed on their broadside. This too seems unlikely, for the projection was only moderate, rarely more than two feet, having little cantilever effect. Moreover this theory would seem to require the jetty to be at both sides or both ends of the building and this rarely occurred.

All or any of these explanations could be correct, but as jettying was usually restricted to the side or ends visible to the public, it may be as Alec Clifton-Taylor in his book *The Pattern of English Building* says, that 'men who could afford to pay for it could not resist a feature so charming in itself'.

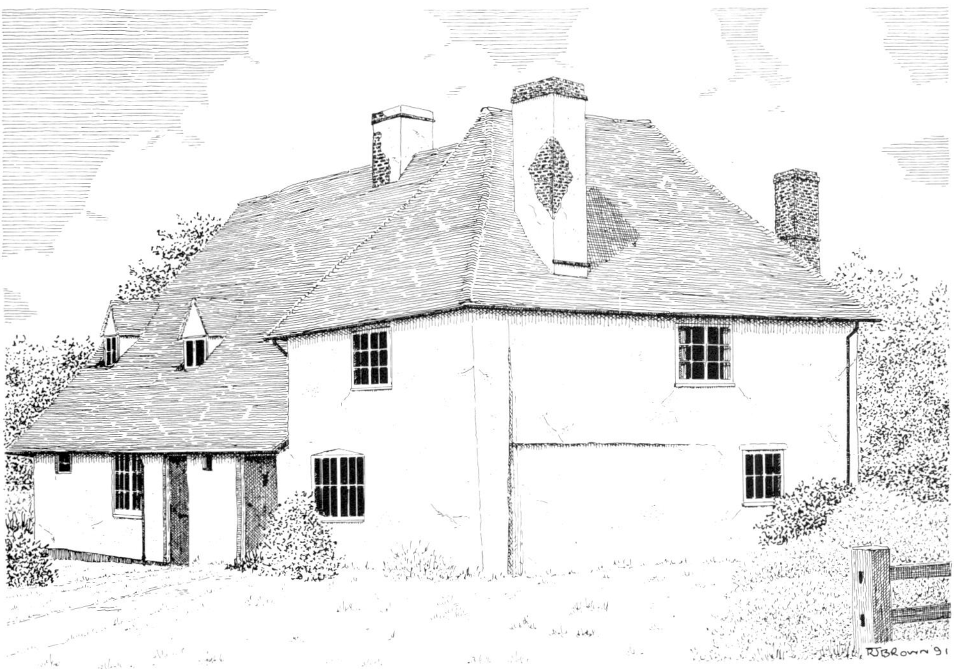

47. Old aisled cottage, Sole Street, Crundale prior to its demolition.

Timber-framed houses of early date are rare within Kent. Up until the 1960s one of considerable age stood on the south side of the lane between Crundel and Waltham, called Sole Street, and directly opposite the inn there (*47*). In its later years it had been occupied as two separate dwellings but after it became empty, planning permission was granted for its demolition as it was then not listed. It was originally thought to be a building of fifteenth-century date but during demolition it was apparent that although the cross-wing was of this date, the aisled post was very much older than at first thought. Mr E.W. Parkin has put a date of not later than 1300 to this part of the building. The frame was taken into store at the Weald and Downland Museum for possible re-erection.

The earliest of these aisled houses surviving today has recently been discovered at Ratling Court, Adisham, by E.W. Parkin, who has dated the building as early fourteenth century. Of similar date is Yew Tree Cottage, at Oad Street, Borden, which has a single aisle. There are a few aisled houses in which the posts are not free standing but inset in the end frames. All appear to be of fifteenth-century date, the most notable being Fairfield, Eastry (*48*). This manor house probably dates from the early fifteenth century, and was built by Christ Church

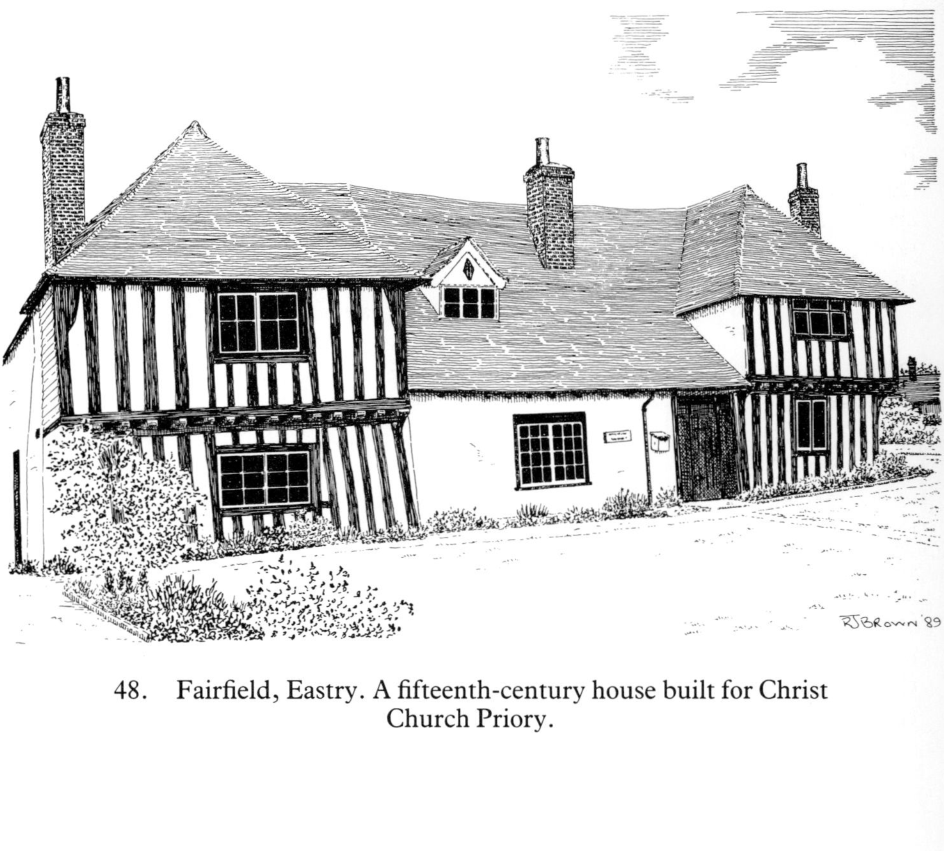

48. Fairfield, Eastry. A fifteenth-century house built for Christ Church Priory.

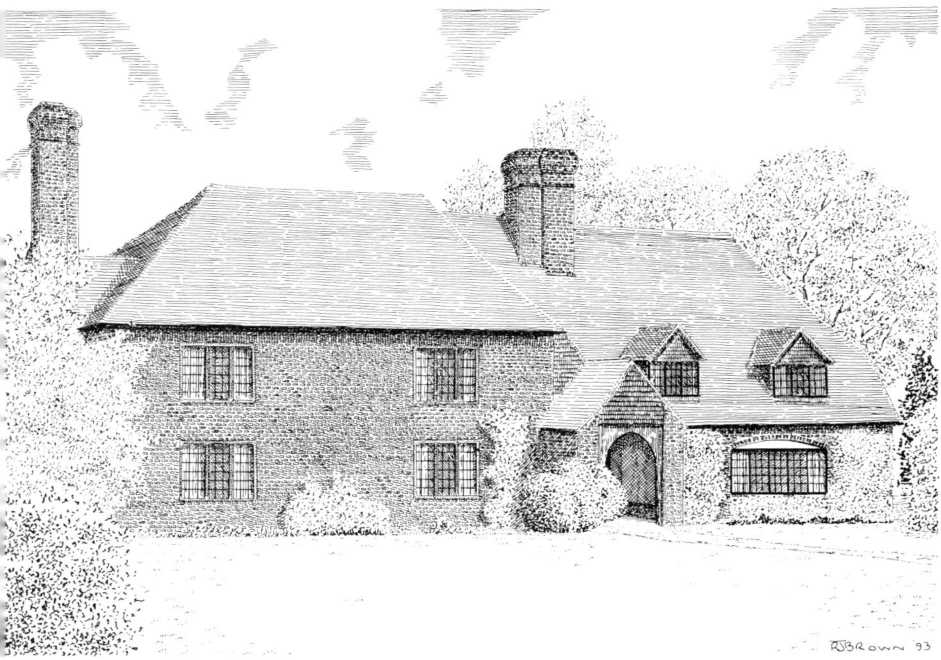

49. Hamden, Smarden. Base cruck house of the fourteenth century encased in nineteenth-century brickwork.

Priory. Unlike, say, Nurstead Court which had an overall hipped roof, the end-bays here were jettied and given separate hipped roofs. There are a few other houses in Kent which have a similar design and outward appearance. Hagbrook, Alkham, is of a slightly later date than Fairfield and is similar in that it too has a two-bay hall.

These fifteenth-century aisled houses were all somewhat old-fashioned, for aisled houses in other parts of the country, namely Essex and Suffolk, had generally been abandoned in favour of hall houses without aisles. Even in Kent there were already houses of mid-fourteenth-century date being built in which the aisles had been abandoned.

As we have seen earlier, one method designed to span the hall was the base-cruck. A few examples survive in the county, the most notable being Hamden, Smarden (*49*), where hidden beneath nineteenth-century brickwork to front and sides and stone to the rear, is an almost complete fourteenth-century hall house, although nothing much of the original hall below head height now survives. Externally the only evidence that the house is timber-framed is the two-centred timber arch to the single-storey gabled porch of the same date as the

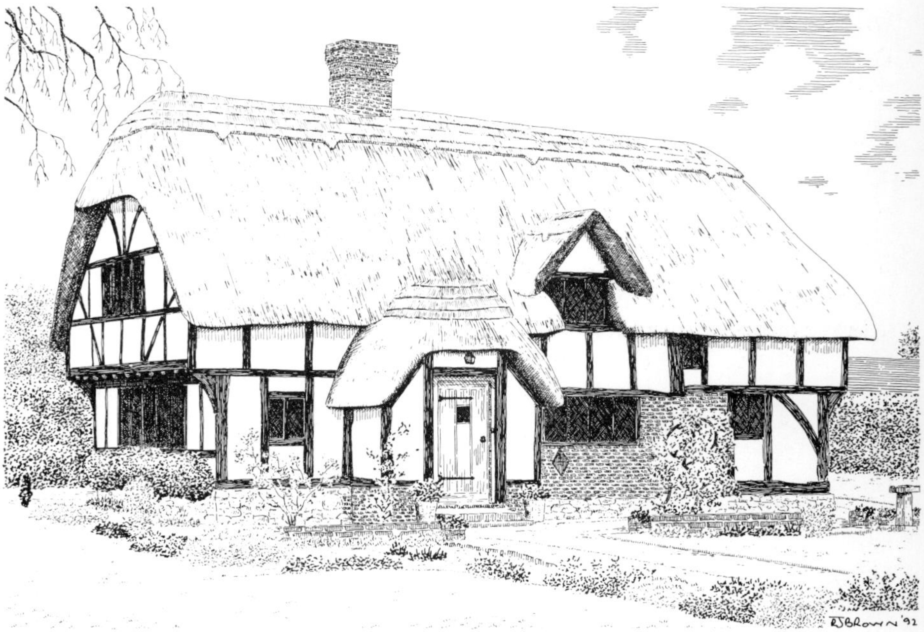

50. Burnt Oak, Benover.

hall. Single-storey porches of this date are a rare occurrence in domestic buildings in England and this example is now unique in Kent. The hall is thirty-two feet long, divided into two equal bays by the base-cruck with arch-braces spanning some twenty-four feet and supporting a tie-beam and crown-posts above. At the lower end is a separately roofed cross-wing possibly of slightly later date than the hall and this has been, perhaps in the seventeenth century, doubled in width. The house may have been built for a John Hamden (or possibly his father) who was rich enough in 1361 to leave the oldest recorded perpetual endowment to Smarden parish, yielding at this time six shillings per annum, a very respectable sum in those days. The estate passed to the Turners in the late seventeenth century and in the late eighteenth century to the Tokes of Godinton. S.E. Rigold has also noted a base-cruck across the hall at Burnt Oak, Benover (*50*), a hamlet a mile or so south of Yalding. A further base-cruck has recently been discovered at Barnes Place, East Peckham (*51*), by Mr Brian Anthony.

Despite the fact that Kent has few early aisled and quasi-aisled timber-framed buildings, the county is extremely rich in late medieval timber-framed houses. An early form, similar in appearance to aisled houses such as Fairfield, are the houses with open halls with either a wing or wings roofed transversely. In Kent these houses were never as popular as in Essex and in East Anglia where the form became dominant at all social levels. Examples can be found, for instance, in the hinterland of Faversham, where Lower Newlands, Teynham (*52*) is a very fine example. Built around 1370, the open hall is flanked at one end by the solar and service combined in a single bay and roofed separately with a higher roof hipped at both ends. A century or so later a new bay was built at the upper end to form a new solar bay. A few miles away at North Street, a hamlet near Sheldwich, alone in a field to the south of the hamlet is a similar timber-framed house. There are a few examples in which there is a separate roofed cross-wing to one end only; one is Old Hall, Petham (formerly Thatched Cottage)(*53*), where the cross-wing houses the service rooms below and solar above.

However, the majority of cross-wing houses are formed by the later enlargement of the solar and/or service ends. Examples are fairly numerous, one excellent example of a cross-wing at the solar end being Hartnup House, Smarden; the cross-wing is of a separate build and probably represents a reconstruction of the upper end. The date of 1671 refers only to the gable and the window below, for the original house is of fifteenth-century date. Olde Manor Cottages, Bearsted, is situated to the north of the large village green. It has the usual medieval arrangement but cross-wings to both ends; the one to the right may well be original but the one on the left has close studding and is clearly of early sixteenth-century date. According to S.E. Rigold, this wing was originally a shop.

The most famous type of open-hall house to be found in Kent is the so-called Wealden house, a misleading name for the highest concentration was not in fact in the Weald but in mid-Kent to the south-east of Maidstone. Although occurring elsewhere in England, in East Sussex and spasmodically elsewhere, this house type is to be found throughout Kent with the exception of areas of marsh, high down and forest, but some three-quarters of the total come from the area between the Medway and Stour and Romney Marsh, comprising the extreme east of the Weald, the southern slopes of the ragstone hills and downs and the plain to the north. The majority of the area was deforested early on and was intensively cultivated. The area immediately south-east of Maidstone contains not only every variety of the Wealden house but also the earliest known examples. To the east of the Stour, there are also many fine examples but they are of rather later date; to the west the number is much fewer – why this should be so is not easy to explain, for other types of open-hall houses are relatively common here. It seems likely therefore that the Wealden house originated not in the Weald but in the heart of Kent, an area of small but wealthy yeoman farmers owning their own freeholds, which

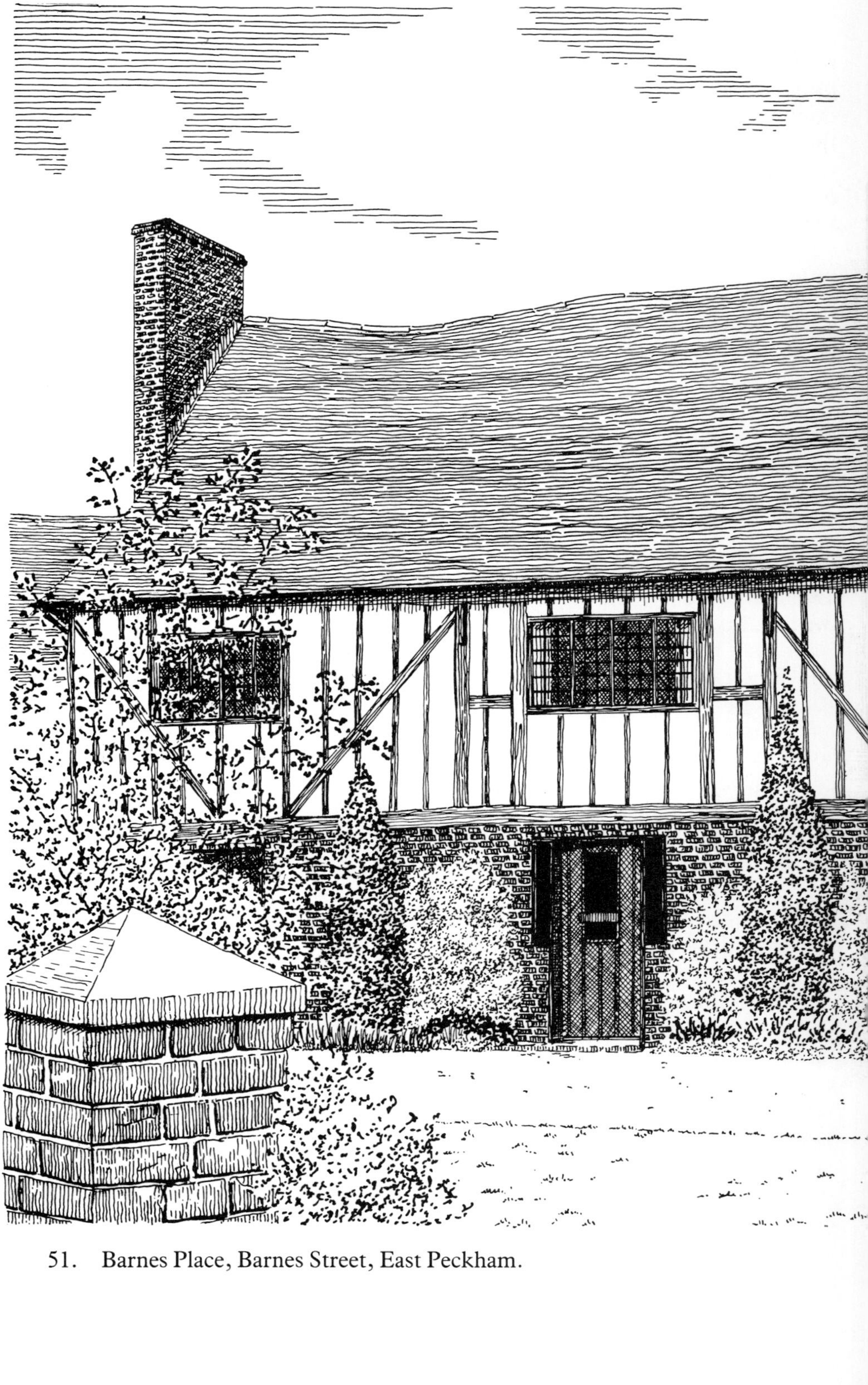

51. Barnes Place, Barnes Street, East Peckham.

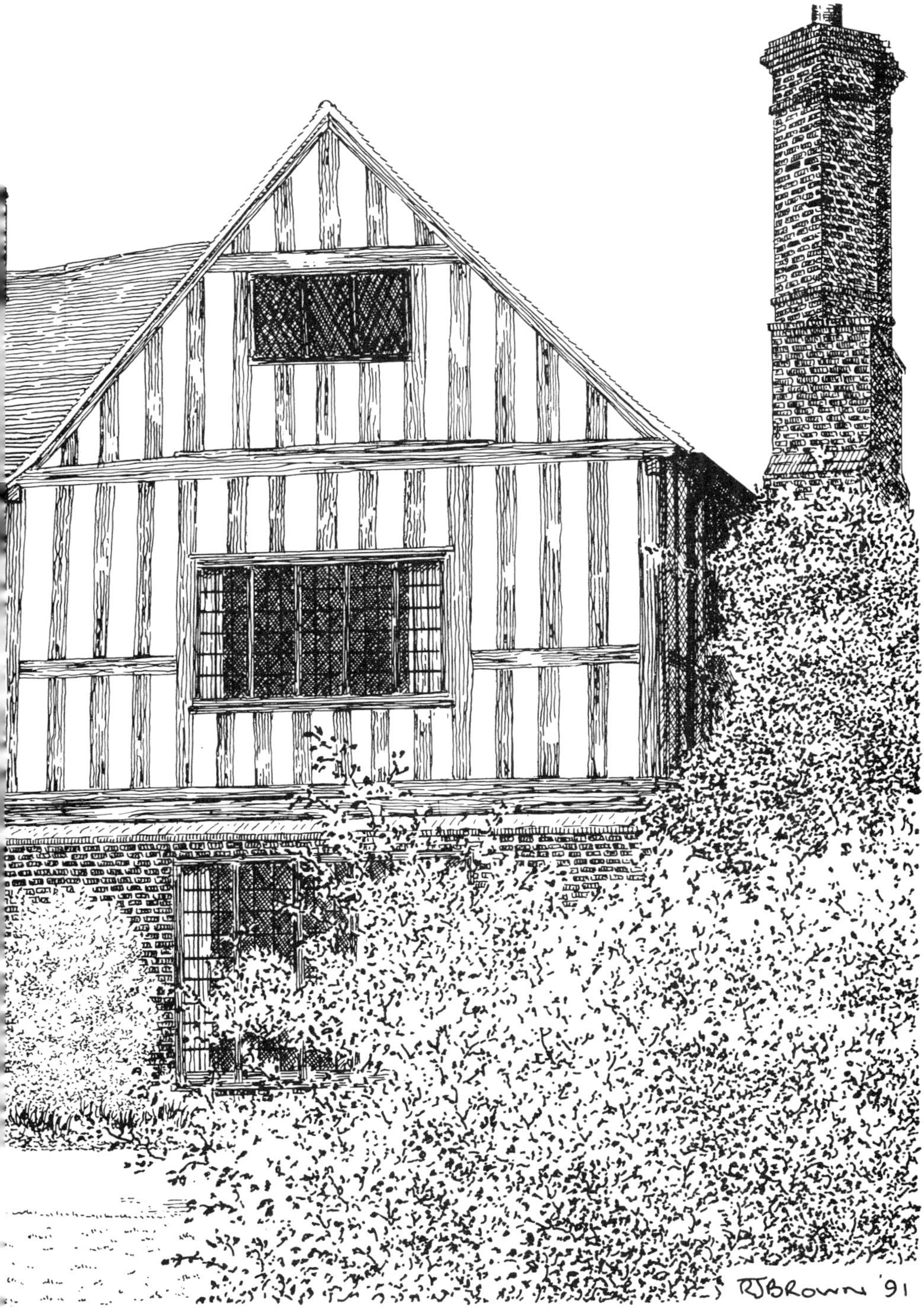
RJBROWN '91

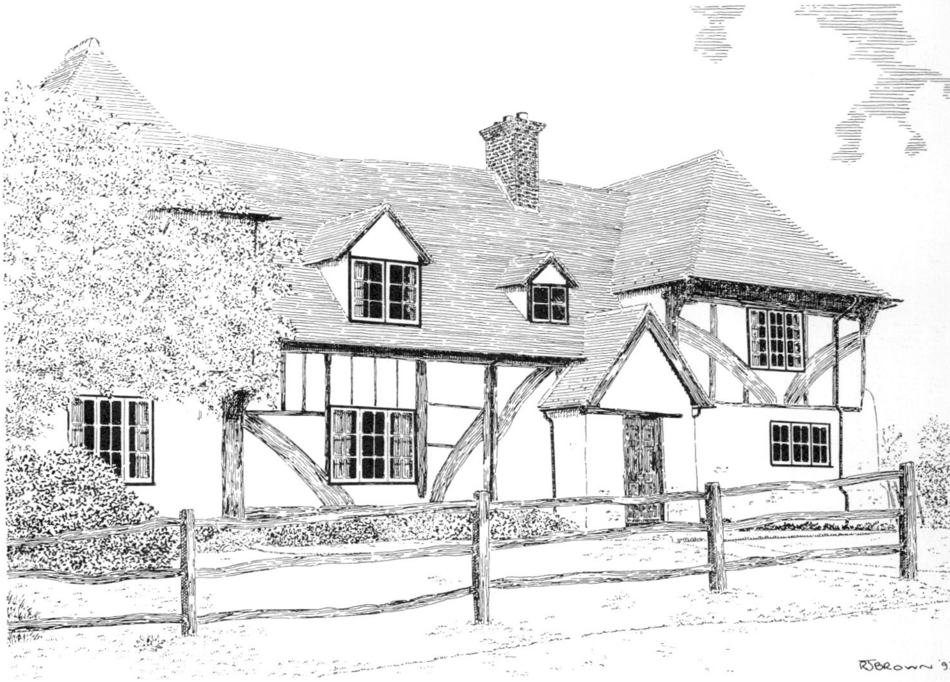

52. Lower Newlands, Teynham. Built around 1370 with a single solar-service bay to one end.

contrasts strongly with the older ecclesiastical estates of the east. The total number of these Wealden houses must run into several hundred for not only are there the obvious ones which retain their characteristic features but there are many others to be found on closer scrutiny hidden behind later additions, and even some such as Chillenden Court Farm, Goodnestone and Furnace Farm, Lamberhurst, which have been totally obscured.

The classic layout of the Wealden house consists of a two-bay open central hall with a two-storeyed jettied end-bay at either end of the hall, with a distinct and recognizable screens passage between the hall and the service end (*54*). The entire building is covered by a single, pitched, hipped roof with the front line of the eaves continuing across the front of the hall, giving the impression that the hall is recessed: hence why it was formerly known as the recessed front type – a term now rejected by most authorities.

There are many variations to this plan. These include a single-bay hall as at Littlecroft, Chilham, a fifteenth-century house, or the Maltings, Sandwich, a house of similar size dated by documented

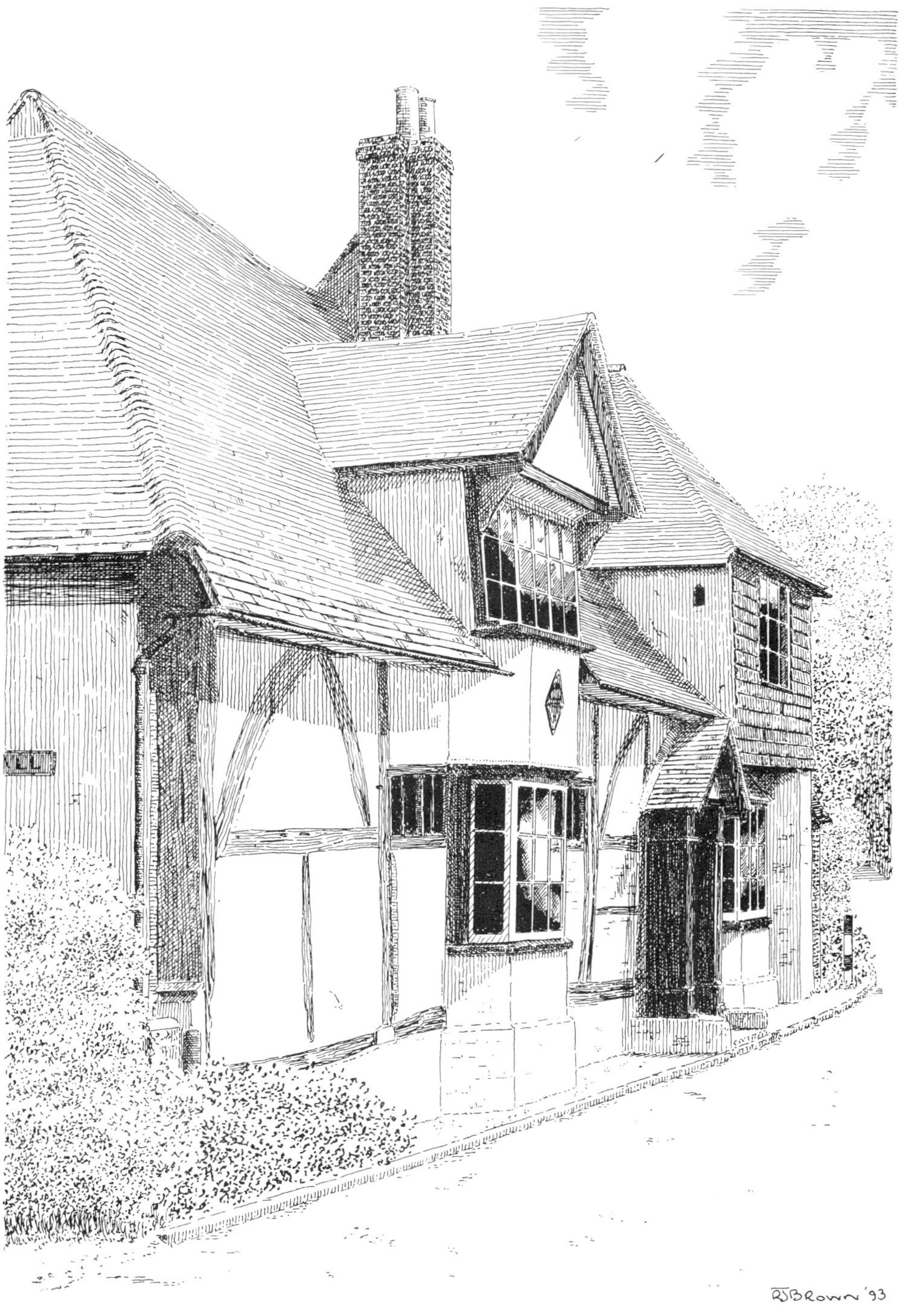

53. Old Hall, Petham.

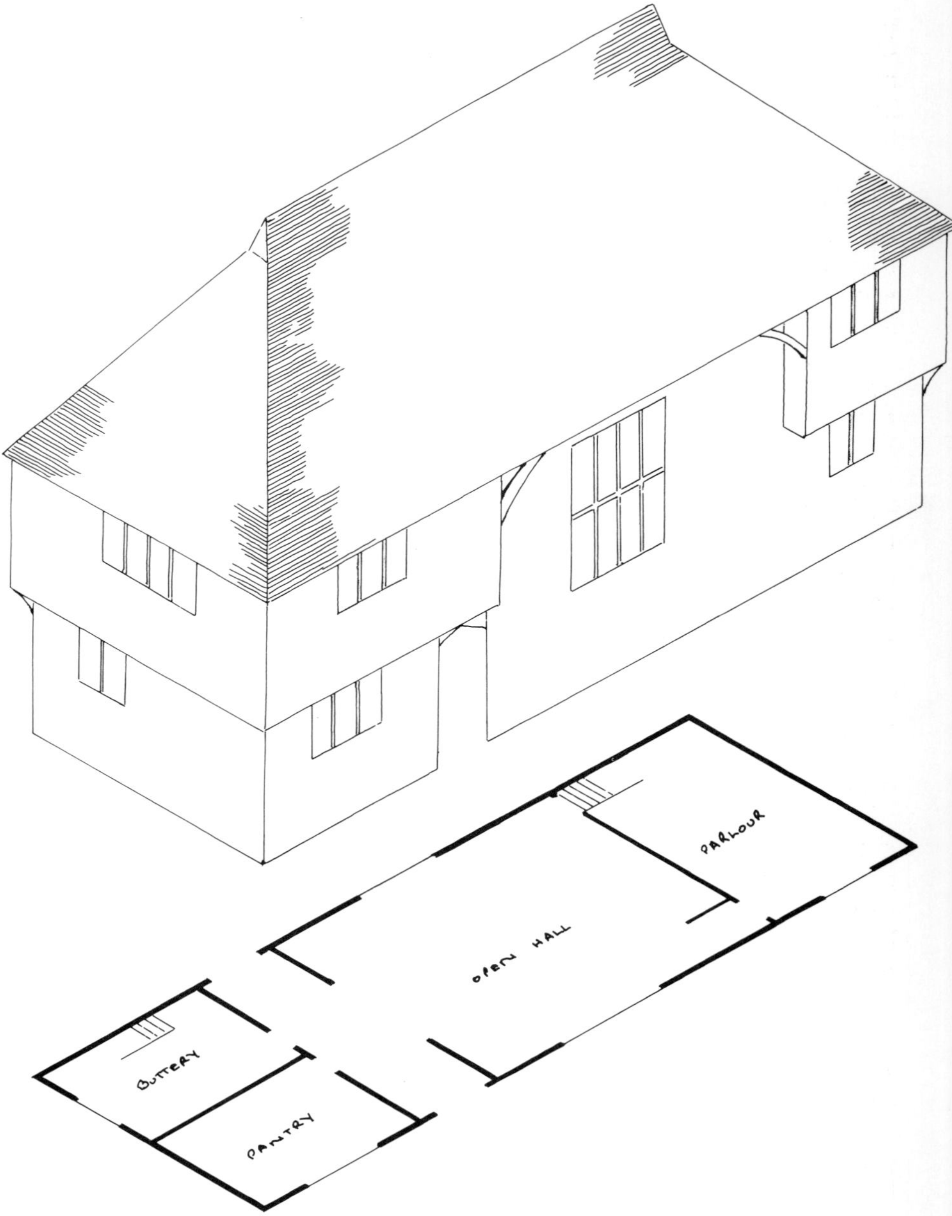

54. Typical layout of a Wealden house.

evidence to 1418. In both cases entry to the house was directly into the hall, there being no evidence of a screens passage. Other examples are Old Hall, Sundridge (55), an early sixteenth-century house, interesting in that Beresford Pite restored the original fenestration including the three-plus-three windows with a dividing transom to the hall.

Another variation to the Wealden house was the position of the screens passage. It was, of course, always situated at the lower end of the hall but in some cases, as for instance at Yardhurst, Great Chart and Headcorn Manor, it is formed by a narrow bay about seven feet wide, often with a spered opening into the hall. This narrow bay is usually structurally separate from both the hall and service rooms, with the wall extending the full height of the hall. In many cases, however, there is no such separate bay, the passage being combined with the hall and separated from it by a screen.

Alternatively the screens passage was contained structurally within the service end and below the chamber above, in which case it is referred to as an 'undershot' passage. This can be seen at Corner Farm, Langley (56), a late fifteenth-century Wealden house restored to its original state, and at Pattenden, Goudhurst, built *c.* 1470 by the Pattenden family (57), who had owned the manor from at least as early as the time of Edward I. When the screens passage was structurally contained it produced jetties of noticeable unequal width, the service end being some one and a half times as wide as the solar bay. This was even more striking where there was an extra service bay, as at Church Cottages, Southfleet. In most instances this additional bay would be a later extension. Although in some cases the solar and service bays were of similar length, as at New Place, Ickham, where both bays are over nineteen feet long, this was generally not the case; sometimes the solar bay was longer and sometimes the service bay, with the lengths varying from as little as ten feet for the service bay at Cotterell Court, Petham to some twenty-one feet at Court House, Bishopsbourne, with the majority between twelve and fifteen feet.

Likewise the open hall varied in size; the single-bay hall was generally about thirteen feet long but those of two bays varied considerably from as little as under sixteen feet at Court House, Bishopsbourne, to some twenty-five feet at the Dower House, Goodnestone. In the majority of cases the length of the hall appears to be around twenty feet. Unlike most aisled halls in which the open truss is placed centrally, in the Wealden house this was never so, presumably because the truss could not be placed under the central hearth and so was moved to one side. In most cases the larger bay was to the solar end.

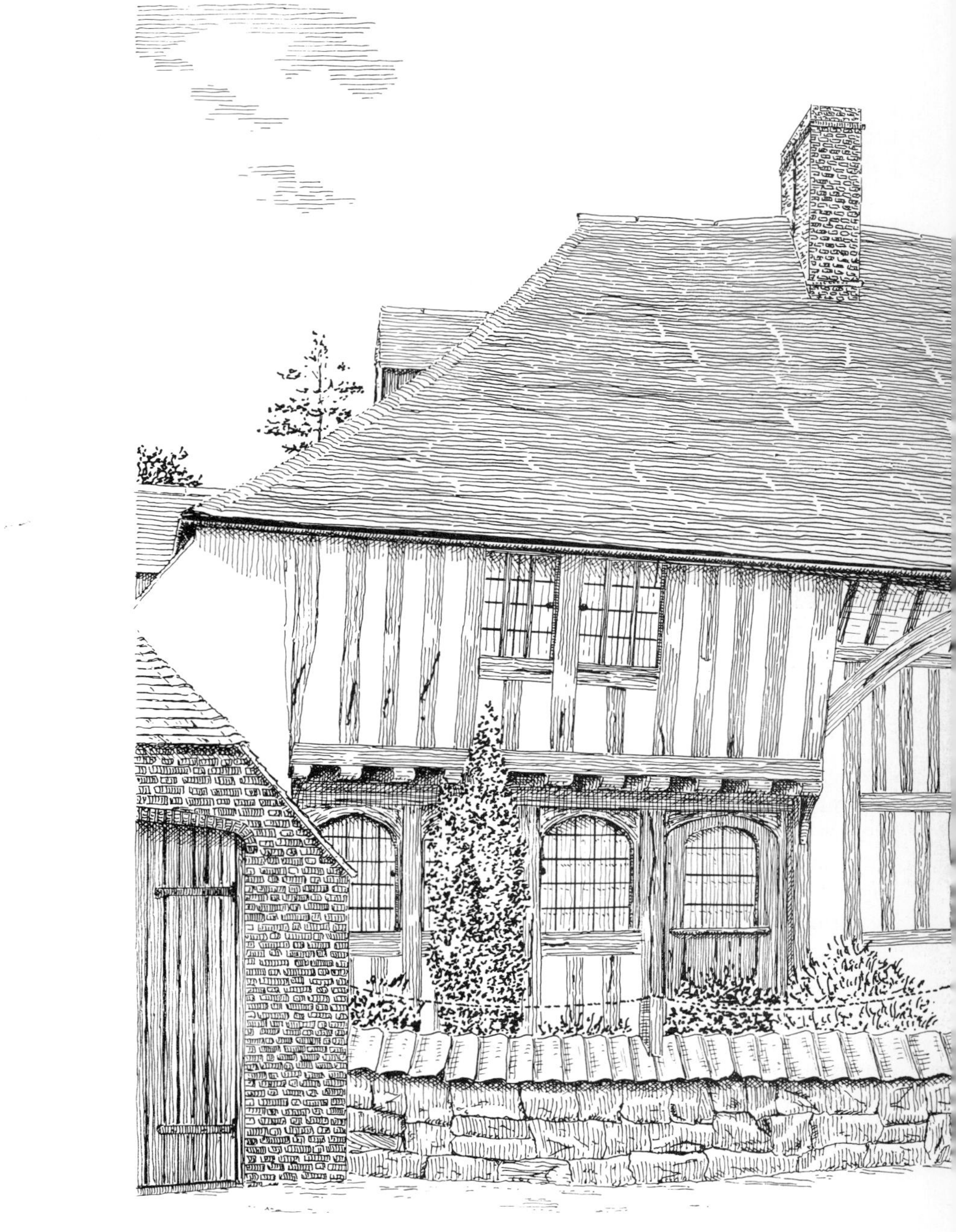

55. Old Hall, Sundridge, with a single bay open hall.

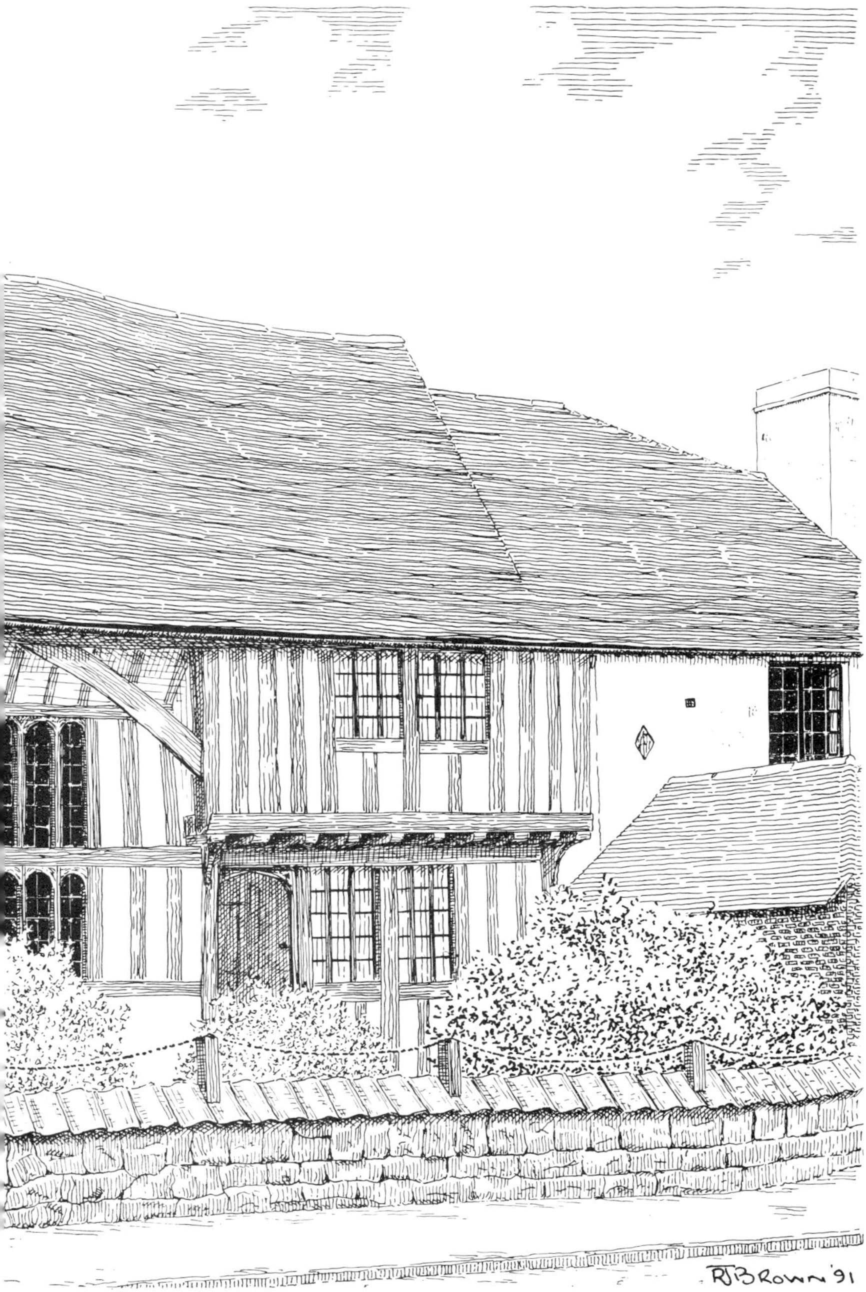
RJBROWN '91

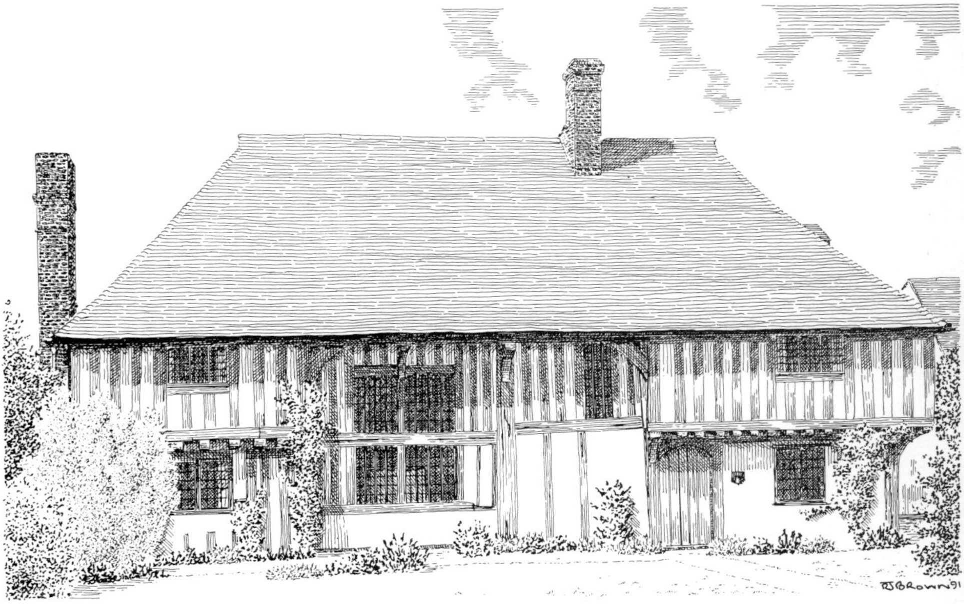

56. Corner Farm, Langley. Fifteenth-century house with 'undershot' screens passage.

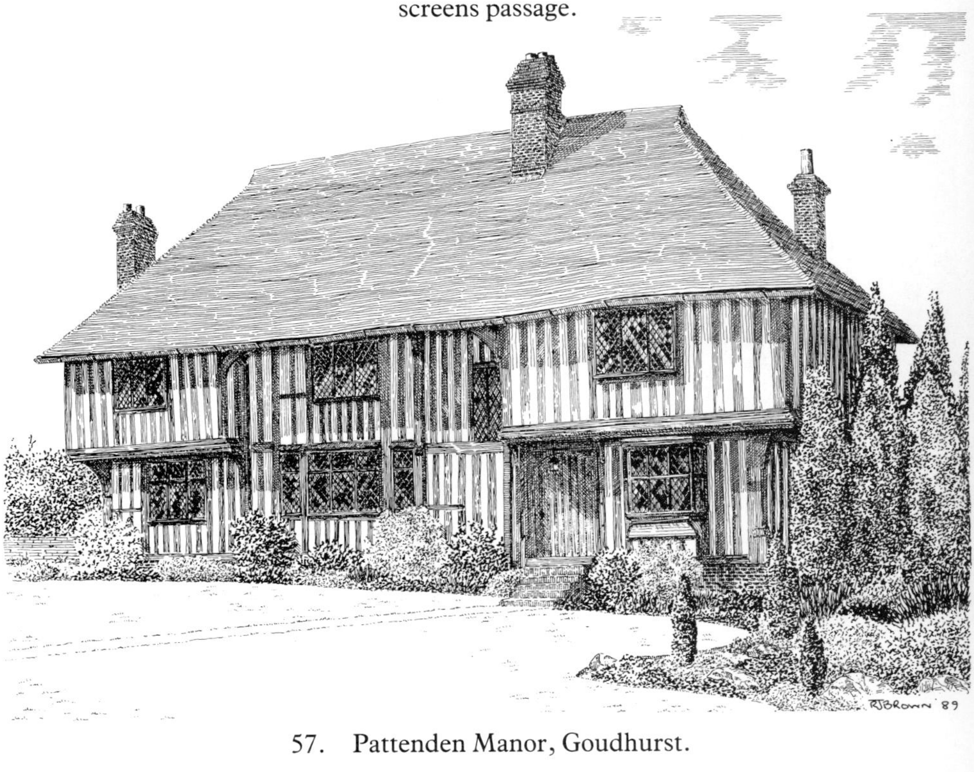

57. Pattenden Manor, Goudhurst.

With such a combination of room sizes the overall length of the Wealden house obviously varied considerably. Chillenden Court Farm, Goodnestone, is a little over forty feet, whereas Deanery Cottages, Chartham, built by Christ Church Priory for the farmer of the estate shortly after 1495, is some fifty-four feet long and Court House, Bishopsbourne, measures fifty-eight feet. The overall depth of these buildings was usually between fifteen and eighteen feet and rarely exceeded twenty feet.

The origin of the Wealden house is obscure. Certainly by about 1400 it seemed to have evolved fully, reaching its peak about eighty years later and continuing to be built for another fifty years or so. Most certainly seem to be of fifteenth-century date. There are some from the fourteenth century, the earliest perhaps being that at Larkfield, on the old A20 four miles west of Maidstone, which is thought to have been built around 1350 and is at present a restaurant called 'The Wealden Hall' (*58*). The building has all the characteristics associated with a house of this date – the widely spaced studs, the

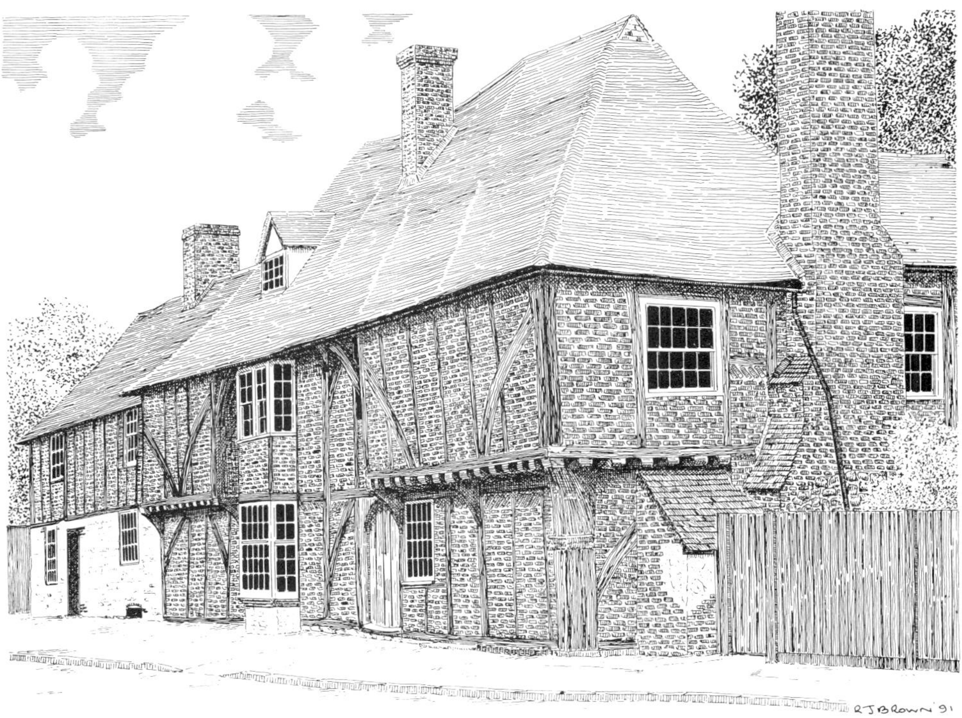

58. 'The Wealden Hall', Larkfield. Probably built around 1350 and now a restaurant.

Kentish framing to the jettied end-bays and the large arch-braces supporting the eaves wall-plate where it crosses the hall.

The house is thought to have been built originally for one of the ecclesiastical establishments, but by the seventeenth century the Bradbourne estate, to which the house belonged, became the property of the Twisdens, an old Kentish family who took their name from their settlement near Goudhurst. It seems likely that around 1850 the house was divided into four cottages, which the Twisdens leased. When the last baronet, Sir John Twisden, died in 1937 the mansion and estate were purchased by East Malling Research Station but this left the old hall house without a secure future and its condition deteriorated. Finally, Malling Rural District Council placed a closing order on it and the house was eventually secured by the Society for the Protection of Ancient Buildings. The Society maintained it until 1979 when they sold it to Peter Malkin who undertook the restoration work.

Another Wealden house of pre-fifteenth-century date is Wardes, Otham (59), said to have been built about 1370. Here too one can see

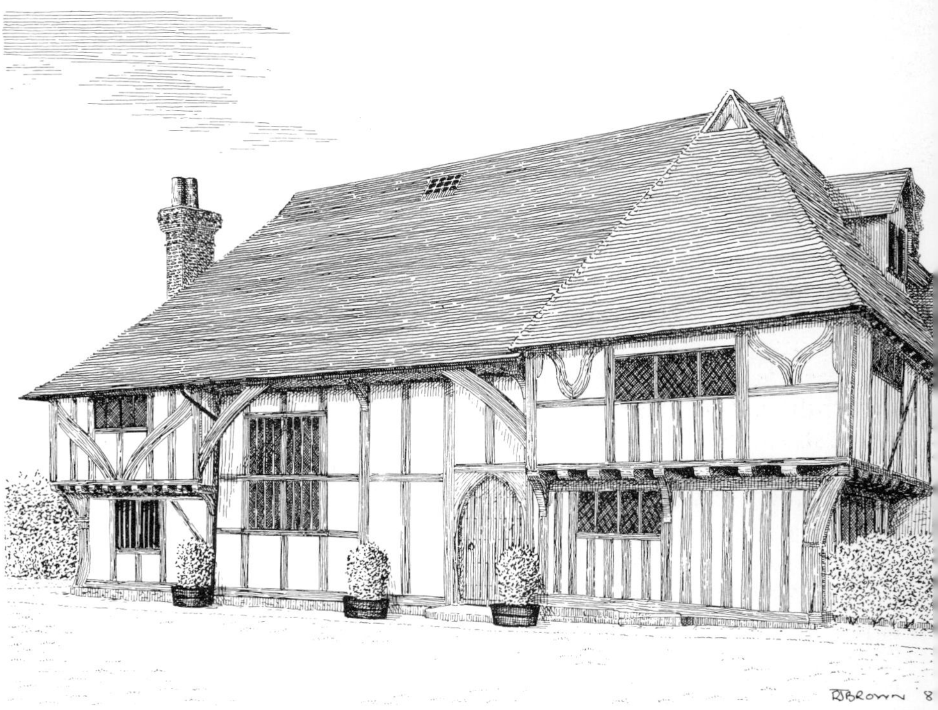

59. Wardes, Otham, a fourteenth-century Wealden house extended in the sixteenth century.

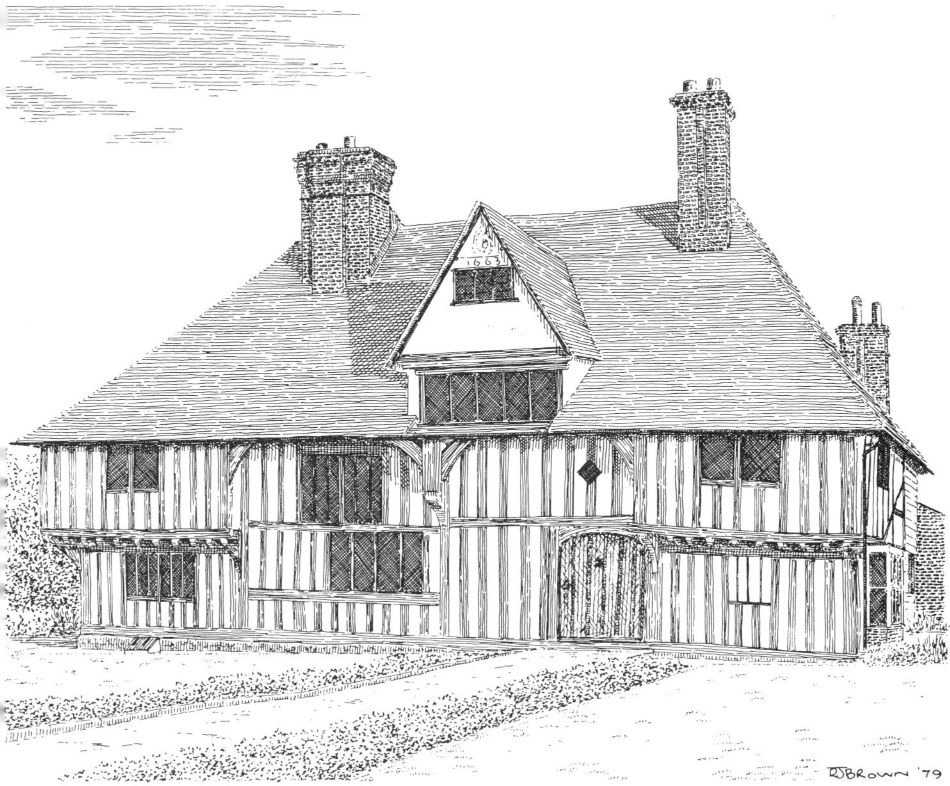

60. Synyards, Otham, a Wealden house, with gable added in 1663.

the Kentish framing to the jettied end-bay and the arch-braces supporting the eaves wall-plate. However, the hipped roof covers only the eastern two-thirds; the cross-wing to the west part is of sixteenth-century date. Hawkenbury, Headcorn, is another Wealden house showing all these early details.

The greatest change to the appearance of the Wealden house was the introduction of close studding which had the visual effect of replacing the square open panels with long, narrow, vertical ones. This became extremely popular after about 1470 and can be seen on many Wealden houses. Although in most cases close studding appeared on all elevations, this was not always so. At Synyards, Otham (*60*), close studding is on the front and sides with concealed braces, while the rear of the building is in large framing, now somewhat altered, with exposed tension braces.

Some Wealden houses such as Elbridge Farm, Littlebourne, were jettied to the front only but jettying was by no means restricted to the

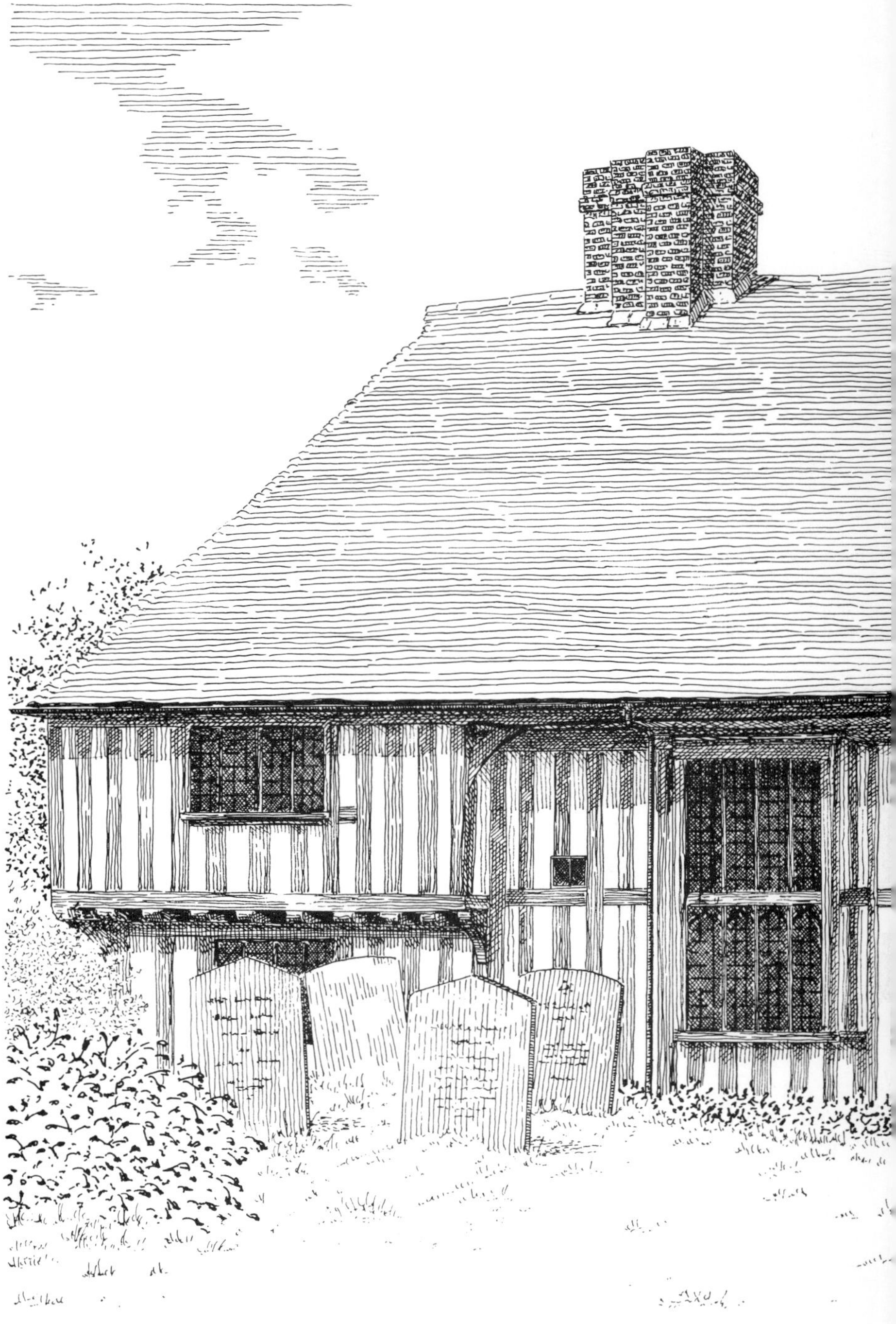

61. Headcorn Manor. Built as a parsonage after 1516.

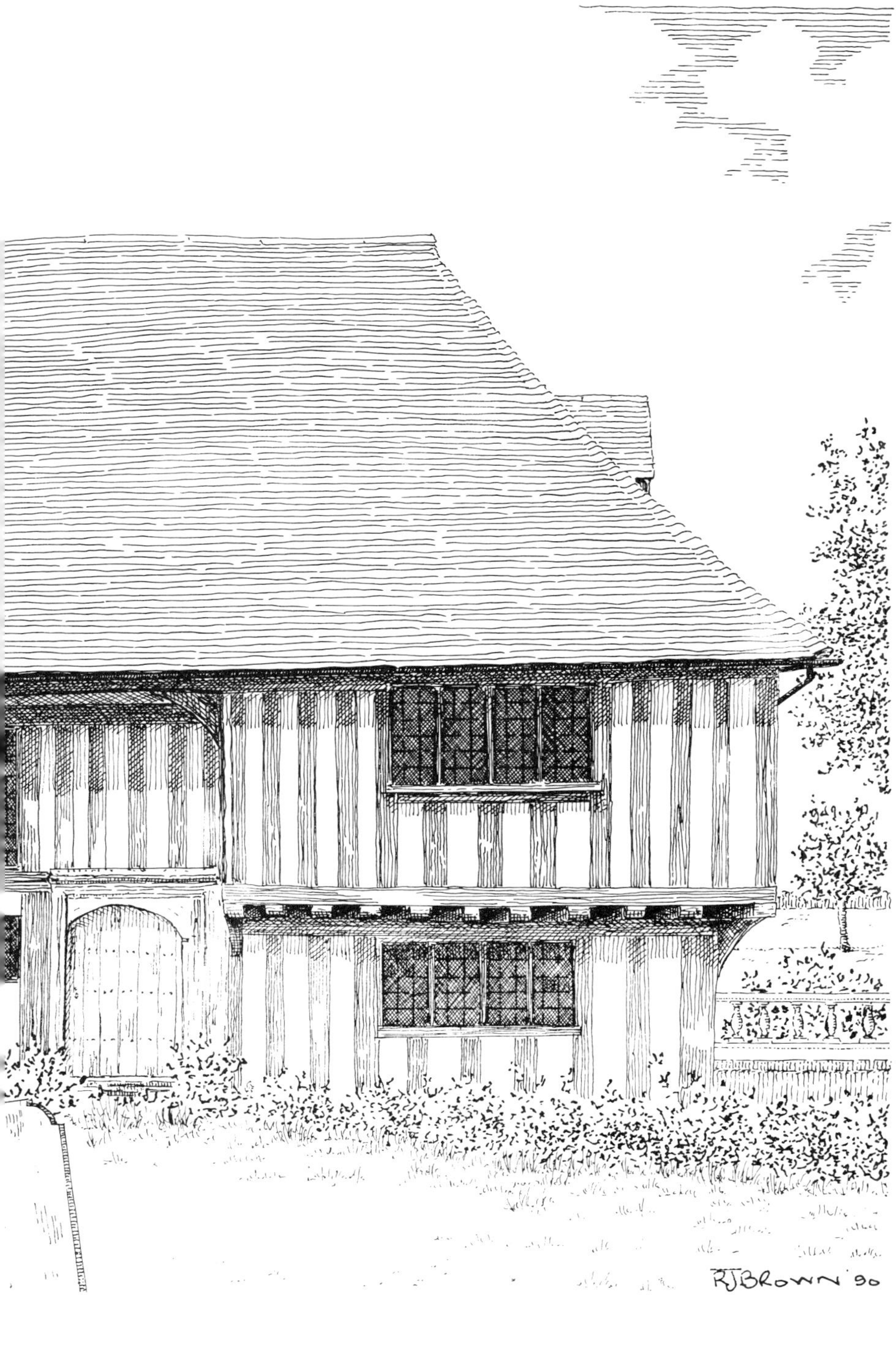
RJBROWN '90

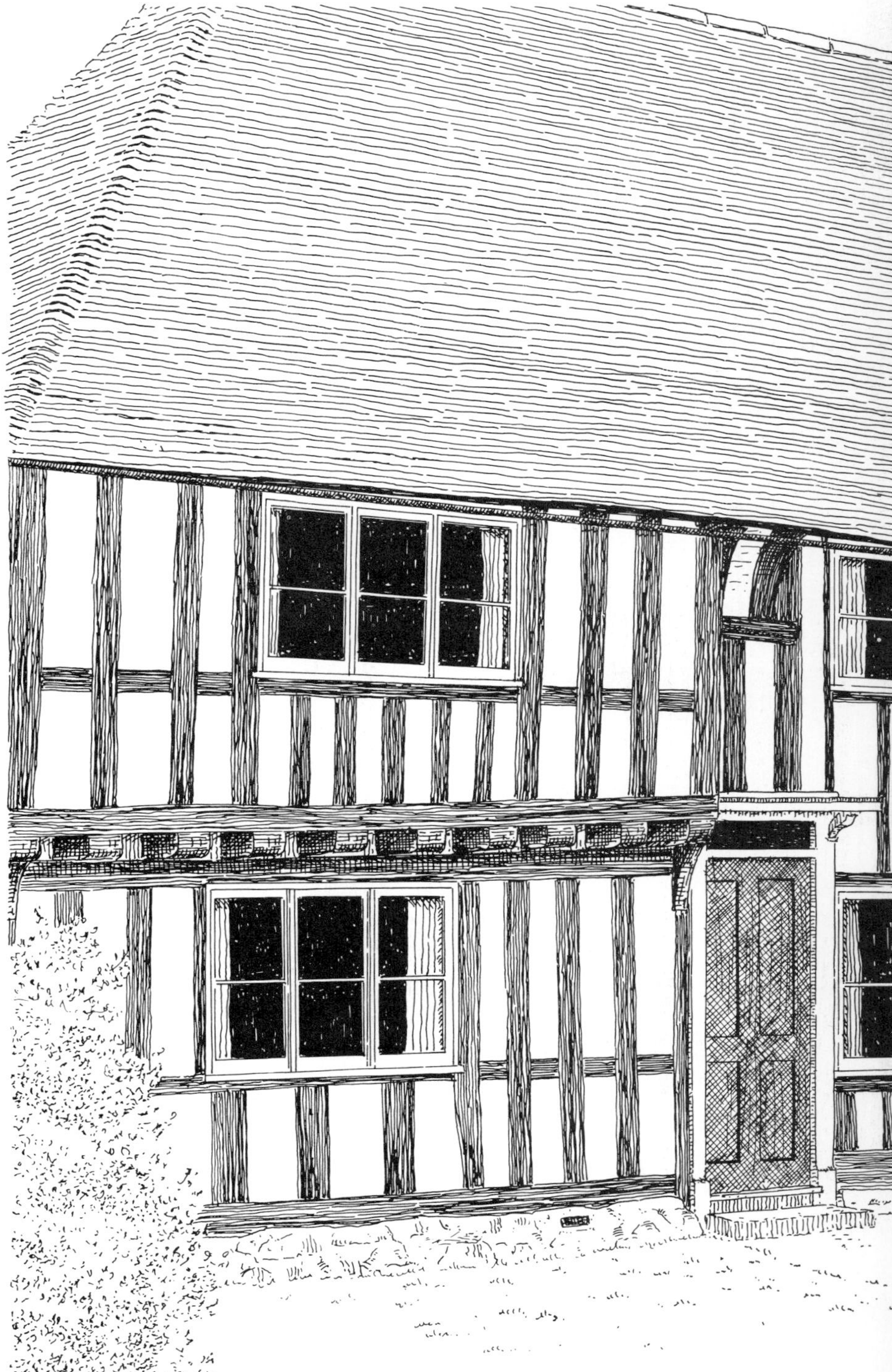

62. Westhoy, near Smarden.

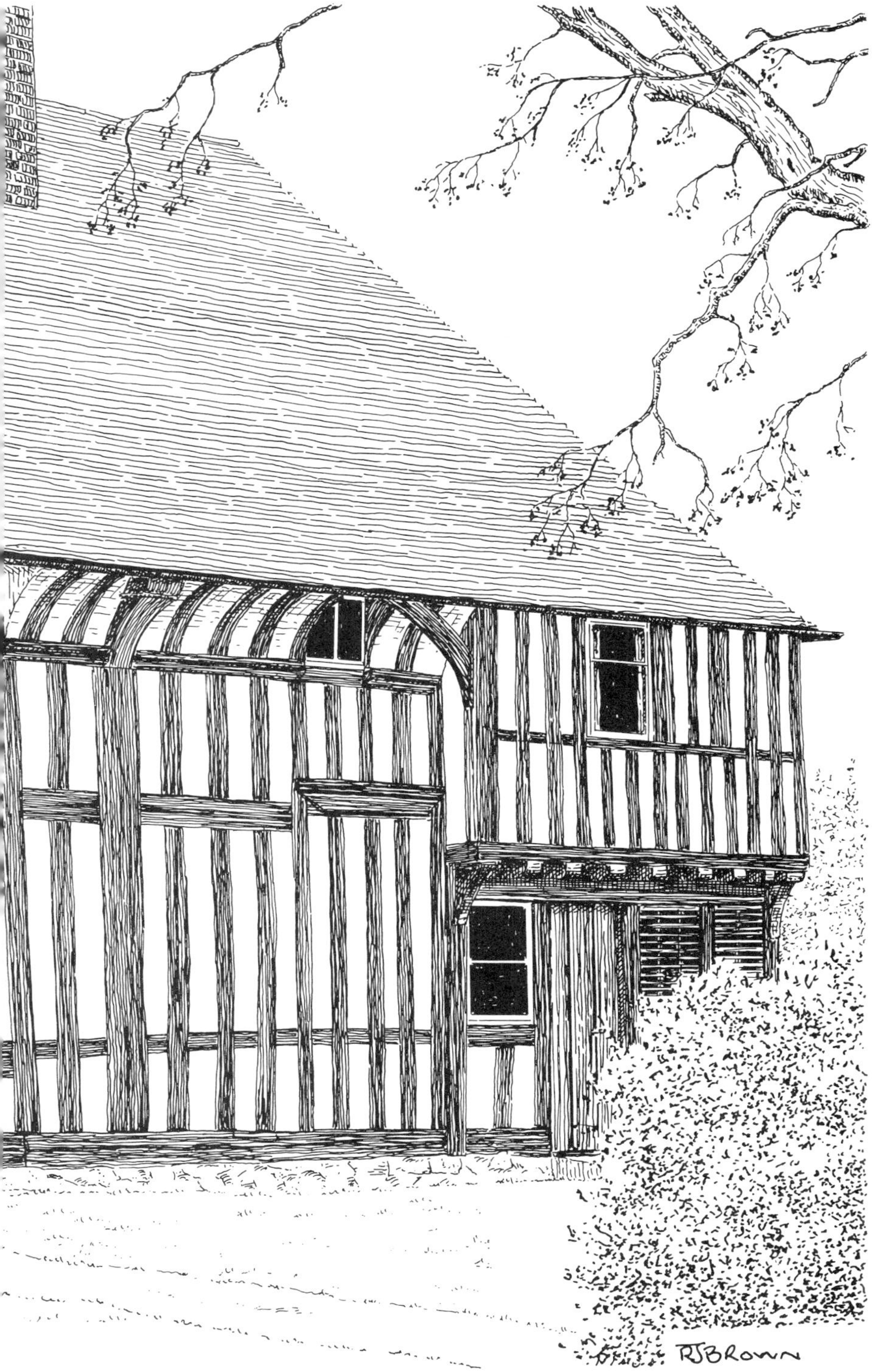
RJBROWN

front. In many cases houses were jettied to the ends as well, sometimes as at Synyards to one end only, but in other cases, for instance Olde House, Harrietsham, at both ends. When one end was jettied, it seems in the majority of cases to have been the service end. Why this was is difficult to know: it may have been because the upper room was used as a solar before the high end was built. Pattenden and Headcorn Manor are double Wealdens, that is to say jettied and recessed at both front and back as well as being jettied to the ends. Headcorn Manor (*61*), which stands almost in the churchyard, was built, it has been discovered by S.E. Rigold, after 1516 as the parsonage. It is truly a spectacular Wealden house, built to a very high standard with a double-bay open hall lit by a two-storey oriel window, and built at a time when the open hall was being abandoned for house types with a first floor throughout.

Another feature which altered throughout the building of the Wealden house was the support to the eaves wall-plate where it crossed the hall. At first there were large arch-braces, but by the time Pattenden was built these had become much smaller, until in the final stages of construction of Wealden houses, around 1500, the braces disappeared altogether and the long eaves wall-plate was supported by a continuous curved cove from the wall of the hall. This can be seen at Olde House, Harrietsham. At Westhoy, near Smarden (*62*), although the eaves beam is supported by a curved cove it still retains the braces to the ends including the central brackets.

Olde House, Harrietsham (*63*), is one of the most complete of these Wealden houses. It was probably built in the late fifteenth century and contains many refinements. It still has its original front door with its four-centred arch, moulded bressummers to the jettied front and ends, the three doors in the screens passage leading to the service rooms, and the staircase still with its original solid-block stairs. The dais was to the south end of the hall with a moulded cornice above which formerly returned along the top of a screen at the sides of the high table. The central open truss has a moulded tie-beam and octagonal crown-post with a moulded cap and base. As mentioned above, the central recess is coved, interrupted by the two-storey bay window to the hall. William Twopeny's drawing of 1828 shows this stone-based window extending to the eaves. A photograph published in W.G. Davie's *Old Cottages and Farmhouses in Kent and Sussex* in 1900 shows the upper part of this bay window filled in, as it is today. The present end-chimney to the parlour was also added between these two dates. The studwork to the upper floor has a horizontal moulded rail, not framed into the studs but planted on. It therefore has no structural importance and is merely decorative, a feature to be found only in Kent.

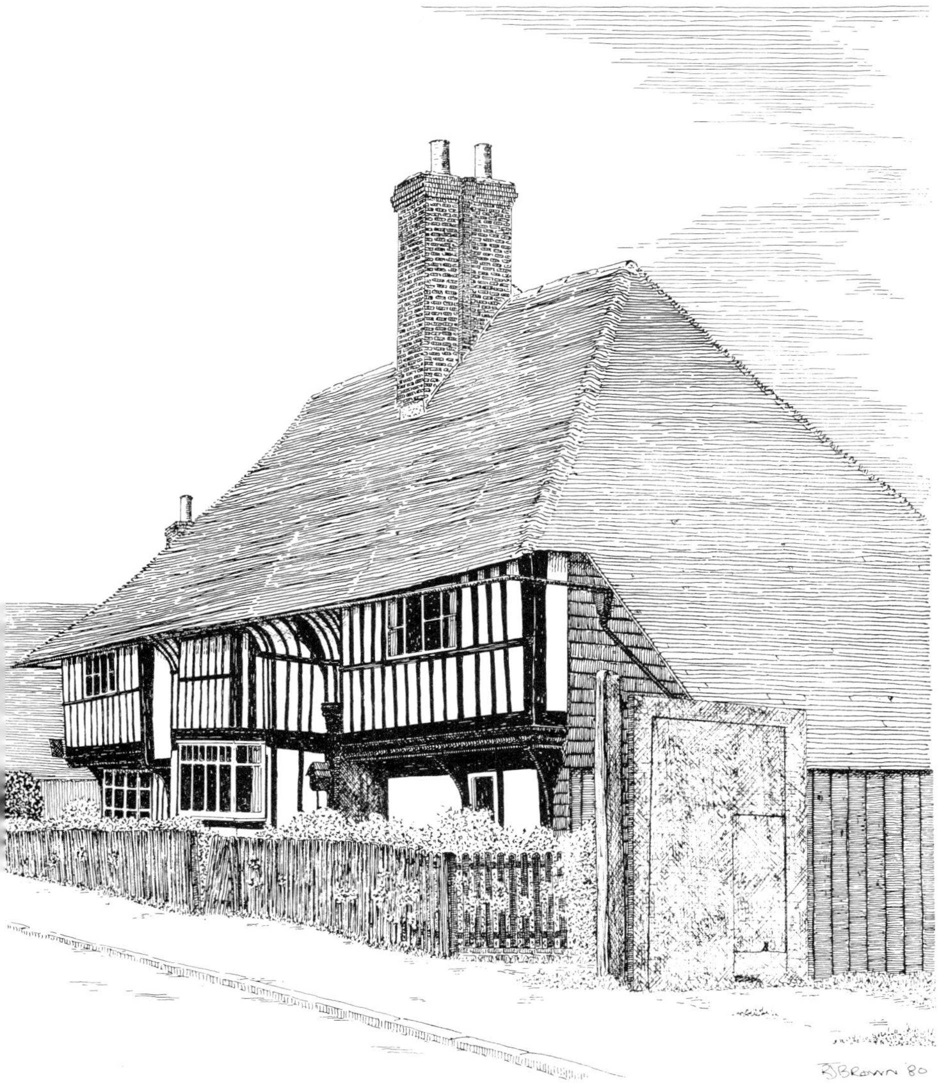

63. Olde House, Harrietsham. A house built late in the fifteenth century and probably one of the finest Wealden houses.

Wealden houses were designed to stand as farmhouses but they are to be found even in villages and towns. They are often free-standing here as well, retaining their hipped roofs as at the Tudor Rose Café, Tenterden. At East Malling there is a Wealden house with a hip at one end and a gable at the other. In places such as Canterbury where space was more restricted Wealden houses are generally gabled.

Although the majority of Wealden houses have jettied bays at both ends this is not always the case. There are a number which are jettied at one end only and in some cases the other end-bay must have been removed as at Pullens Farm, Horsmonden, and Little Robhurst Farm, a house probably of fourteenth-century date which has lost its service ends. At Ivy House, Marshborough, a house of mid-fifteenth-century date, not only has the solar end been removed but also the hall has been truncated. There are too many examples of these single-ended Wealden houses which have had their end bays removed for this to have been always the case. Many must have been built from the start with only one end bay. This was proved when Bayleaf Farmhouse was dismantled and re-erected at the Weald and Downland Open Air Museum (*64*). The house was originally built by Henry Bayly in around 1405 and there is clear evidence that the solar

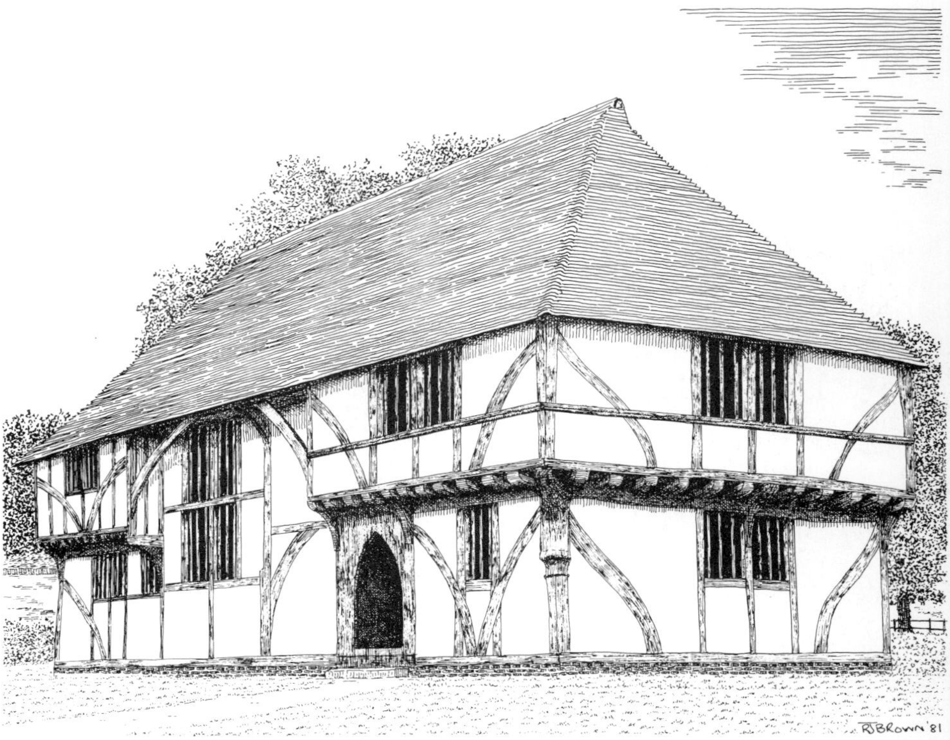

64. Bayleaf Farmhouse. A fifteenth-century Wealden house formerly situated at Bough Beech and moved to the Weald and Downland Open Air Museum, Singleton.

bay was built at a later date than the remainder of the house. Also, the chamber above the service rooms is of such a high standard that it seems likely that this end of the house was for a time at least used as a combined solar service wing. In addition, many of the details and features of the solar wing differ from those of the remainder of the house, clearly indicating a different building date for this end. Examples of two-thirds or single-ended Wealden houses are Rose Farm, Broomfield, Harts Heath Farm, Staplehurst, and in Lower

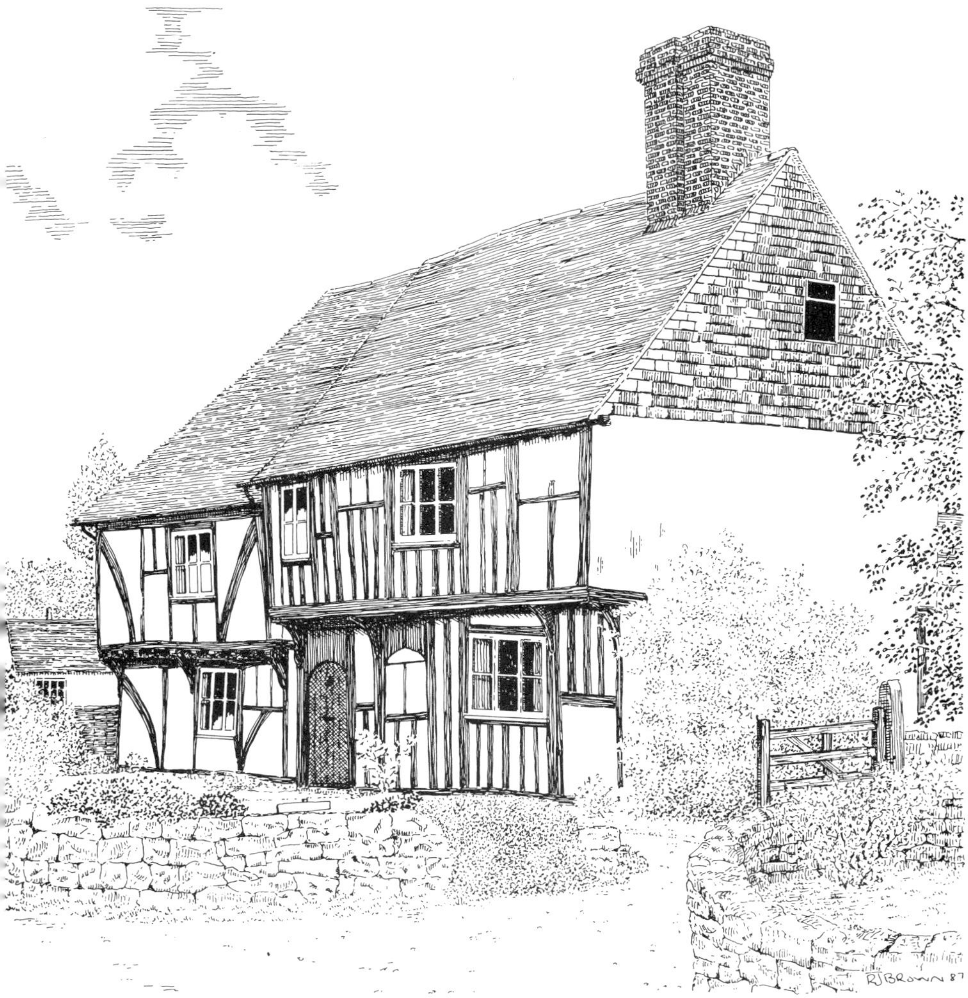

65. Westenhanger, Horsmonden.

Street, Leeds, the Manor House.

Many of these single-ended Wealden houses have been reconstructed at one end. One such example is Westenhanger, Horsmonden (*65*). Here, when the house was modernized in the sixteenth century with the insertion of the first floor over the hall, the central recess was blocked in, the south bay built and continuous overhang formed. Another and more famous example is Wardes, Otham, where the west wing of the house was also added in the sixteenth century.

There are other houses which display only one forward jetty. At Woodchurch overlooking the green is Hendon Place (*66*), a close-studded late fifteenth-century house with a combined jettied service bay with solar above and the eaves carried across the two bays of the former hall; but here the house stops, with the balancing bay at the right-hand end of the house missing. The typical Kentish hipped roof suggests that there was never another bay. At Cotterell Court,

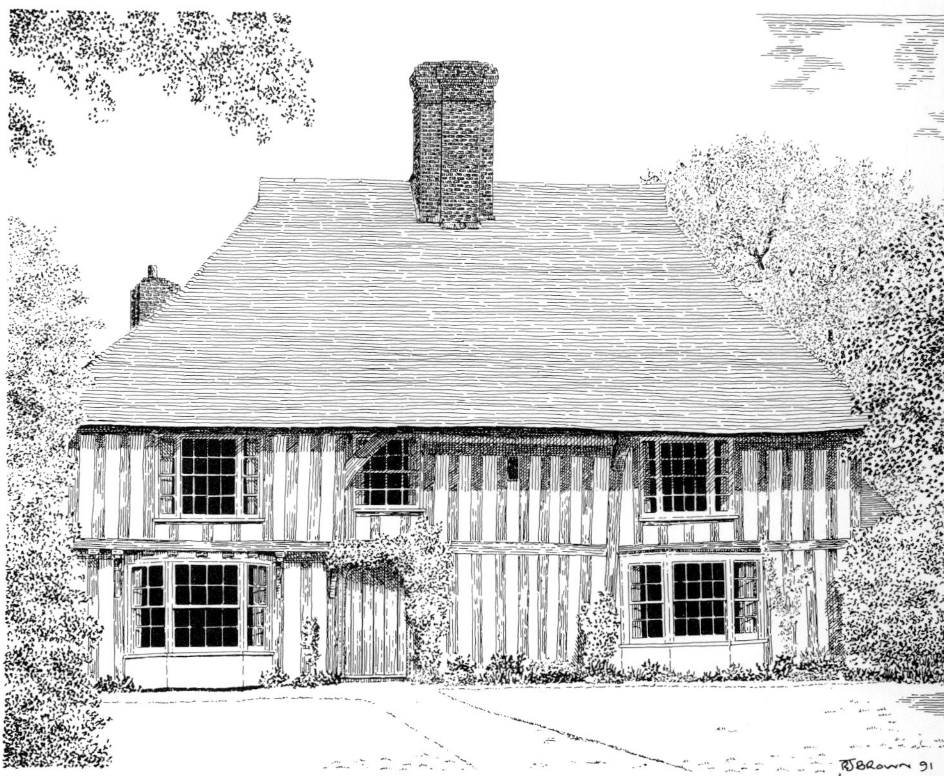

66. Hendon Place, Woodchurch. A two-thirds Wealden house of late fifteenth-century date.

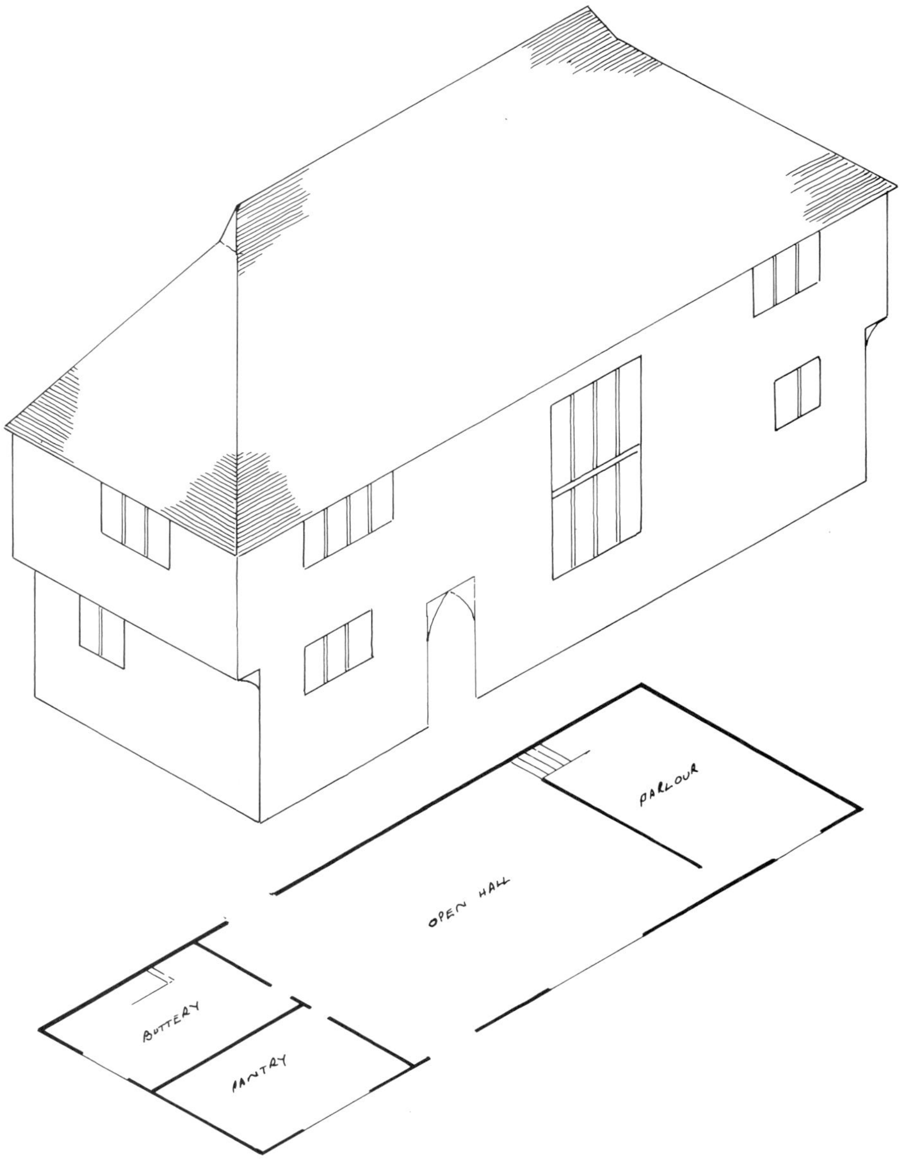

67. Typical layout of an end-jettied house.

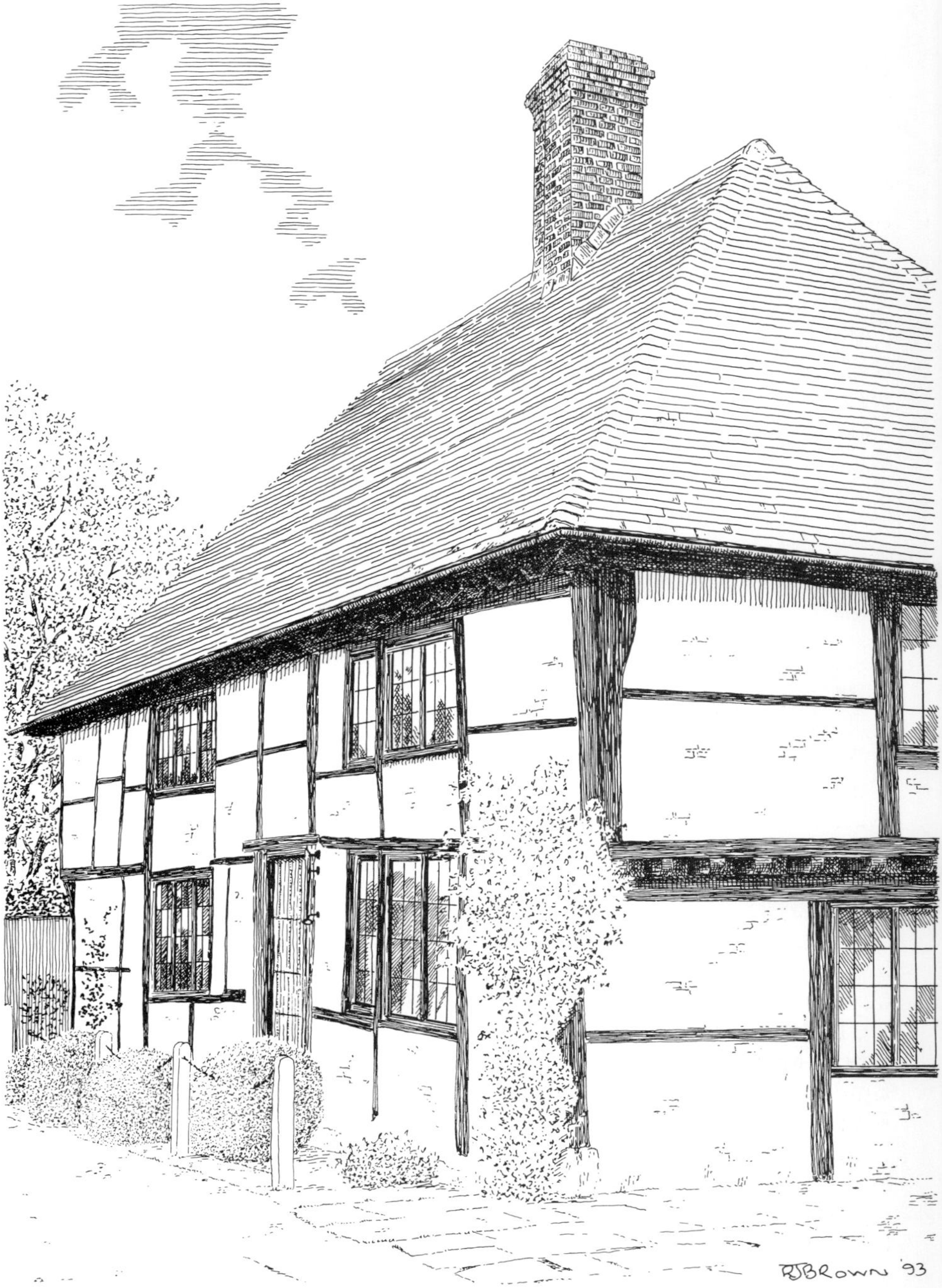

68. The Old Cottage, Bishopsbourne. A house said to have been built in 1480.

Petham, a house of slightly earlier date than Hendon Place, only the solar end is jettied, with a small single-bay service end approximately ten feet long.

Although the Wealden house is justifiably famous as a house type for its quality of workmanship and style, there is another timber-framed house type which is thought to be generally of older date and more common than the Wealden house. This is known as the end-jettied house (*67*). This house type shares the same basic plan as the Wealden house, that is an open hall flanked by a service bay at one end and a solar bay at the other, all gathered under a single hipped roof. Here the likeness ends, for externally the appearance differs greatly. Whereas in the Wealden house the end-bays are jettied to the front and often to the ends and very occasionally to the rear as well, the end-jettied house is jettied, as the name suggests, at the ends only. This jettying may occur at one end only, as at the Old Post Office, Goodnestone, or at both ends as at Old Cottage, Bishopsbourne (*68*), said to date from 1480, the house at Stanford's End, Edenbridge, and Burnt Oak, Benover. When one end is jettied it is generally the solar end, while houses jettied at both ends are less common and are generally of a later date. Again, whereas in the Wealden house the screens passage is often clearly defined by a separate bay or contained within the service bay, in the end-jettied house it is almost without exception formed within the open hall.

Examples of these end-jettied houses survive most thickly in the south and east of the Weald. In general they are smaller than the average Wealden house and there are a number which appear to predate the earliest Wealden house. One such example is Frogholt Cottage at Newington-next-Hythe (*70*), a small thatched house with an overhang to one end for which a date of before 1350 has been suggested by E.W. Parkin. The house was of four bays with a two-bay hall open to the roof, a two-storeyed solar bay with an end-jetty to the north and a service bay open to the roof. In the seventeenth century the hall was floored and in the eighteenth century the service end was rebuilt open to the roof, reflecting its previous arrangement. Others of similar, certainly fourteenth-century date, are Barton Cottage, Kennington, Walnut Tree Cottage, Lynsore, near Upper Hardes and Southdown Cottage, Nonington, a cottage which is now completely encased by Victorian brickwork.

Like the Wealden house, the end-jettied house has variations to the basic plan. In some cases there was only a two-storey bay to one end, so the solar was above the service room. This can be seen at Walnut Tree Cottage, where the house originally comprised three unequal bays with a two-bay open hall complete with a crown-post. The overall length of this house was originally only some thirty feet. At Upstreet

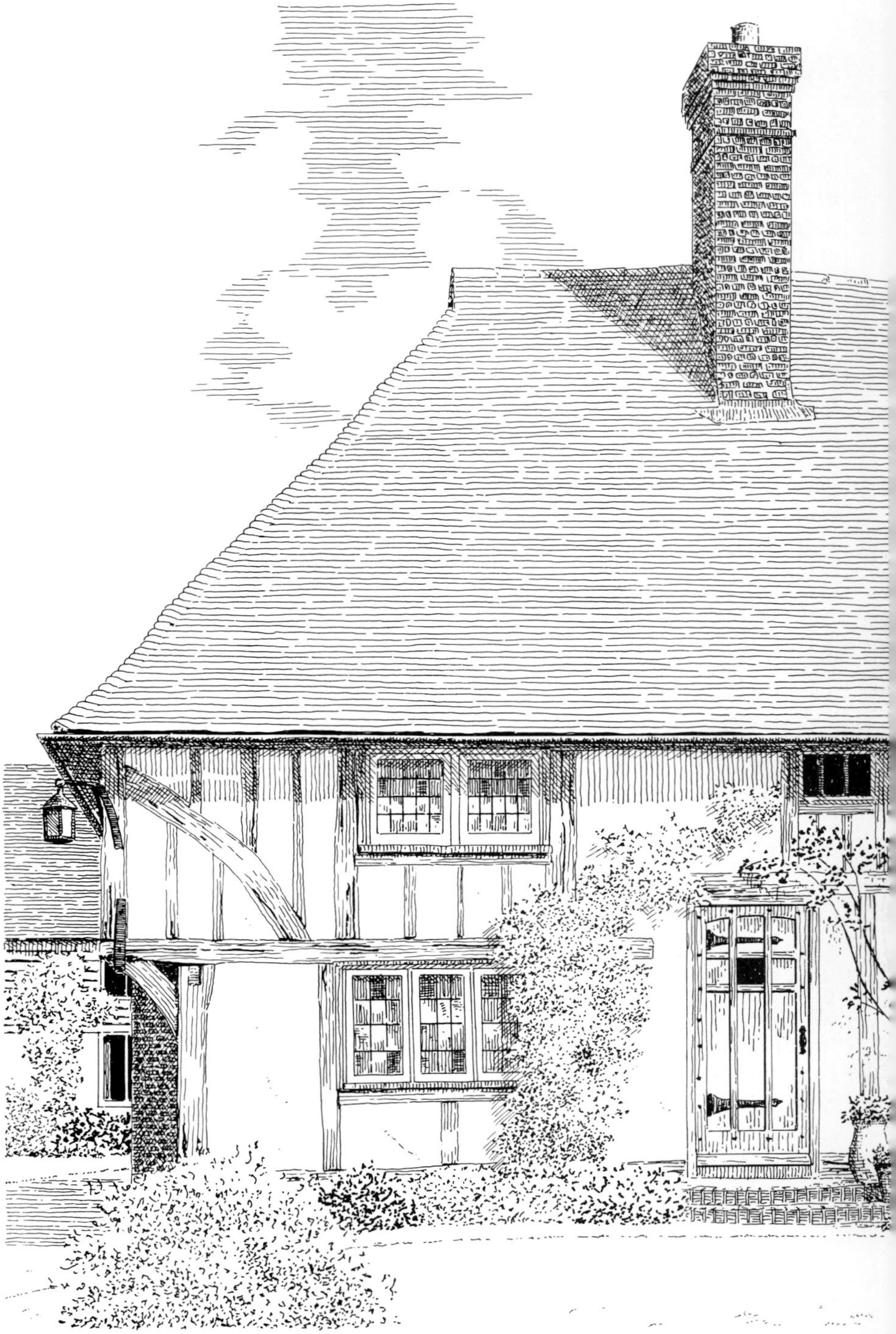

69. Groome Farm, Egerton, an end-jettied house.

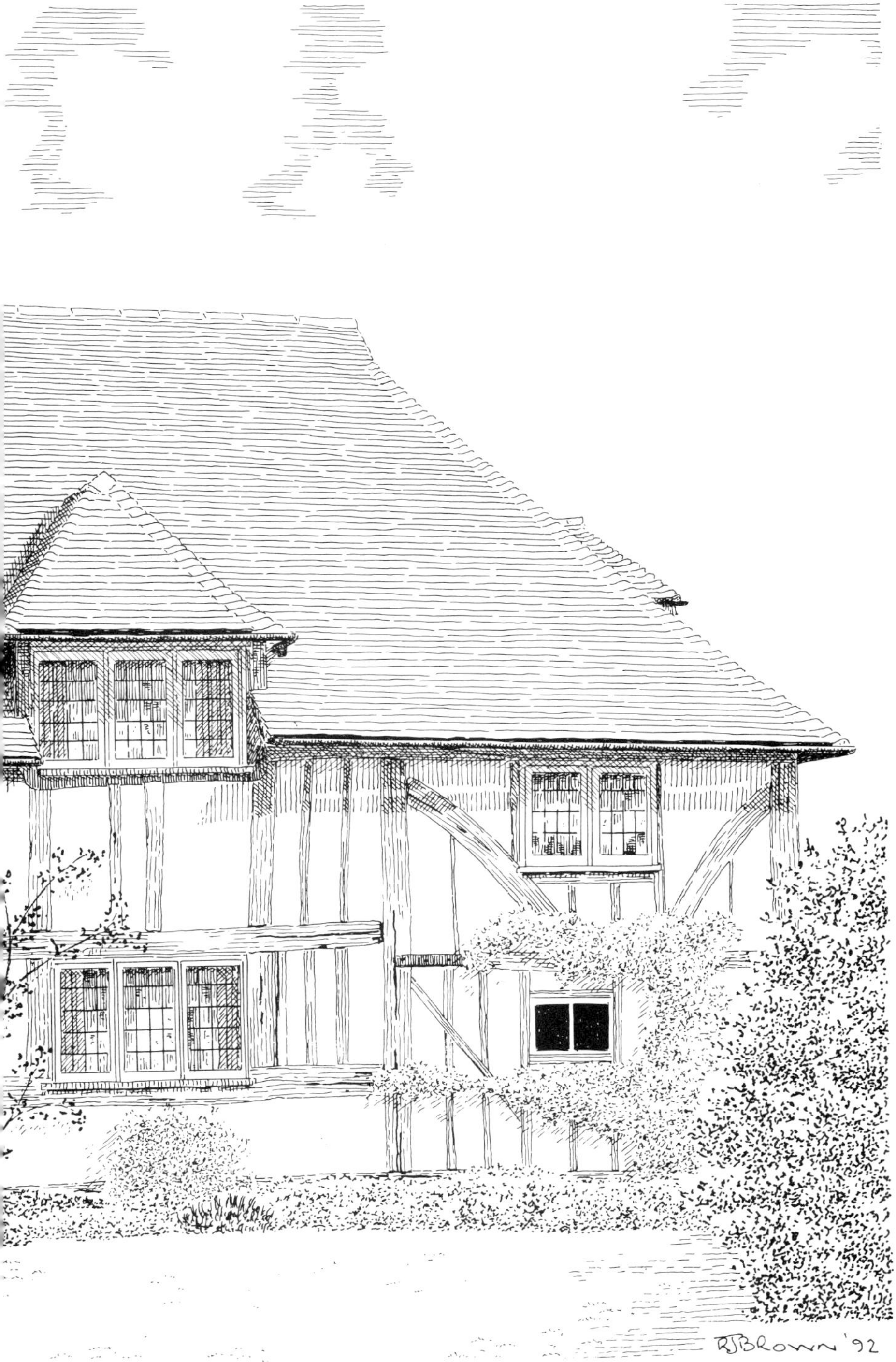
RJBROWN '92

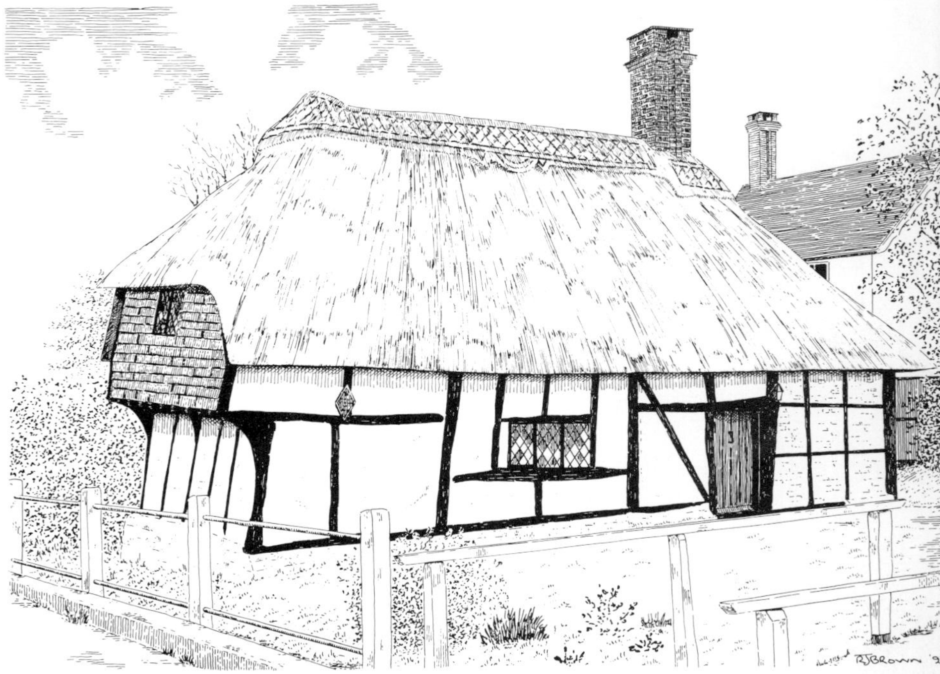

70. Frogholt Cottage, Newington-next-Hythe. End-jettied house thought to be built before 1350.

Cottages, Etchinghall, Lyminge, originally one house but later converted to three cottages, instead of the usual two-storeyed service bay, the service bay was only single-storeyed and open to the roof. Like the Wealden house, most end-jettied houses had an open hall of two unequal bays but open halls with a single bay were by no means rare. The Old Post Office, Goodnestone, and the Old Cottage, Bishopsbourne, are two instances.

As previously stated, the end-jettied house is considered a predecessor of the Wealden house, but the former were not replaced by the latter and continued to be built alongside them. End-jettied houses are far more numerous than we would at first observe today, for while the Wealden houses remained for the most part distinguishable because they retained their recessed fronts, the end-jettied houses have often been mutilated from their original forms, their jetties underbuilt or the whole building clad in brick or brick and tiles. In fact, unlike the Wealden house, which was abandoned when houses with open halls became obsolete, houses with end-jetties continued to be constructed. One such example is Ivy

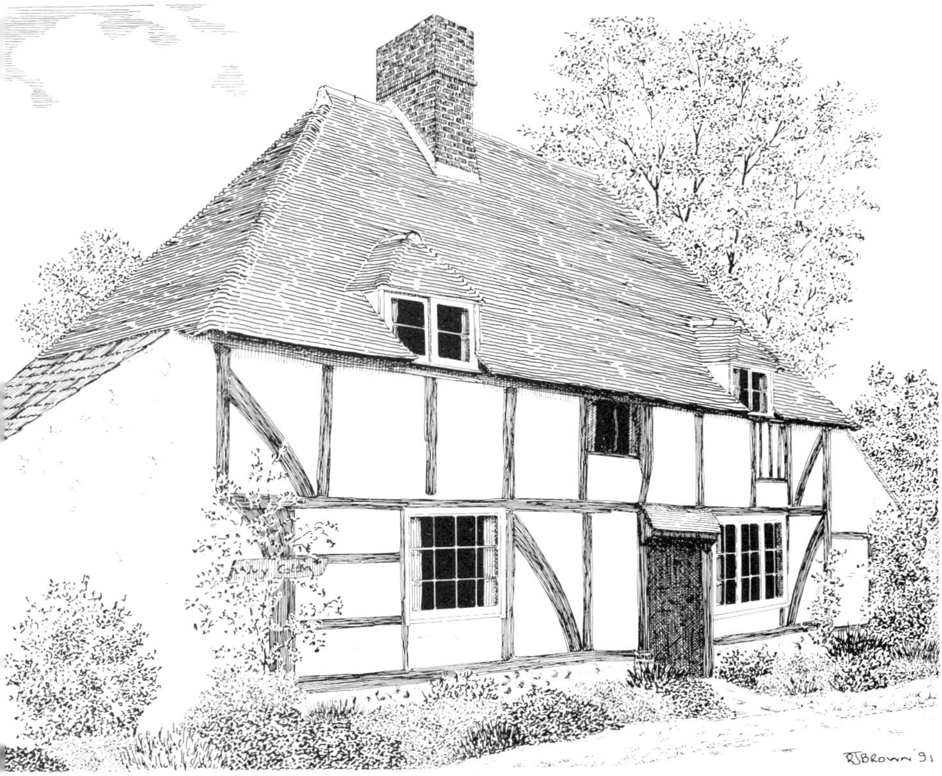

71. Ivy Cottage, Elham. A house built in the second half of the sixteenth century.

Cottage, Elham (*71*), a house of three unequal bays built in the second half of the sixteenth century with a two-storeyed end-jettied bay, a small central bay which appears to have been originally a smoke bay, and a two-storeyed bay which was the hall with a chamber above.

Not all medieval open-hall timber-framed houses in Kent were jettied. Winkhurst Farmhouse, as previously noted, was dismantled on the formation of Bough Beech Reservoir and on examination it was discovered that one wing of what appeared to be an ordinary timber-framed house of the sixteenth century was in fact a house dating from the fourteenth century. It comprised only two bays – one was the hall open to the roof and the other a service bay, divided from the hall by a screen, with a solar above. It must represent a typical substantial house of that period prior to the development of the end-jettied and Wealden houses. Other similar houses most probably still exist hidden within later additions and yet to be discovered. When

Winkhurst Farmhouse was re-erected at the Weald and Downland Open-Air Museum it was built in what was considered its original medieval form, clearly indicating the life led by people occupying a house of this kind in the fourteenth century.

Up to now we have discussed timber-framed medieval houses which, as they survive today, must have been substantial buildings with an upper floor over at least part of the house and erected for yeoman farmers, merchants or traders, but there must have been many smaller houses built for the ordinary folk which have been swept away. These would have been of a single storey throughout with no upper floor at all. Dormer Cottage, Petham (*72*), is one very rare example, thought to be of fourteenth-century date. It originally had three bays, the hall with the solar bay to one end and the service bay to the other all open to the roof. In the seventeenth century the upper floor was inserted and a dormer provided in the thatched roof. It still retains in use its timber and plaster chimney inserted at this time. Another house survived until the 1960s and before its demolition was recorded; this was St Mary's Grove Cottage at Tilmanstone (*73*), of late medieval date, which in its original state was of two bays, the hall and a service room both open to the roof, the single-bay hall heated by a central hearth. It had been subsequently extended at one end and two small rooms squeezed in under the thatch. A fireplace with a bread oven had been added in Tudor times. On demolition, hidden beneath the plaster was discovered one of the old hall windows which was never glazed but was fitted with three oak bars with peg-holes for a hinged shutter.

Towards the end of the fifteenth century the importance of the open hall as the dominant and principal room in the house began to decline. Hall houses continued to be built in Kent until around the middle of the sixteenth century but the decline in the importance of the open hall is clearly indicated by the number of single-bay, open-hall houses being constructed by the beginning of the sixteenth century – for instance, Old Hall, Sundridge. So the open-hall house type was slowly replaced by an entirely new house type which was constructed with two storeys throughout. The initial impetus may have come from the desire for greater privacy that the greater number of smaller rooms provided, coupled perhaps with the desire to make better use of the upper storey, rather than any wish to get rid of the open hearth.

Because of the open hall, it had up until this time only been possible to form jetties to the end-bays but now, because the hall was floored over, it became possible to extend the jettying throughout the entire length of the building. Known as the continuous-jettied house (*74*) this is the only house type which can be classed as transitional, for it lies between the medieval and modern, incorporating the characteristics of

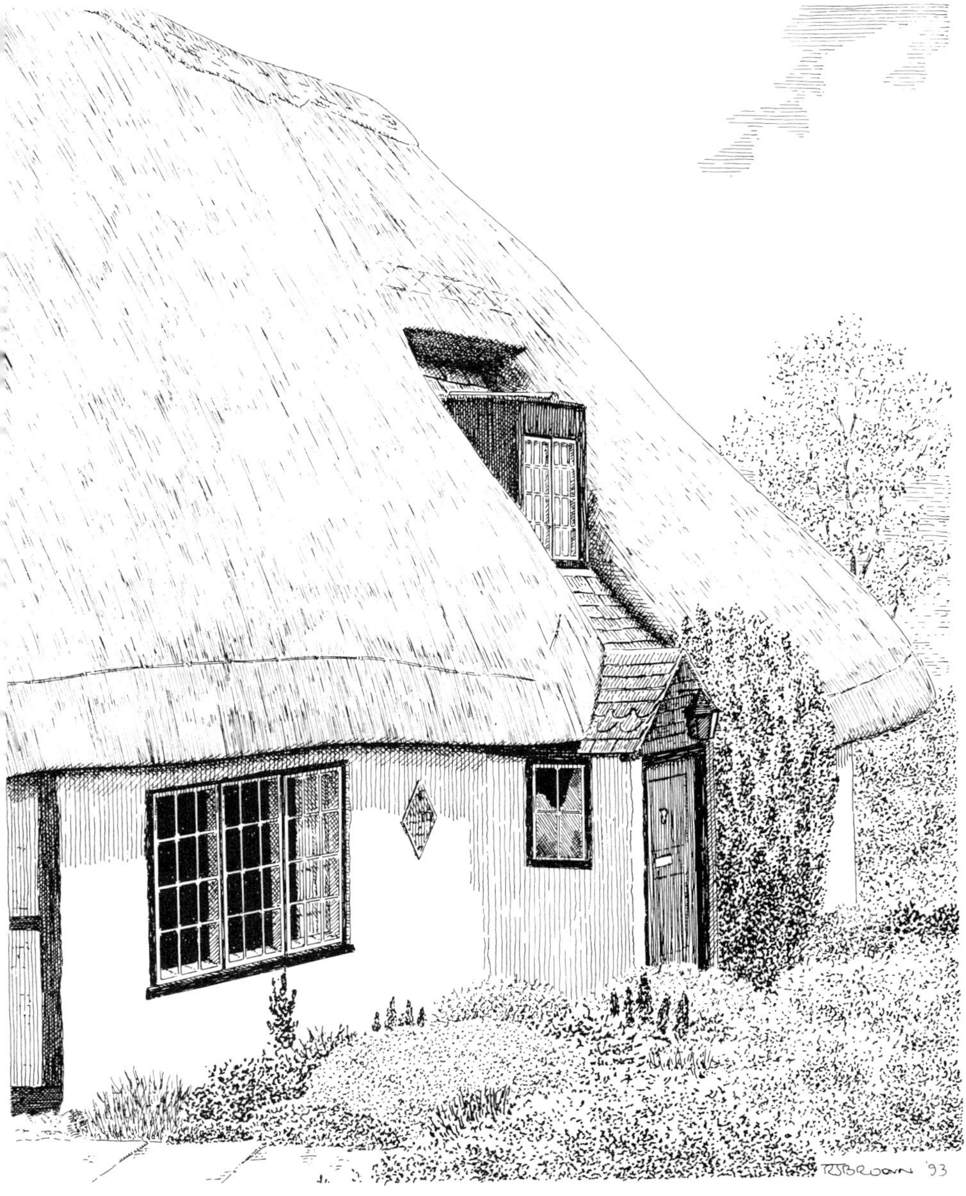

72. Dormer Cottage, Petham.

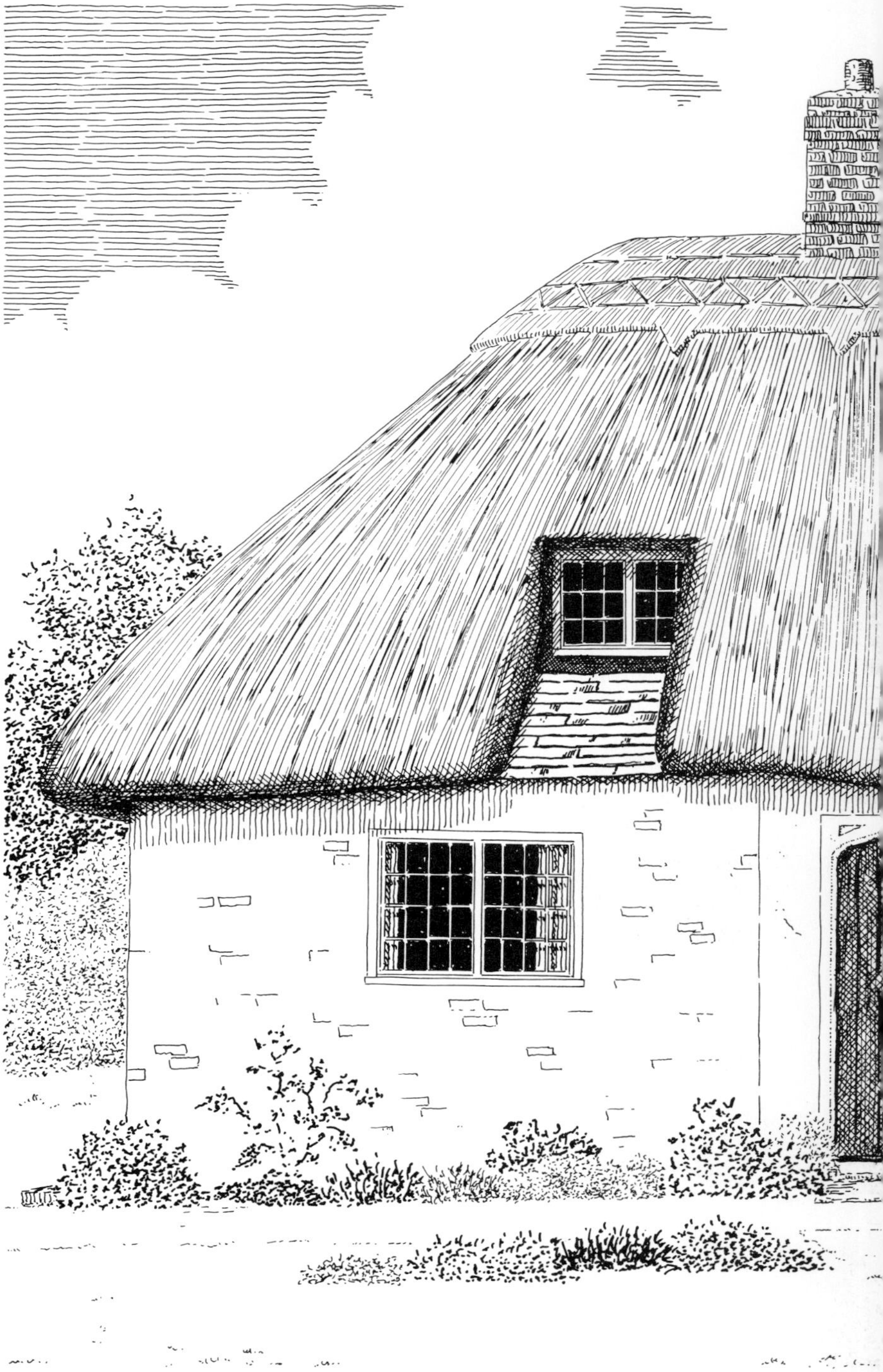

73. St Mary's Grove Cottage, Tilmanstone.

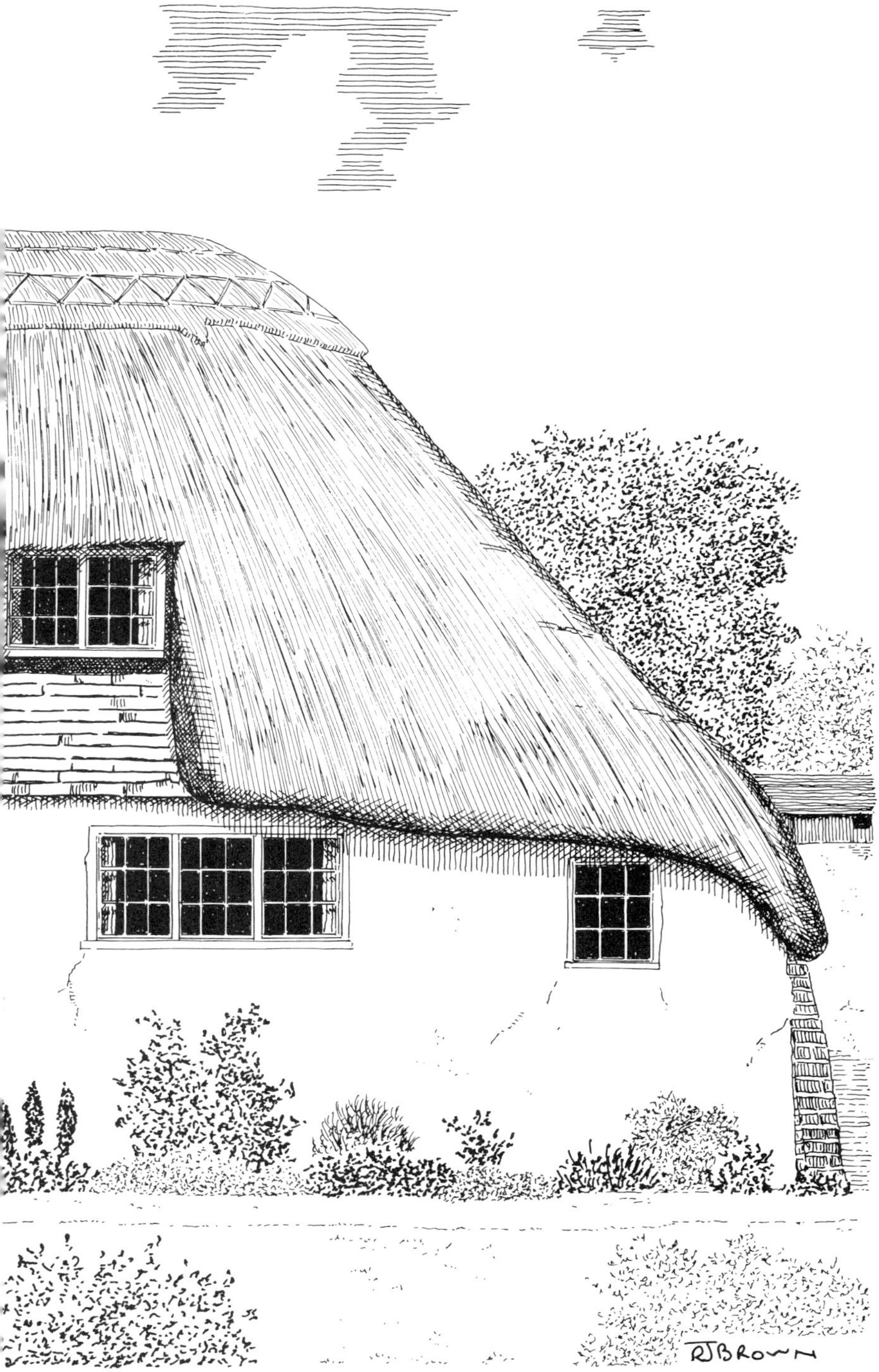
RJBROWN

both. It retained the medieval ground-floor plan, that of a ground-floor hall, a screens passage, service rooms to one end and a parlour to the other end, with the hall still keeping its distinction between the upper and lower ends. This is without doubt because of the influence that the open hall, which was not only an old but also a superior form, had on smaller houses long after it had disappeared in larger ones. On the other hand, the continuous-jettied house also incorporated elements of the post-medieval house: fireplaces and chimneys were provided from the outset and the number of private rooms increased. The crown-post roof was invariably retained, persisting alongside houses built with the newly introduced side-purlin roof. Also in accordance with the medieval practice were the usual two service doorways leading off the screens passage and at the upper end a single doorway giving entry to the parlour. Again the screens passage is equally as defined as in some of the Wealden houses and a wide spered opening is to be found between the passage and the ground-floor hall. With the upper floor now being continuous it was necessary to have only one staircase, either from the upper end of the hall or from the parlour. The use of the chamber over the hall is problematic; in some cases it is referred to as the upper hall and treated with all the lavish decoration which was once given to the open hall, yet in others it appears to have been little more than a store. The position of the chimney also varied; the most popular position was between the hall and the end room when there was also an opportunity to heat this room as well. Other positions were against the rear or front wall as can be seen at Court Lodge, Orlestone (*75*) or backing on to the screens passage, as at Sunderland, Lynsted (*76*).

In some houses it seems that the medieval arrangement of hall with the parlour at the high end and service rooms at the lower end was abandoned when the stack was placed at the high end of the hall. The fire was used for cooking and so it proved inconvenient for the service rooms to be at the lower end of the hall beyond the screens passage, because of the constant 'comings and goings' past the high table from the service rooms to the hearth. It seems, therefore, that with the stack at the upper end of the hall the room beyond was almost certainly the service room, thus easing the problems of cooking and serving the food in the hall. The room beyond the screens passage then became the parlour. This arrangement can clearly be seen at Smallhythe Place, Tenterden (*77*), where the hall, originally the only heated room, was used for cooking, with the service room behind the chimney and off the screens passage a highly finished room which was obviously the parlour with, originally, an oriel window looking south towards the harbour. The house was built perhaps soon after the great fire of 1514 which destroyed most of Smallhythe. Known locally as the

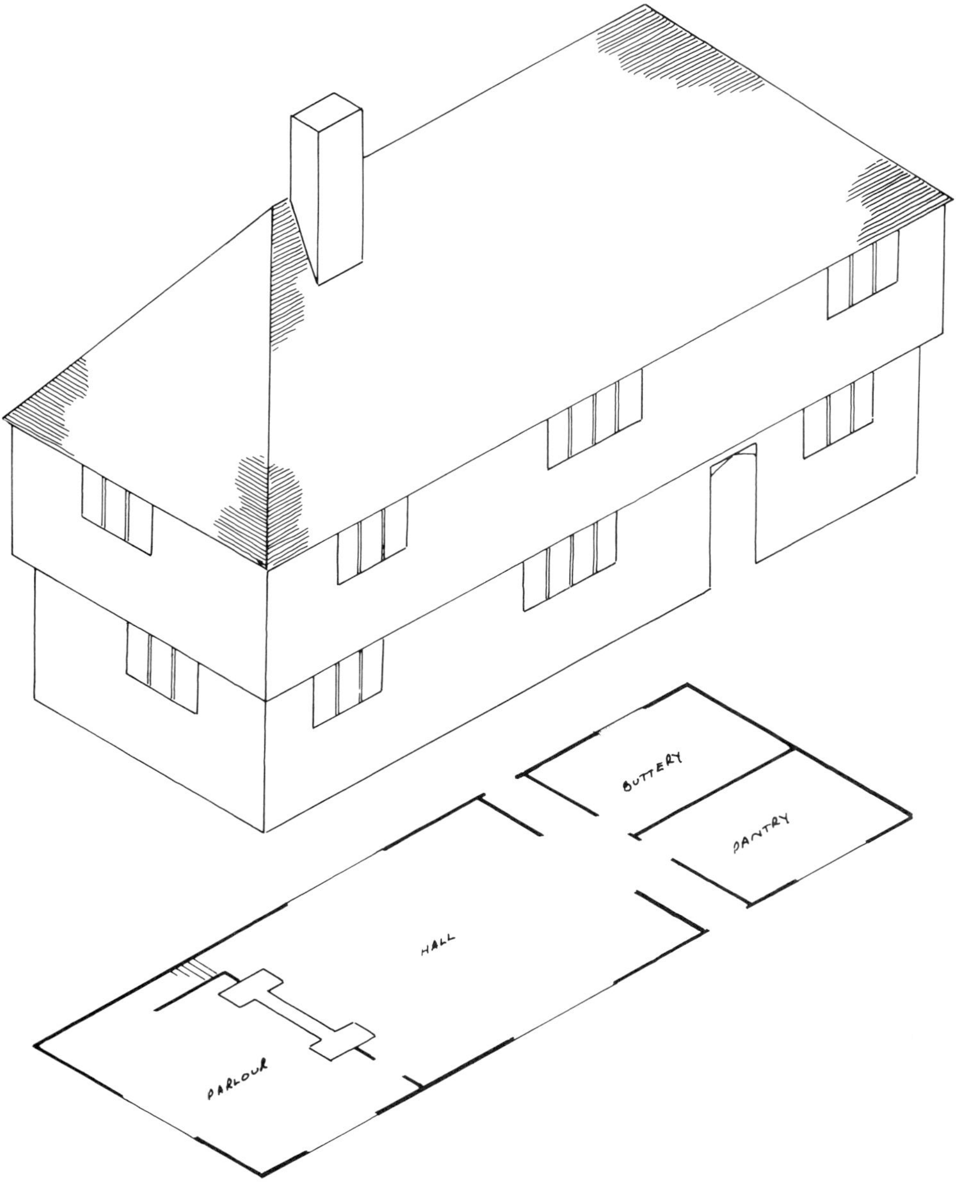

74. Typical layout of a continuous-jettied house.

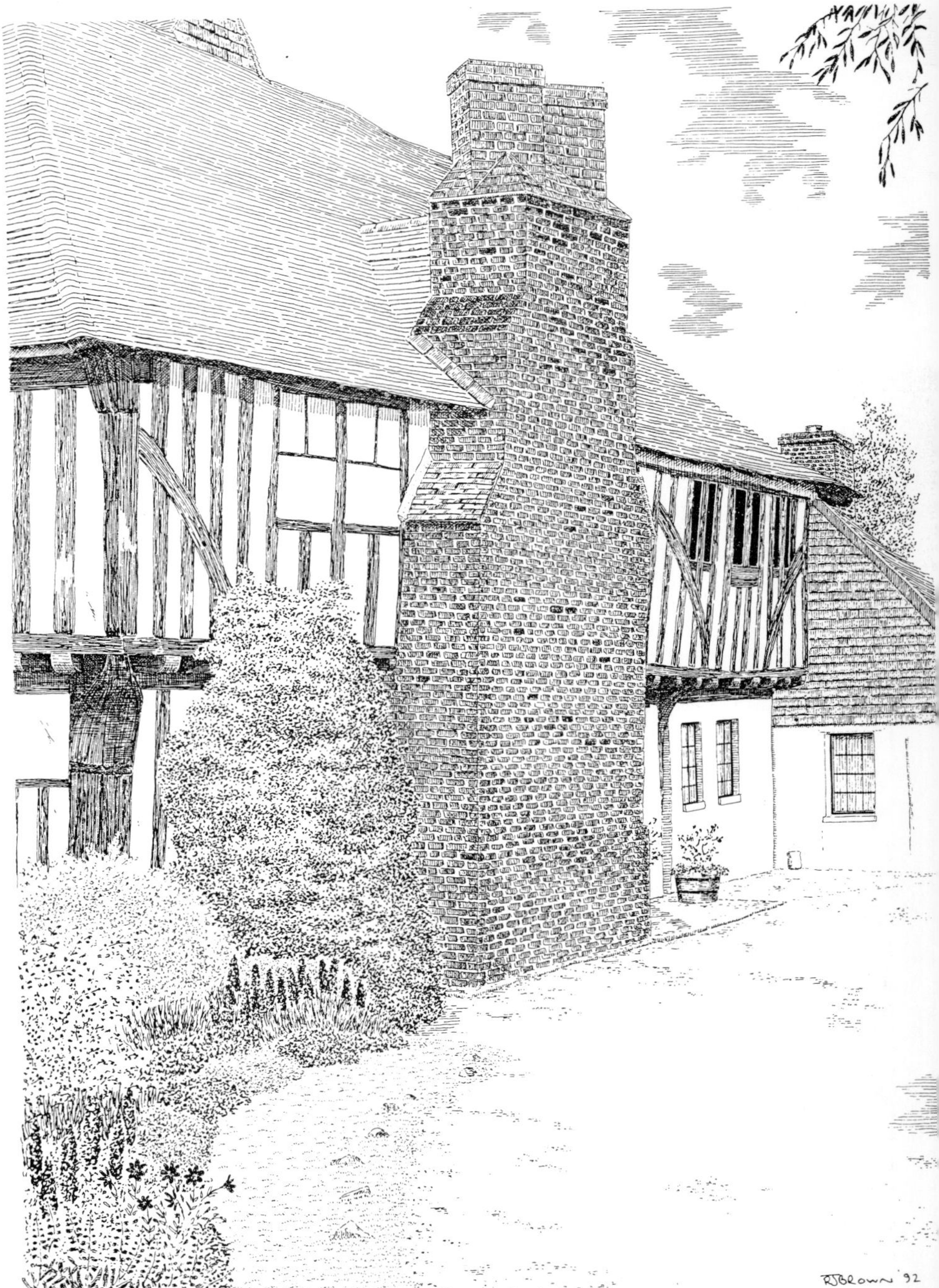

75. Court Lodge, Orlestone.

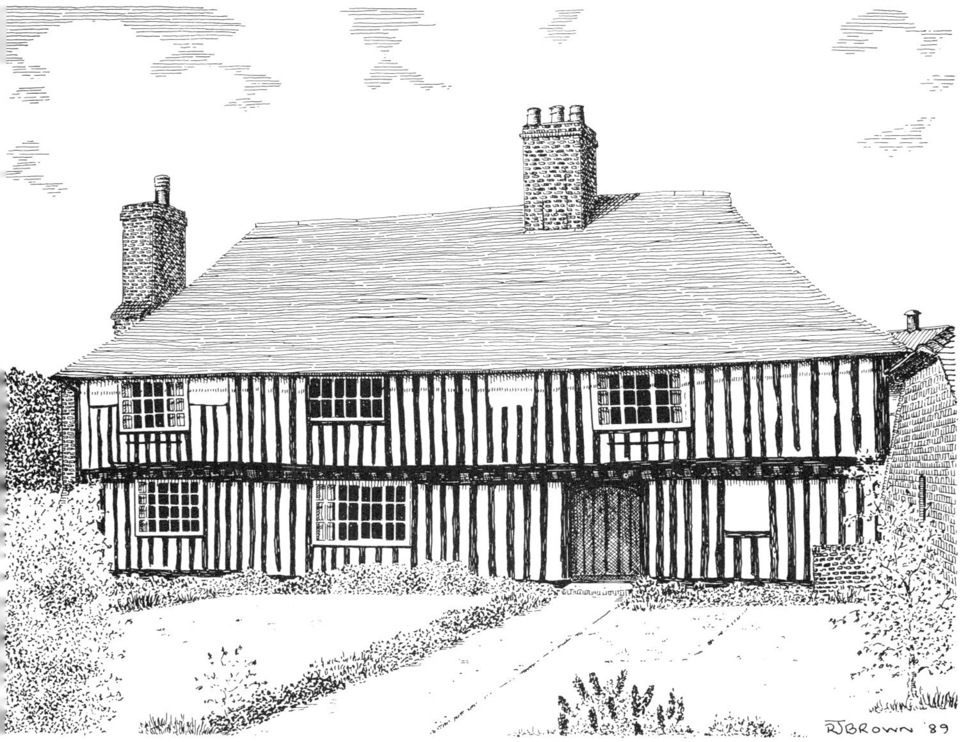

76. Sunderland, Lynsted, an unrestored sixteenth-century continuous-jettied house.

Farm, it served first as the Port House to what was then a thriving shipyard, acquiring its new name when the sea receded and agriculture replaced navigation. Later the house became the home of Dame Ellen Terry, the actress, and is now owned by the National Trust. When the stack was positioned against the screens passage the medieval arrangement remained undisturbed, with the parlour at the high end and the service rooms beyond the screens passage, but conveniently placed near the fire.

The continuous-jettied house first began to appear towards the end of the fifteenth century, but Kent was generally slower to accept this house type than Essex and Suffolk, and it never gained the popularity which it did in those two counties; nevertheless Kent has some early examples. Although sometimes to be found in isolated locations in the countryside, the continuous-jettied house tends to be an urban house type found mainly in villages and towns.

Although the chief distinguishing feature of the continuous-jettied

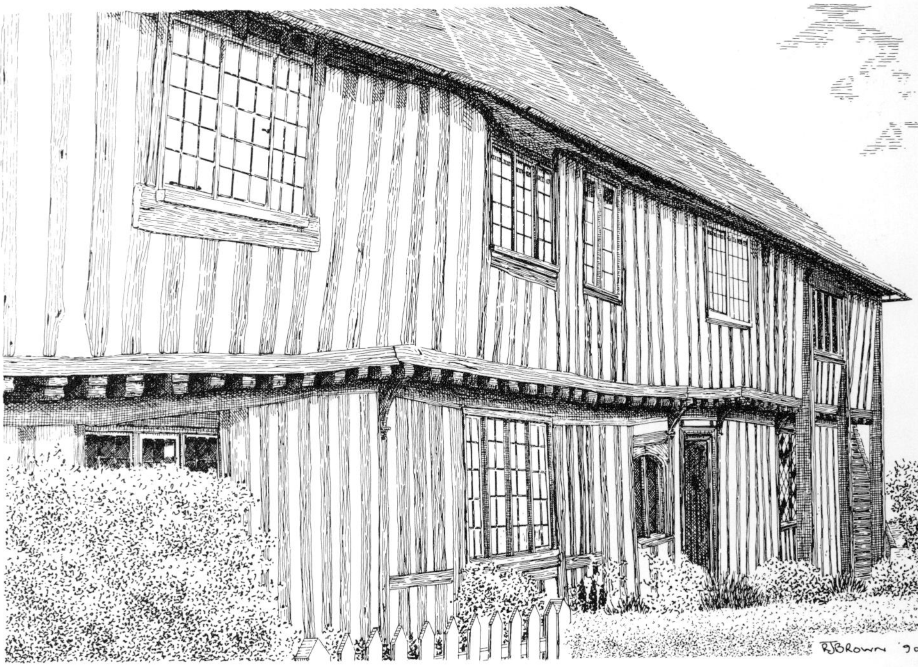

77. Smallhythe Place, near Tenterden. A continuous-jettied house built soon after 1514.

house is that the jettying extends throughout the whole front elevation, in some cases it may well return along a flank wall. This can be seen at Hushheath Manor, Staplehurst, a handsome house with two gables, one small, the other large, forming a cross-wing with oriels beneath. In Kings Street, Margate, is Tudor House (*78*), a rare example of a timber-framed house which is jettied on all four sides. Built in the sixteenth century the house is now a museum, and was built to a very high standard with a moulded fascia beam with oriel windows beneath, all under a fully hipped roof. The ends of the tie-beams are supported on shaped brackets, and the eaves soffit is of considerable width in order to accommodate the feature.

Brick Houses

Considering the fine quality of brick-making clays in the county, it is somewhat surprising that there are no brick buildings even in towns prior to the fourteenth century. Even after this date the use of brick was sporadic and it was not used systematically, either in towns or in supra-vernacular buildings, until much later than, say, in Norfolk or Lincolnshire. There are examples of early brickwork from the fourteenth and fifteenth centuries but they are by no means common. There is Salmeston Court, Margate, one of the most important granges of St Augustine's Abbey, and the vaulted undercroft to the chapel to Horne's Place, Appledore, both of fourteenth-century date. From the mid-fifteenth century (before 1445) are the bricks and knapped flints in a pattern of alternate bands at Dent-de-Lion Gatehouse at Garlinge. All these buildings are constructed with the small buff-coloured bricks often associated with Flanders, which may well have been imported.

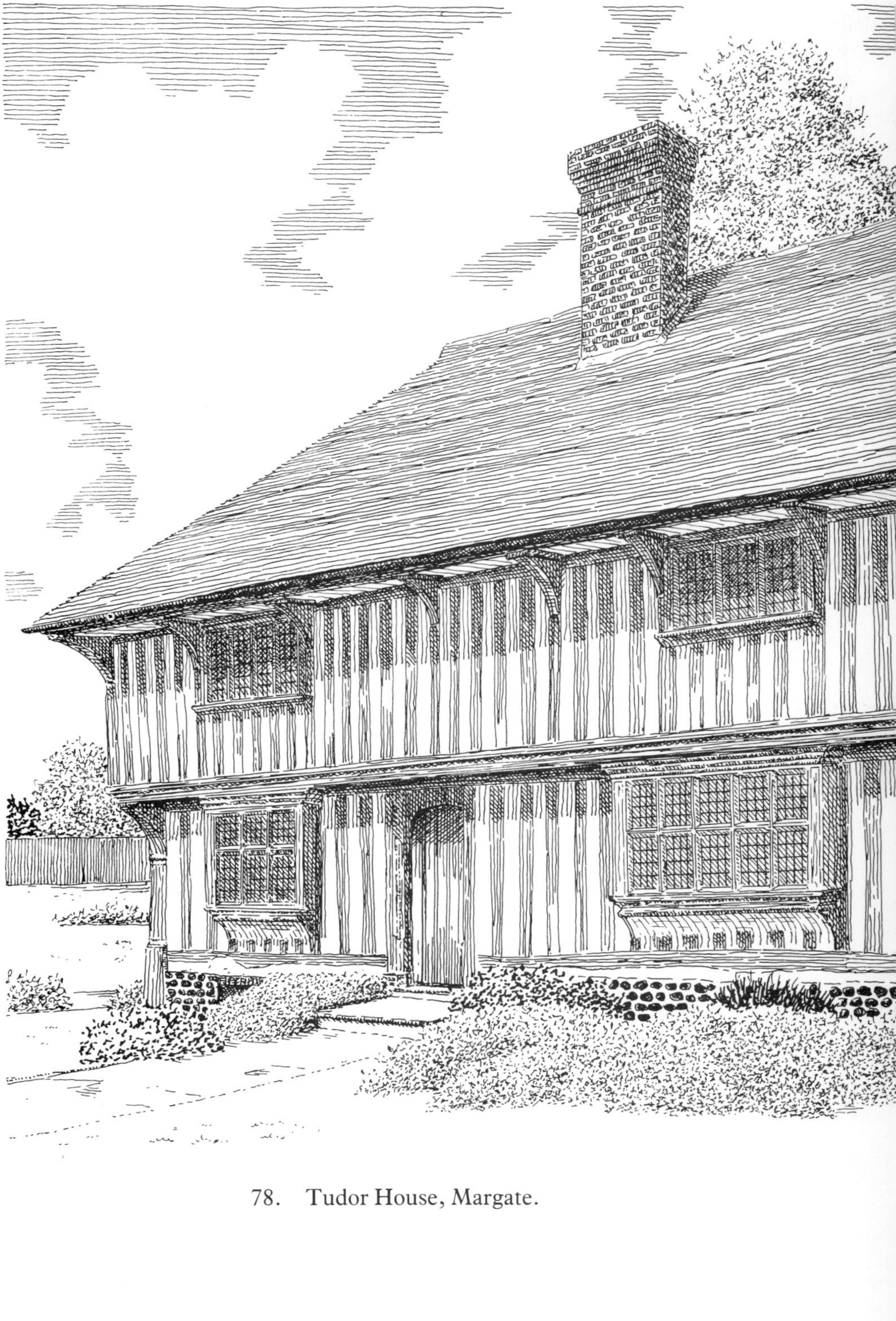

78. Tudor House, Margate.

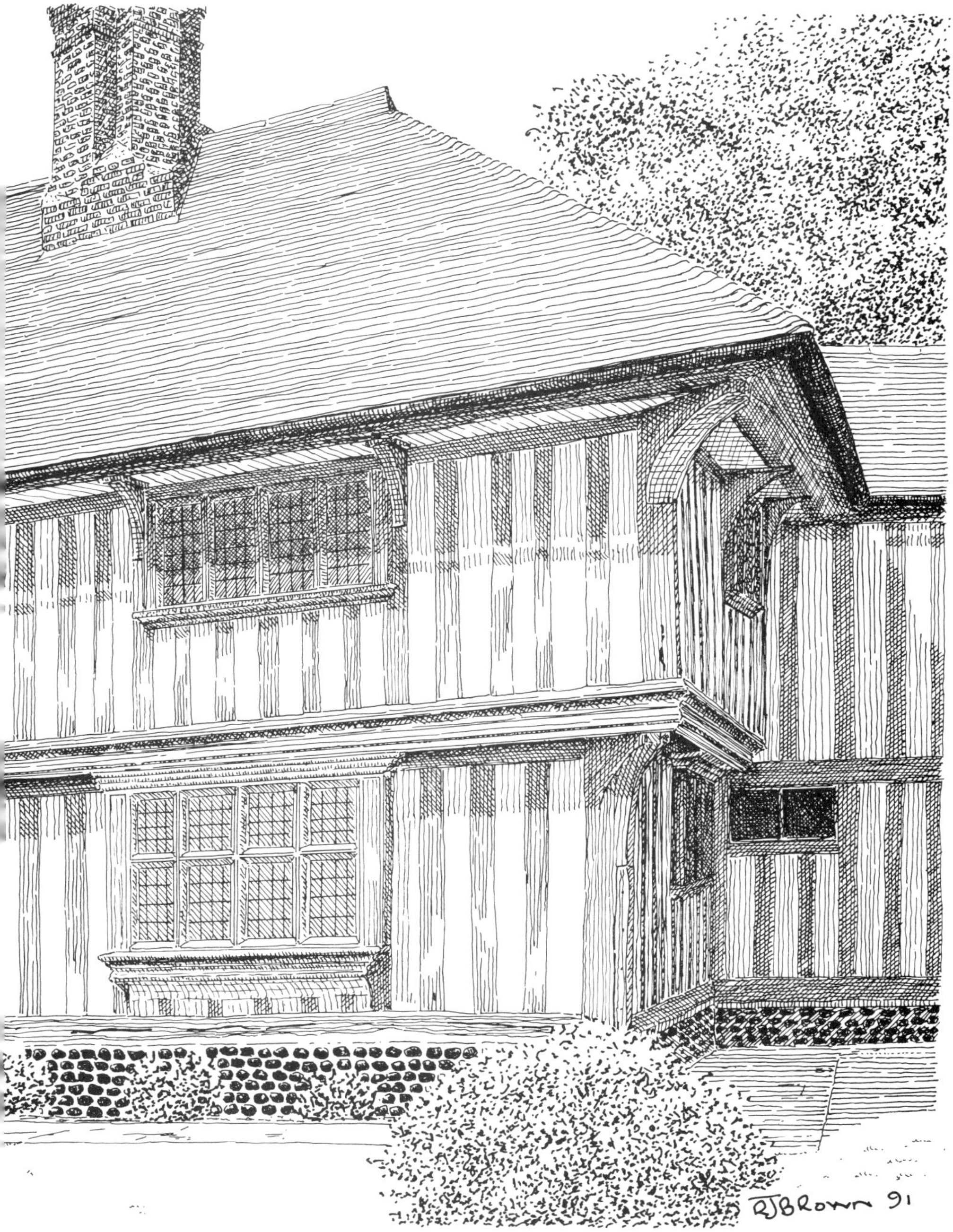
RJBROWN 91

4

Post-medieval Houses

The sixteenth century was a period of great change for the houses of Kent. The Great Rebuilding of England of the sixteenth and seventeenth centuries described by Dr W.G. Hoskins came to Kent a century or so before the Midlands and South-west and so by about 1540 the vast majority of the old, poorly constructed houses of the previous centuries had already been swept aside to be replaced by substantially constructed ones. In Kent the sixteenth century brought about a demand for the adaptation of old buildings as much as for the construction of new.

The greatest change was the abandonment of the central open hearth and the increasing popularity of some method of removing the smoke from an enclosed hearth, which enabled the hall to be subdivided to make a continuous upper floor. This reached its peak in the second half of the sixteenth century and is clearly confirmed by the Revd William Harrison, who in 1577 observed in his book *Description of England* that one of the notable features in the village of Radwinter in Essex, where he was vicar, was the 'multitude of chimnies latelie erected'.

We have already seen the use of some form of stack with the introduction of the continuous-jettied house at the beginning of the sixteenth century. This house type continued to be built, along with those with open halls, but such was the popularity of the new house type that there was an increasing desire to modernize the open halls, to provide a chimney stack and insert a floor. It can be assumed that practically every open hall was modernized, although this was spread over a period of a hundred years or more, and the few open halls in Kent that exist today are probably without exception twentieth-century restorations. Old Hall, Sundridge, was restored by Beresford Pite for Mr Munn in 1926; Wardes, Otham, was repaired and restored by Sir Louis Mallet in around 1910; and the Yeoman's House at Sole Street, near Cobham, was restored by Sir Herbert Barker.

The position of the inserted stack within the open hall varied, as it did in the continuous-jettied house. One of the most popular positions was backing on to the screens passage. This can be seen at such Wealden houses as Olde House, Harrietsham, Corner Farm, Langley and Link Farm, Egerton. This position was perhaps less popular in the end-jettied house but it is by no means rare, examples being Monkton Manor, Chilham and Marley Farm, Kingston.

As has already been noted, the position of the stack did not affect the medieval layout when it was close to the service rooms. Its position along the screen varied; usually it was placed more or less centrally but sometimes, as at Olde House, and Pattenden Manor, it was located towards the front entrance with one return built against the wall to the front. Nearly half of the stacks inserted in the open hall were, it appears, built against the screens passage.

Another and perhaps almost as common position was to site the stack at the high end of the hall against the partition dividing the hall and parlour. Synyards, Otham, Headcorn Manor and Old Hall,

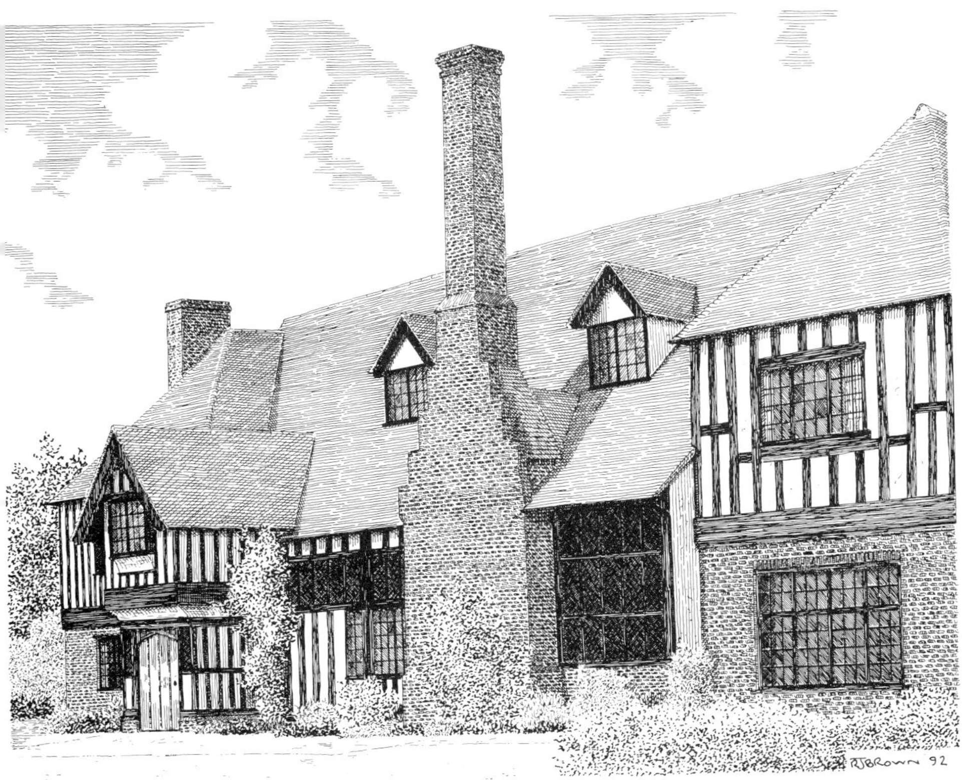

79. Singleton Manor, Great Chart.

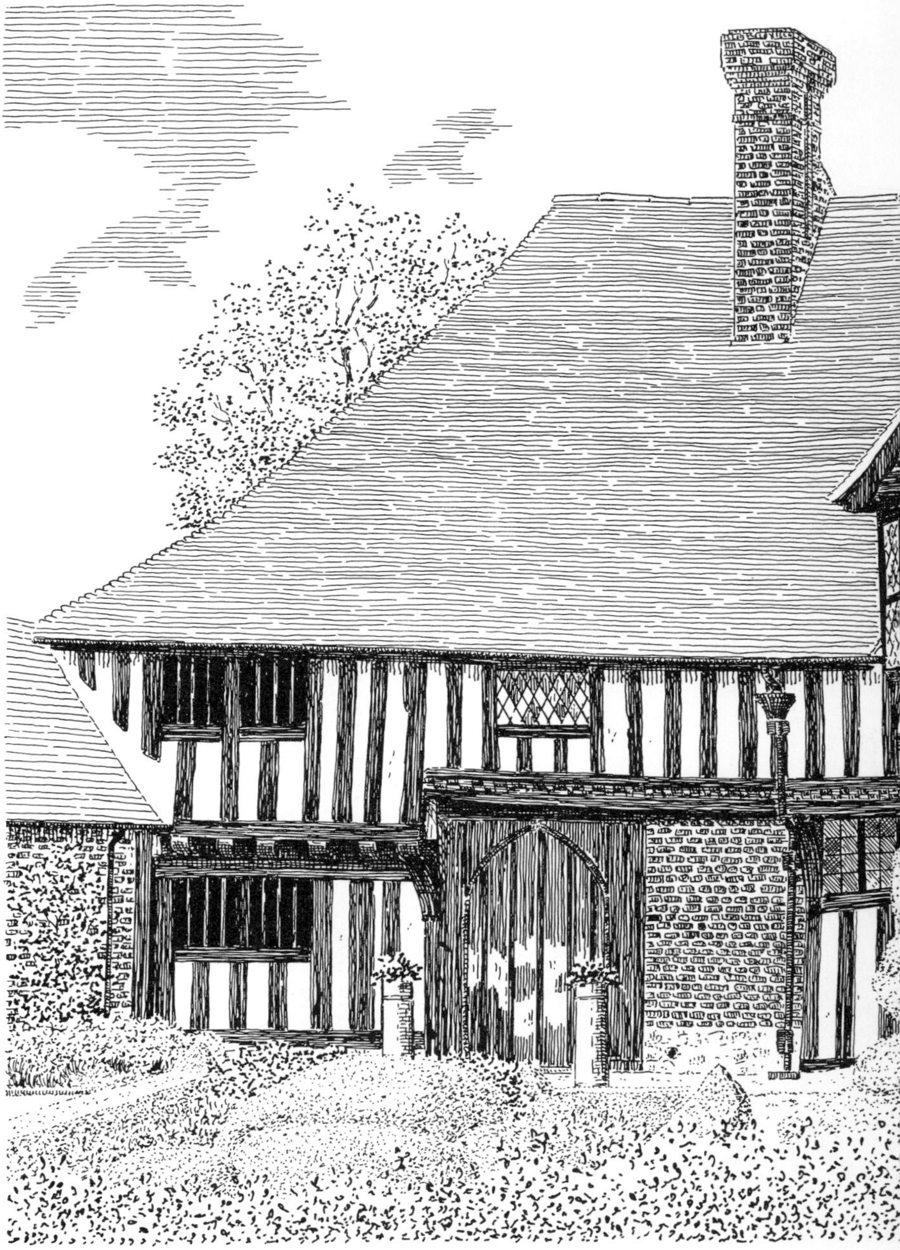

80. Kite Manor, Monks Horton.

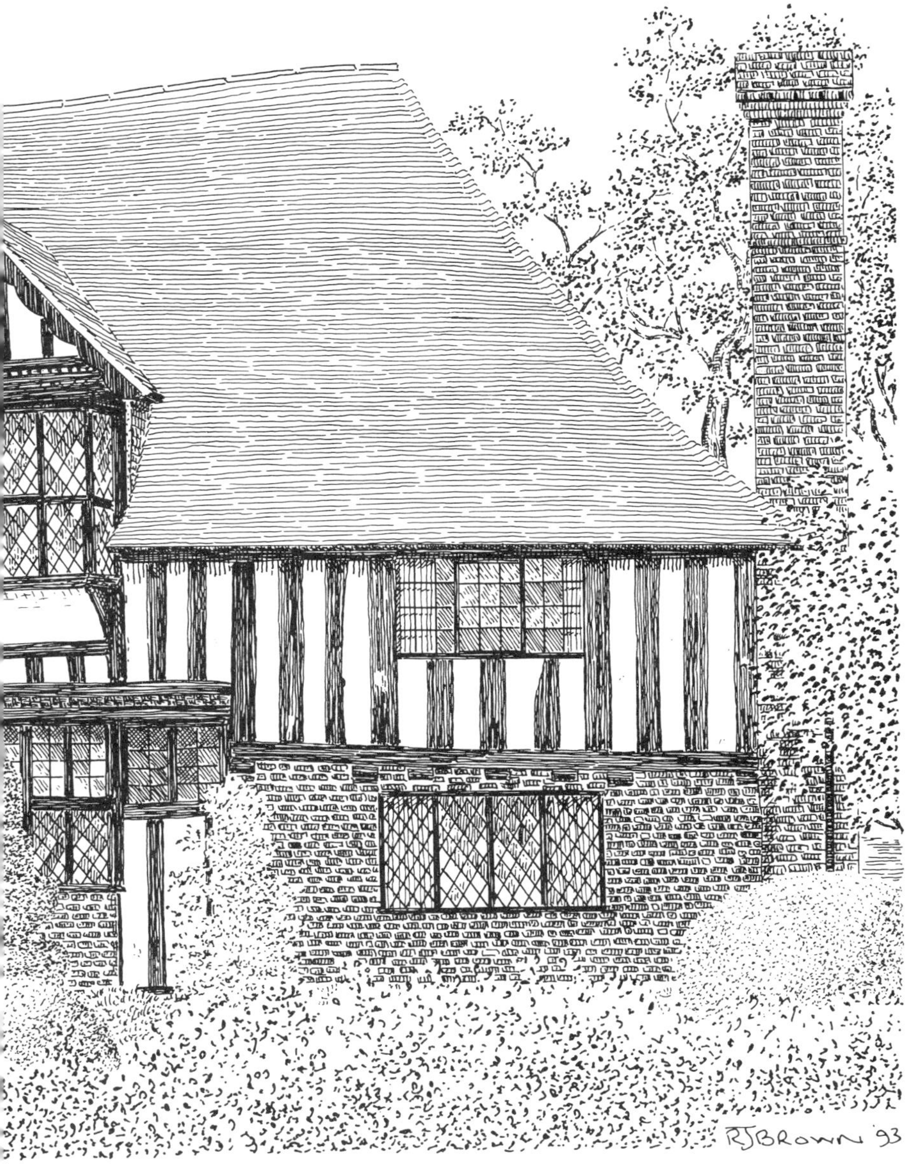
RJ BROWN '93

Sundridge, are all examples of Wealdens with this arrangement while for end-jettied houses one can cite Old Post Office, Goodnestone, and Walnut Tree Cottage, Lynsore, Upper Hardres. This position obviously upset the medieval concept of having the service rooms at the far end of the house and there is evidence that in some cases the parlour was converted into the service room and a new parlour built beyond the screens passage.

Perhaps less common but by no means rare was to place the stack within the screens passage, thus blocking the passage and so forming a lobby entrance. This seems to be more common in the end-jettied house than the Wealden house, perhaps because in end-jettied houses the screens passage is usually found within the open hall. Good examples of this arrangement in end-jettied houses are the Old Cottage, Bishopsbourne, Bagham Farm, Chilham, and Gander End, Staple.

Alternatively the stack could be positioned outside the house, with the fireplace built on the front or rear of the house. This was less common and seems to have been reserved for larger houses. It can be seen at Singleton Manor, Great Chart (*79*), a large, moated house with an exceptionally large hall. At Durlock Grange, Minister-in-Thanet, the fireplace was to the rear wall with brick ovens to both sides. These stacks serving the hall and perhaps the adjacent room were at first the only stacks to be built, whether in the former open-hall house or in the continuous-jettied house. The chimney stacks usually inserted on the outside of the gable or rear walls serving the end room, which may have been either the former service room or parlour, were later additions, of perhaps late seventeenth-, eighteenth- or even nineteenth-century date.

With the elimination of the open hearth it became possible to insert a floor over the whole of the open hall to provide a continuous first floor throughout the house. Such was the popularity of the continuous-jettied house that some Wealden houses were often assimilated to it by having the upper part of the recessed front filled in. This is invariably easy to observe, for the floor is often inserted at a different height to the adjoining solar and service bays. One of the most well-known examples is the house in the High Street at Tenterden known as the Tudor Rose Café, another is Kite Manor, Monks Horton (*80*), where the floor was inserted in 1574. At Cowden in the village street is a Wealden house which clearly shows its building history (*81*); the house was built in the fifteenth century, the floor was inserted in the sixteenth century and the recessed centre filled in, and finally in the following century the jetties were underbuilt in brick.

The use to which the newly formed room above the hall was put is

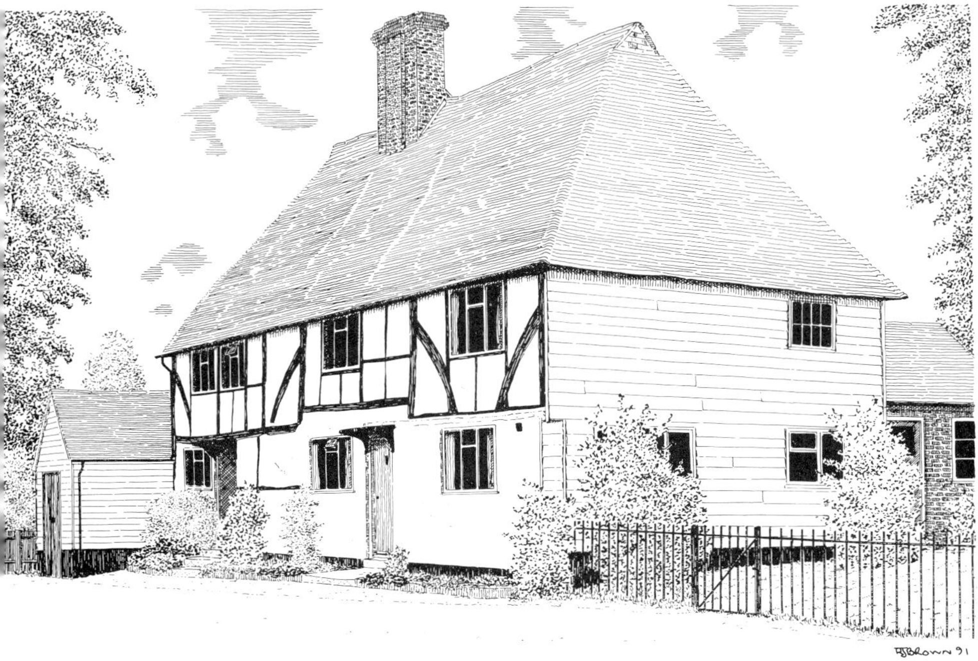

81. Wealden house at Cowden.

not clear. In many instances it is merely called the 'chamber over the hall' while in other cases it is referred to as a loft. The distinction between a chamber and a loft is difficult to define but presumably a chamber was superior, having a floor at such a height to enable a window to be installed, while a loft was no more than a triangular space made by the insertion of the floor at more or less eaves level. In any case the crown-post would in many instances restrict the head-room. It seems from surviving probate inventories that whether referred to as a chamber or loft the room was used as a store for a combination of foodstuffs, seeds for the farm and articles such as tools, needed perhaps only once or so a year. M.W. Barley in his book *The English Farmhouse and Cottage* gives the example of Thomas Whitfield of Eastry who used the room for storage of 'wood and russet yarn, hemp seed, mustard seed, oats, cheese, butter and apples; an eel snare and a rook net, his armour and hunting gear and fifteen sickles and hooks'.

It was not always the case that the insertion of the floor into the open hall was carried out at one time. In Kent, in perhaps as many as a third of the hall houses a floor was partly inserted into the open hall, thus providing a smoke bay, open to the roof, from which the smoke from the open hearth could escape, and also an upper chamber of reasonable size. This evidently happened at Kite Manor, where the floor was inserted in 1574 but it was not until four years later that the hall chimney was formed, clearly indicating the presence of a smoke bay. One disadvantage of this arrangement was that the upper floor of the house was still split and so access from the ground floor was still required at both the solar and service ends. In some instances this was overcome by the provision of a gallery linking the new floor over the high end to the chamber above the service rooms at the lower end. E.R. Swain in *Medieval Archaeology* mentions his discovery that in Kent this was by no means rare and notes nine examples, the best being the Old Farmhouse, Fawkham, Payne Street Farm, Charing and Barrow Hill House, at Upper Bush, Cuxton, while at Tonge Corner Farmhouse, Sittingbourne, there was a gallery across both sides of the smoke bay.

The provision of a smoke bay was a transitional arrangement between the open hearth and the brick-built stack, but its use often continued well into the latter part of the seventeenth century before a brick-built stack was constructed, perhaps inserted into the smoke bay itself as at Netherhall, St Nicholas-at-Wade. By the end of the seventeenth century all open halls would have been floored and a brick-built stack inserted. Perhaps the last hall house in the county where this happened was at Hoggeshawes, formerly the Old Post Office, in the village of Milstead, which had to wait until 1700 for the whole process of modernization to be completed.

An alternative method of removing the smoke from the open hall was the provision of a smoke hood – a chimney made of timber with a wattle-and-daub infilling and usually plastered internally to protect the timbers. The structure itself, which tapered to an outlet in the roof, was built against a timber-framed partition, usually with two return walls, and was supported at the front by a mantel beam above the fireplace. The smoke hood was probably first introduced at the end of the fifteenth century when it was inserted into the open hall, usually prior to the insertion of the first floor, and probably continued to be built in many smaller houses until the beginning of the eighteenth century. How widespread its use was in Kent is debatable, but an example remains at Marley Farm, Smarden, and is illustrated in N. Lloyd's *A History of the English House*. Another and perhaps the finest in Kent is in a continuous-jettied house near Headcorn, which has been left untouched, with a seventeenth-century brick chimney actually built within the original plaster one.

At the same time as inserting a floor and stack into the open hall it was not unusual also to provide a bay window serving both the ground and newly formed first floor, replacing the large, open windows of the hall. Often the bay was extended into the roof space and a gable added.

Features of the Post-medieval House

HOUSE PLANS

Despite the adaptation of existing houses in the two generations from about 1570 there is also a visible ripple of the more famous Great Rebuilding previously mentioned. Many new rural halls and even new settlements began to appear and this was particularly true in the prosperous cloth-industry areas around Biddenden, Staplehurst, Goudhurst and Cranbrook.

The rebuilding brought about a new house type, the lobby-entry house, in which the service rooms were incorporated within the house unlike the old house type, in which the service rooms were separated from the living-quarters by means of a screens passage. We have seen

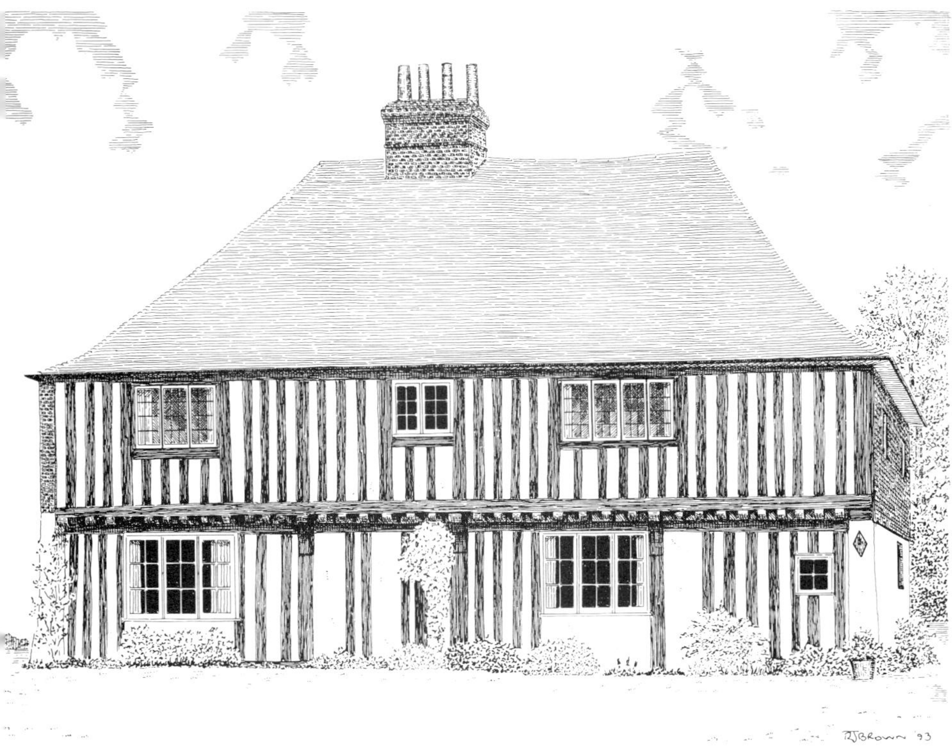

82. Cobb's Hall, Aldington. Built between 1509 and 1526 for Thomas Cobb, Steward of the Archbishops of Canterbury.

that a number of old open-hall houses were converted into lobby-entry houses either by the insertion of an axial chimney stack or in other cases by the rebuilding of the lower end. However, the vast majority were new houses and although there are several types of lobby-entry houses, in Kent the type most commonly employed was the central-lobby-entry house. The earliest example in the county is perhaps Cobb's Hall, Aldington (*82*), built as a combined lodging and court house for Thomas Cobb between 1509 and 1526. From about the middle of the sixteenth century until the eighteenth century the central-lobby-entry house became almost the universal house type for smaller houses in Kent.

The basic type had an entrance towards the centre of the front lateral wall, leading into a small lobby formed between two main rooms by the introduction of a central axial stack, the lobby being in general the width of the stack. This layout had two main advantages over those houses which contained a screens passage: the lobby reduced draughts, providing greater comfort to the two principal rooms, while giving independent access to the bedrooms above. In addition both rooms were heated either from their own fireplace or, when only the hall had a fireplace, from heat radiated through the stack from the fire in the hall.

Most of the earliest forms of this house type had two ground-floor rooms: the hall or the hall-cum-kitchen, as it had now generally become, and the chamber. These two-roomed houses continued to be built throughout the seventeenth century, although by this time both rooms had a fireplace using the same stack. The hall would have been used for cooking and towards the end of the seventeenth century began to be referred to as the kitchen. The other room was still referred to as the chamber; few people called it the parlour, for no one in Kent had abandoned the habit of using this ground-floor room as the principal bedroom, and it was sometimes called the 'chamber behind the hall'. This use of 'chamber' for ground-floor rooms, including bedrooms, distinguished the south-eastern counties from the rest of England where such names as parlour, buttery, pantry were in general use in Elizabethan times.

From these two-roomed houses evolved what can be termed the classic central-lobby-entry type which in Kent was almost universally adopted for all larger houses (*83*). The house comprised simply three rooms – a heated chamber, a heated main room (the hall or hall-cum-kitchen) and, at the opposite end to the chamber, an unheated service room, with the entrance lobby situated between the chamber and the main room. Entrance to the service room was directly from the main room. The service room was commonly subdivided into two, entry being gained either by two separate doors

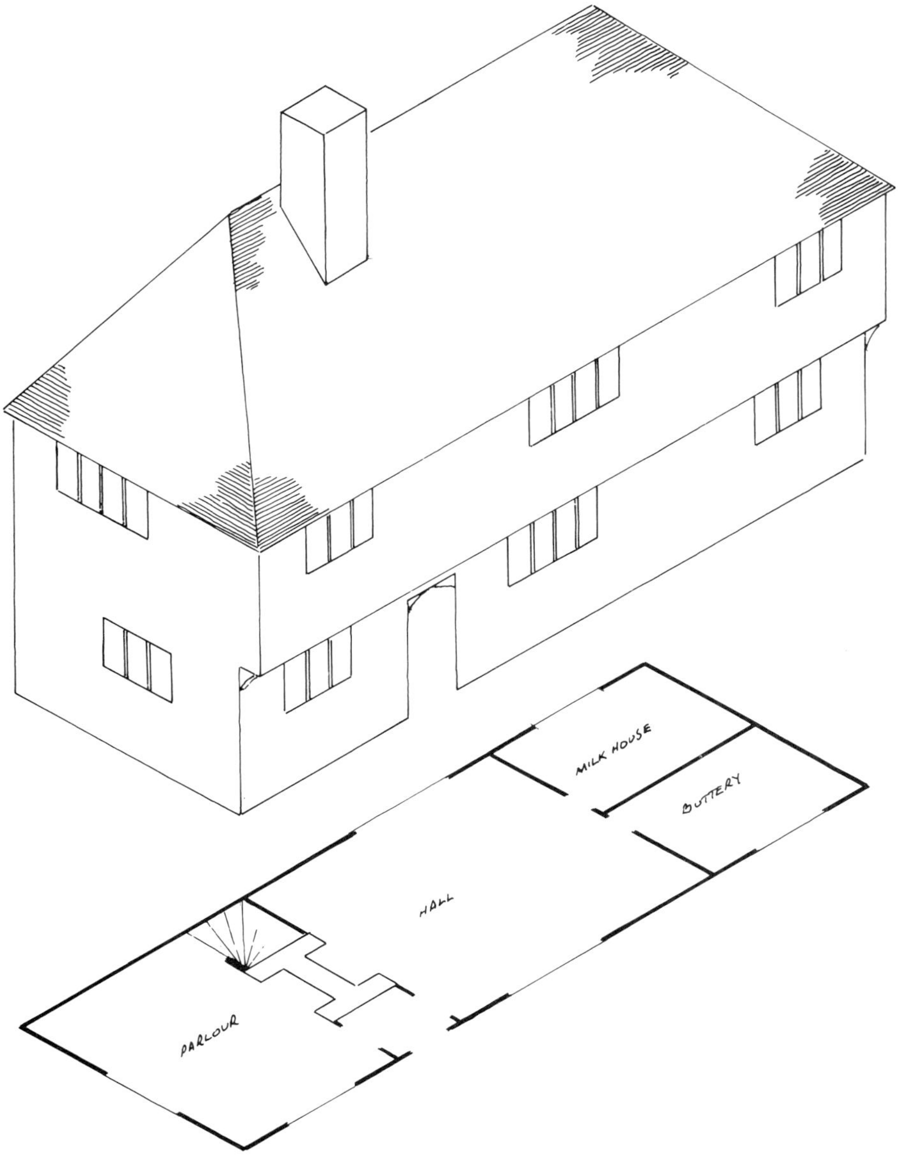

83. Typical layout of the classic three-unit, lobby-entry house.

from the main room or by a single door from the main room with a communicating door between the two service rooms.

To the basic two- or three-roomed plan there were several variations. These, as with other house types, generally revolved around the position of the chimney stack and its relationship with the stairs. The stack could be placed centrally within the depth of the house so that the return wall of the stack formed one wall of the entrance lobby – the one opposite the entrance door – with the stair either a newel or straight flight, positioned between the stack and rear lateral wall. Another layout was to place the stack against the rear lateral wall with the stairs elsewhere. Often the stairs were situated in the entrance lobby, sometimes adjacent to the stack itself, but in the two-roomed unit they were generally placed in the hall while in houses with three rooms they were commonly in the service room. In some three-roomed houses an additional flight of stairs can be found in the service room to give independent access to the third bedroom without going through one of the other rooms.

Although these central-lobby houses, especially the two-unit ones, produced an elevation with some degree of symmetry, towards the end of the seventeenth century there came about an increasing desire for complete symmetry (*84*). This was achieved by the omission of the central stack, the entrance door being placed in the centre of the front elevation and opening directly either into a small entrance hall, extending the full depth of the house, or into a small lobby. The entrance hall or lobby, in which was situated a straight flight of stairs, divided the house; there would be two rooms – one on either side – both reached independently from the hall or lobby. The two rooms were each heated by a fireplace situated on the gable walls. By the 1730s houses built to this general layout replaced the central-lobby house as the most popular house type. The entrance hall or lobby was often increased in width and the simple straight flight was replaced with an open-well or dog-leg staircase. This house type is commonly referred to as the vestibule plan to distinguish it from the lobby-entry house.

The basic lobby-entry or vestibule plan had no service rooms. In the larger houses these were sometimes contained within a wing to the rear, but more often than not they were housed in an outshut either at the side, or, more commonly, to the rear. This can be seen at Godfrey House, Hollingbourne (*85*), a large, timber-framed, three-unit, lobby-entry house built in 1587 with a continuous-jettied front broken by the three-storey porch. To the rear, as indicated in William Twopeny's drawing of 1827, is the outshut under a catslide roof containing the service rooms. The outshut was in Kent referred to as the cove, which in Kentish dialect meant a shed or lean-to. These

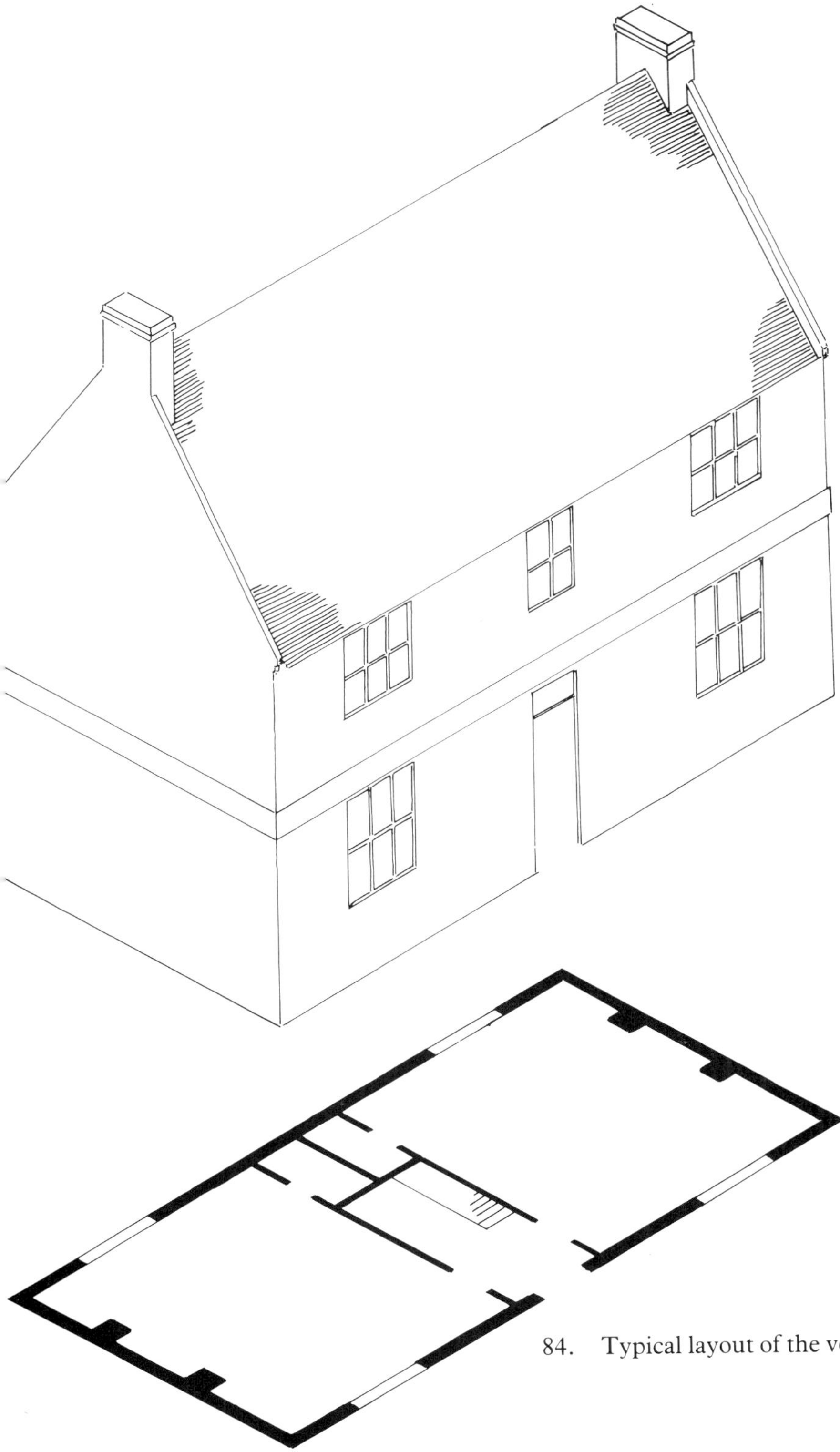

84. Typical layout of the vestibule plan.

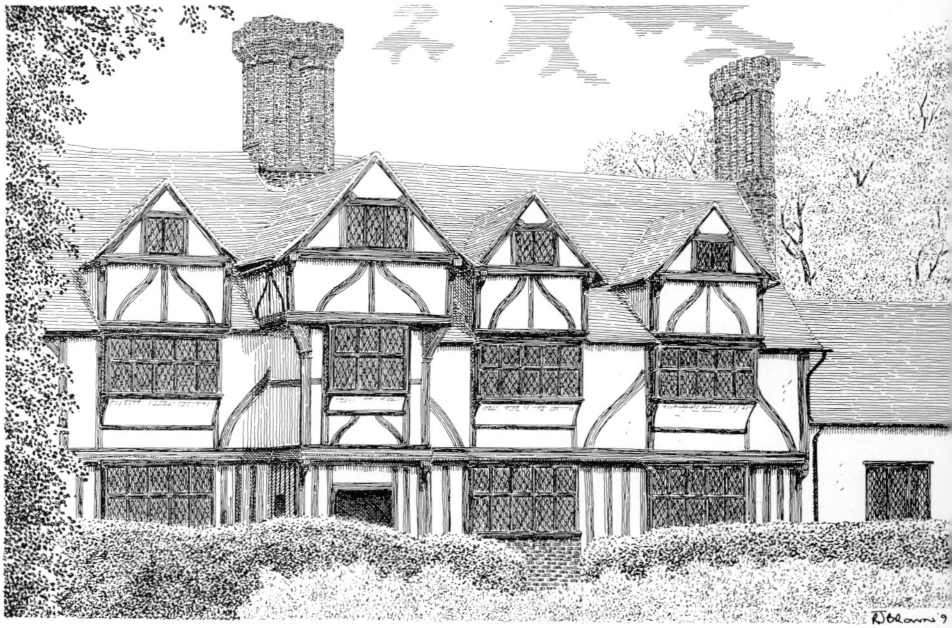

85. Godfrey House, Hollingbourne, built in 1587.

outshuts to the rear produced the picturesque catslide roofs to be seen on many houses in the county.

In some three-unit houses the service room was converted to form a kitchen, and a chimney stack was inserted into the gable end. This happened at Brunger Farm, Tenterden, where the external stack is tied back to the brick gable with a number of iron straps. Additional rooms were sometimes added by building a two-storey extension to provide not only additional ground-floor accommodation but a chamber over as well. Similarly, a cross-wing could be added to either end of the house to provide additional accommodation. In most cases these additions to the basic two- or three-unit house would be later extensions rather than part of the original plan.

The evidence from the probate inventories at the end of the sixteenth century gives some indication of the number and uses of the service rooms provided by these extensions. They varied greatly and it would now be difficult to generalize on their plan, for many would have been former open-hall houses, much altered and enlarged and therefore varying greatly in arrangements. Most of the better-off people, who were calling themselves yeomen, had, it appears, a kitchen, a buttery, often referred to as a drink buttery, and a milk-house. Those slightly further down the social scale – either small farmers (husbandmen) or craftsmen – had, it seems, a buttery, drinkhouse or milk-chamber; few had a kitchen, the cooking still being carried out in the hall. Few labourers living in two or three ground-floor rooms had a kitchen or a milk-house.

Fifty years or so on these two-roomed houses still survived – a hall with a chamber beside it, though now the hall was often called the fire-room. However, most husbandmen in the county at this time had two service rooms – a kitchen and milk-house, or buttery and milk-house – and in a few cases all three. The number of service rooms thought desirable by the average yeoman-farmer continued to increase. One such room was the wash-house, differing from other service rooms in that it had a water supply (i.e. a well); another becoming increasingly popular was the boulting-house in which was kept the flour which had to be sieved through a linen boulting-cloth to produce a fine flour, so determining the quality of the bread or pastry. The brewhouse too became a feature of some large houses. So in addition to the normal three service rooms – kitchen, milk-house and buttery – more facilities for baking, brewing and washing began to appear. Whether these additional service rooms were housed in extensions to the main building or in separate buildings is not clear from the probate inventories of the time. By this time, around 1640, the chamber next to the hall began to be known as the parlour and had for the first time chairs and a table or two; yet in most cases it still retained a bed.

Towards the end of the century the yeomen class together with wealthy clothiers began to place greater emphasis on the status of the parlour, clearly indicating the changing lifestyle of the family and the importance now beginning to be placed on hospitality. Few people, particularly in east Kent, referred to this room as a chamber and, though some retained a bed, the wealthier families had removed it from the parlour; only when there were two parlours would one be retained as a bedroom. Upstairs too there was a corresponding increase in the number of rooms now clearly always furnished as bedrooms. Only a few people, those generally requiring space for the storage of materials for their trade, continued to use an upstairs room as a store, although a few farmers still used the loft over the hall or the chamber over the parlour for the storage of corn; but some were now using the garret or attic for storage. The service rooms too continued to develop, the new emphasis being, it seems, related to the needs of the inhabitants of the house rather than those of the farm. The term 'buttery' began to be replaced by the drinkhouse or drink buttery. Two butteries were not uncommonly referred to as 'best drink buttery' and a 'small drink buttery' and Mr Barley quotes Thomas Gibson, a clothier from Hawkhurst, as having three – one by the parlour, a small drink buttery and a third buttery next to the kitchen.

Cellars too began to appear from around 1600 onwards especially outside the Low Weald, for the wet clays there would have made this sort of accommodation impossible to provide. By the second half of the seventeenth century the practice was well established not only for new houses but also for existing ones, which would have a cellar put in, usually under the parlour. Mr Barley gives the example of Stone Street Farm, Petham, purchased in 1666 by a merchant escaping from the plague, who 'improved' the house by having a fireplace inserted in the hall, the jetties underbuilt, a porch added, a cellar formed under the parlour, and an outshut and other extensions built on the rear.

Up until now all the house types described had one common feature: the principal rooms were the depth of the house, although in many cases, such as the service rooms, they might well have been divided. In addition the service rooms were in nearly all cases situated at one end – the lower end. Towards the end of the seventeenth century a change began to develop to this medieval layout which had lasted for over five hundred years. Houses more than one room deep began to be built with, for the first time, the service rooms relegated to the rear of the house behind the principal rooms – a house type known as the double-pile house.

We have seen previously that houses with outshuts began to appear towards the end of the sixteenth century and continued to be built until the end of the seventeenth century. These were the forerunners of the double-pile house. In some cases these single-storey outshuts would be raised to provide two storeys but most double-pile houses appear to have been purpose-built and clearly a development of the vestibule plan. The basic double-pile house is of four rooms, the two principal living-rooms – the dining-room and parlour – at the front and at the rear the kitchen and another service room. In nearly all cases the living-rooms were deeper than the service rooms. Between the two living-rooms was the front entrance, placed more or less centrally along the front elevation, from which access to the two living-rooms was obtained. It also contained the staircase to the upper floor. The two living-rooms were generally heated by end-gable stacks although it is not uncommon to find the fireplaces backing on to the partition walls between the living- and service rooms. Although the kitchen was always heated, the service rooms rarely were.

The double-pile house was the ultimate development in house design at the vernacular level, providing a degree of comfort not generally found in earlier houses. In most, and especially the later ones, access to each room was gained from the central hall, and there was no need to pass through one room to gain access to another as with previous house plans. The hall-cum-kitchen became the new dining- or living-room, the parlour became the sitting-room and the kitchen became for the first time an essential part of the house. Unlike previous house types in which only the hall or at most the hall and parlour were heated, in the double-pile house it was possible to heat all the ground-floor rooms as well as the main rooms upstairs. The old, steep, newel or straight-flight stairs were replaced with the fashionable framed staircase. The general result is all these improvements provided a house which was for the first time designed for the needs and comfort of the family.

The double-pile house was better suited to brick or stone construction, rather than timber. For many centuries builders had both built and extended timber-framed houses by means of a wing either at the rear or set at right angles to the main block to form an L- or T-shaped plan, but it was not until the seventeenth century that an attempt was made to build a house of two sections, one containing the living-quarters and the other the service rooms, side by side. Because

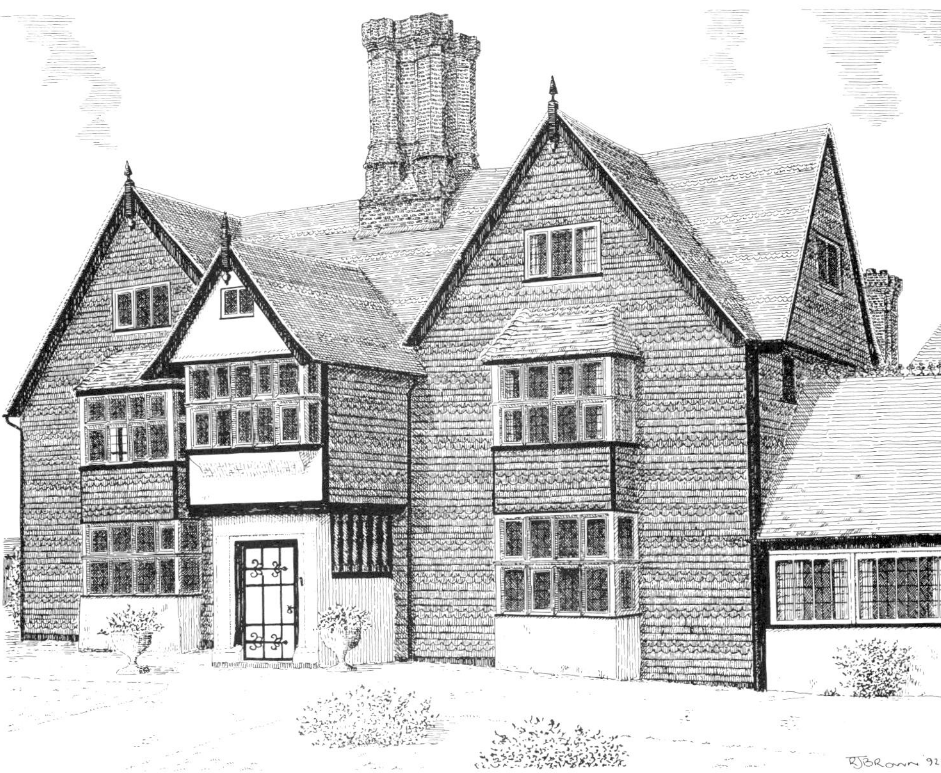

86. Marle Place, Brenchley, a half-timbered house dated 1619, but clad with nineteenth-century tiles.

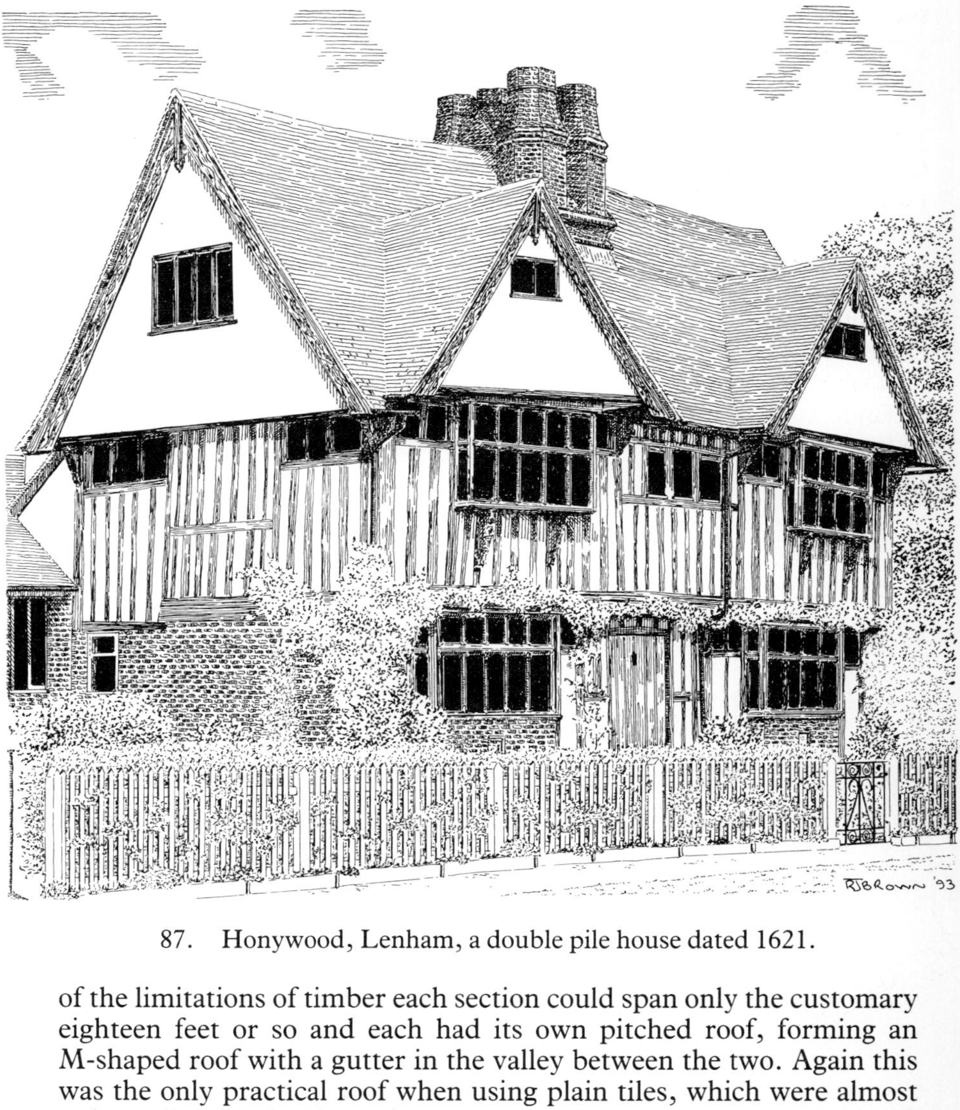

87. Honywood, Lenham, a double pile house dated 1621.

of the limitations of timber each section could span only the customary eighteen feet or so and each had its own pitched roof, forming an M-shaped roof with a gutter in the valley between the two. Again this was the only practical roof when using plain tiles, which were almost universally used in Kent, for the required pitch for plain tiles would have produced a roof of unacceptable height which would have been expensive to frame. However, there are a few timber-framed houses built at the beginning of the seventeenth century to the double-pile plan which did not have this M-shaped roof. At Marle Place, Brenchley (*86*), built in 1619, the house is almost square on plan with four rooms centred around a four-shafted stack. Anthony Honywood's house at Lenham (*87*), dated 1621, is similar with a symmetrical front, two rooms deep with a central stack now, alas, deprived of its octagonal stacks.

ROOFS

With the adoption of these new house plans and the abandonment of the open hall, the importance of the crown-post declined. Although immensely strong, it was expensive in the quantity of timber used and as it was no longer intended to be viewed from the hall the decorative function was superfluous. It also became impracticable, for in the lobby-entry house the centrally placed stack would have obstructed the collar purlin. In addition it became desirable to utilize the roof space and for this both the crown-posts and collar purlins with the collars to each rafter were a hindrance. Slowly the crown-post was replaced by a cheaper roof type using side purlins which left the roof space free from obstructions between the trusses. The side-purlin roof

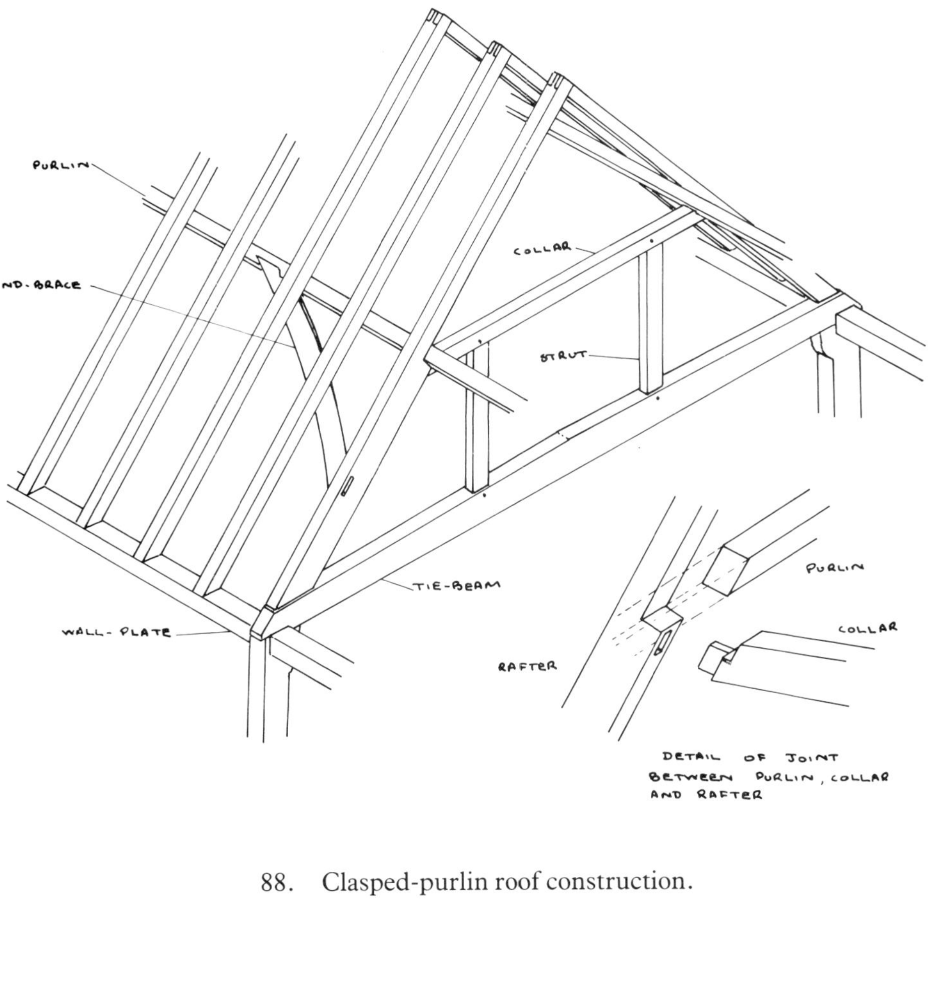

88. Clasped-purlin roof construction.

appeared first in the West Midlands, entering Kent from the west around 1530 and slowly moving eastwards, finally reaching Canterbury and Sandwich in about 1600.

There are several detailed variations to the side-purlin roof. At first the side purlins were butted and mortise-and-tenoned into the principal rafter which formed part of the roof truss. Alternatively instead of a mortise-and-tenoned joint a through splayed-scarf or a through halved-scarf joint was used. These roof trusses comprised a tie-beam, two principal rafters and a collar-beam, the collar-beam generally being supported off the tie-beam by a central strut, similar to the crown-post but devoid of its collar purlin and known as a lower king-strut. This roof truss was soon superseded by the queen-strut roof, with the through-purlins clasped at the angle between the

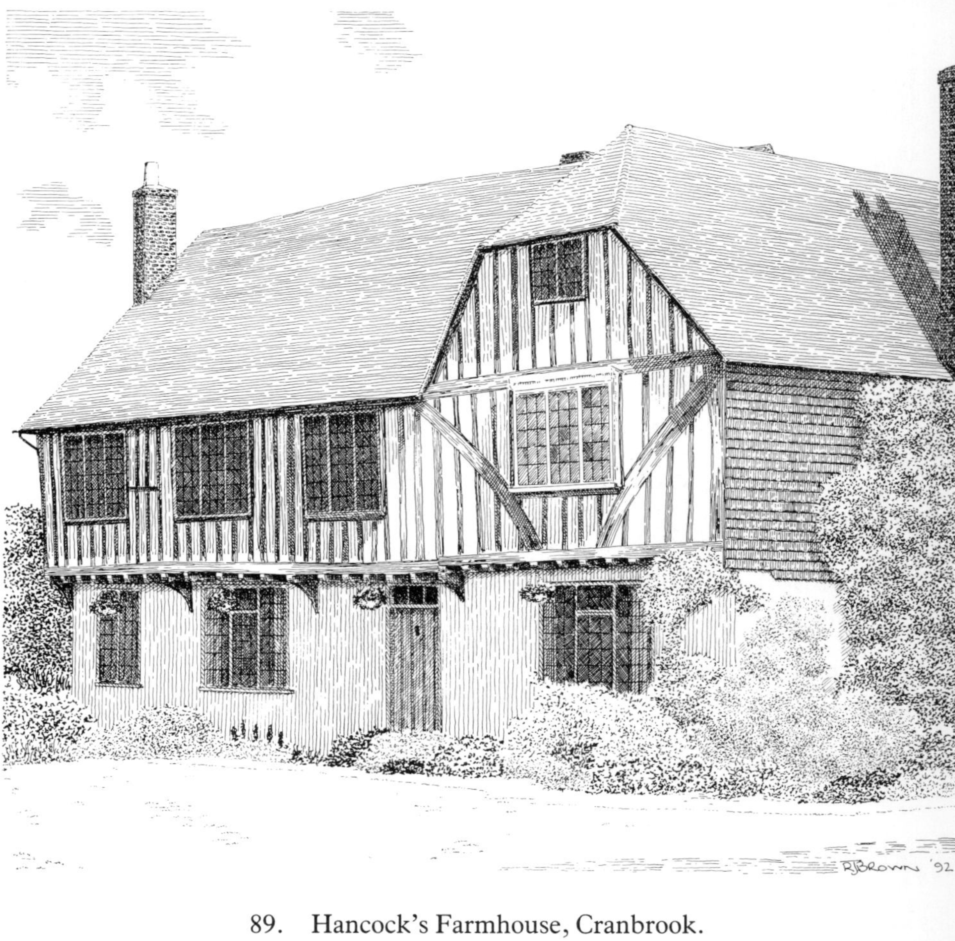

89. Hancock's Farmhouse, Cranbrook.

principal rafter and collar (*88*). At first the queen-struts were straight and set vertically but later they tended to be curved and set at an angle. Above the purlin the principal rafter was often reduced in depth to the same depth as the common rafters.

A much rarer roof type is where the members are arch-braced, supporting both side purlins and a collar purlin. Only two examples are known at present in Kent; one, the finest example, is Shakespeare House on the south side of the High Street at Headcorn, where the arch-braces can clearly be seen. The other example, much disguised, is in Goudhurst High Street. Both examples date from the early sixteenth century and both were reputedly built by men connected with the cloth trade, so that the attic was used for storage. Shakespeare House was formerly known as the Old Cloth Hall.

With the introduction of these new roof types came the abandonment of the steeply pitched hipped roof which had been the predominant feature of the medieval house in Kent. For the first time houses with gables replaced in popularity those with hips. The reason was two-fold: one structural, for it was easier and cheaper to construct a side-purlin roof with the purlins supported by the gable wall; the other social, for with the increasing demand for more space the gabled roof provided greater practical attic space for either storage or accommodation for servants. In Kent the half-hipped roof became popular; this gives a part-gable at the end of the house which often incorporated a window to light the roof space or attic (*89*). A feature of some houses in Kent, especially the Weald, was to provide a hip or half-hip to one end and a gable to the other.

CHIMNEY STACKS AND FIREPLACES

The chimney stack was the most significant feature of the early post-medieval house and around it the house plan developed. Until the seventeenth century it was normal to provide only one fireplace, that in the hall. This was not only the case when the stack was inserted into the open hall, but also when the continuous-jettied houses began to be built. A central stack could serve both hall and parlour as well as the two rooms above, and so by the end of the sixteenth century it was not uncommon to have four or more shafts. By the middle of the seventeenth century even in houses of moderate size there might be three or four shafts rising above the central stack. The number of shafts did not necessarily indicate the number of fireplaces, for sometimes large fireplaces were served by two shafts.

The width of these early inglenook fireplaces was seldom less than eight feet and was often in excess of twelve (Kite House, Monks Horton, is thirteen feet). At Olde House, Harrietsham, the overall width of the fireplace is around fourteen feet with an opening of about ten feet, leaving some five to six feet for access into the hall from the screens passage. This obviously explains why the stack was so often placed against the front or rear wall of the hall, for if placed centrally access to the hall would be restricted to an opening of no more than two or three feet. The width of the fireplace in the chamber above was generally much smaller, probably only three feet or so.

The appearance of these fireplaces depended on the status of the house as well as their position within the house. The beams of the earlier fireplaces were usually carved into a flat Tudor arch, often with the carved 'flower and fern' pattern in the spandrels on each side (*90*). Later, in Stuart times, the fireplaces were wider but the beams were generally plain except for a chamfered edge, because spit machines were mounted on them. The beams of many Jacobean fireplaces bear the peg-holes and grooves where the spit machines were fitted, usually to the right-hand end, although occasionally to the left. Fine examples of these machines can still be seen at Hampton Court and in the Ann of Cleves House museum at Lewes. Within the brick sides of some of

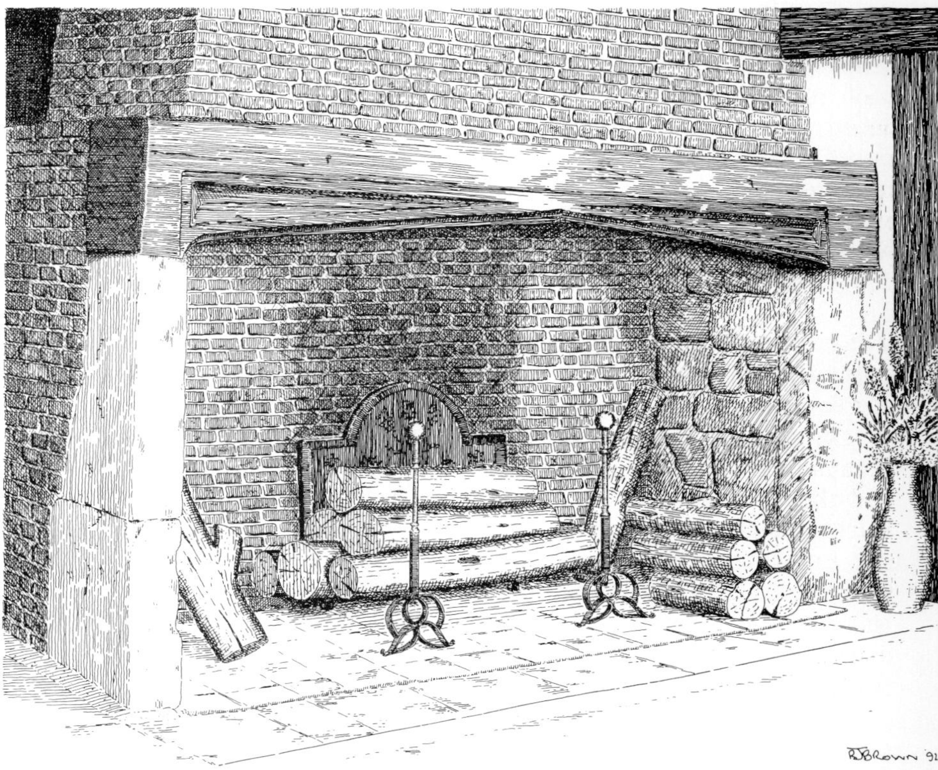

90. Hall fireplace, 'The Wealden Hall', Larkfield.

these fireplaces are still to be seen recesses, very occasionally with their original oak cupboard doors. The niches and side cupboards in these old fireplaces were used to keep certain articles dry, such as salt and the tinder box, an essential part of any household. A favourite material for putting in the tinder box was cotton, obtained from old stockings, which kept tinder dry. The box also contained a couple of flintstones and a U-shaped striking-iron. A spark was struck into the tinder, any glow being encouraged by blowing it. When it was glowing enough the striking-iron was touched by the end of a sulphur match which would burst into flame, enabling the candle to be lit.

The brick jambs were either plain, chamfered, rounded or on occasions moulded. The brickwork of the hearth and the back was frequently laid in herringbone pattern. Occasionally the surround of the fireplace was wholly in brick, plastered over and lined to simulate stone. Stone surrounds or overmantels inserted into a brick stack can also be found. Pre-Elizabethan examples are arched with a square head. The arch is either four-centred, or less often elliptical or segmental. The jambs are generally stop-moulded, the moulds carried around the arch with the spandrels enriched with foliage or shields. In the upper chamber, where the opening was much smaller, surrounds were often constructed with a four-centred brick arch or less often with stone. Within the hearth the log fire was supported on iron dogs to improve the draught and to the rear a cast-iron fireback was provided to reflect the heat of the fire and protect the brickwork from excessive heat.

Externally the stack above the roof received some form of decoration. The almost endless variety of plans and the ingenuity of the arrangements indicate the importance placed upon these structures. The highly exuberant shafts of the reign of Henry VIII are to be found mostly in East Anglia, and in Kent the designs, although often lofty and of admirable proportions, are usually less ornate, moulded and carved bricks being seldom used. This may have been because the open hall in Kent lingered on longer than in East Anglia and the shafts inserted into the open hall in Kent are generally of Elizabethan date. Although the shafts of these stacks were no longer decorated they often retained the basic design of a base, shaft and cap. Octagonal shafts of mid- to late sixteenth-century date are to be found here and there. Often the shafts were square and not infrequently set diagonally on their bases. This became common at the beginning of the seventeenth century.

The majority of chimneys were not individual shafts but composite stacks in which a number of flues were collected in one square or rectangular structure above the roof. These too often received some form of decoration. All of them would have projecting courses at the

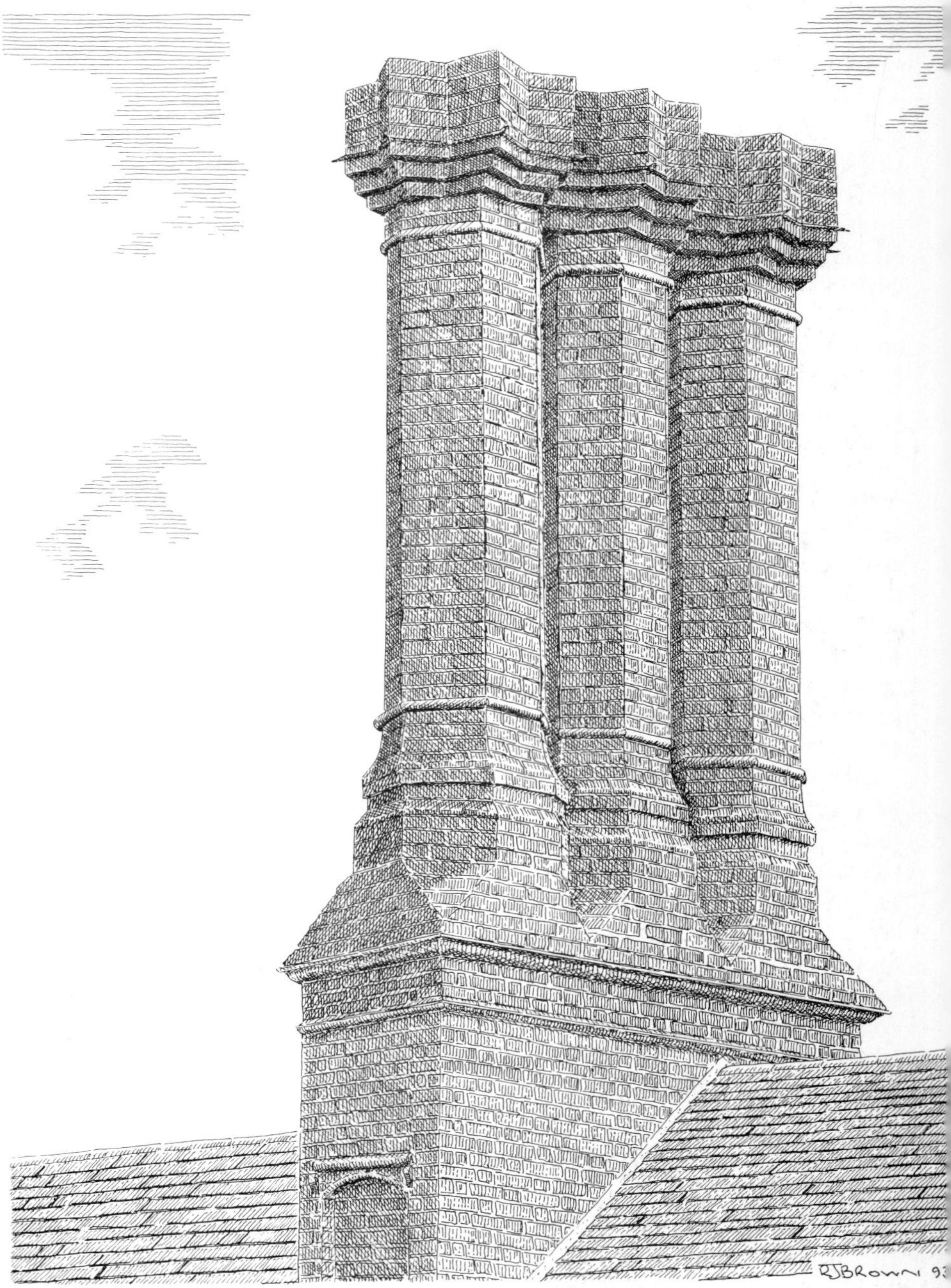

91. Late sixteenth-century stack, Winchcombe Manor, Crundale.

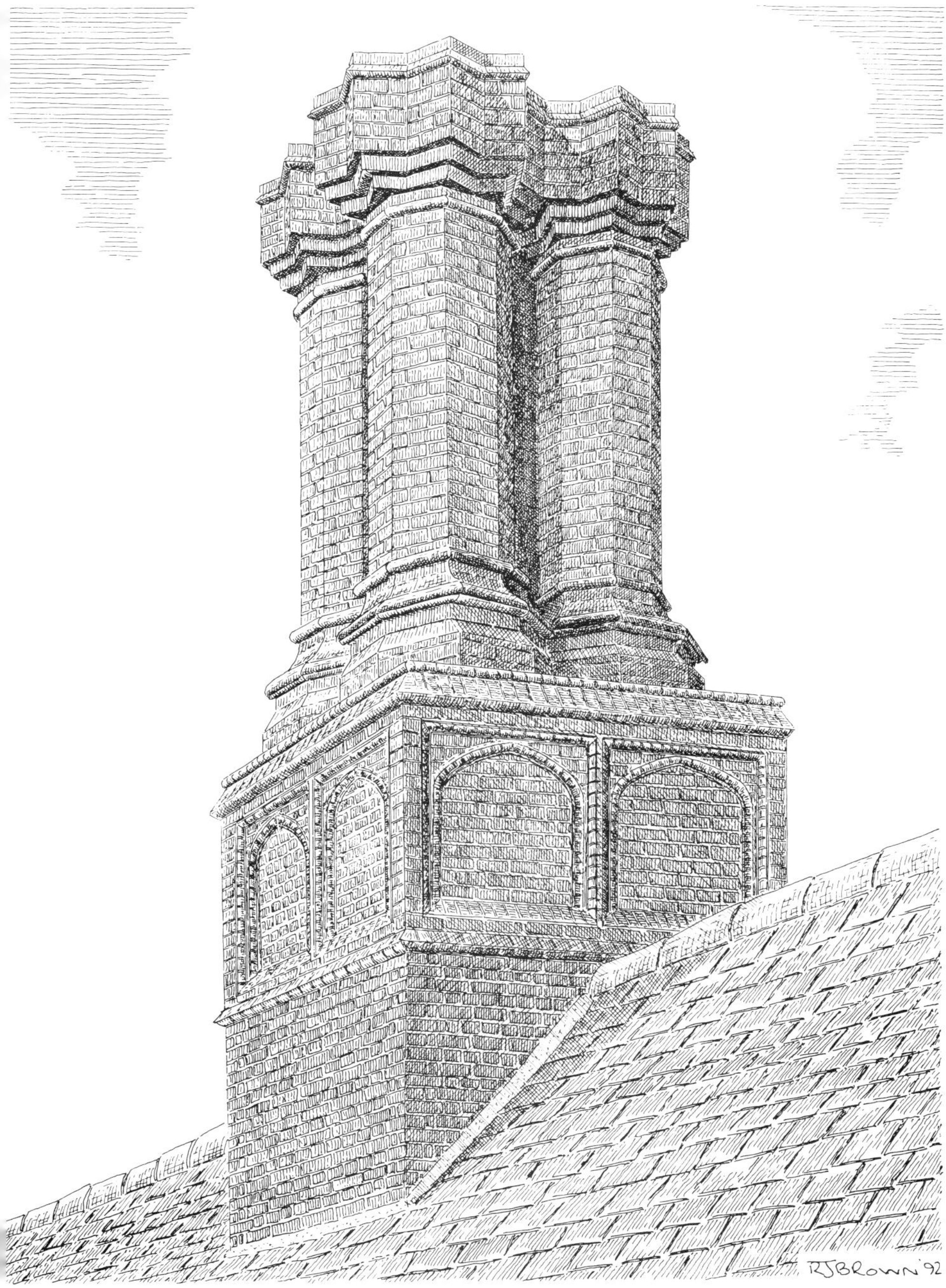

92. Shafts of Manor Farm, Cliffe. From an old photograph.

top but often other decorations would be incorporated as, for instance, recessed or projecting vertical bands, those projecting vertically often being set diagonally to form a pointed projection. A transitional arrangement was employed from the late sixteenth century, in which they were conjoined, either at base and top or along the entire length. Octagonal and diagonal shafts both lent themselves to this close coupling, sometimes to the extent of producing what was virtually a composite shaft. This can be seen at Winchcombe Manor, Crundale (*91*), which has three octagonal shafts with their base and star tops joined. Another excellent example is to be seen at Marle Place, Brenchley, which has a group of four octagonal shafts on a square stack with star tops linked to a square core. Originally the base and the brickwork linking the shafts were decorated with moulded bricks. A similar arrangement can be seen at Manor Farm, Cliffe (*92*), here the shafts are set close together with both the octagonal bases and the star tops joined, and so the brickwork between the stack is less. Also the square stack projects well above the ridge line and is decorated on all four sides with recessed panels formed with moulded bricks.

FLOORS

The solid ground floor made from earth or chalk remained in use until the eighteenth century in Kent, but by the seventeenth century it was being replaced by other materials of a more substantial nature. Bricks of a similar size to those manufactured for walls but laid flat became established in Kent. They were laid either directly on to the ground, often on top of the old earth floor, bedded perhaps on sand. Clay tiles, so popular in East Anglia, did not, it seems, gain much popularity in Kent. Stone flags, where available, were also used in Kent and were regarded as superior to brick paviors. At Durlock Grange, for instance, when alterations to the house were undertaken early in the eighteenth century the old earth floor to the hall was covered and paved with stone flags, while the other downstair rooms were paved with brick paviors.

These solid floors were cold and damp, for they relied solely on the impervious nature of the floor and rarely was any form of damp-proof membrane introduced. At the beginning of the eighteenth century boarded ground floors on joists began to be introduced into both old and new houses. Even so, this was at first restricted to the parlour, the other ground-floor rooms still retaining the old solid floors. As often as not these boarded floors were constructed with the joists resting directly on the ground, so few survive today. Oak was the material used for flooring, when available, whether to the ground or upper floors, but in the sixteenth century elm began to compete with it and in the eighteenth century softwood replaced both as a flooring material.

STAIRS

The newel stairs remained the most popular form of stairs in the vernacular house until the eighteenth century. Since the lobby-entry house was so widely adopted in Kent and the stack was placed centrally within the house, the most convenient position for the stairs to rise was between this and the external wall. With such a confined position the newel stair was the only practical solution, although when space permitted straight flights were still preferred. However, by the beginning of the seventeenth century solid stairs had been replaced by framed stairs with separate strings, treads and risers.

With the adoption of the vestibule plan and the framed stair it became possible to incorporate other stair types into the central entrance hall. The dog-legged staircase was particularly common in the seventeenth century, as was the open-well staircase from the middle of the seventeenth century. The open-well stairs often incorporated winders at each turn of direction, forming in effect an open newel stair rising around a small square well. The Elizabethan and Jacobean staircases were of heavy construction, generally with heavy square newels which projected above the handrail, and finished with a carved or moulded cap; the end below the strings had a similarly fashioned pendant. Wide, moulded handrails and closed strings with the turned balusters housed into the strings and handrails were also characteristic of the period. At the vernacular level the splat baluster, flat balusters either shaped or tapered and occasionally pierced, which could easily have been made by the local joiner, became common. By the end of the seventeenth century these had been superseded by turned balusters, although often the splat balusters were retained in secondary positions out of view to the visitor. So one might find turned balusters on the lower levels giving way to splat balusters on the upper floors. The twisted baluster – the well-known 'barley-sugar' twist – was also a feature of staircases constructed after the Restoration.

Towards the end of the eighteenth century, as joinery techniques improved, the delicately cut string stair constructed of softwood was developed. The outer string was cut to the profile of the treads and risers, with fret-cut brackets applied to the face of the open string and the treads extended beyond it, the nosing of the tread being returned at the end. The balusters, two or three to a tread, were now lighter in section, often square, with only the newels, also of light construction, turned. Each baluster would be framed into the tread and handrail, which was generally mahogany and extended over the newel to end with a scroll. The bottom step was frequently curtailed and the space beneath the stairs filled in with panelling. However, in most small houses the closed-string staircase, being easier to construct, continued to be used.

CEILINGS

As previously stated, the ceilings in the medieval house were left with the joists and boards exposed. It was not until the late fifteenth and early sixteenth centuries that in some of the greater houses the exposed joists and beams were moulded and in some instances carved. In many cases, in the average house, the decoration was generally restricted to a chamfered or ovolo mould to the edge of the timber. Even so this was invariably confined to the principal timbers, the joists remaining plain. The fashion of plastering between the joists first occurred in the sixteenth century; timber laths were nailed to the underside of the boards prior to plastering.

This type of ceiling, with the beams exposed and plaster between, remained in general use throughout most of the seventeenth century but from the beginning of the seventeenth century onwards there was an increasing desire in both old and new houses for the ceiling to be 'underdrawn' in plaster. In many of the older houses the deeper main beams remained exposed, but early on it became fashionable to plaster these as well; the ceiling would often be finished with a continuous moulded cornice which ran around the beam and adjoining wall. Even during the seventeenth century beams projecting below the ceiling line were avoided, with, on occasions, separate ceiling joists framed into the main beams and independent of the floor joists above.

These plastered ceilings were often decorated with ornamental moulded plasterwork. Moulded ceilings first appeared in the principal rooms of the great houses during the sixteenth century and soon spread into larger domestic houses. Those of the Elizabethan period are usually characterized by small moulded ribs applied in geometric patterns. At the intersections of the ribs are often ornamental bosses and between the ribs a somewhat restrained use of decorative motifs, usually restricted to heraldic bosses, shields, sprigs of foliage, the Tudor rose and the fleur-de-lis. The finest of these Elizabethan ceilings is perhaps to be seen in the hall at Singleton Manor, Great Chart, with the moulded ribs making patterns of interlocking circles with small rosette bosses at the intersections. The moulded ceilings of the Jacobean period are far more ornate, and are divided into panels by moulded trabeations – wide ribs in high relief – providing greater space on the soffit for running ornamentation.

In Upper Street, Sandwich, in the Old Customs House, a fifteenth-century Wealden house altered in later centuries, the ceiling to the ground-floor room is moulded and painted with foliage and flowers. The room above also has a very fine moulded ceiling incorporating the emblems of the four apostles, for instance the lion of St Mark. The Tudor House, Margate, has a plaster ceiling in the solar with a frieze of Prince of Wales feathers. Later, moulded ceilings became more dignified and restrained, with simpler patterns employed. A centrepiece became a common feature. At first this was in high relief and richly decorated but later towards the end of the seventeenth century, although the centrepiece was retained, the mouldings were often plain and in low relief. The centrepiece remained a feature throughout the eighteenth century, again in low relief and often connected to the moulded cornice by a delicate moulding.

DOORS AND DOORWAYS

As we have seen, the four-centred arch made its appearance in the fifteenth century and this developed into the so-called depressed pointed arch in late Tudor and Jacobean times. This was particularly true in the timber-framed house where a false timber arch, usually with sunken spandrels, was let into the head of the frame. This shape continued to be used well into the seventeenth century but even by the end of the sixteenth century, as brick houses began to gain popularity, doorways with square heads had begun to appear. The door frame was often heavily moulded, with the moulding stopped near its foot. The square head frame, although not so heavy as in late Elizabethan times, remained popular until the beginning of the eighteenth century when the main entrance became the focal point of the front elevation. It was moved to the centre to conform with symmetrical Renaissance planning, and the attention it received bears testimony to the importance attached to it.

The doorway was often flanked by pilasters or pedestals supporting a frieze or cornice. In some instances this cornice projected to form a hood, which could be either curved or flat, supported by large carved brackets known as consoles. The brackets sometimes took the form of grotesque corbels, especially where there are traces of Low Country immigrants. A pair can be seen at Hales Place, Tenterden (*93*) and again at a house in Bridge Street, Wye. At Delaware, Edenbridge, can be seen a late seventeenth-century shell-hood on richly carved brackets – a feature rarely to be found in Kent, the most usual arrangement being a flat hood, often accompanied by a simple fanlight over the door. Of early eighteenth-century date is the use of the pediment, both triangular and segmental; later in the second half of the century these pediments would sometimes be broken or open, often with a fanlight over the door. Another feature that gained

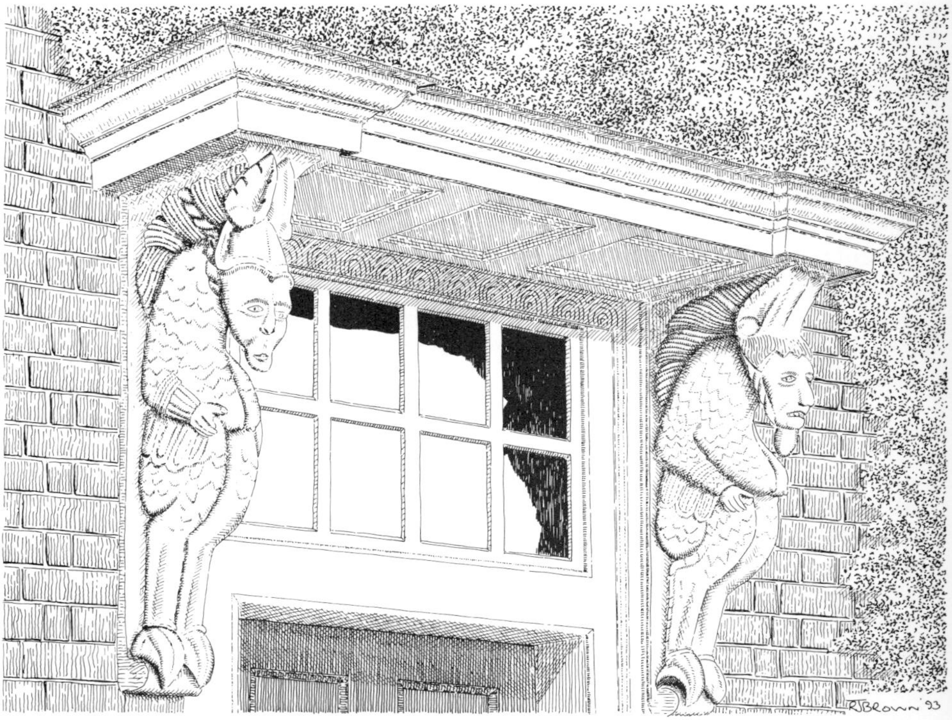

93. Grotesque corbels, Hales Place, Tenterden.

popularity at the end of the eighteenth century was the fluted pilaster, with the entablature over resting on the abacus of the caps of the pilasters.

The battened door, sometimes taking the form of the so-called creased door which had vertical mouldings so designed to create a shadow, remained in common use for the main entrance door until around 1700, when, in conjunction with timber doorcases, the panelled door gained popularity. Transitional forms of panelled doors were used; one method was to construct a battened door in the usual way and then apply to its outer face mitred mouldings to simulate the panels. Another was to form a frame with a middle rail incorporating solid mouldings with vertical boards fixed to the back. By the 1740s the six-panelled door became more or less a standard form of main entrance door. Even so, battened doors continued to be used elsewhere in the house, for instance in the kitchen or other entries of little significance.

Internal doors followed much the same development as external doors but were of lighter construction. Panelled doors were often plain with no moulding around the panel. In late Tudor and Jacobean times internal doors were often panelled to match the wall-panelling which was then becoming popular in the larger houses. Like the external battened door, by the eighteenth century the internal battened door was relegated to doorways of little significance, although the use of panelled doors may in many of the smaller houses have been restricted to the parlour.

WINDOWS

Another significant improvement that occurred during the sixteenth and seventeenth centuries was the increased use of glass in houses. We have already seen that before the time of Henry VIII the use of glass was restricted to royal palaces and a few great houses and it was not until the sixteenth century that its use began to be more widespread in Kent. Cylinder glass continued to be used, as did imported crown glass from the Continent, but in 1567 the Privy Council issued a patent to introduce the foreign glass industry into England, and so for the first time crown glass began to be made in Kent. A Wealden glass-making industry flourished, expanding during the second half of the sixteenth century with the increased demand before somewhat abruptly ceasing in around 1618. This was undoubtedly because of a new process which used coal instead of wood in the manufacture of glass. Glass was therefore supplied from sources where coal was readily available, outside the Weald. It may have come from the West Midlands to which a number of glassmakers emigrated or from the north, where on the Tyne there developed from the early seventeenth century a glass-making industry using chalk from Kent brought as ballast in collier ships returning from London. These developments increased supply and so reduced the price of glass sufficiently to allow its use in quite modest houses. Yet despite this, glass remained an expensive material.

The quarries were still small and like those of the medieval period were set in lead cames to form a light of reasonable size. Diamond-shaped quarries continued to be used, but with the improved quality that was achieved after 1618 they came to be replaced by square ones. In many of the larger houses quarries of a variety of patterns were used and made into lights.

When fixed, leaded lights were stiffened by horizontal saddle-bars set inside the glazing and housed into the mullions and jambs, the leaded lights being secured to them with lead tape or later with wire. When installed in a timber window, these lights were often secured by nailing directly to the mullions of the previously unglazed windows. The lights were therefore narrow, usually around six to eight inches wide. In new buildings, however, the windows were designed to take slightly wider lights, often between eight and ten inches, fitted to the mullions and supported by an intermediate vertical square bar set diagonally.

Opening lights, even in larger houses, were kept to a minimum, and in smaller dwellings, or where the number of open lights was inadequate, ventilation was provided by omitting a quarry and replacing it with a pierced lead plate. Opening lights were made from wrought iron. Those of late sixteenth- and early seventeenth-century date comprised an inner frame often one inch or more wide and in some cases only one-eighth of an inch thick, mounted on hinges in an outer frame usually of a similar section. The saddle-bars were welded outside the plane of the frame for diamond-shaped panes but later, in the seventeenth century, when square panes became popular, these were butt-welded in the plane of the frame and so arranged to correspond with the horizontal line of the lead cames. Latch-plates were elaborately decorated, but towards the end of the seventeenth century became more compact. Stays were not provided to early wrought-iron casements, for since they were narrow and generally less than two feet high, it was not necessary to do so; but later, when the size of windows increased, a stay comprising a twisted square rod was generally provided, engaging with a ring in the base of the tulip-leaf handle. The tulip-leaf handle, a feature throughout most of the seventeenth century, was replaced by a round rod ending in a spiral or boss. At first the leaded lights were secured to the casement with lead tape or wire in the usual way but later they were often riveted to the wrought-iron frame.

Full-height bay windows are a feature of many timber-framed hall houses, and were inserted when the hall was floored over. They were built off a brick or stone base and often dominated the front of the house. In many cases they extended beyond the roof line, finishing with a gable, and in some cases this too had a window to light the attic. Less common was the introduction of an oriel window to the first floor; this occurred at Kite Manor, Monks Horton, which has a large oriel window with a gabled dormer in the roof.

Oriel windows became a feature of the sixteenth century and they had an advantage, particularly in timber-framed buildings, in that they could be placed anywhere in the building – under the projecting overhang of the gable, beneath the eaves or at ground level. An early feature of these windows was the corbelled timber base wrought out of the solid which could be either moulded or carved. Later, towards the end of the sixteenth century, it became customary to support the sill on shaped brackets. The brackets of Honywood, Lenham, are carved with grotesque human figures. Unlike the mullioned windows of the previous centuries these windows were generally divided with a transom.

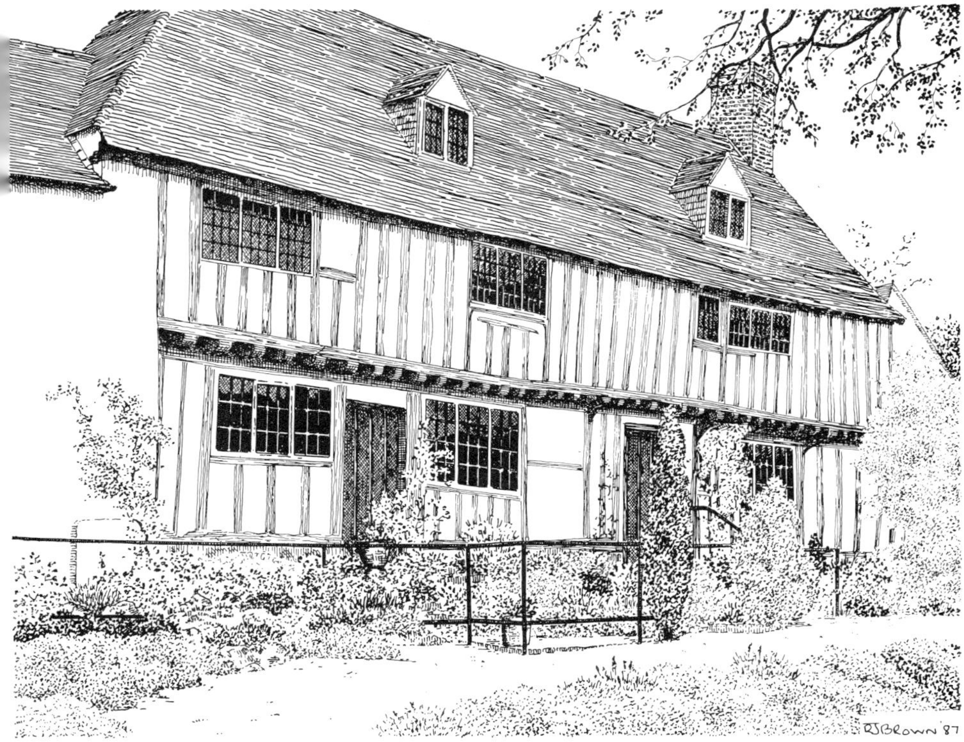

94. Bank House, Little Chart. Built 1480.

The long horizontal ranges of mullioned windows began to give way to these transomed windows. They could be up to six lights wide although they were frequently only two lights wide, divided by a mullion vertically and a transom horizontally to form a cross. Opening lights made from wrought iron continued to be used.

Towards the end of the seventeenth century the vertical sliding sash window made of softwood was first introduced; each sash was divided into small panes by glazing bars which were often rectangular in section and heavy in appearance. At first the upper sashes were fixed; only the lower ones slid in grooves and the window was held open by means of a wedge or hook. It was not in fact until the end of the eighteenth century that the now familiar double-hung, counter-balanced sash replaced this older system. Later, with the general improvement in glass and joinery techniques, the glazing bars began to be reduced in size and were moulded.

The introduction of the sash window coincided with the decline of timber-framed buildings, but in many of these houses built before the

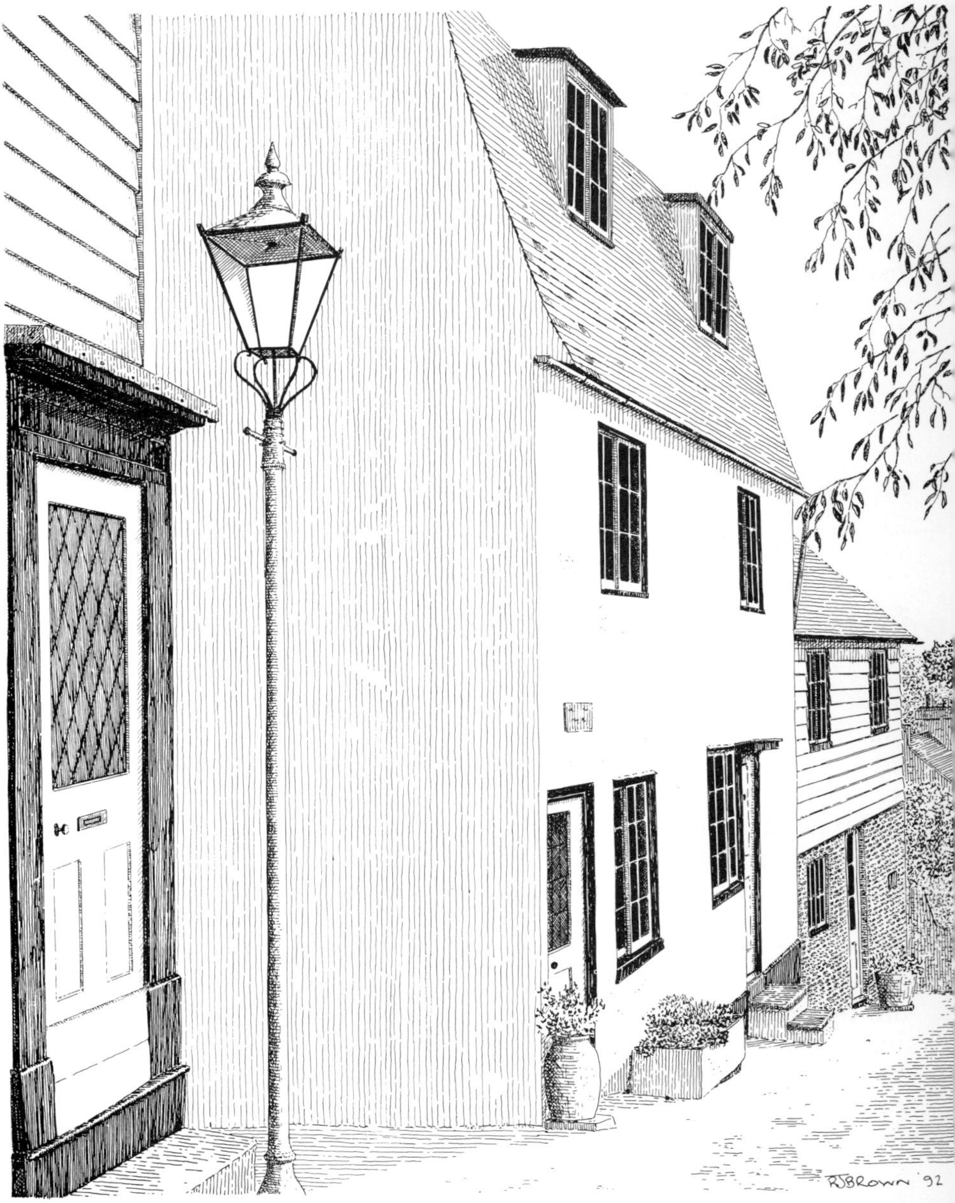

95. Cottages at Six Bell Lane, Sevenoaks.

end of the seventeenth century, sash windows replaced the earlier mullioned ones, and in many cases they may have been the first glazed windows the houses received. It was a comparatively easy process to cut a new opening in the studwork and to block in the existing windows, and it is not uncommon to see these earlier blocked windows alongside later sash ones. The old mullioned windows were often concealed beneath plaster and tiles when the process of modernization took place and in recent years some have been rediscovered beneath the cladding almost intact. In many houses the installation of sash windows was confined to the front and other important elevations, with wrought-iron casements continuing to be used in less conspicuous positions.

Sash windows were not, however, universally adopted. Throughout the county timber casements or wrought-iron casements within timber frames continued to be used in many of the smaller houses where the low ceilings made the tall, vertical sliding sash impracticable (*94*). A cheap alternative to the vertical sliding sash was the horizontal sliding sash, the so-called 'Yorkshire' sliding sash, in which one light was fixed and the other sliding. It was first introduced at the beginning of the eighteenth century and became extremely popular in many small houses and cottages, for it was particularly suited to houses with low ceilings (*95*).

To overcome the difficulty of low ceilings, some houses have vertical sliding sashes with the sashes of unequal height, the upper one smaller than the lower one. This alters the overall proportion of the window from vertical to horizontal. Sometimes this horizontal window shape is obtained by the use of narrow false sashes to either side of the main sliding sash.

INTERNAL WALL DECORATIONS

From about 1600 onwards the use of wall-panelling gained in popularity, finding its way into converted medieval houses as well as new ones where it was often included as a matter of course. This was the normal Elizabethan/Jacobean rectangular panelling and many, even quite small urban houses, were literally lined with it throughout. The characteristic embellishment was linenfold: panels were carved with vertical grooves to resemble folded linen. A feature of some Jacobean panelling was its division into bays with pilasters supporting a rudimentary frieze. With it went the carved overmantel and fireplaces of greatly reduced openings.

Towards the end of the seventeenth century the panelling became plainer, the feature of early Georgian panelling being raised and fielded panels framed with bolection mouldings, with large panels above a dado rail and squat ones of the same width below. By now pine had replaced oak as the principal material for panelling. In the eighteenth century the bolection mouldings were replaced by a simple moulding run out of the solid. Later panelling was often taken up to dado height only.

In the absence of panelling, painted wall-hangings of cloth or canvas, which first appeared in the yeomen's houses during the fifteenth century, continued to gain in popularity in the sixteenth century, as far as can be deduced from the evidence of the many domestic inventories of the period which frequently refer to 'painted cloths' and 'painted hangings' for walls.

From the middle of the sixteenth-century wall-paintings also gained popularity. These early paintings were generally executed in colours in which the pigments were diluted with glue or alternatively mixed with the white of eggs to form a distemper. The earliest of these paintings were pictorial, often of a religious nature. At Cobb's Hall, Aldington, built in the first quarter of the sixteenth century, in one of the upper rooms is a remarkable overmantel in plaster, once coloured, showing in relief the Garden of Eden in three panels. In the centre one is the Tree of Knowledge of Good and Evil; Adam is depicted on the left-hand panel and Eve holding the apple on the right. Twined about the tree is the serpent, and all around are birds and beasts; the face of God looks down from above. This house also contains other wall-paintings ranging from simple repeat designs to very elaborate designs with flowers and birds.

Floral patterns, sometimes in an all-over design but more frequently of a repetitive nature in panels or bands, often within a decorative border, became fairly common. At Watergate House, Fordwich, can be seen a very fine design incorporating cherubs, flowers and fruit. In an upper room at Long House, Strand Street, Sandwich, the walls are decorated with a design of flowers, foliage and at intervals brightly coloured butterflies. Again a house in Bogle Lane, Lynsted, has two rooms with floral decoration, one dated 1587 and the other 1605. Although many of these patterns were repetitive, most repeats appear to have been undertaken free-hand and it was not until the Reformation that stencilling became widely accepted. These decorative paintings were not only restricted to plasterwork but also occurred in those partitions where the timbers were exposed; it was not unusual for the studs to be whitened and the painting carried across.

Although panelling had already become fashionable in the wealthier houses, wall-painting continued in vogue throughout the seventeenth and into the eighteenth century. The floral designs of Tudor times gave way in the seventeenth century to geometrical patterns. Examples from the reign of James I are numerous and are of course especially grand in large houses, such as Ightham Mote, where one can see a very rare example of seventeenth-century decoration which includes Chinese hand-painted wallpaper. Among smaller houses the finest example of these geometric patterns is to be found in Paramour Grange, Ash near Sandwich, where all four walls of an upper room are covered with a geometric pattern surrounded by a frieze incorporating the initials J.R. – James I – and a date 1603, together with various emblems and in Gothic lettering the beatitudes (Matthew 5:3–11): 'Blessed are the Peacemakers …'.

At 11 Harnet Street, Sandwich, when a box-room was being converted into a bathroom a large painted panel was discovered beneath the plaster, with parts of the panel in relief. It showed on the left a Tudor rose and on the right a Scottish thistle, while in the centre was the former owner's monogram and emblems and underneath '1611 anno'. Again in Sandwich in the Old Customs House in Upper Street, over the fireplace is a large coat of arms of James I. The provision of wall-paintings above the fireplace occurs in many houses in the county.

Sometimes the wall-painting represents panelling; good examples can be seen at Lynsted Court, at nearby Calico House, Newnham, and a house at Golden Green, near Tonbridge, which has texts above set in a decorative border.

In some instances timber wall-panelling itself was also decorated. The most famous example can be found at Old Wilsley, Cranbrook, for here one room is panelled with large fielded panelling of late seventeenth-century date and entirely painted. The mouldings are painted in an imitation of grey-green marble; in each panel of the dado is a continuous procession of harriers and on the door the hare they are pursuing. The main panels, including the doors, have representations of spiritual subjects. A small panel in the corner next to the door depicts Mr Weston, the owner, in sporting attire. It appears to be the work of a Flemish or German artist.

Wall-paintings continued throughout the seventeenth century. One example of late seventeenth-century date can be seen at the head of the staircase at Kite Manor, Monks Horton, depicting the house and its garden. The eighteenth century marked the transition between the popularity of wall-paintings and that of wallpaper – the latter came into use towards the end of the century as hand-painted Japanese paper. In smaller houses, before the manufacture of wallpaper in quantity, there was for a time a vogue for stencilled patterns on walls. At Millwall Place, Sandwich, during redecoration a stencilled fleur-de-lis design was found on the walls of the entrance hall. As the house dates from the late eighteenth century it presumably was the original decoration. The designs for eighteenth-century wallpapers were usually block-printed on sheets of rectangular paper which, though small in size, were the largest capable of being produced by the hand methods then employed. Colour was added to the design either by hand-painting or more commonly with the aid of a stencil. It was not until the beginning of the nineteenth century with its improved methods of paper manufacture that the use of wallpapers began to increase and it was only in the 1840s, when an effective machine was produced, that machine-printed papers began to replace hand-painted ones. Such was the demand for this new wall-covering that its mass production was soon established.

Timber-framed Houses

Timber, and by that we mean oak, remained the principal material for the construction of houses for the first hundred years or so of the post-medieval period. Two external features remained popular throughout much of this period. One was jettying and, with the abandonment of the open hall, houses could be constructed with a jetty along the entire front of the building, whether the house type was the older continuous-jettied type or the later lobby-entry or vestibule types. The other external feature was the continuing use of close studding. Examples of these houses are to be found throughout the county although datable instances are indeed rare. The earliest is the forementioned Cobb's Hall, Aldington, built between 1509 and 1526. At Ightham opposite the Town House is another, the left-hand part of which was built in 1555 when according to documentary evidence a Thomas Skynner was fined for building his house so that it encroached on the highway. Another is Standen, Biddenden, which has a date of 1578 on one of the fireplaces. These houses, like their medieval predecessors, still retain their hipped roofs.

Around 1600 houses with gable ends began to appear, made possible by the revised roof design – that is, the abandonment of the crown-post roof in favour of those with side purlins. This change, as we have seen earlier, was primarily to gain additional space in the attic, either for storage or additional rooms. The continuous overhang remained as popular as ever but dated examples are again rare. An early and very fine example is Yew Trees in Scotton Street, Wye (*96*), which has a date of 1605 on a rainwater head set in the east wall; although there is some doubt about its authenticity, the date of construction must be around 1600. Crippenden Manor, Cowden, which has one gable, that to the east part, was built, according to an inscription in the hall, in 1607. Seven years later is the date ascribed to Abbott's Fireside (formerly the Smithie's Arms) at Elham, an extremely long house, the upper storey overhanging its entire length supported on brackets in the form of grotesque caryatids. The deep

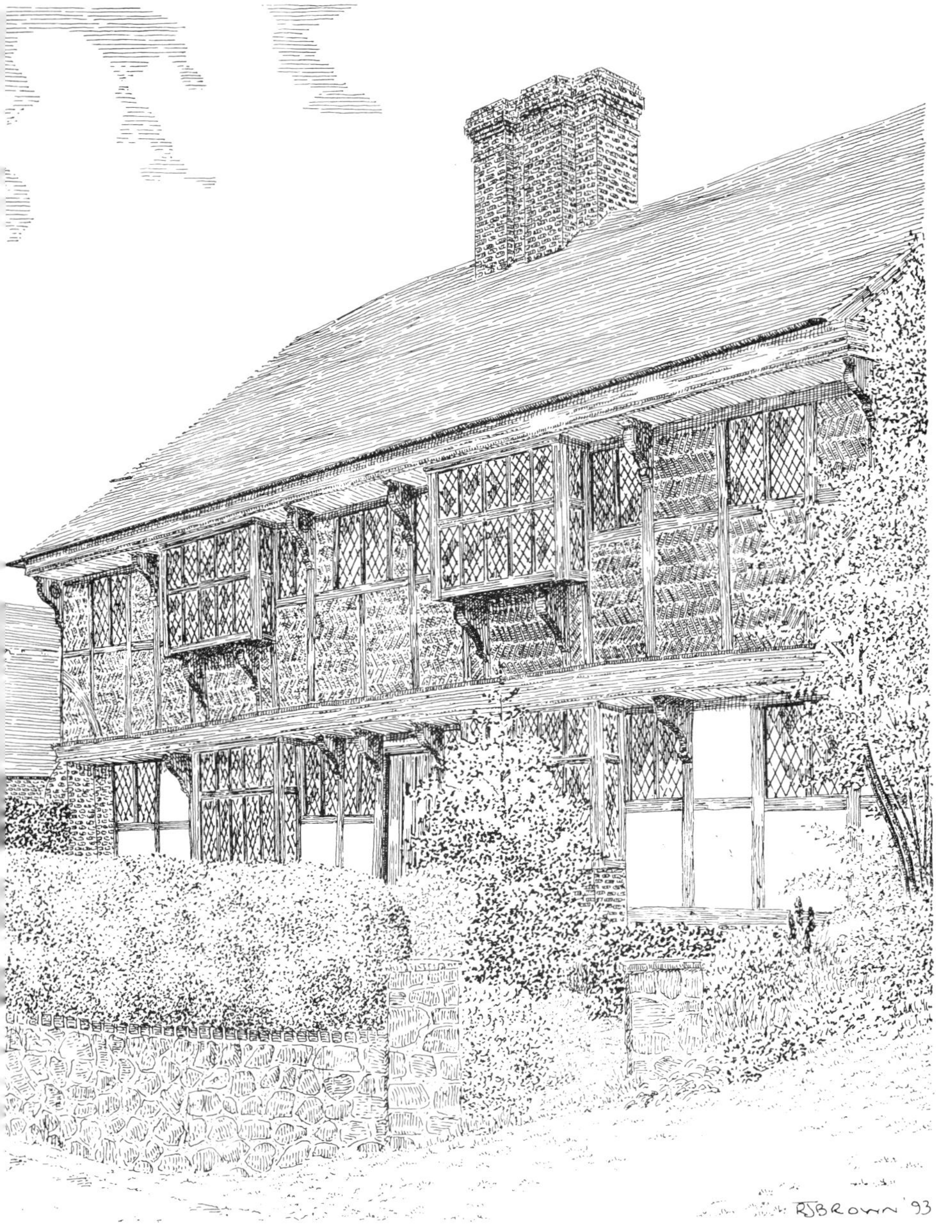

96. Yew Trees, Scotton Street, Wye.

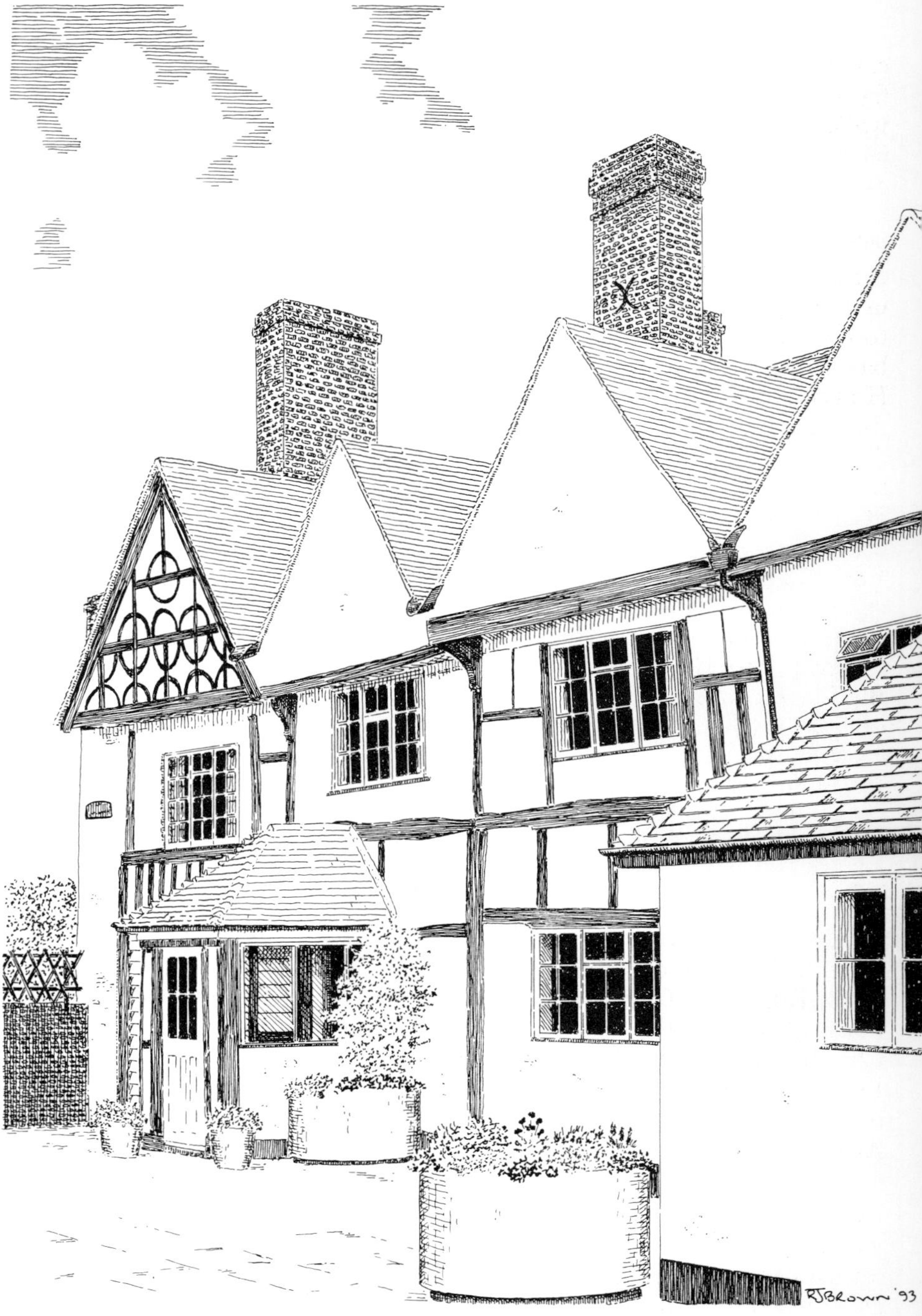

97. Frognal Farmhouse, Teynham, dated 1668, a late example of timber-framing.

eaves are also supported on similar brackets. Grotesque crouching figures can be seen at a group of houses, 134–40 Bridge Street, Wye, while at Yew Trees the brackets are carved supporting not only the jetty but the eaves as well. Dane Chantry, Petham, has a date 1638 carved on one of the studs while Bogle, Lynsted, is dated 1643.

It was not only end gables that became fashionable; secondary gables along the pitch of the roof also became a feature not only in cramped sites in towns but also on many houses in the country. These invariably incorporated a window to light the attic rooms within the roof-space. Sometimes, as at Birchley, Biddenden, they form part of a bay window, or in the case of Godfrey House, Hollingbourne, and Honywood, Lenham, first-floor oriels. More often than not, however, these gables would project from the eaves as at Frognal Farmhouse, Teynham (97). The number of gables at the eaves varied greatly, many houses, such as Birchley, having only one while others such as Honywood had two. Marle Place, Brenchley and Valence House, Sutton Valence, also have two, if one excludes the gabled porch. Foxenden at Seed to the south-west of Newnham has three; the central, most heavily timbered one has a date of 1604. Hawkhurst Place also has three symmetrical gables, each with an oriel beneath. Frognal Farmhouse has no less than four while Old Cloth Hall, Biddenden, has six; but here the structure is not of one build and is obviously a composite construction of sixteenth- and seventeenth-century date, the gabled east end dated 1672 being the final addition. It was built for clothworkers who occupied it as workshops.

Most but not all of these houses with secondary gables have a continuous jetty: Godfrey House has, so have Honywood and Hawkhurst Place, but Valence Place has not and neither has Marle Place or Frognal Farmhouse. These houses with secondary gables first appeared towards the end of the sixteenth century, the earliest dated example being Godfrey House of 1587, followed by Valence House of 1598, Rumwood Court, Langley, of 1599, Foxenden of 1604, Marle Place of 1619, Honywood of 1621, Birchley of 1632, Old House, Chiddingstone, of 1637, Grovehurst, Horsmonden, of 1641 and Frognal Farmhouse which is dated 1668 – a late date for a new timber-framed house. Even later is a town house in North Street, Ashford, which has a date of 1671 on a gable.

These gables are often jettied. In the case of end gables these might be jettied to first-floor level and again to roof level, especially if this was facing the road. However, in most cases the gables would be jettied only at eaves level and the tie-beam often moulded or carved, as, for instance, on the cross-wing of the Dragon House, Smarden, which has a twice-projecting gable to the road, the upper overhang decorated with a row of carved dragons. The gable here is half-hipped.

These overhangs are often supported on consoles or brackets not infrequently carved either with some form of strapwork or occasionally with grotesque figures.

On a timber-framed building the gables were often provided with bargeboards to protect the exposed ends of the roof timbers as well as to afford some protection for the walls below. The carpenter therefore had an additional opportunity to display his skills and the bargeboards were often elaborately carved, shaped and pierced, forming an important part of the decorative treatment of the building. The earliest surviving examples belong to the fifteenth century; those which were foiled, possibly with carved spandrels and often cusped in the Gothic tradition, are generally of pre-Reformation date; later they usually had straighter sides and were simply moulded or moulded and carved. Towards the end of the sixteenth century running designs based on the vine were largely replaced by scroll-work, strapwork, dentils, the guilloche pattern and other Renaissance forms of decoration. The pendant, both carved and moulded and very occasionally pierced, was frequently used in the Elizabethan and Jacobean period, usually at the apex but sometimes at the eaves as well. Finials are somewhat rare and are generally replacements of earlier ones like those at Marle Place, Brenchley; the original ones were pierced. In some cases the finials have been replaced with pendants. This can be seen at the Picture House, Pounds Bridge, Penshurst, where in 1829, according to William Twopeny's drawing, the house had moulded and carved finials; they have now been replaced with pendants. The use of decorative bargeboards declined during the seventeenth century when timber-framed houses began to be clad with other materials, and the distance between wall and bargeboard, formerly around eight to ten inches, diminished until in the eighteenth century the bargeboard was fixed flush to the wall, the former overhang at the gable being no longer required to protect the wall beneath.

Because of their vulnerable nature many bargeboards have now been lost but there still survive many excellent examples. The Old Canonry, Wingham, said to have been one of three houses in the village occupied by the canons of Wingham College, has a very elaborate example. Another is to be seen at Honywood, Lenham.

Although close studding still remained the predominant form of construction for Elizabethan and Jacobean houses ornamental framing, usually associated with the West and North, in particular Shropshire and Cheshire, began to make small intrusions. This ornamental framing was, from the evidence of the Streatfeild Collection reproduced in Kenneth Gravett's *Timber and Brick Building in Kent*, much more widespread than appears today. The use of ornamental framing was almost entirely restricted to curved braces to form what one would describe as hollow-sided lozenges. The use of straight diagonal braces within square framing, a common feature in Shropshire and Cheshire, is rare in the county but one example, that of the post office at Milton Regis, still survives. This house, of early seventeenth-century date, would be more at home in one of the towns of Shropshire, for instance Ludlow, than in Kent. Maintaining ornamental curved bracing was obviously difficult and even those examples that remain today contain a high proportion of replacement timber. Today Waystrode Manor, Cowden, formerly Wood Farm, shows none of the ornamental framing which still remained when Howard Gaye drew it from a photograph dated 1867. The gable which displays the ornamental framing at Taylor House, Edenbridge, has also disappeared, pulled down together with the wagon entrance before 1895, although the major part of the old house still remains. The house was originally built for Sir William Taylor, Lord Mayor of London in 1469. The finest example to be found in the Streatfeild Collection is at Bore Place, Chiddingstone, but this was removed by Aymer Vallance and replaced by a classical brick façade. Aymer Vallance used this gable while constructing the north wing of Stoneacre, Otham, when he restored and enlarged the former semi-derelict Wealden house in 1920. The house was originally larger than most Wealden houses, the great hall being flanked by cross-wings running at right angles to it. The one to the south has a gable and overhanging storey, while the one to the north was remodelled around 1550. The hall was divided at about the same date but Mr Vallance restored it to its original state, revealing once again its great open roof with its massive crown-post and collar purlin. From these timbers the new wing was added to the south. The property was given to the National Trust in 1928 and is open to the public.

The house that today possesses the most ornate framing is Standen, Biddenden (*98*), which when sketched by Howard Gaye from a photograph taken in 1867 was partially tile-hung, which obviously helped to preserve it. The upper part is decorated with curved braces making the typical hollow-sided lozenges in panels, some wide and some narrow. Again at Frognal Farmhouse, Teynham, one of the gables today shows arches and squares forming a geometrical pattern; the façade was plastered when drawn by Howard Gaye, probably in the late 1870s.

Another fine example is at Wickens Manor, Charing (*99*), which amongst the close studding has a band of square framing filled with hollow-sided lozenges. The porch has not curved braces but straight ones forming diamonds, which are probably replacements of earlier framing. To either side of the entrance, filling the gap between the

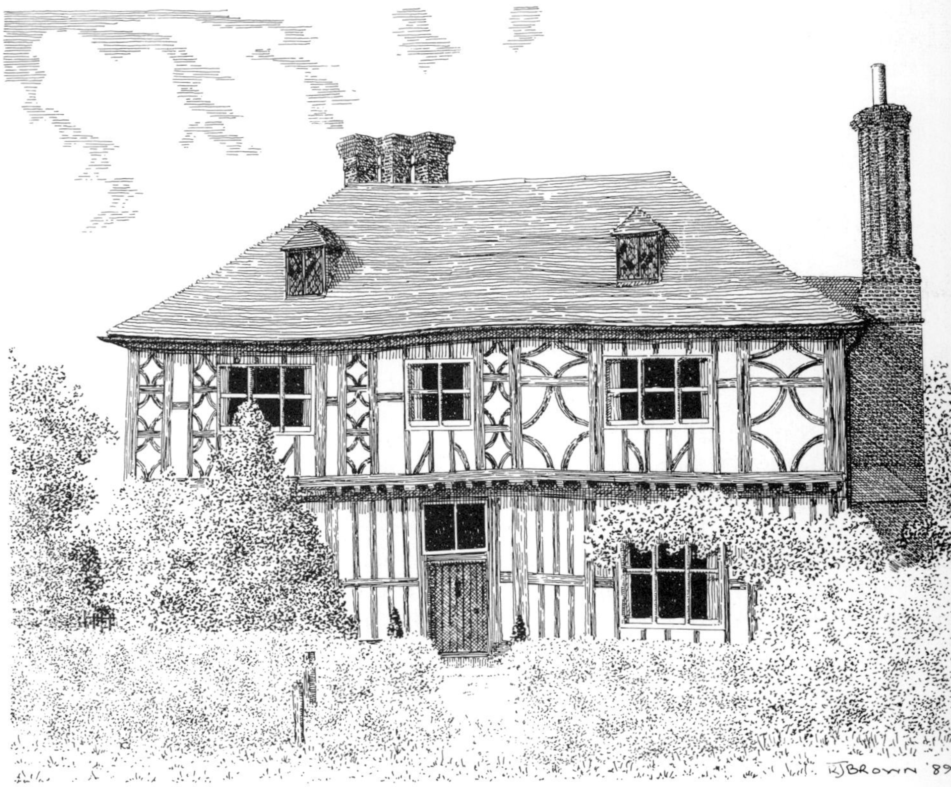

98. Standen, Biddenden.

frame and the corner posts, are a series of diagonal braces. The house appears to be from the outside late Elizabethan or early Jacobean but is the result of at least four rebuilding or modernization phases up until the seventeenth century, with additional work in the eighteenth century to the north-east end and a mid-nineteenth-century flint and brick wall to the front by the north-east end. The earliest parts of the house are at the north-east end, which is in all probability of late fifteenth-century date. The footings and some of the timbers of the central part of the house, which is now the dining-room, appear to be the remains of the open hall of an earlier hall house. At the north-east end there is above and slightly to one side of the present brick fireplace an earlier timber-and-daub smoke bay. It is thought that this smoke bay was a mid-sixteenth-century insertion within the fifteenth-century house, the centre of which was then largely rebuilt in the late sixteenth century to form the continuous-jettied house seen today. It would

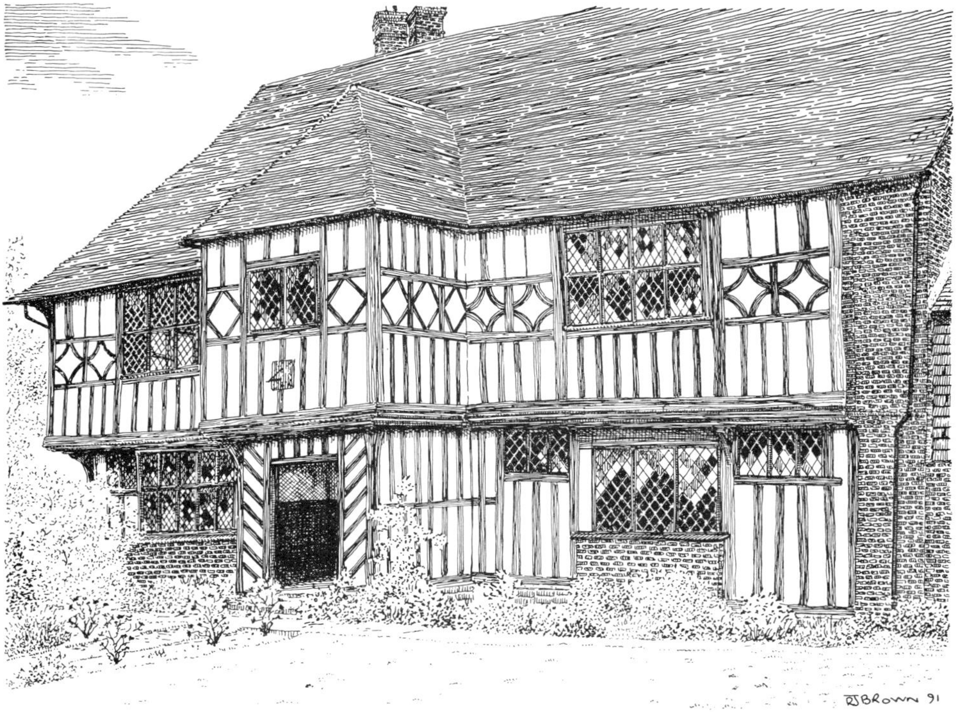

99. Wickens Manor, Charing.

have been around this time that the two-storey porch was added. The house was completed with an outshut which has now largely disappeared; it once extended the length of most of the rear and was covered by a catslide roof. The rear wing was not constructed until 1974 from an earlier eighteenth-century farm building. Wickens remained in the Brent family of Charing and then through marriage in the Dering family for over six hundred years before being sold in 1926.

An early example of curved braces forming hollow-sided lozenges is to be found on Queen Down Warren, Hartlip, built, it is thought, in 1566, the date over the door, although this date is not original. On a fireplace within the house are the initials of the owner of the house between 1558 and 1573. An interesting fact about the house is that it was moved in 1841 to its present position from a site nearer the village.

Porches are a feature of many Elizabethan and Jacobean timber-framed houses. They are nearly always of two storeys (*100*), for single-storey porches on timber-framed buildings are rare. The finest example is perhaps Bexon Manor, Bredgar, possibly built in

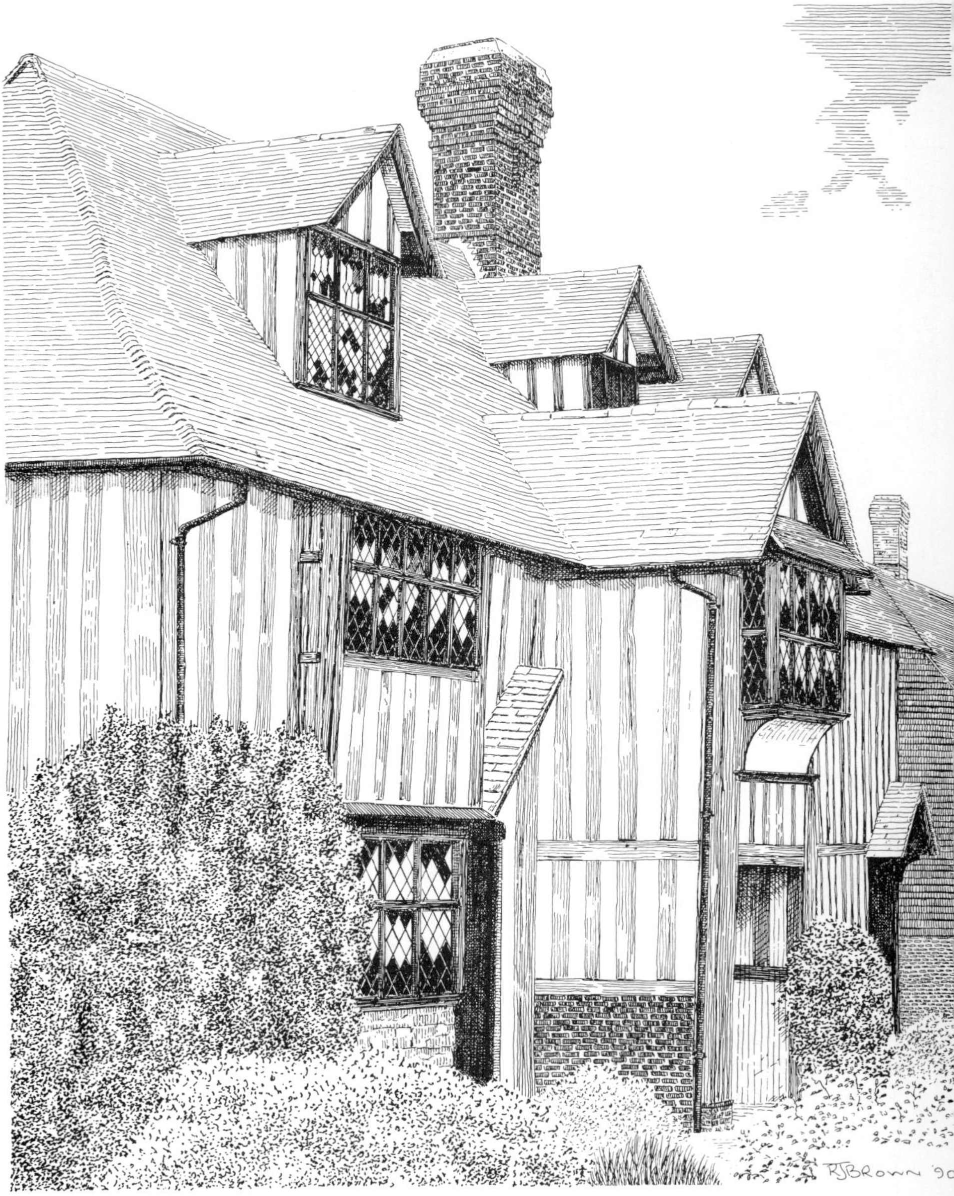

100. The Old Workhouse, Brenchley. Early sixteenth-century house with porch on posts with oriel window.

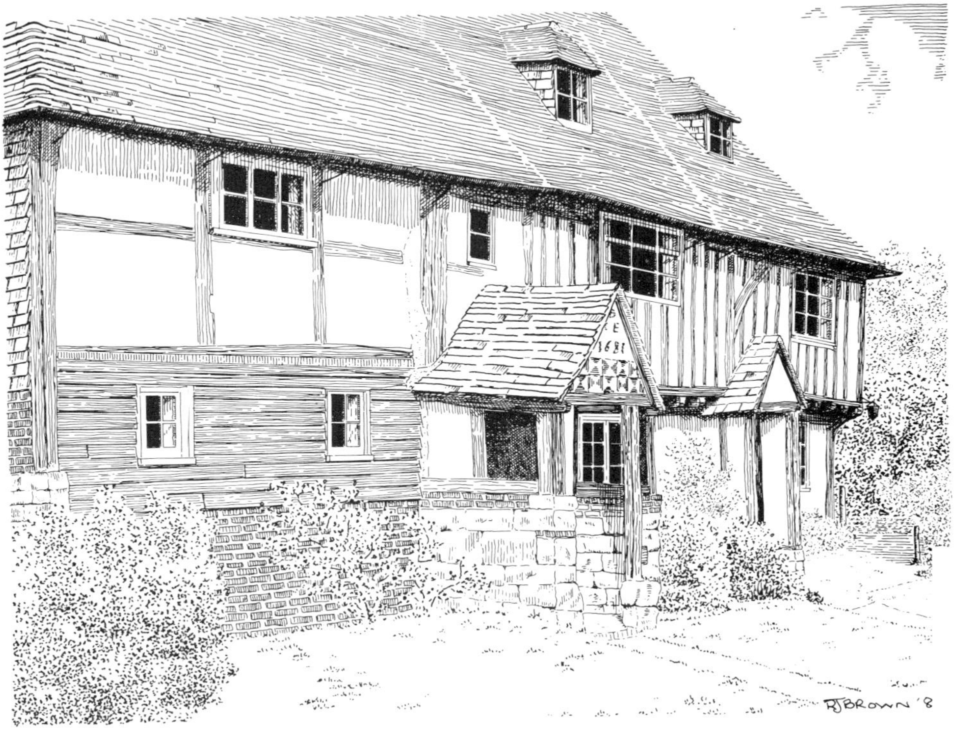

101. Four Wents Cottages.

1617: this is the date on the central gable, and it is probably when the floor was inserted into the open hall. At Four Wents Cottages, near Wingham (*101*) the single-storey porch carries the date 1681. On occasions one finds three-storey porches such as at Godfrey House, Hollingbourne, a house built in 1587, the third storey being formed in the main roof. This use of the roof-space to form a third storey can be seen elsewhere, for instance at Marle Place, Brenchley, and also at Rumwood Court, Langley. Here the third storey appears to be a later insertion, for a drawing by William Twopeny dated 1822 shows no such window and so it probably dates from 1896 when the wing to the west of the house was added.

These porches first appeared at the end of the sixteenth century and were frequently the first part of the house to exhibit the new Renaissance ornamentation and detail. The reason for the introduction is not clear, but certainly they would have suggested a high social status for the owner; certainly the main practical reason was to reduce the draught from the main doorway, consequently increasing the comfort of the inhabitants of the house. Porches of two or three storeys could also provide additional accommodation. They rarely had doors and those that have today are modern and generally inappropriate, as can be seen at Marle Place. It was not uncommon for the porches to have open balustraded sides to the ground floor which would undoubtedly hinder their effectiveness in reducing draughts. These open balustraded porches can be seen at Marle Place, which carried the date 1619 on the porch gable, at Valence House, Sutton Valence, and on the single-storey porch at Bexon Manor, Bredgar. At Porch House, Chiddingstone, a former Wealden house, the upper storey is carried on two posts. Most two- and three-storey porches are jettied on all three sides of each floor level, but the one at Valence House is jettied to the front only, while the three-storey porch at Godfrey House is jettied to the front at the first floor but at the second floor on all three sides, while the gable has a further jetty. Most of these porches have gabled roofs but a few are hipped; the most striking are probably at Wickens Manor, and at Eastling Manor, Eastling, which according to Edward Hasted was rebuilt in 1616.

The influence that brickwork was beginning to have on timber-framed buildings increased. Its use in the construction of chimney stacks was well established by the sixteenth century and in the seventeenth century, with the ever-increasing popularity of this material, timber-framed houses with brick gables began to appear. Abbotts Fireplace, Elham, is one example where one of the end gables, that to the south, was rebuilt and is a fine example of late seventeenth-century brickwork. Bogle, Lynsted, is another house, built in 1643, with the gabled end walls built entirely of brick.

We have seen earlier that during the sixteenth century the old medieval open-hall houses were modernized with the insertion of an upper floor and chimney into the former open hall. This modernization and improvement of old timber-framed houses continued throughout the seventeenth century and into the eighteenth. Now, however, it was not so much concerned with the upgrading of the accommodation, although this continued, but with the outward appearance of the house.

Clearly the close-studded framework and the ornamental timber-work of the Elizabethan and Jacobean periods were intended to be seen and yet, in common with later timber-framing, they are today frequently hidden from view by some form of cladding. The reason for this change from exposed timbers to one in which the timbers were covered was two-fold – partly to add greater comfort for the inhabitants by making the building draught- and weatherproof, and partly, in the name of fashion, to provide a 'face-lift' in an attempt to match the plainer brick and stone façades of the Georgian period without the expense of rebuilding.

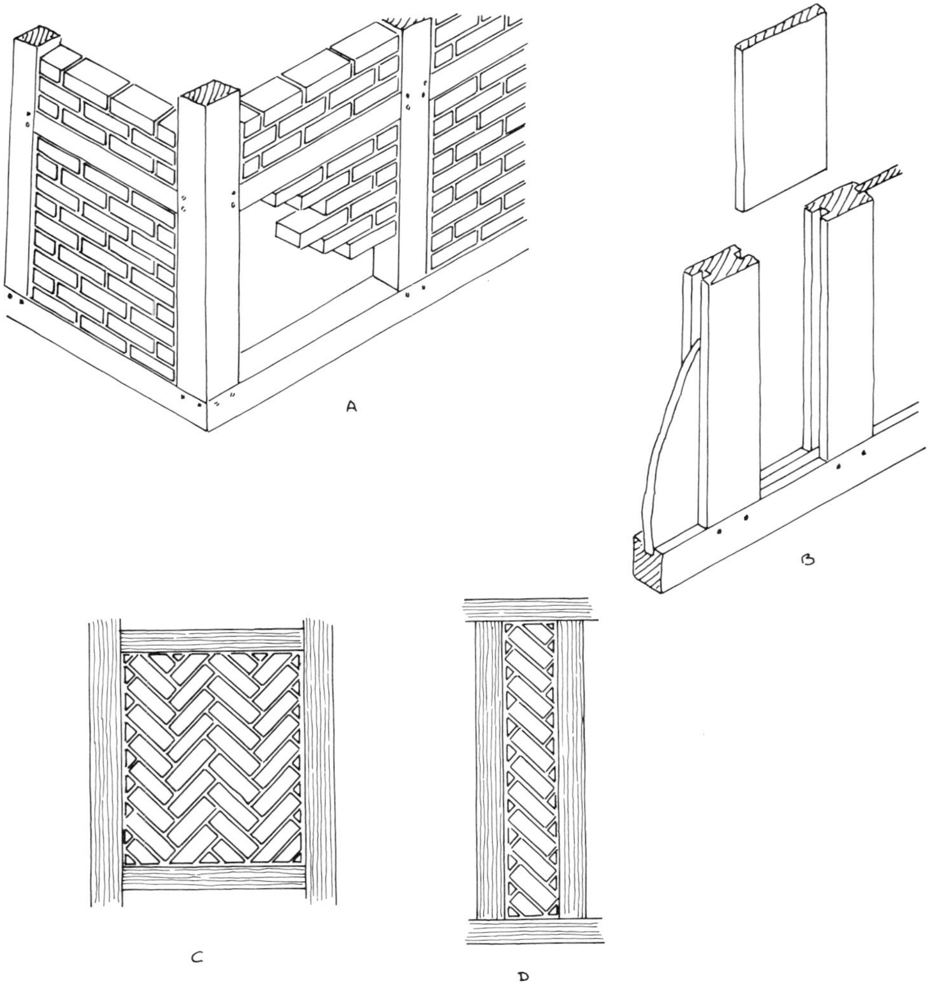

102. Brick-nogging and boarded infilling. A. brick nogging to open panels; B. infilling with vertical boards; C. brick herringbone pattern; D. brick nogging to closely spaced studs.

Formerly the infilling between the studs was wattle-and-daub but with the constant movement of the frame and the shrinking of the daub not only damp but also draughts could get in. Although the oak studwork could withstand the dampness, the infilling made of hazel would finally decay and so the panels needed to be replaced. As the production of bricks increased it became fashionable to replace the old panels with brickwork, a process known as brick-nogging (*102*). This

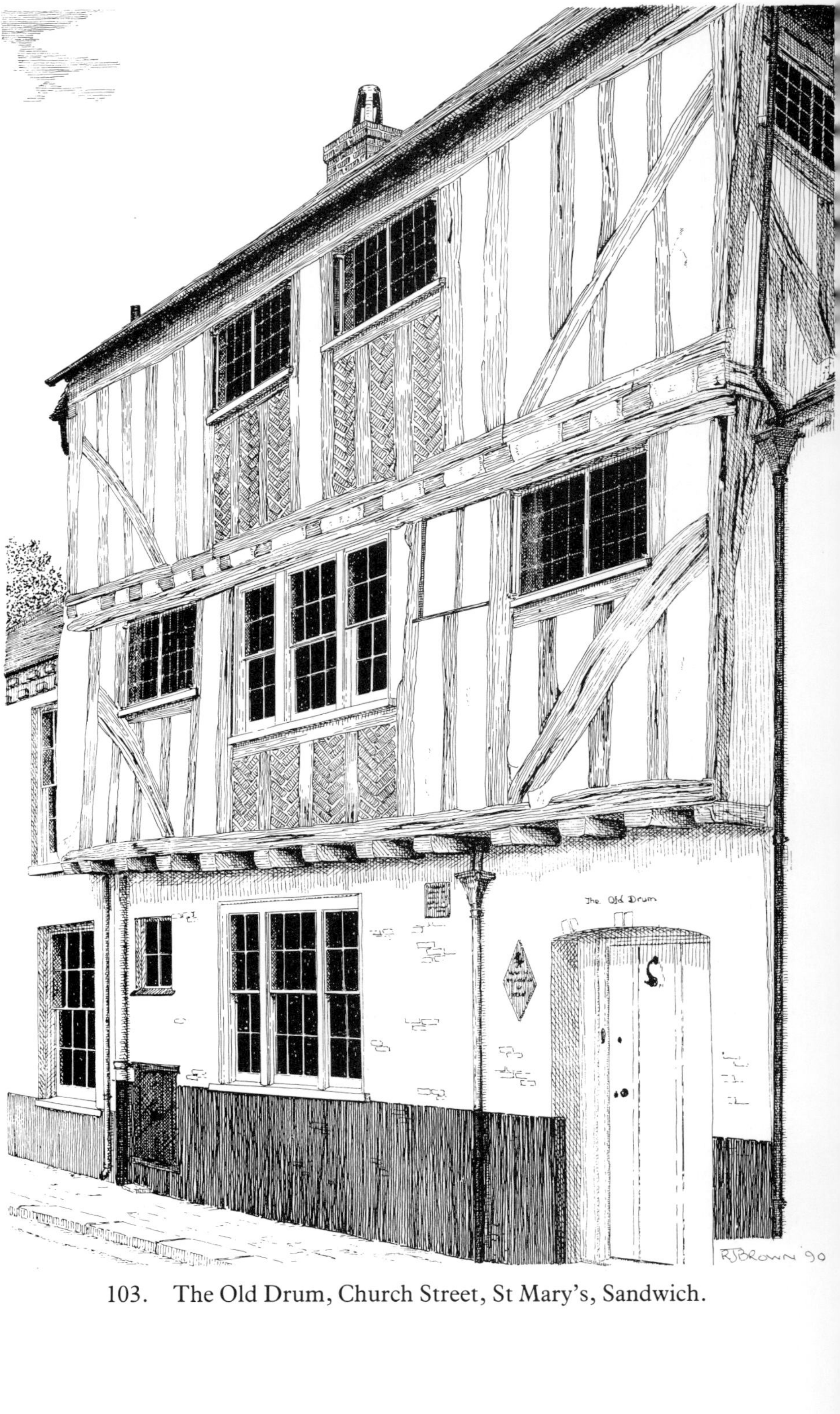

103. The Old Drum, Church Street, St Mary's, Sandwich.

first appeared during the latter part of the sixteenth century and was sometimes carried out in a piecemeal fashion, the panels between the studs being replaced as and when necessary. Why this transition took place is difficult to explain, for most old bricks are more porous than good plastered daub, so dampness tended to be encouraged, while the increased weight of brickwork caused structural problems. The bricks were generally laid in stretcher bond but herringbone and basket-weave and other patterns were incorporated within the same building. At 28–32 Church Street, St Mary's, Sandwich, no fewer than six different patterns are displayed. In some instances it appears that houses were built with brick-nogging infilling from the outset, a common feature in Hampshire but less so in Kent. One excellent example is Yew Trees, Wye, with bands of diagonal bricks rather than a true herringbone pattern. Another house clearly originally built with brick-nogging is Bogle, Lynsted, a large house with a symmetrical timbered front. Herringbone brick-nogging was particularly suitable for close-spaced studs, the bricks having a tendency to be forced out against the timber. This can be found on Pierce House, Charing and again on the Old Drum in Church Street, St Mary's, Sandwich (*103*). Brick-nogging in the county is for the most part painted white. This is especially true of many town houses to be seen, for instance, in Sandwich and Faversham.

Although the replacement of the old wattle-and-daub infilling with brick-nogging was an improvement it was still not completely satisfactory. As well as the structural problems already mentioned there was also the difficulty of providing a suitable joint between the frame and the rigid panel. The house could therefore remain damp and draughty. To overcome these problems the houses were clad. One method was the plastering of the external face, a technique which first appeared in Kent in the second half of the sixteenth century (*104*). The old wattle-and-daub often remained, the external face being only covered with closely spaced riven oak laths nailed to the face of the studs, and subsequently plastered over, leaving the timbers exposed on the inner face. During the seventeenth century, with the improved quality of lime plaster and the availability of sawn laths, the rendering of timber buildings gained popularity so that by the end of the seventeenth and throughout the eighteenth century it was common practice.

Although this was the principal method of cladding in East Anglia because there was a plentiful supply of good lime and sand, it was also used fairly often in Kent. It was particularly popular in many towns – Faversham, Canterbury and Sandwich – where many of the timber-framed houses are rendered. It is also to be found in many isolated timber-framed houses; Charlton Court Farm, on the road to

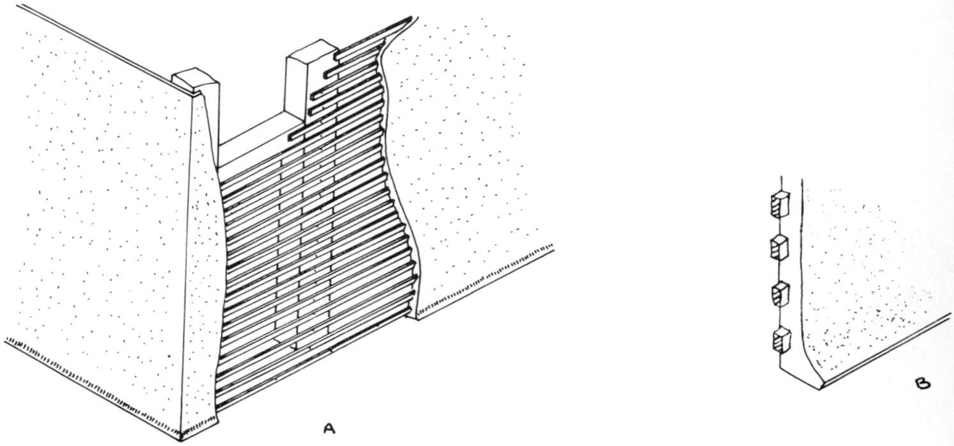

104. External plastering. A. isometric view of plaster and riven timber laths; B. detail of plaster and lath showing bellmouth.

Hearnden, is a fine example of a Wealden house that is plastered over. Close by at Chartway Street is Blue House, another large Wealden house which has received the same treatment. One of the finest Wealden houses to be rendered is Old Wilsley at Wilsley Green, Cranbrook, a house formed of two parallel half-timbered ranges, joined by a modern wing. The main range facing the road was, it seems, a large fifteenth-century Wealden house to which large gables have been added; all its timbers are hidden by a 'warm ochre rendering' as John Newman says.

Not all external rendering was plain, for such was the quality of old lime-haired plaster that it was possible to form ornamental enrichments to the face of the plaster, a process known as pargeting. Two forms were employed, incised or inscribed work in which patterns were impressed into the surface of the wet plaster, and the more ornate, but less common, raised or relief work, which required considerable skill.

Pargeting was widely used in eastern England but is found less often in Kent than in other counties. Much original work has been lost, undoubtedly because of the nature of the material and the difficulty in making satisfactory repairs. The plaster was sometimes incised to imitate rusticated stone, the finest example in the county being Sir John Boys' House, Canterbury (*105*). This attempt to imitate stone is again to be found in the town on Queen Elizabeth's Guest Chamber in the High Street. From Howard Gaye's drawing reproduced in Kenneth Gravett's book *Timber and Brick Building in Kent*, Frognal

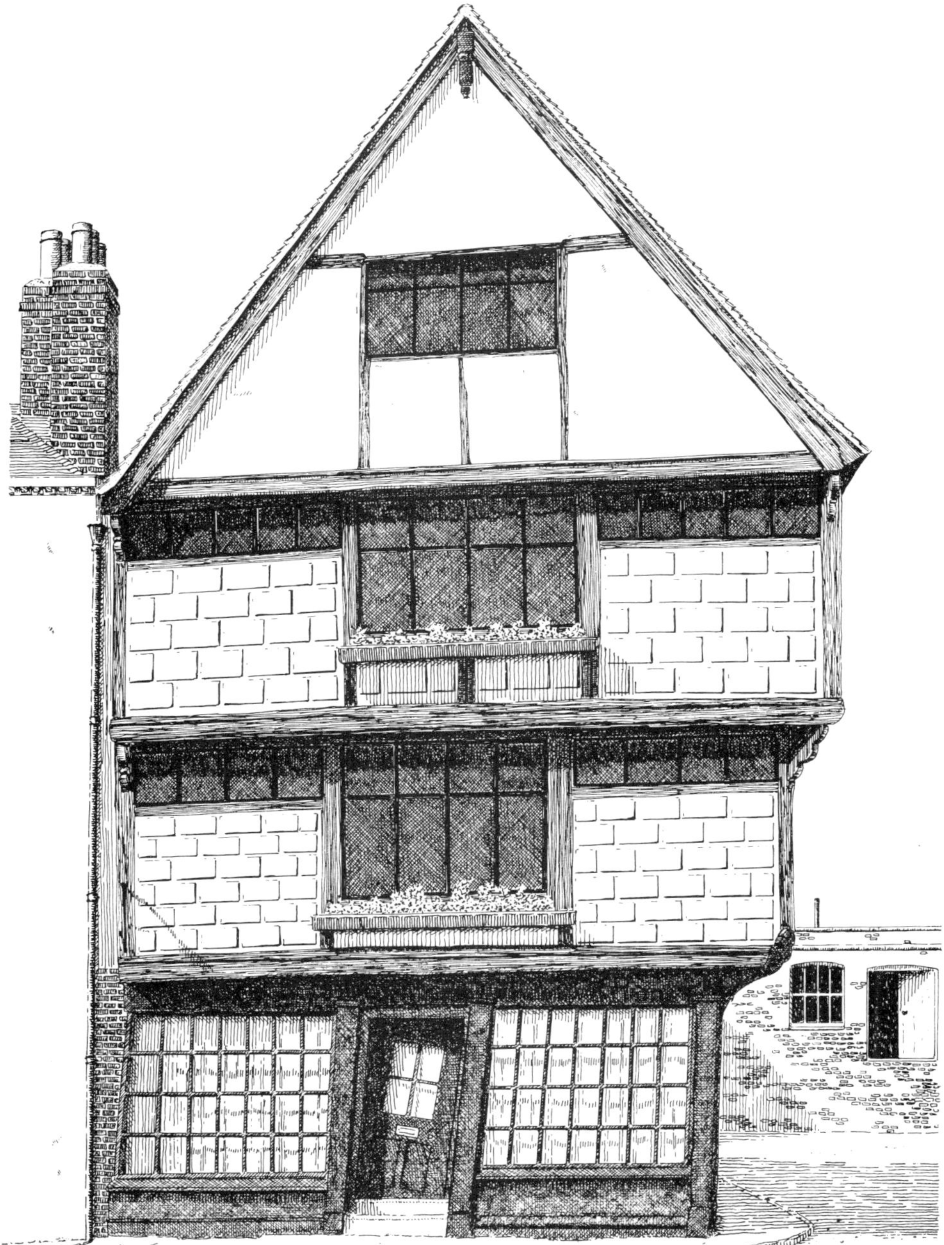

105. Sir John Boys' House, Canterbury.

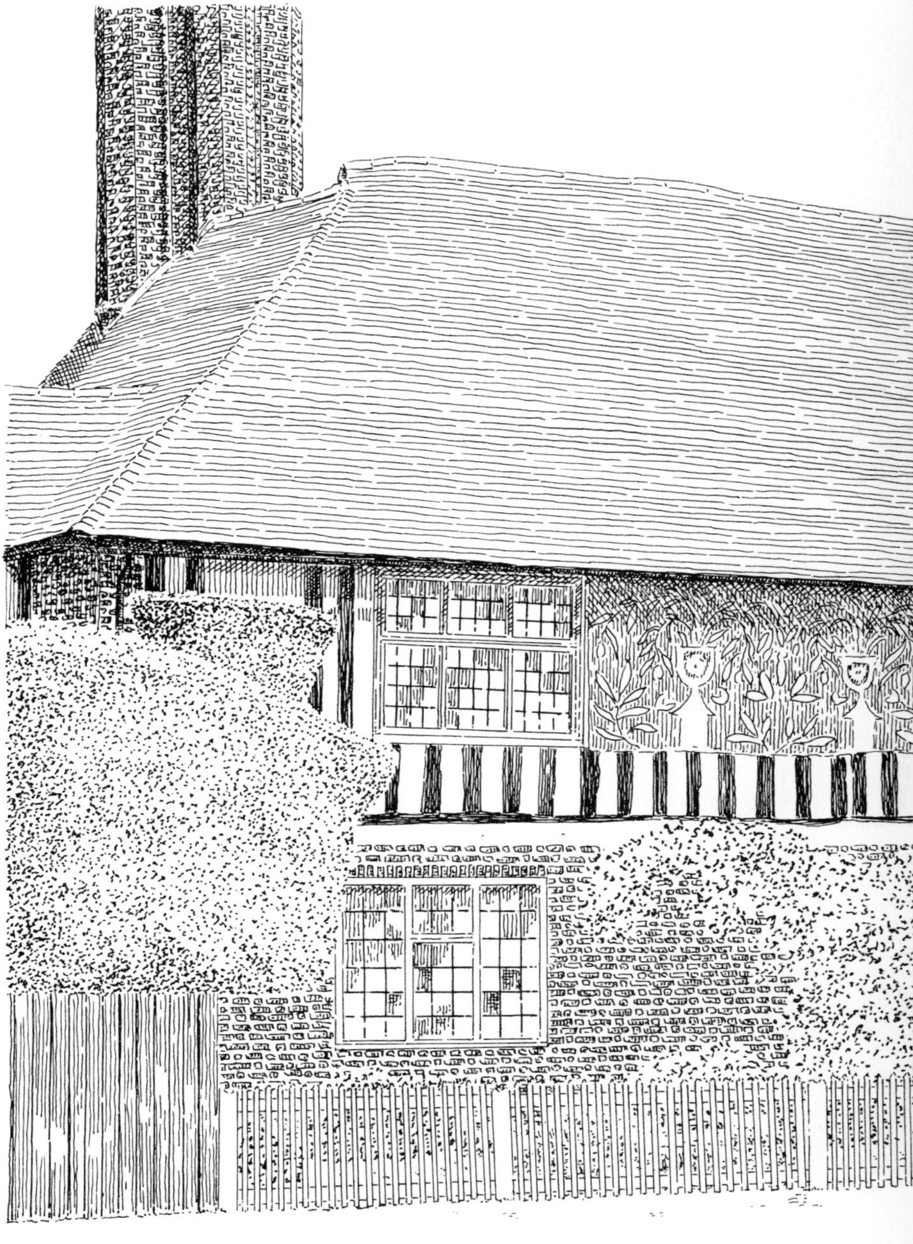

106. Calico House, Newnham.

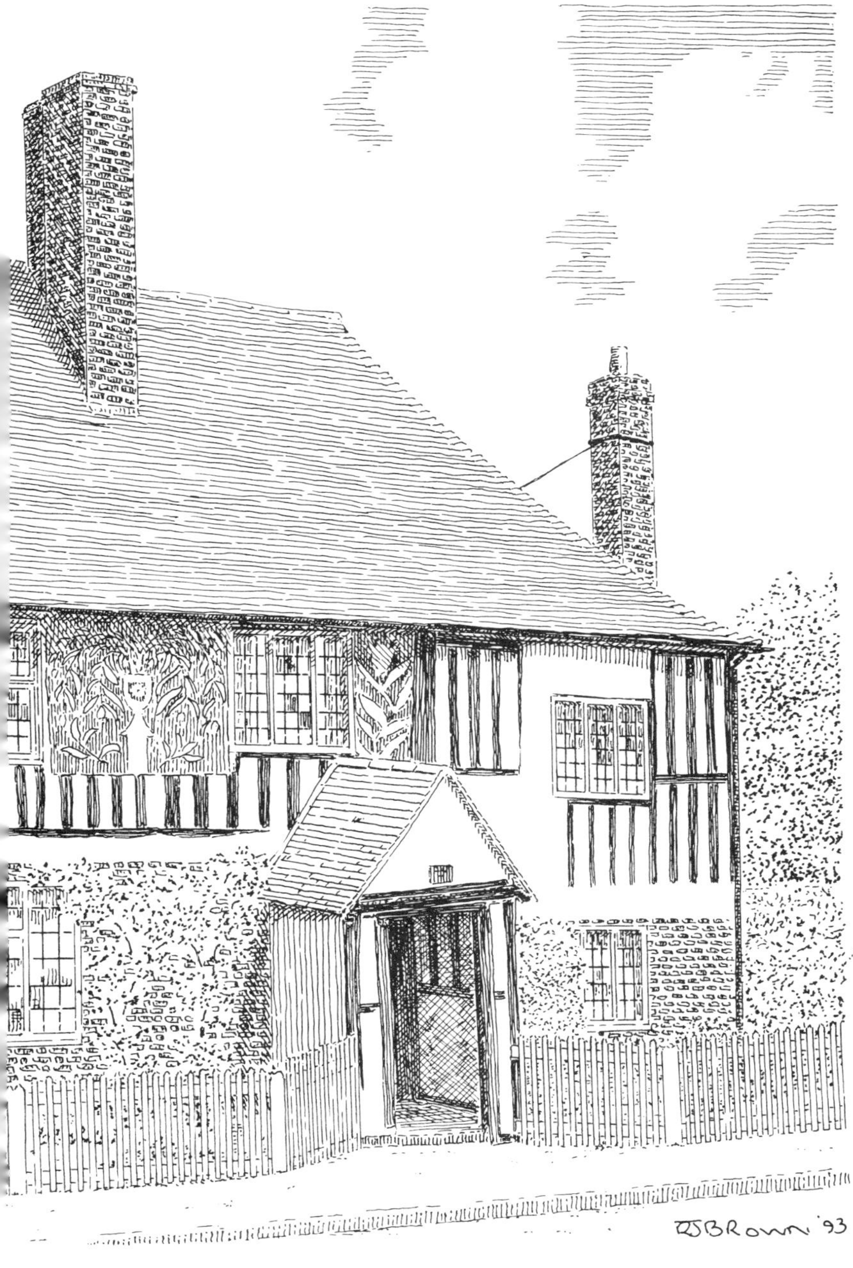

Farmhouse, Teynham, had this type of rendering to the upper storey but today little remains. This house in fact has two fronts, for fifty years or so after the original house of 1668 was built a second half was constructed in brick to form a double-pile house. This latter part of the house has a classic front of two storeys and five bays, and a fine doorcase with an open scrolly pediment.

Raised pargeting became fashionable in the seventeenth century and because of its expense is to be found mainly in towns. One of the earliest, date 1611, and certainly the finest example, is to be found in Bank Street, Maidstone, showing the Royal Arms and Prince of Wales feathers. Also in Maidstone in Week Street, no. 55 displays another good example. Dated 1680, it is less ambitious than that at Bank Street, comprising swags between vases on the first floor with ovals separated with pilasters above. Of similar date, 1697, is the pargeting in the form of large vegetable scrolls found on 121 West Street, Faversham. At Canterbury a good example, now highly coloured, is to be found on the walls of Queen Elizabeth's Guest Chamber. Pargeting could also be very simple as can be seen on one of the houses opposite the churchyard at Chiddingstone which has a date of 1697 in the pargeting.

This tradition of covering a house with bold, eye-catching designs was carried on into the eighteenth century. At Calico House, Newnham (*106*), between the timbers the plaster has been painted with rust-coloured patterns of leaves flowing from vases. On the east wall the pattern includes the date 1710. Much of the rendering and painting is obviously a replacement of earlier work.

More common in Kent as a cladding material to keep the weather at bay is tile-hanging. First appearing towards the end of the seventeenth century tiles were, as previously stated, fixed by means of pegs hung on laths nailed to the face of the frame. Generally their use was restricted to the upper storeys and in many cases the opportunity was taken to underbuild the jetty with brick, thus gaining some extra space for the ground-floor rooms. This type of modernization is to be seen throughout the county especially in the Weald, so that the external appearance gives no indication of the age of the building behind.

Often the tile-hanging is restricted to one or more elevations, as at Great Job's Cross Farm, Rolvenden (*107*), where the front is completely covered, with both upper halves of the gable walls also tiled. In many cases only one gable end is tile-hung as at the Old Cloth Hall, Smarden, or only the gable itself as at Westenhanger, Horsmonden, perhaps to give protection to the end facing the prevailing winds. In some cases the tiles could cover almost the entire house as at Marle Place, Brenchley, where the house is now clad, except for part of the porch, with three rows of plain tiles, alternating with two rows of ornamental tiles. The tiling here is probably Victorian, for in William Twopeny's drawing of Marle Place in 1822 the front elevation was then rendered with pargeting in the form of square geometrical patterns, although in some disrepair, to the gables. The moulded plastered date of 1619 over the initials T.S. on the porch gable has sadly also gone.

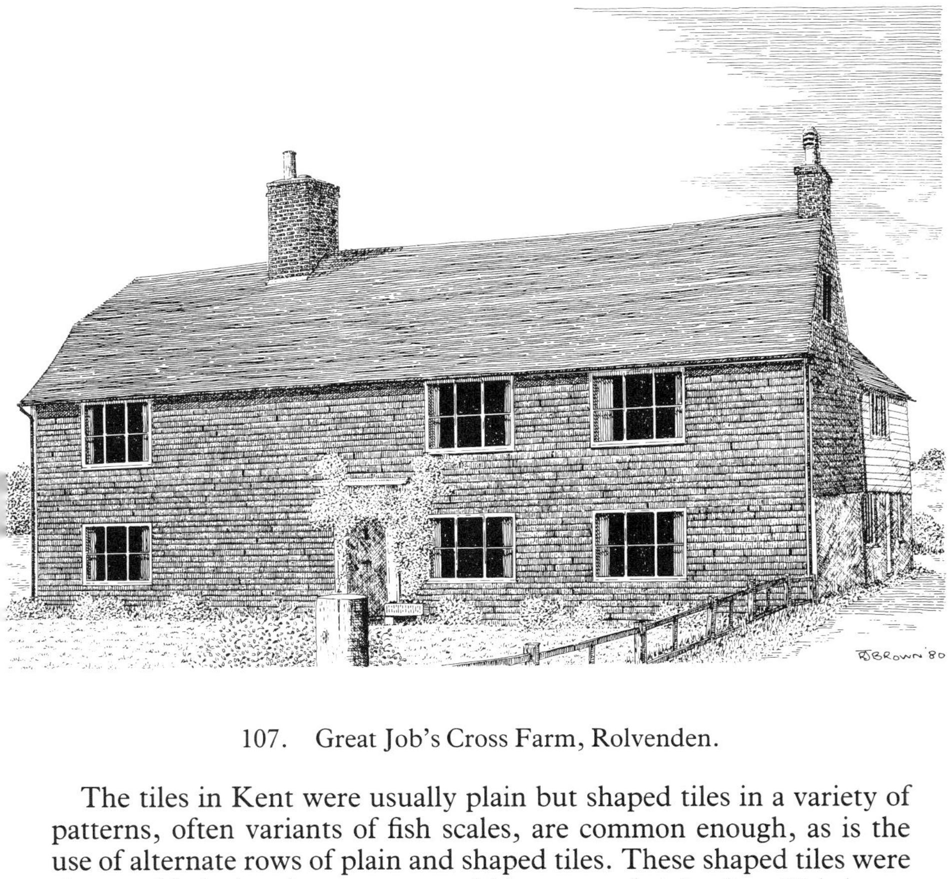

107. Great Job's Cross Farm, Rolvenden.

The tiles in Kent were usually plain but shaped tiles in a variety of patterns, often variants of fish scales, are common enough, as is the use of alternate rows of plain and shaped tiles. These shaped tiles were also used in isolated patterns set within a row of plain tiles. This is not all that common in Kent but can be seen for instance on a house at Old East Side, Hamstreet, where the shaped tiles are set in triangular-shaped panels. At Leigh Green Farmhouse, Tenterden (*108*), the panels are square between the windows with a band of ornamental tiles beneath. This farmhouse is typical of many hundreds in Kent, for behind the brick and tile façade is an old timber-framed building probably dating from the sixteenth century.

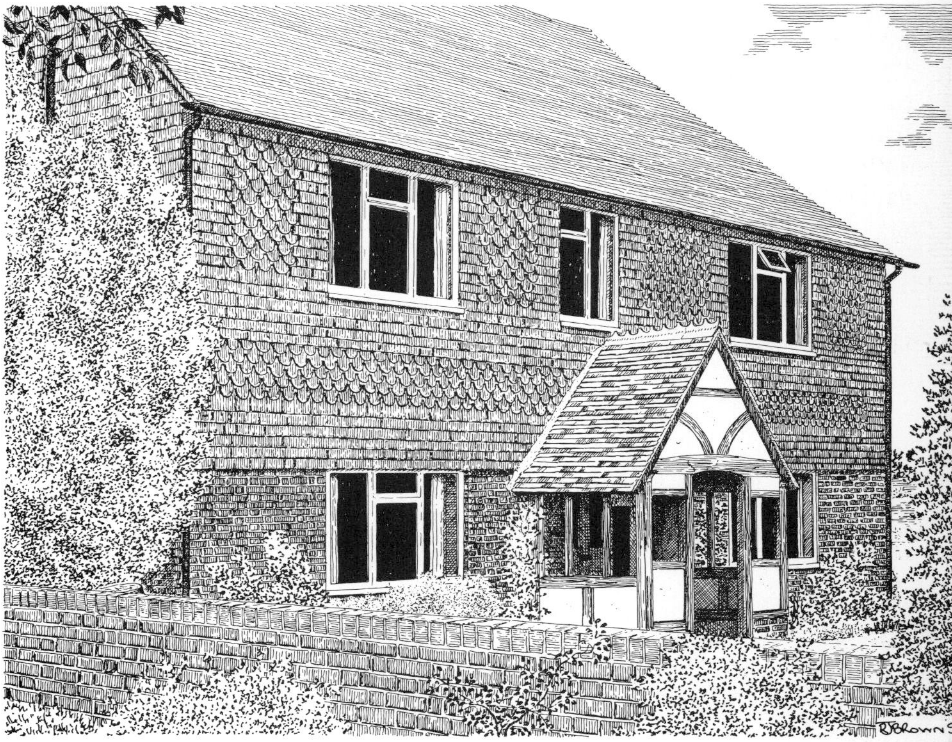

108. Leigh Green Farmhouse, Tenterden.

There are only some eight hundred or so buildings in England where mathematical tiles survive; nearly half are in Sussex, mostly in Brighton and Lewes, about a quarter in east Kent, particularly in Canterbury (which has 138) and Faversham, while there are also a number in west Kent, notably in Tenterden. In Faversham they can often be seen on the upper floors of jettied houses, giving the appearance of brick to the upper floor but reducing the weight on the jetty. Their use is almost exclusively restricted in Kent to villages and towns and they are rarely to be found in rural areas. They could be hung on battens nailed to the face of the frame as with plain tiles or alternatively, and it seems more usually, they could be fixed to softwood square-edged boarding.

Weatherboarding is to be seen to great effect in many of these delectable Wealden villages and towns, such as Rolvenden, Tenterden and Smarden (*109*). Domestically, like tile-hanging and plastering, weatherboarding was first used to render old timber-framed houses weatherproof. In many cases the entire house is clad from eaves to

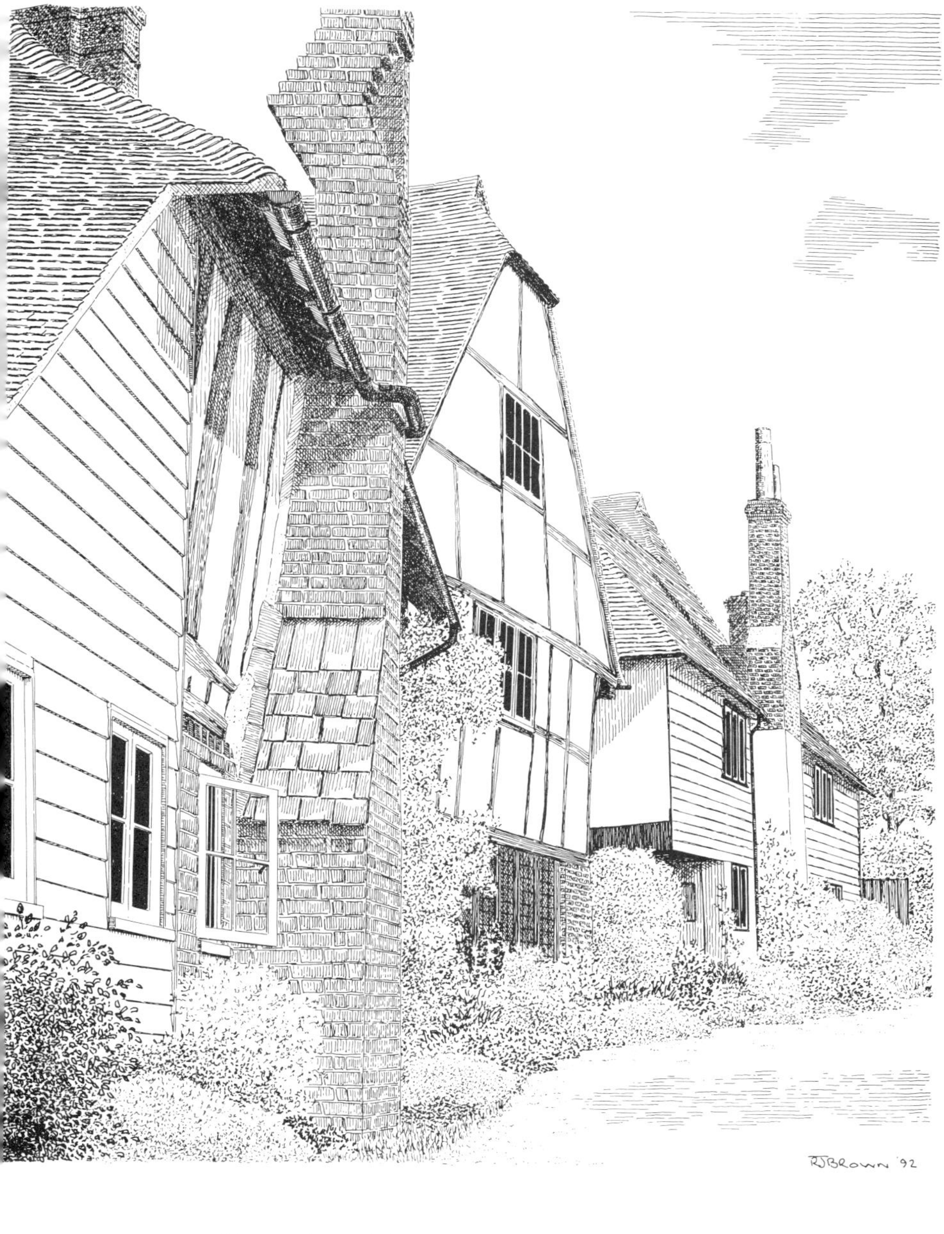

109. Weatherboarded and timbered houses overlooking the churchyard, Smarden.

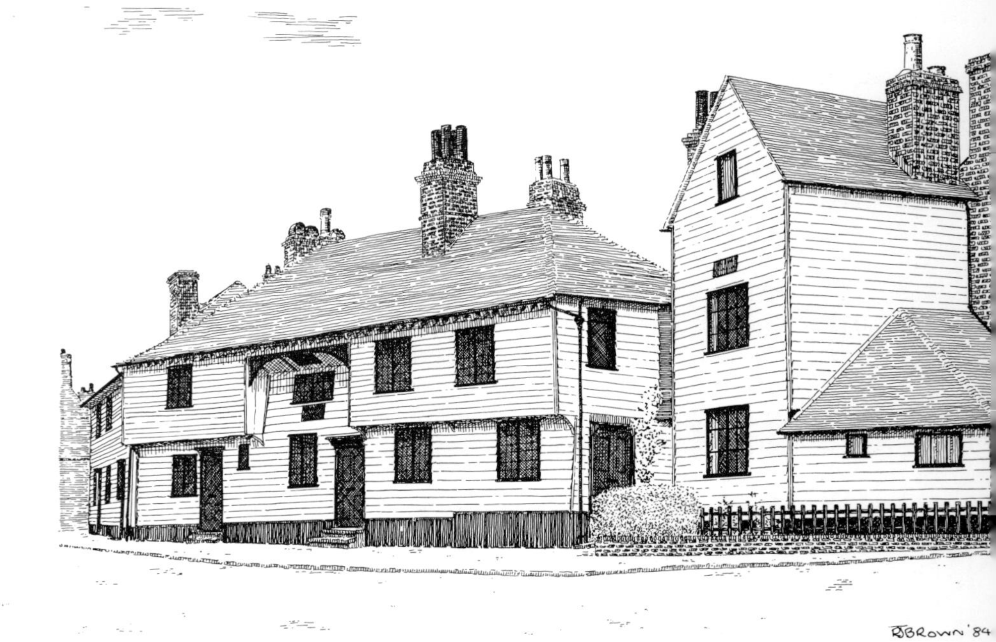

110. Weatherboarded Wealden house, Eynsford.

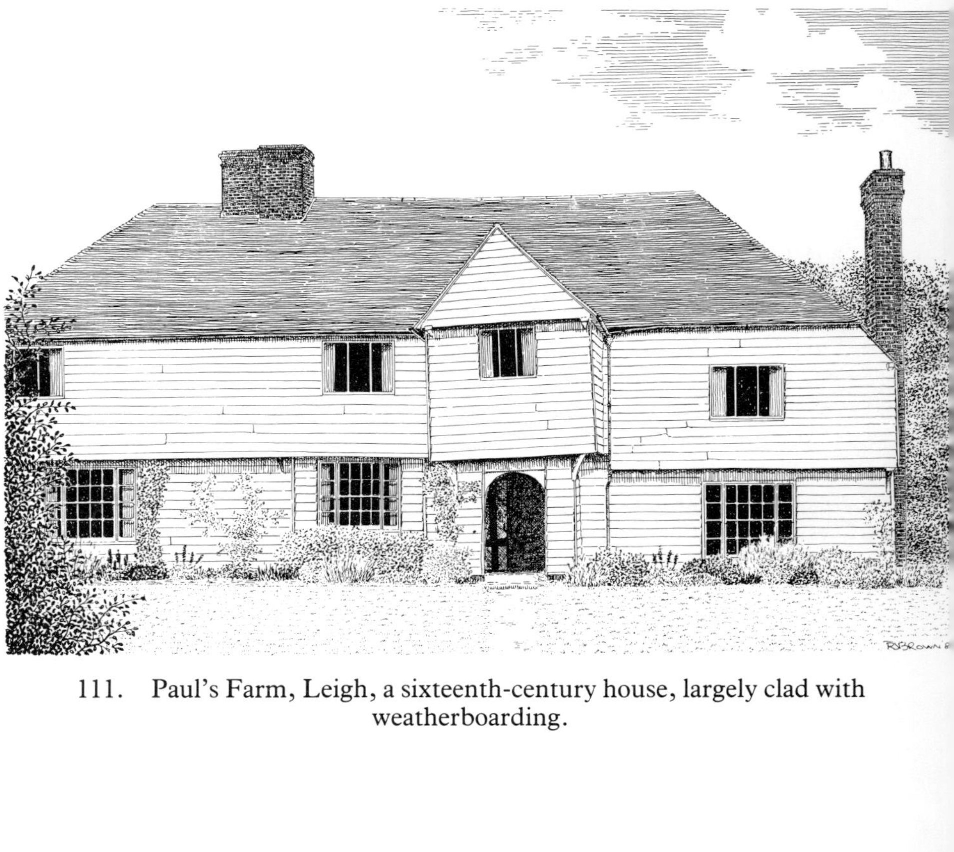

111. Paul's Farm, Leigh, a sixteenth-century house, largely clad with weatherboarding.

ground and this is often the case with older houses, as on the Wealden house at Eynsford (*110*). At Paul's Farm, Leigh (*111*), a sixteenth-century continuous-jettied house, the entire front is clad, including the two-storeyed porch. In other cases these old houses are clad perhaps on the gable end as on the house at Cowden (see illus. 81) or on the upper storey, like 'The Brothers' at Smarden (*112*). The ground floors of many of these houses were built or rebuilt in brick or stone, the boarding being restricted to the upper storeys.

Occasionally boarding was used in such a way as to simulate stone. Here the horizontal boards did not overlap but were rebated and scored vertically at regular intervals to suggest the use of blocks. This can be seen on a number of buildings along the Pantiles at Tunbridge Wells, on some houses and cottages at Rolvenden and at Church House, Brenchley (*113*). The scoring had by necessity to be shallow and so the illusion of stonework is easily dispelled. At Craythorne House, Tenterden, the suggestion of stonework is more convincing for here it is obtained by the use of individual blocks each carefully chamfered on all edges to give the desired rusticated effect.

In some cases more than one cladding material was used. Weatherboarding and tile-hanging is one popular combination as at the house at Lamberhurst (*114*), where the upper storey of the front elevation is tile-hung and the remainder of the house, including the ground floor of the front elevation, weatherboarded. The combination of tile-hanging above and weatherboarding below can also be seen at Church House, Goudhurst. Sometimes this combination is what can only be described as a 'patchwork' of the two.

At the aforementioned Church House, Brenchley, where the weatherboarding to the front is lined out to resemble rusticated stone, tile-hanging was used for the entire gable wall.

Another combination is mathematical tiles and tile-hanging, where the mathematical tiles are to the front elevation with tile-hanging to the remainder.

During the seventeenth and eighteenth centuries, as bricks became cheaper and consequently more widely used, it became popular to modernize old timber-framed houses by completely refronting them with a false brick front, often with a parapet, with the old building behind remaining almost untouched. The overall Georgian effect is sometimes lost if, for structural reasons, the desired perfect symmetry is not quite achieved. This can be seen at Cobrahamsole Farmhouse, Sheldwich (*115*), a former open-hall house built at the beginning of the sixteenth century for the Belk family in whose possession it remained until 1779. The Georgian façade was added in around 1750; the date 1753 and the initials 'BB' are inscribed on one of the bricks over the entrance. In other cases the entire house has been encased or

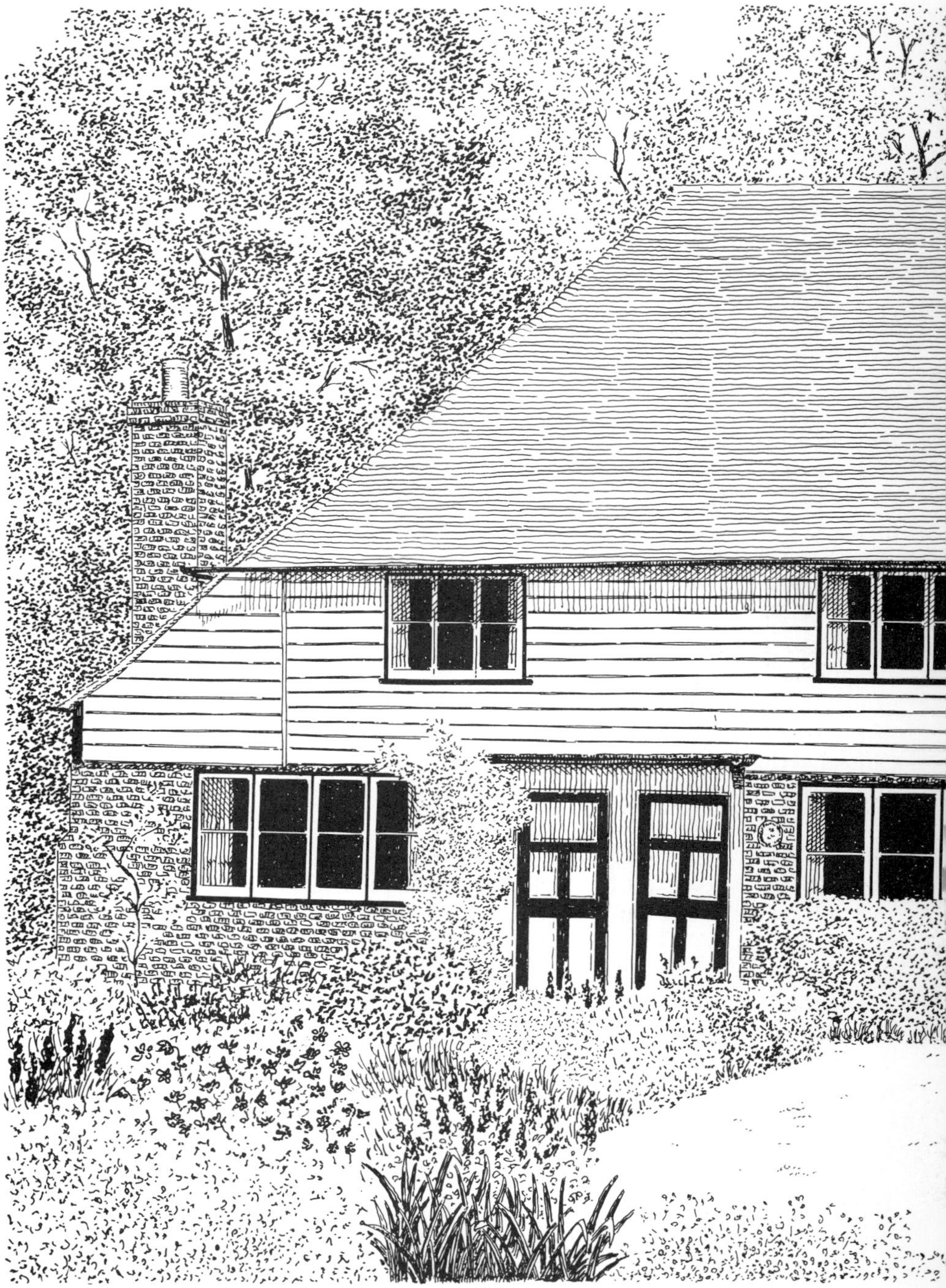

112. 'The Brothers', Smarden.

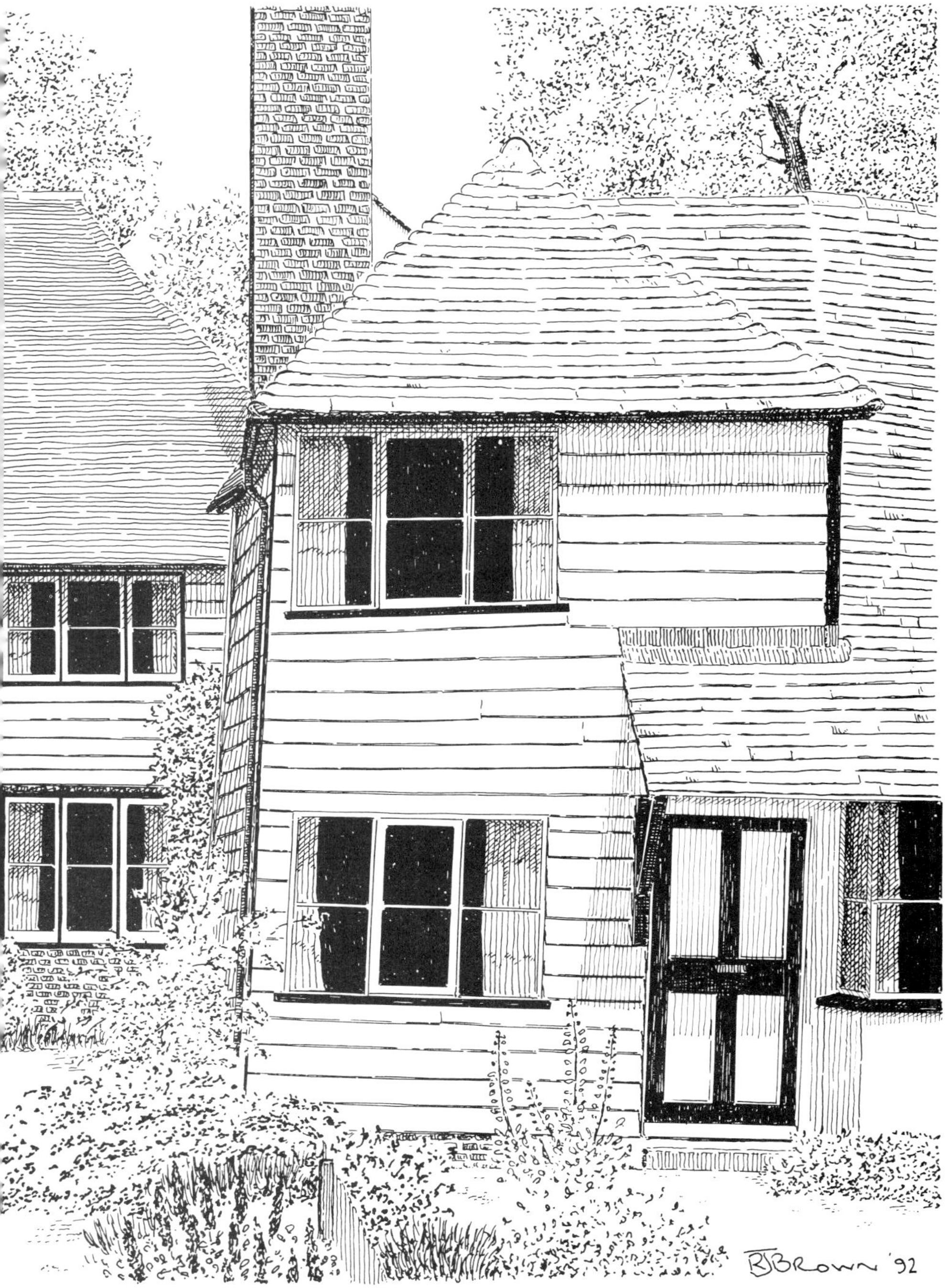
RJBROWN '92

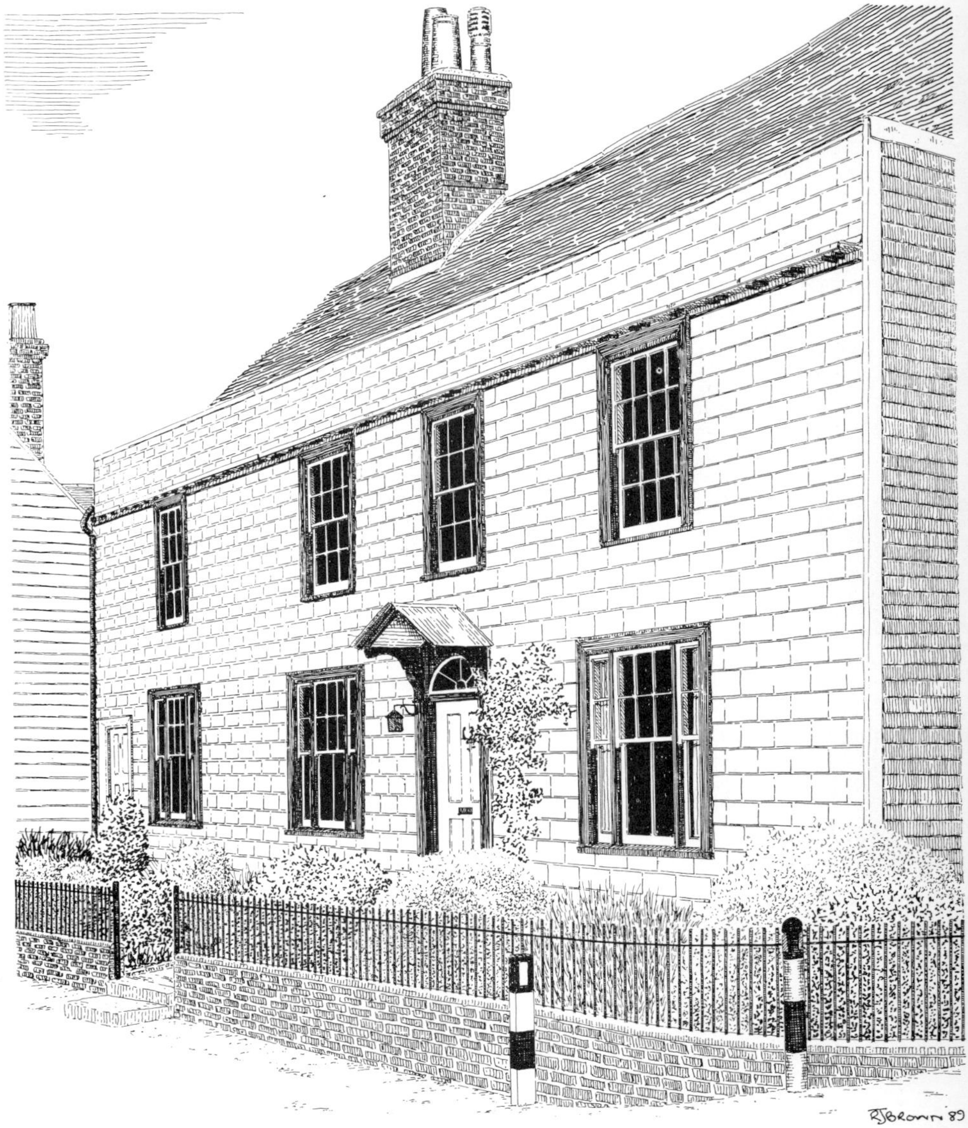

113. Church House, Brenchley.

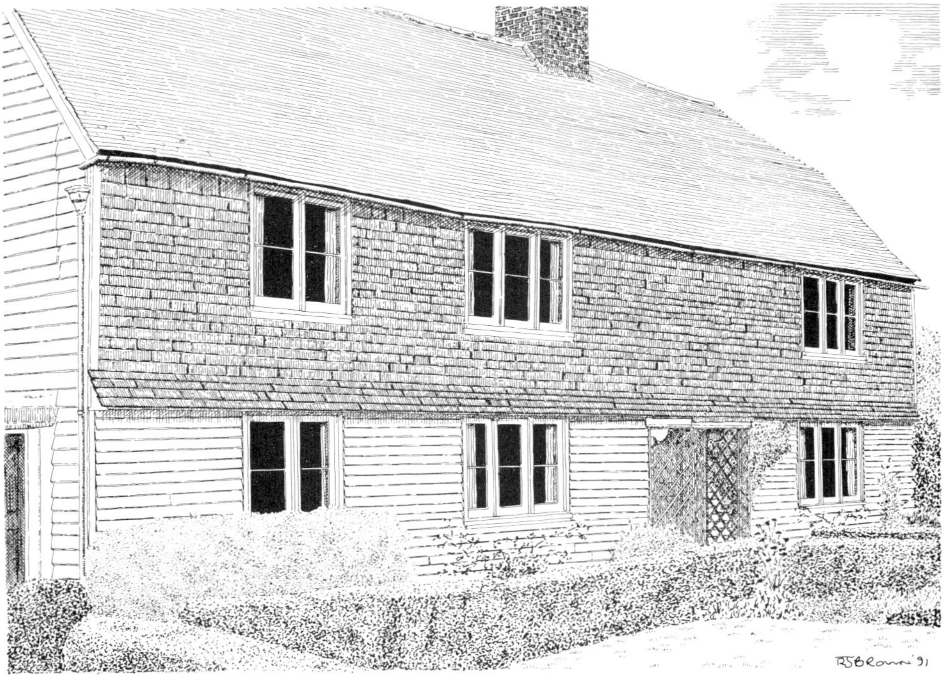

114. House at Lamberhurst.

largely encased in brick so that the character of the original house has been lost. One excellent example is Chillenden Court Farm, Goodnestone (*116*), a Wealden house of mid-fifteenth-century date, completely encased in the seventeenth century in brick with shaped gables and gable chimneys inserted to each end room. Tonge Corner Farmhouse is another former open-hall house which was completely encased in brickwork in the eighteenth century, only the hipped roof giving a clue to its origin.

From the late sixteenth century onwards it became common practice to underbuild the jetties, and many houses which today appear on first evidence to be plain brick or tile-hung houses are on closer examination found to be former jettied houses. The reason for this was two-fold, for it provided extra space to the ground-floor rooms – usually eighteen inches or so – and at the same time the front of the house could be modernized. Generally a brick wall was constructed under the jetty to support the ends of the projecting joists. When a Wealden house was so treated the brickwork was carried up to eaves level between the projecting bays to support the wall-plates. When all the timbers were securely fixed, the front wall beneath the

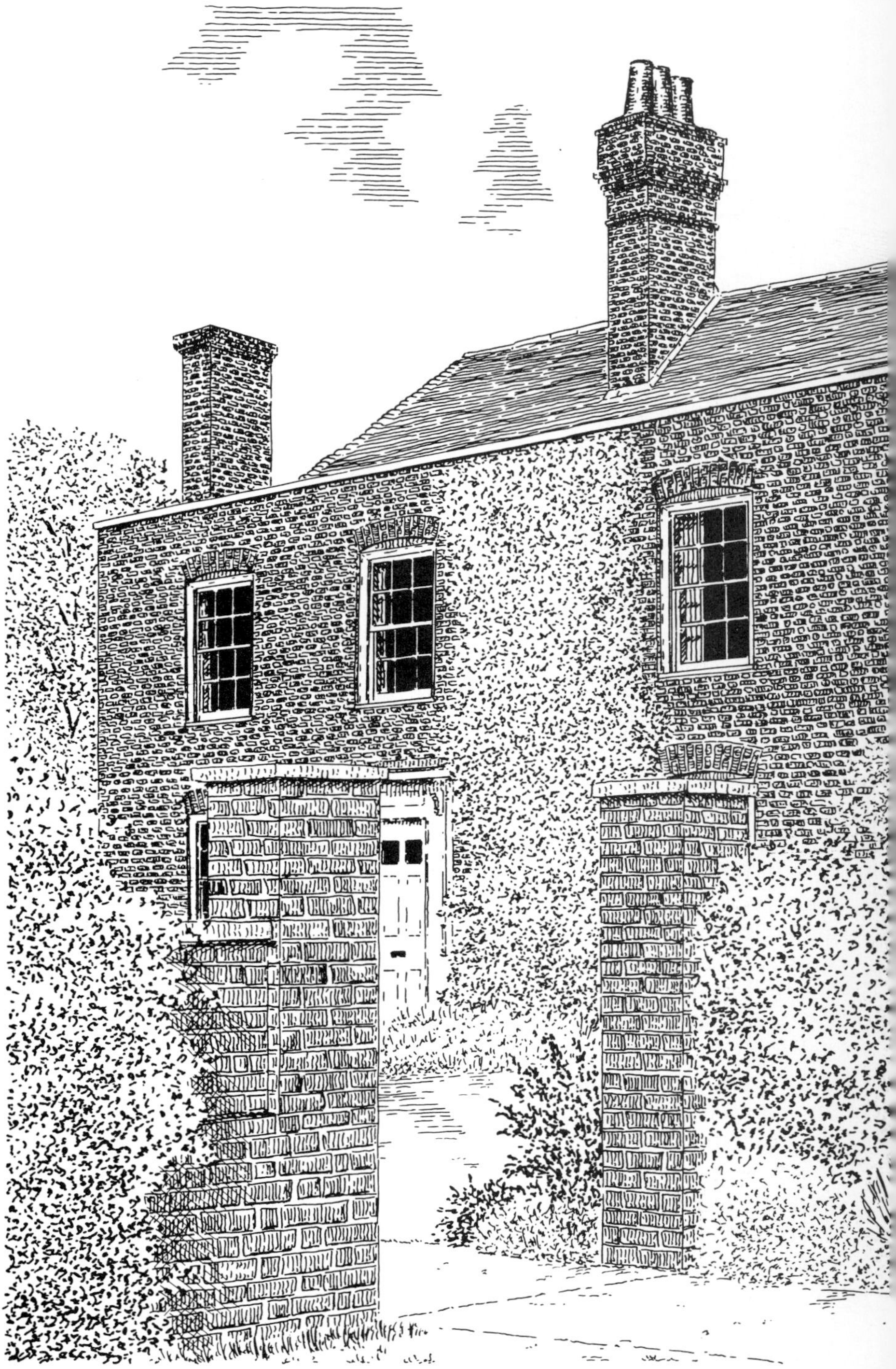

115. Cobrahamsole Farmhouse, Sheldwich.

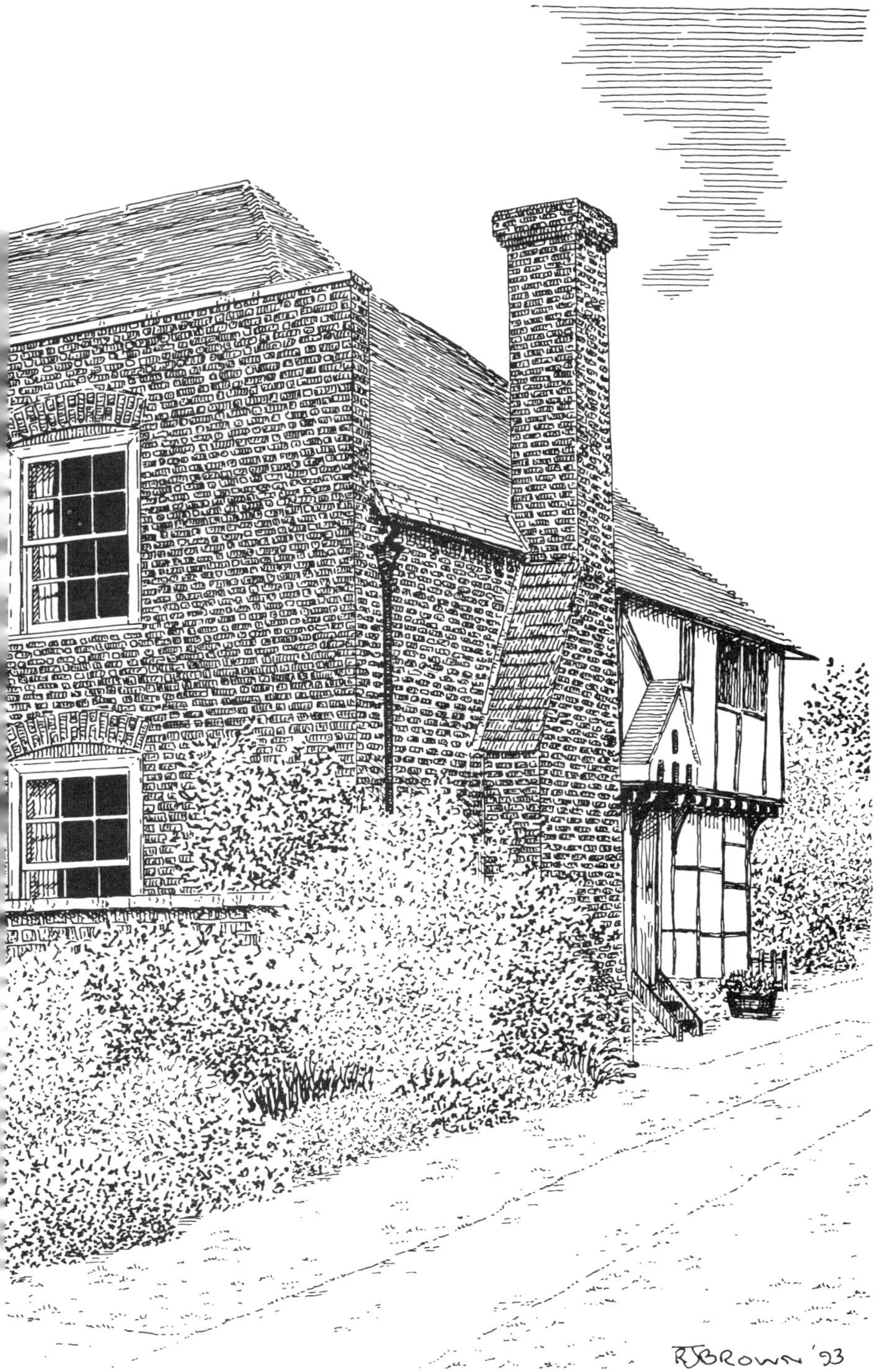
RJBROWN '93

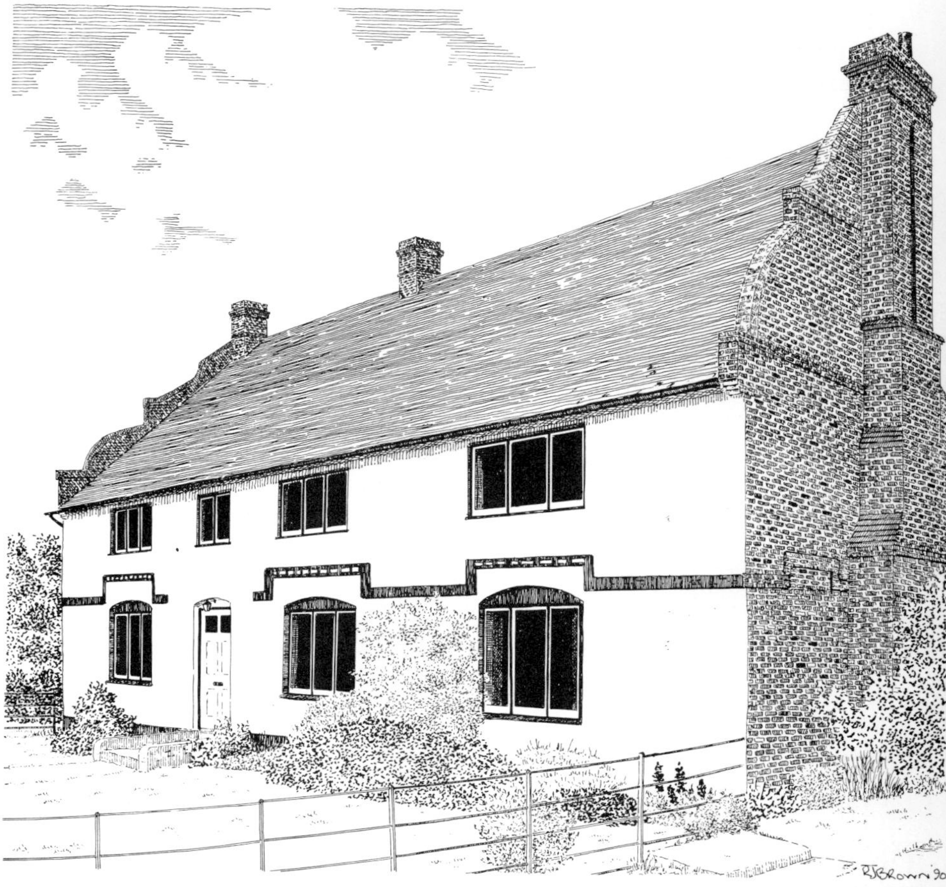

116. Chillenden Court Farm, Goodnestone. A Wealden house encased in seventeenth-century brickwork.

jetty or wall-plates could be subsequently removed without fear of structural damage. The upper storey could then be clad with tiles or weatherboarding and with the insertion of contemporary double-hung sash windows and door cases the modernization could be completed and the medieval façade become either Queen Anne or Georgian. In many cases only the jetties would be underbuilt, the timbers to the first floor remaining exposed. This can be seen at Kite Manor, Monks Horton and the house at Cowden.

The cladding of timber-framed houses with stone in Kent is rare. An example is Twissenden, Goudhurst, where a late sixteenth-century Wealden sandstone façade with a centrepiece of 'a very crude form' was added to the rear of a Wealden hall house.

In the seventeenth century the supply of indigenous oak began to decline as a consequence of the house-building boom of the previous century, coupled with the consumption of wood for fuel for the Wealden iron- and glass-making industries, and the continuing growth of ship-building, both for the navy and merchant fleet at Chatham and elsewhere in the county. As the supply of suitable timbers declined the price increased and it became necessary to economize on the size and spacing of timbers. It became important not only to make the available timber go further but also to be less particular in the selection of wood for the framework; this resulted in the lack of uniformity observed in many seventeenth-century houses. Another way to economize in the use of oak was to obtain the timber from old buildings which for some reason had been demolished, cut it up into smaller scantlings and re-use it for larger or perhaps two or three smaller buildings. All these buildings still built of oak, or possibly chestnut, were intended from the outset to be clad with either plaster, tiles, weatherboarding or mathematical tiles.

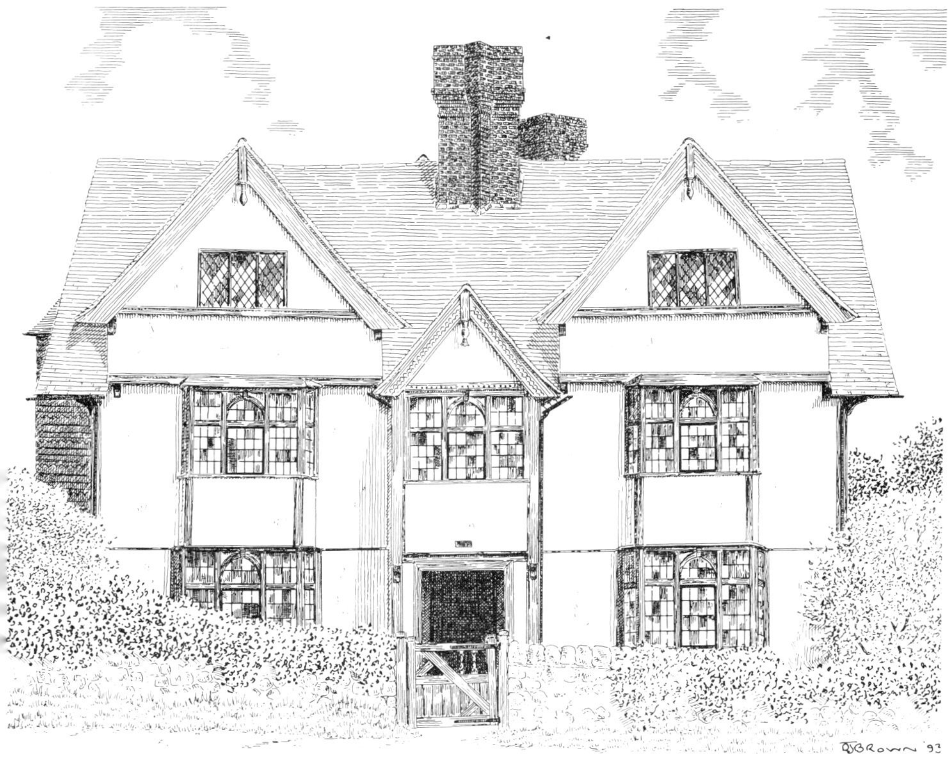

117. Valence House, Sutton Valence.

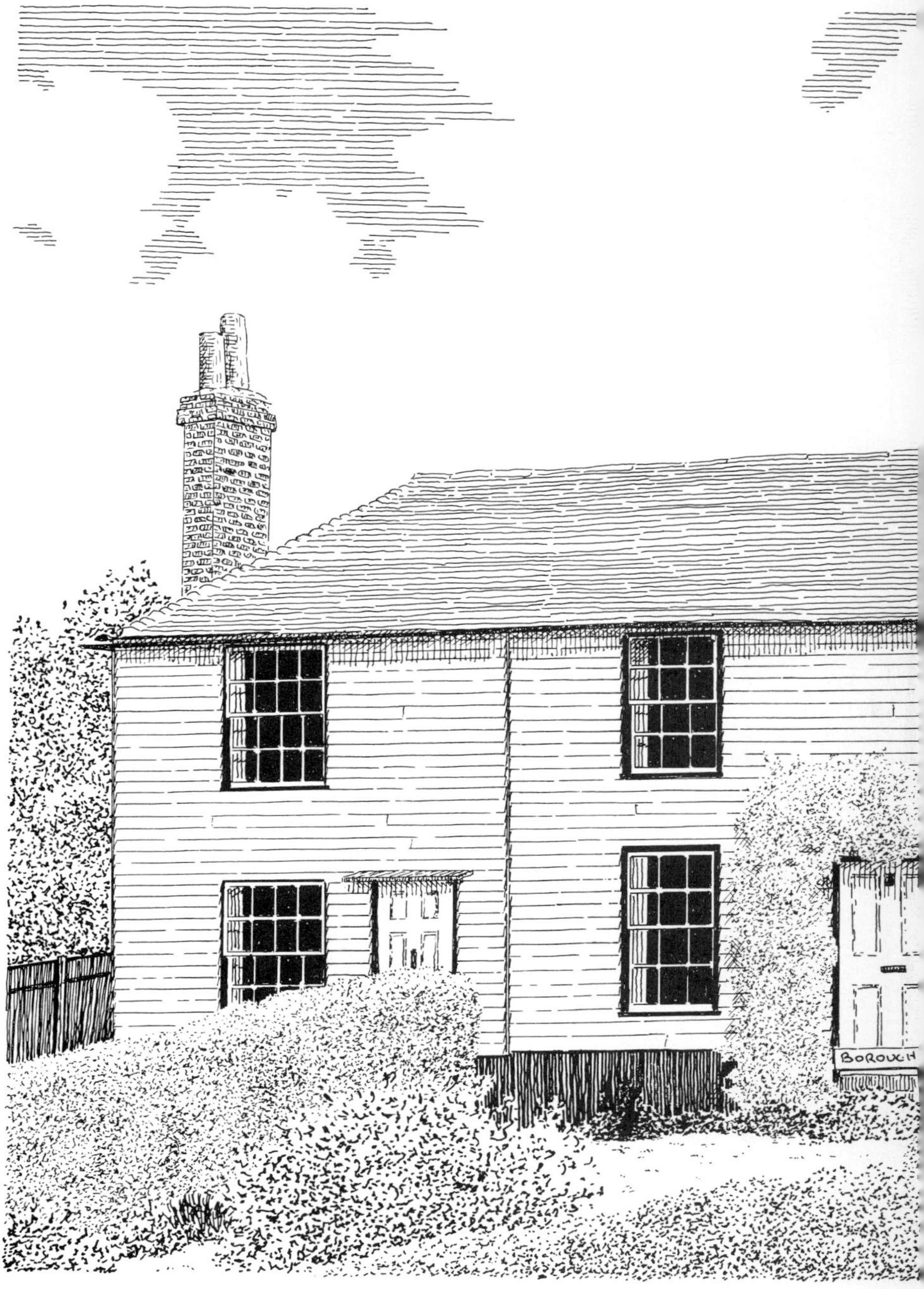

118. Borough Cottages, Cranbrook.

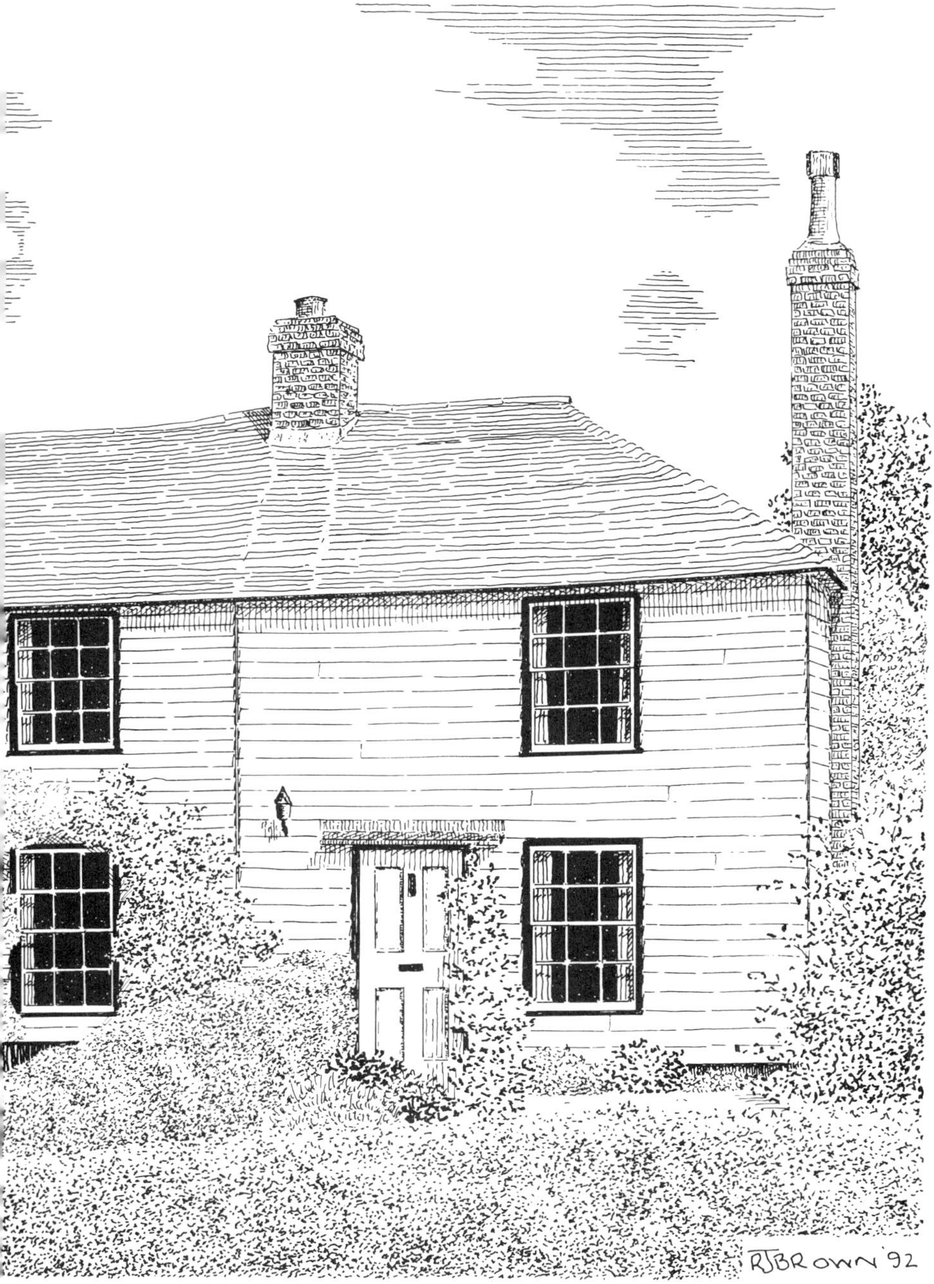
RJBROWN '92

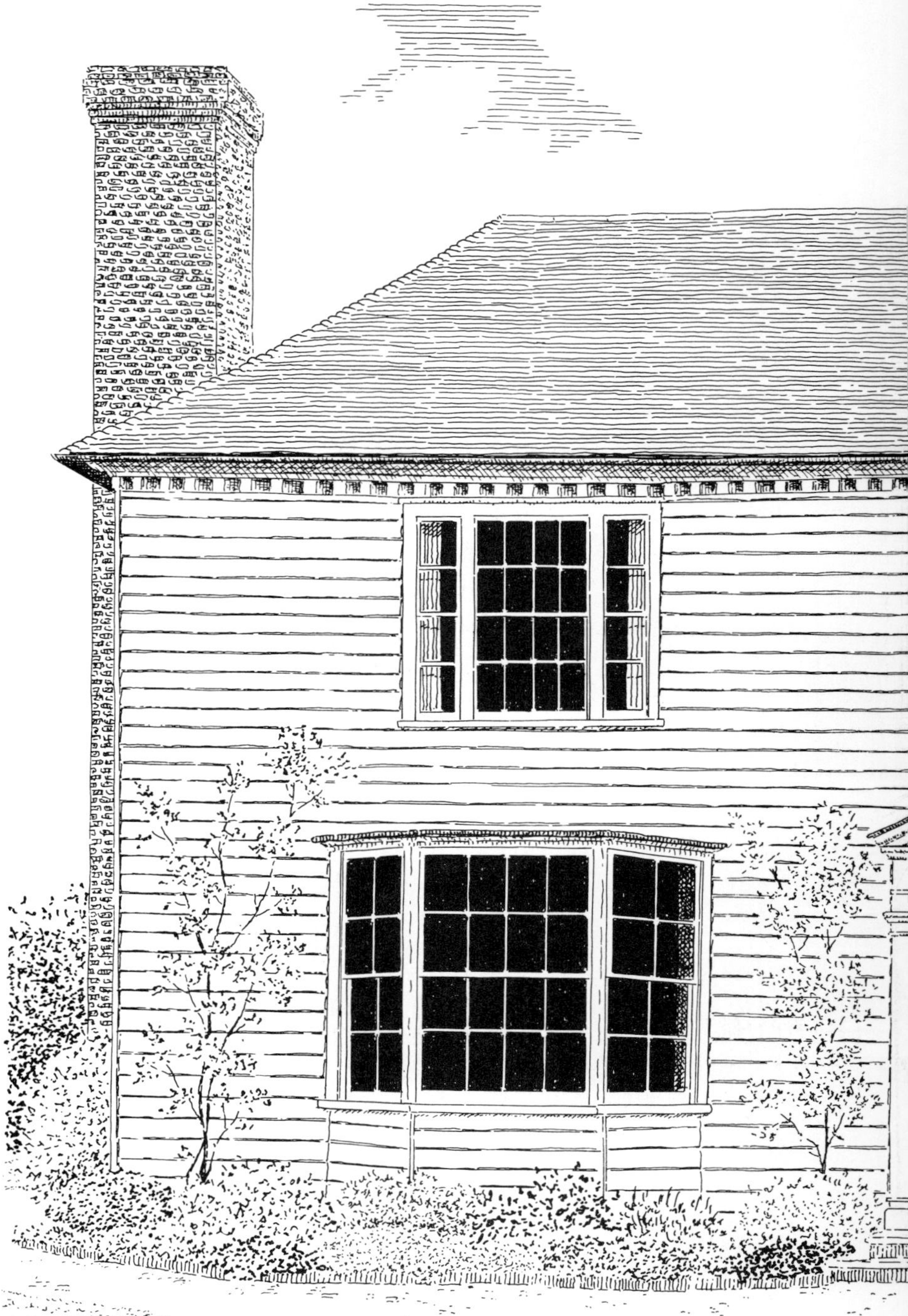

119. House near Rolvenden, built around 1780.

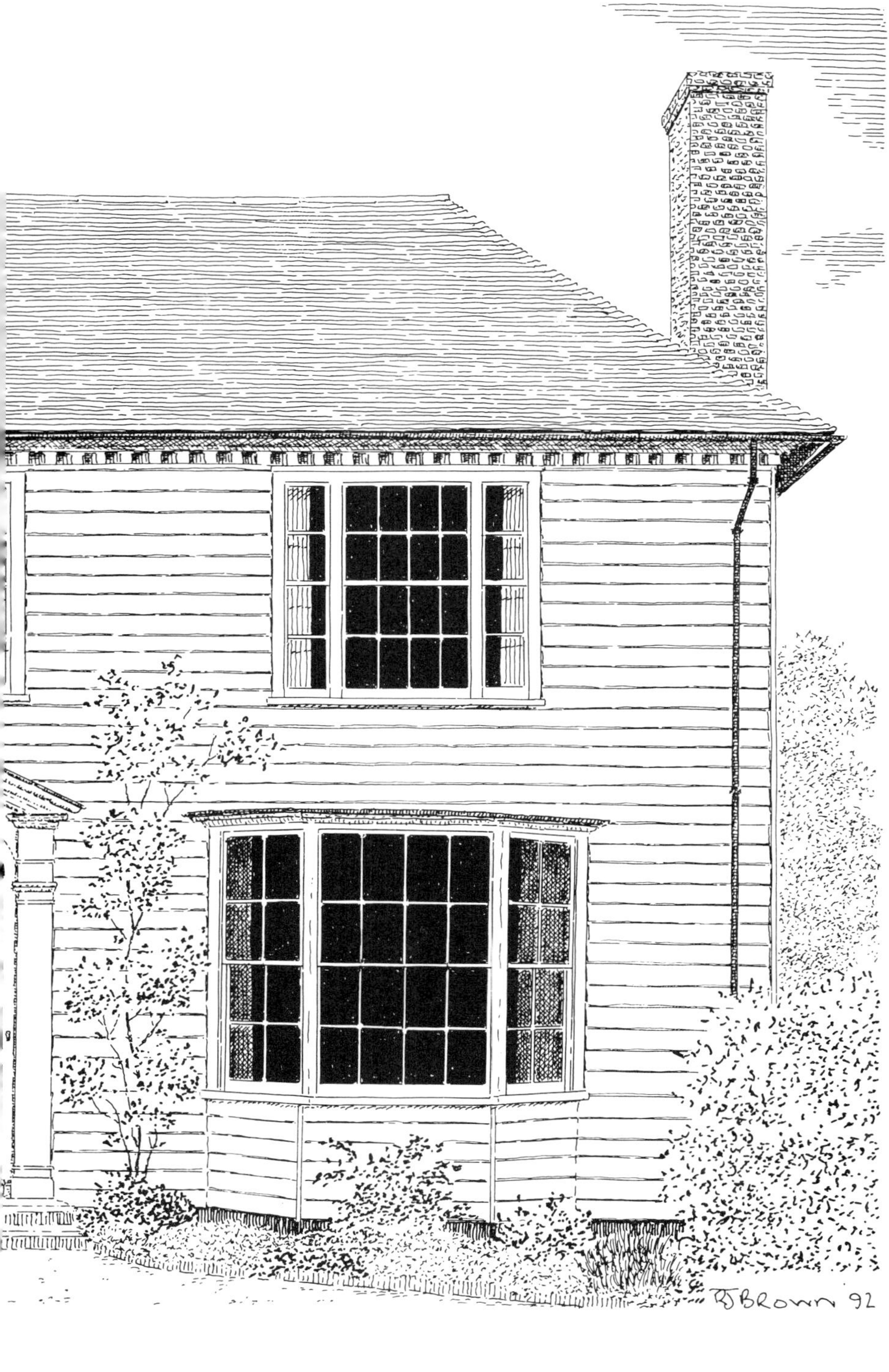

TJ Brown 92

One excellent example is Valence House, Sutton Valence (*117*), a house with the timbers concealed beneath plaster. The symmetrical north front, casement windows with arched transoms to the centre light in each window, a central brick chimney stack, are all typical of the seventeenth century and suggest a date of the second quarter of that century despite the date of 1598 on a finial. It has been suggested that it was possibly a rebuild of an earlier house.

Today many people have a desire to strip away these cladding materials to expose the underlying timbers, but in many cases the timbers were never intended to be exposed, and are constructed of light scantlings. Even on buildings subsequently clad, the fixing of battens or laths necessitated the driving in of numerous nails, leaving unsightly holes disfiguring the face of the timbers. Fortunately in Kent the stripping process is not so common as in East Anglia but it is to be seen all too often.

In some instances the cladding has been removed to good effect, exposing the original timbers as they were intended to be seen. At Standen, Biddenden, the house was at one time hung with decorative tiles to the first floor; these have now been stripped away to expose the ornamental framing previously mentioned.

By the eighteenth century the county's natural forests were so depleted that imported softwood from the Baltic and Scandinavian countries, supplemented later, in the nineteenth century, with supplies from Canada and the United States, came into ever-increasing use. This imported softwood was of uniform section and with the manufacturing of cheap, machine-made nails, oak was no longer regarded as a necessity and the elaborate joinery techniques of earlier timber-framed buildings were no longer required. There are many houses built with a brick ground floor with a softwood frame tile-hung above. Houses of this type continued to be built until around 1850. They could be of surprising size as at Delaware, Edenbridge, which is of late seventeenth-century date. It is a large square house, tile-hung to the front, with a shell-hood to the front door on richly carved brackets.

Fostered by the tax on bricks, first imposed in 1784 and increased from time to time before being finally abolished in 1850, the use of softwood framing flourished to house the ever-increasing population. Small houses, like Borough Cottages, Cranbrook (*118*), built entirely of a softwood frame, were quick and cheap to erect, particularly when clad with painted weatherboarding on the outside, lath and plaster on the inside and with an air space between, ensuring a house that was warm in winter and cool in summer. Not only small houses were constructed using this method but also houses showing some pretence to the classical design. The house near Rolvenden (*119*) was built in around 1780 and shows all the elements that would have been found in

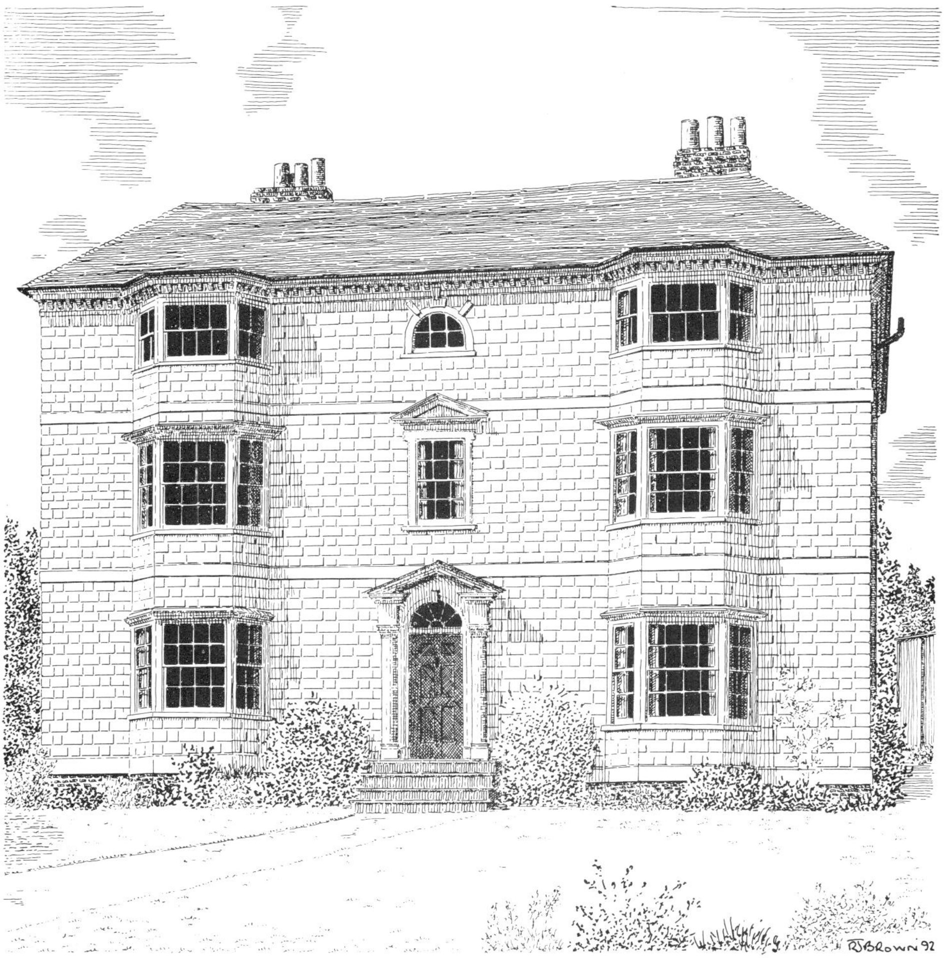

120. Craythorne House, Tenterden.

the brick-built houses of the period. The doorcase, cornice and joinery show some of the crudeness often associated with local tradesmen's work. As previously noted, Craythorne House at Tenterden (*120*) is clad with softwood blocks cut to suggest stonework but the frame is of softwood. The house was built about the same time as the one at Rolvenden, for Hasted states that it was newly built in 1790. Like the house at Rolvenden this house is of three wide bays but unlike Rolvenden it is of three storeys. Again the house has the refinements of the period – the doorcase with Doric columns and a pedimented window above, a lunette (a semicircular window) above that and a deep cornice. The windows to the second floor have now been enlarged.

Cottages (*121*) with a softwood frame, weatherboarded on the outside and lath-and-plaster internally, continued to be built until the middle of the nineteenth century when bricks, now mass-produced, took over as the principal building material. Weatherboarding in preference to tile-hanging or plaster for these cottages was undoubtedly used as it was both cheaper and quicker to install.

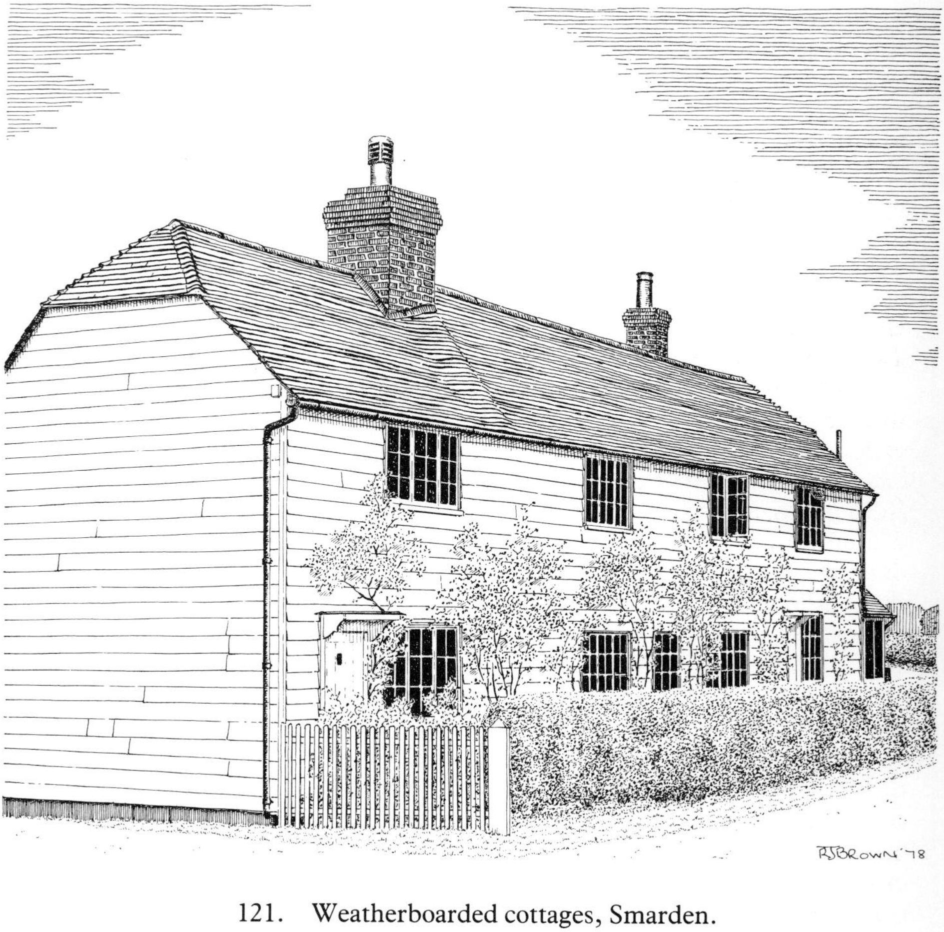

121. Weatherboarded cottages, Smarden.

Brick houses

As we have seen, the use of brick in medieval Kent was rare. In other counties in eastern England, for instance Norfolk and Lincolnshire, its use was gaining popularity from the fifteenth century for major buildings – Tattershall Castle, Lincolnshire of mid-fifteenth-century date, Oxburgh Hall, Norfolk of 1482. These counties lacked other building materials – stone and timber – but in Kent there remained until well into the seventeenth century a plentiful supply of home-grown timber and this continued to be the principal building material.

It was not until the beginning of the sixteenth century that buildings constructed of brick began to appear in any number in the county – Smallhythe Church of 1516–17, built of red bricks following a fire in 1514, is an excellent example of Tudor brickwork, its principal features being its brick tracery windows and crow-stepped gables. The continuing preference for timber in the county is clearly indicated at the domestic level by the rebuilding of the nearby Priest House and Smallhythe Place, in timber, after the fire. Another early sixteenth-century brick building was Royden Hall, East Peckham, where the entrance range and the terraced gardens survive from the house of 1535. The gatehouse to Lullingstone Castle is perhaps the first major building built entirely of bricks. Of mid-sixteenth-century date, it indicates how far Kent was behind other areas, for the details are similar to those used elsewhere in the country, for instance Tattershall Castle, a century or so before.

Gradually the use of brick spread to the vernacular level although timber remained the predominant building material. Its use was encouraged by immigrant Flemings who began to settle in Kent in the fourteenth century, bringing with them the traditions and innovations from centuries of brick-building in their own country. Brunger Farm, Tenterden, is one early example; probably of mid-sixteenth-century date, it is built entirely of bricks with a crow-stepped gable to one end and a different crow-stepped gable to the porch. These crow-stepped gables were a feature of the brick-built sixteenth-century houses in Kent, and originated in the Netherlands. The stepped gables could be constructed of ordinary bricks formed in steps as on the gable at Brunger Farm, or more commonly with bricks so arranged to provide a weathered capping, as on the porch to Brunger Farm and the gable at Bax Farm, Tonge. The latter is a remarkable house dated 1567, constructed of flint and stone with a close-studded upper storey and crow-stepped brick gable end wall with two modern brick stacks on large stone chimney breasts. Before about 1840 there was a second stepped gable. At Wickhambreux the delightful medieval flint-and-stone chequered building beside the stream, known as the Old Stone House, has had its end gables and the gables to the two projecting porches rebuilt in brick with crow-steps. A brick end-gable wall with crow-steps was added in 1584 to the mainly ragstone Boughton Malherbe Place, much of which dates from about 1560. These stepped gables can also be seen at Whorn's Place – the late fifteenth-century house has gone, the present house being a former outbuilding – and at Old St Alban's Court, Nonington. Stepped gables continued to be built until the end of the sixteenth century; two excellent examples are Sir Roger Manwood's almshouses at St Stephen's Green, Canterbury, of 1570 and his school-house Manwood Court, Sandwich, with six stepped gables towards the road built around 1580. One of the last to be built was in the 1590s at Ford Place, Wrotham.

Straight-sided gables were also a feature of the Elizabethan brick house. Sometimes they were set on projecting corbels and had a finial at the apex but generally they had no ornamentation. Their use continued until the seventeenth century and one can cite such dated examples as Ash Manor at Ash near Wrotham of 1637 and Bicknor Court of 1628, a former timber-framed house, still to be seen at the rear, partly encased and rebuilt in brick (the date is scratched in the plaster on one of the roof partitions).

Slowly the use of brick gained momentum for whilst the supply of home-grown timber declined, resulting in an increase in price, the price of bricks was falling, so by the middle of the seventeenth century brick began to replace timber as the principal building material in the county. This is particularly true of east Kent where timber was less plentiful than, say, in the Weald. This reduction in price and consequently the increased popularity of brick was due in no small part to the improved method of manufacture. No longer were the bricks made locally, often from clay dug close by the new building, but they were produced at small local brickworks. The method of production was further improved towards the end of the seventeenth century when a machine known as a 'pug mill' was invented. This machine, which was powered by horses, removed the necessity for men to tread out the earth with their bare feet. The increasing popularity of brick was further encouraged by the influx of immigrants from Holland and the Low Countries.

Yet the adoption of this new material was a tentative process. The average country bricklayer, competent in laying a foundation to a timber-framed house, constructing a brick chimney or filling in the panels of a timber-framed house, would have found the construction of houses built entirely of bricks a much more difficult task. At first he would have used brick in conjunction with timber, for instance putting brick gables to a timber-framed house as at Abbott's Fireside, Elham, and Bogles, Lynsted. As confidence in the new material increased the walls would be largely constructed of brickwork but with timber tie-beams within the walls. Eventually with mounting skill and experience in the capabilities of brickwork, the builder finally dispensed with timber, relying on the quality of the bricks and mortar for strength.

These new brick-built houses departed from the traditional Kent house in appearance and proportions rather than interior design. At first the houses remained one room deep and were either of the lobby-entry type with a central stack or the vestibule plan. Gabled roofs instead of hipped became the normal form of construction, having the advantage of providing usable garrets. A string-course indicated the height of the ground- and first-floor ceilings, the upper one being higher than the eaves and appearing only at the gable end, as at Ickham. The string-courses represent the clearest superficial proof that the chambers were now required to be as lofty as the ground-floor rooms. The proportions of these brick-built houses mark more than anything else the difference between them and the timber-framed houses of previous centuries.

The Flemish influence on the external appearance remained up until the end of the second quarter of the eighteenth century and it was in the gables where this could best be seen. Shaped and Dutch gables became a feature of the smaller Kent brick-built house in the second half of the seventeenth century in east Kent and in particular the Isle of Thanet. They were incorporated into small houses both at Littlebourne and Finglesham, where shaped gables can be found on single-storey cottages which are themselves unusual – most seventeenth-century brick houses in Kent are two-storey. The Dutch gable at Littlebourne has a broken top pediment and an open pediment below superimposed on the wall, an elaborate arrangement for such a row of small cottages.

Let us first look at shaped gables. They can be found at Ford Place, Wrotham, probably from around 1600; the Earl of Dorset added them to Knole in 1605, but these were of course in stone; while those at Charlton Court, East Sutton, are from 1612 and those at Godinton, near Ashford, 1628. As previously mentioned, it is on the domestic houses of east Kent and in particular Thanet and its hinterland where shaped gables are indeed a special feature. The designs are endless, the so-called 'double compass' gable being perhaps the most common; it is produced by a series of segments or circles, a semicircle at the top, then a step, then one or two quadrants each separated by further steps. In some cases the upper quadrant is concave as at Perry Farm, Preston, or convex like Treasury Farm, Ickham (*122*), which carries a date of 1663. At Bonnington Farm, Bonnington, there is no step between quadrants, the convex quadrant and the top meeting the concave quadrant at the bottom in 'S' curves. In some instances the semicircle at the top is surmounted by the chimney stack as at Perry Farm and Bonnington Farm. Sometimes the upper quadrant – as at Chillenden Court Farm, Goodnestone – is omitted and replaced with a straight gable which can sometimes be stepped. Most 'double

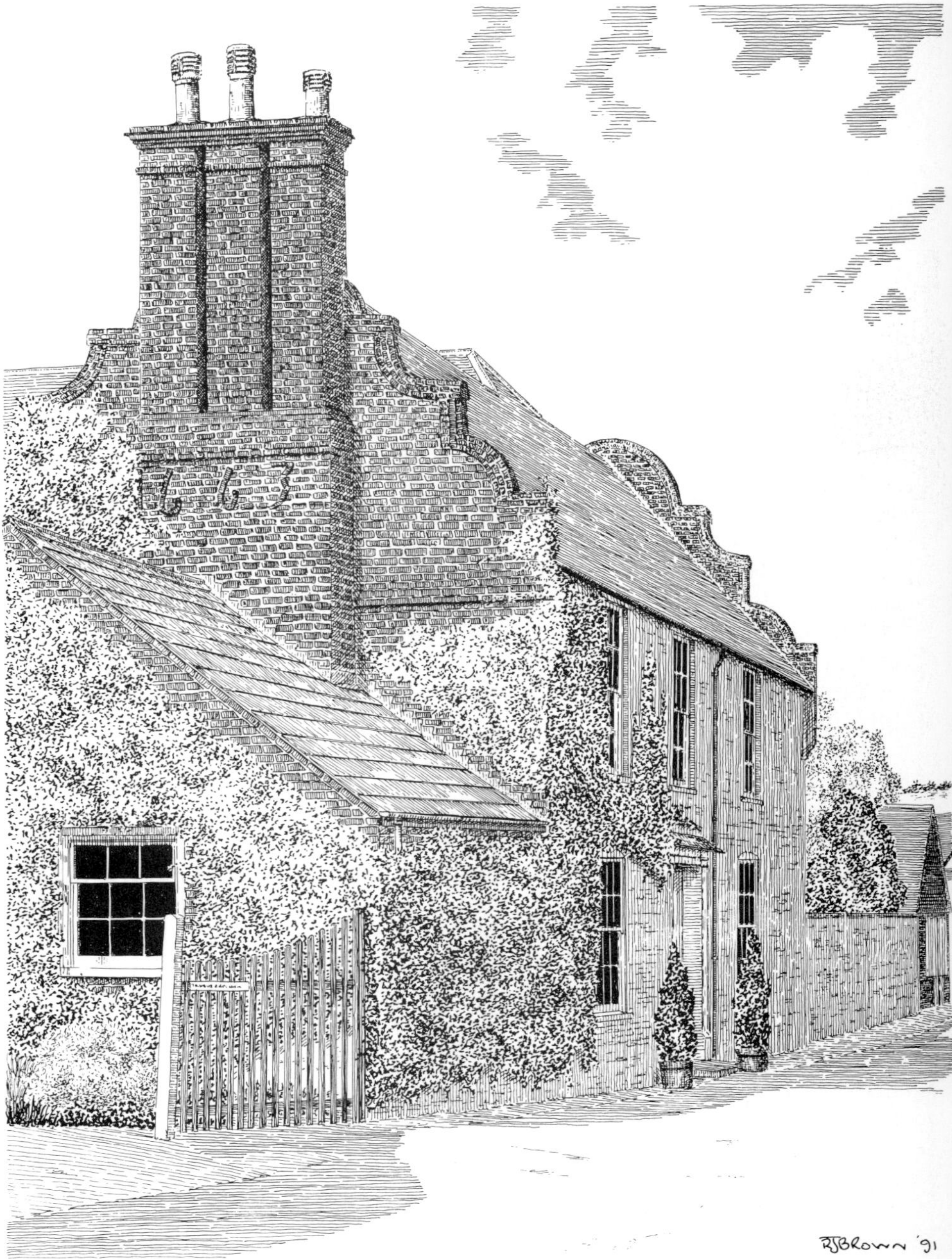

122. Treasury Farmhouse, Ickham, dated 1663.

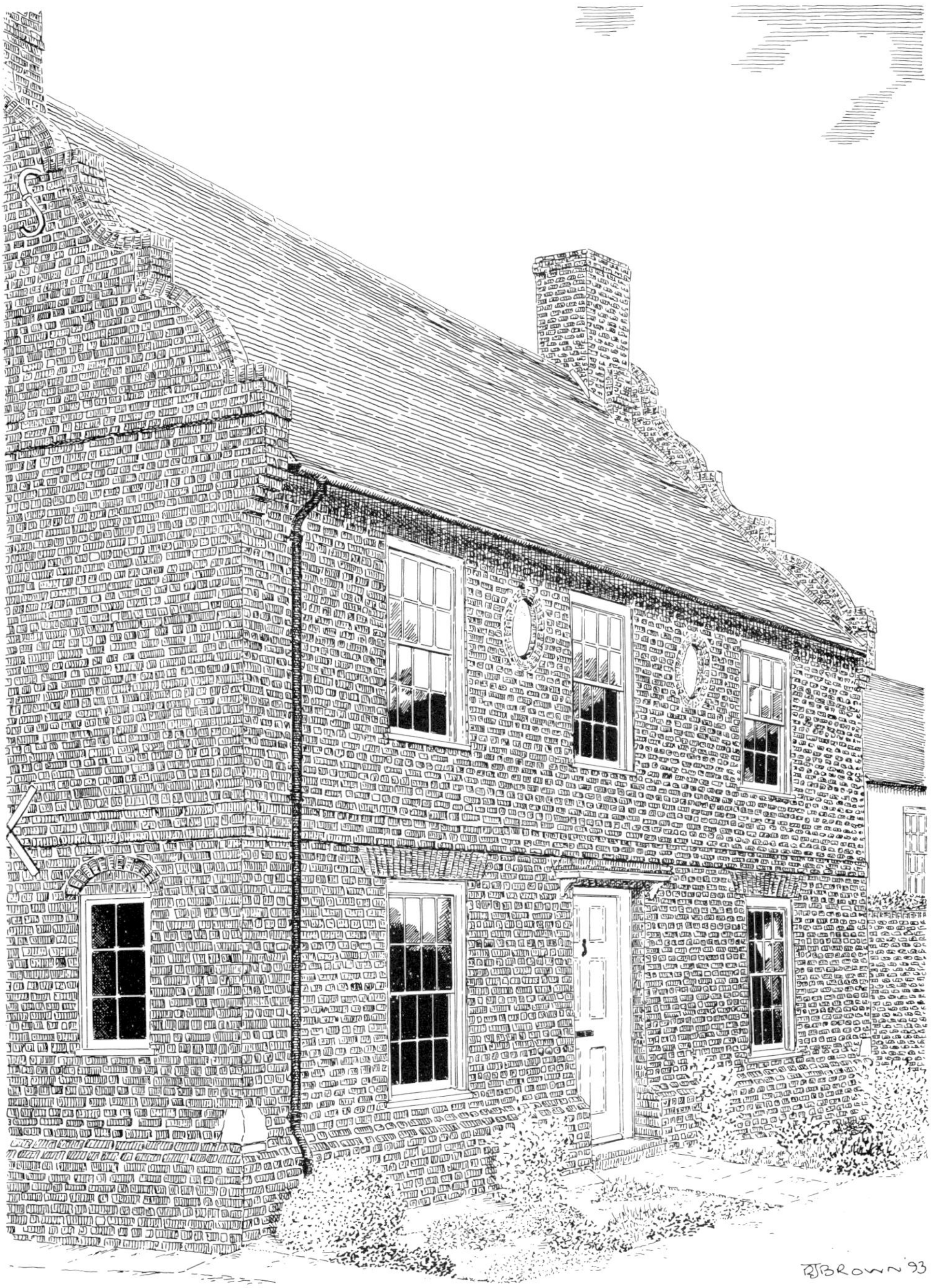

123. Worth Farm, Worth, dated 1675.

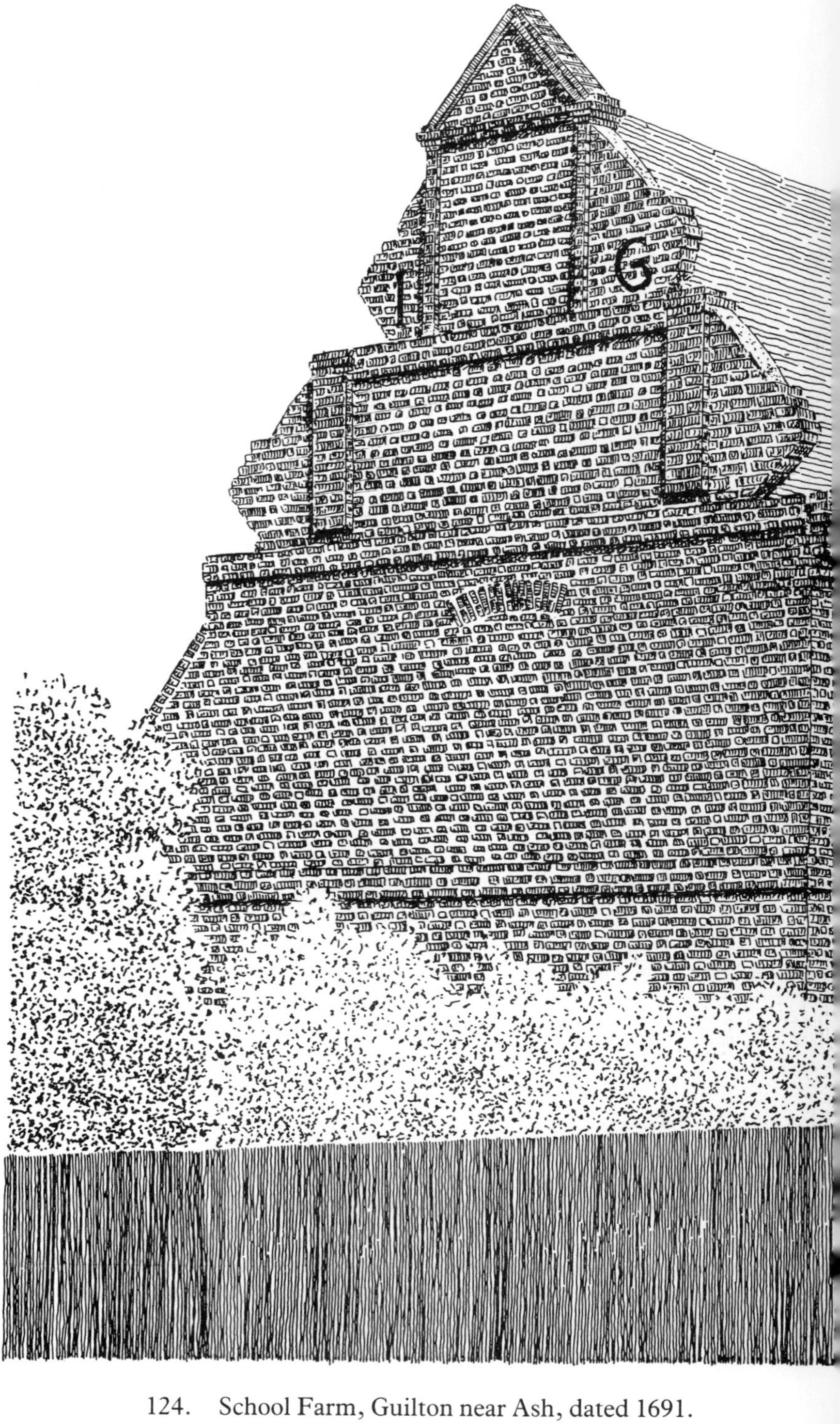

124. School Farm, Guilton near Ash, dated 1691.

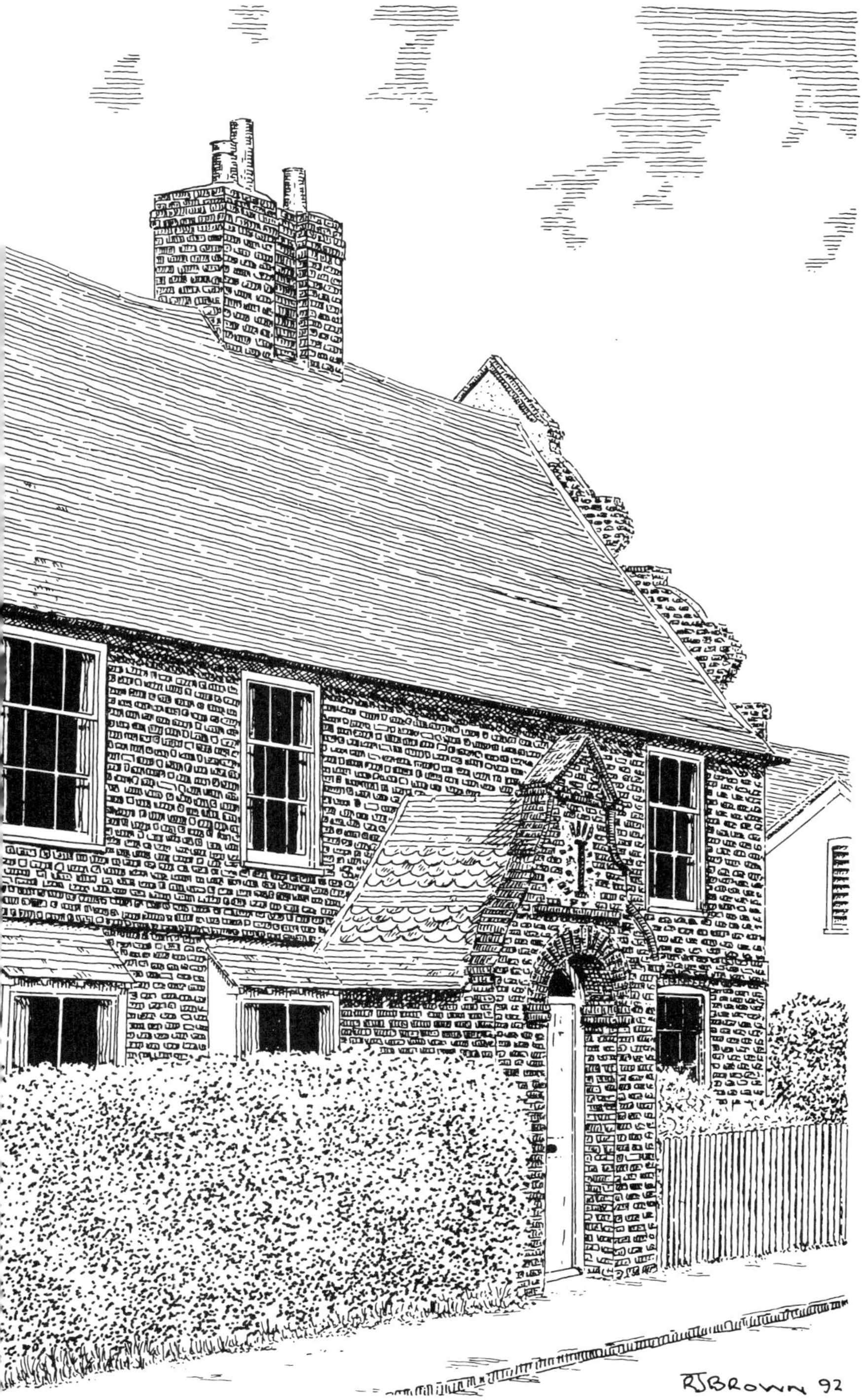
RJBROWN 92

compass' gables date from the second half of the seventeenth century. Rushbourne Manor, Hoath, is the earliest dated example, being built in 1659; Treasury Farm is dated 1663; Hode Farm, Patrixbourne is of 1674; at Finglesham, near Ham, there is a single-storey cottage with a date of 1690. The last dated example in the county is Rose Cottage, Combe, near Ash, which is from 1723.

Dutch gables, which are shaped gables crowned with a pediment, are far less common, although they are by no means rare. Despite their name they may have originated in Belgium or north-east France. They first appeared at Broome Park, near Barham, a house built for Sir Basil Dixwell in 1635–8 which is the finest and most elaborate brick house not only in Kent but probably in the country. A copy of these gables at Broome can be seen at the domestic level on a cottage at Wingham Well, near Wingham. It has giant pilasters to the left and right, with the gable crowned by a broken pediment above an open pediment. A house at Goodnestone also incorporates pilasters to the gable wall, with a simple pediment to the gable. Dated examples of houses with Dutch gables are rare; one example is Worth Farm, Worth (*123*), which carries the date of 1675. At Broadstairs, in the old village of St Peter's, there is Old Farm House; the house is dated 1710 while the porch with another Dutch gable is dated 1686.

Of all the shaped gables the most unusual is to be found at Guilton, near Ash, where School Farm (*124*) dated 1691 (16 on one gable and 91 on the other), has two Dutch 'halsgevels' – stepped gables with volute scrolls on the steps.

A building method generally used on humbler buildings, although it can be found on Sissinghurst Castle, was a Dutch device known as 'tumbling-in'. It was employed to provide a straight gable which was both cheap and reliable by using bricks set diagonally at right angles to the slope of the roof to form a series of triangular wedges, thus producing a straight gable. First introduced into England in the seventeenth century it did not gain popularity in Kent as it did in other counties on the eastern side of England and can only be found on rare occasions (the Farrier's Cottage, St Nicholas-at-Wade). In Kent its use was almost entirely restricted to the construction of external chimney stacks, being employed in the set-backs of the stack when it was reduced in size.

The use of brick continued to flourish and by the end of the seventeenth century it had become firmly established, ousting timber as the most popular material. It was a suitable material for the new double-pile houses and examples can be seen throughout the county. Its popularity continued even in the construction of cottages until the latter part of the eighteenth century, when in 1784 a brick tax was imposed at the duty of two shillings and six pence per thousand; it was

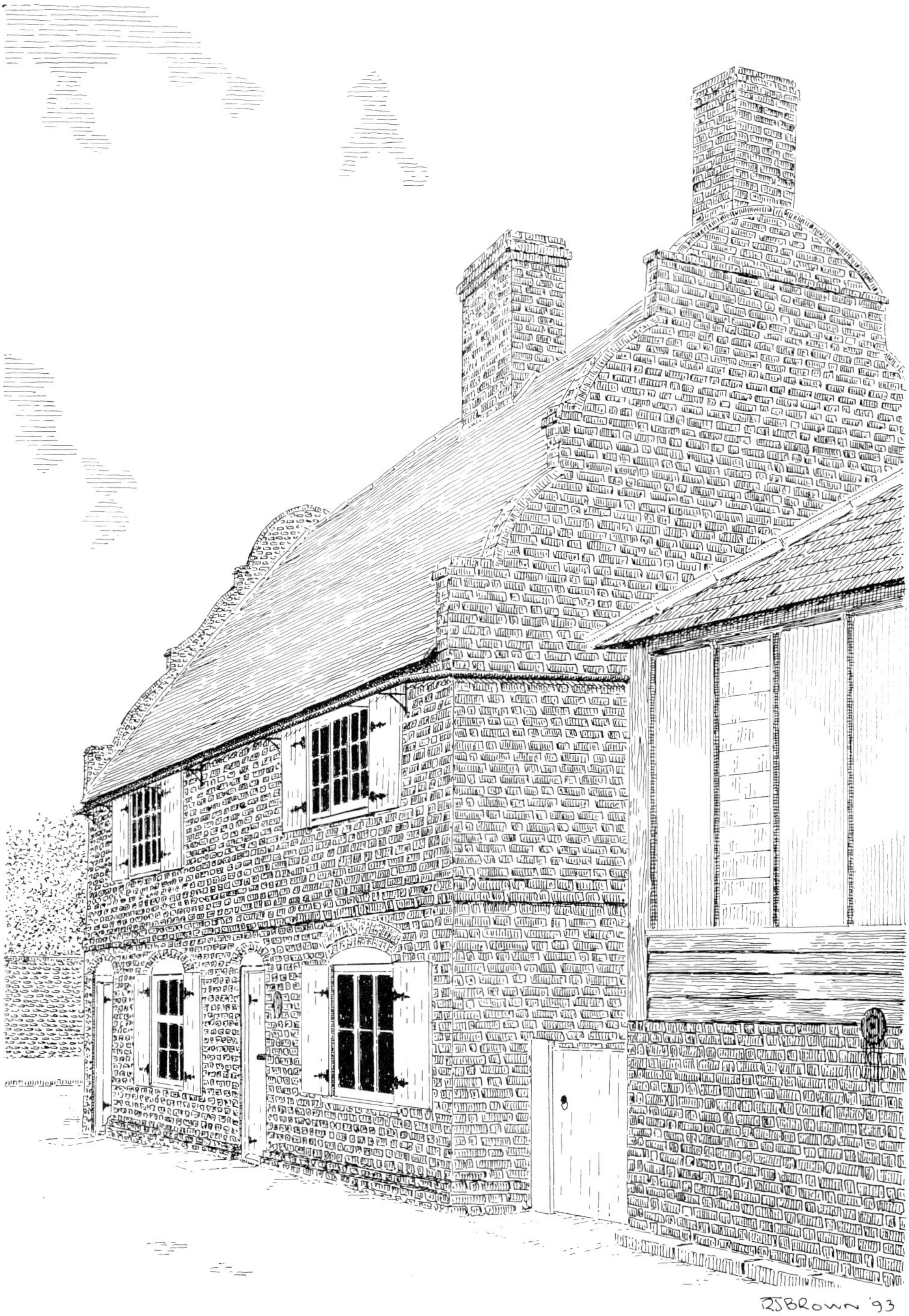

125. Church Cottage, St Nicholas-at-Wade, with double-compass end-gables.

increased in 1794 to four shillings per thousand and again in 1803 to five shillings per thousand. In some areas of the country this resulted in a temporary increase in the size of bricks but fortunately not in Kent, for these larger bricks are aesthetically disastrous. As we have seen earlier, in Kent the tax brought about a revival of timber-framework, although now in imported softwood, for the construction of houses and cottages clad with weatherboarding and tiles. The tax was finally abolished in 1850 and this coincided with the vastly improved methods of manufacture which were the beginning of the mass production of bricks and the beginning of the end of the manufacture of locally produced bricks.

Much of the early brickwork was built with little regard to either bond or pattern, and this remained the case on lesser buildings during the seventeenth century, when much of the brick walling was laid in a bond that defies any classification. At Church Cottage, St Nicholas-at-Wade (*125*), the bond generally comprises one course of stretchers and one course of alternate stretchers and headers, although additional headers have sometimes been introduced. Yet much of the charm of early brickwork lies in this haphazard use of headers and stretchers. If a bond was used it was always English – alternate courses

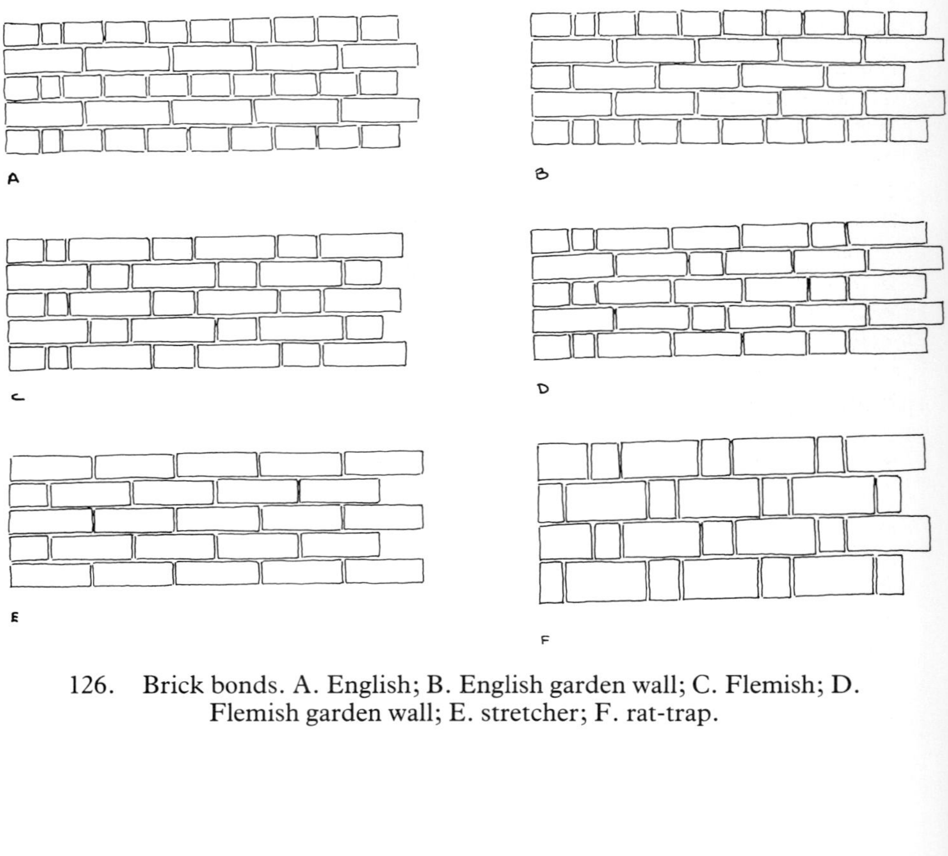

126. Brick bonds. A. English; B. English garden wall; C. Flemish; D. Flemish garden wall; E. stretcher; F. rat-trap.

of headers and stretchers (*126*). This bond remained in use throughout the fifteenth and sixteenth centuries but by the end of the seventeenth century it was gradually replaced by Flemish bond – a bond comprising alternate headers and stretchers within the same course. By the beginning of the eighteenth century this change from English to Flemish bond was almost complete. A late example of English bond is to be found at Fordwich, where a row of three cottages is dated 1736. Although less strong than English bond, as there are more straight joints, Flemish bond has two advantages: first, it was more pleasing to the eye and secondly, it used fewer faced bricks.

Flemish bond has remained the most popular bond for all walls one brick (nine inches) thick and over, but there are other variations of both English and Flemish bonds to be found. English garden-wall bond, comprising three or five courses of stretchers to one of headers, did not gain popularity in the South-east, but Flemish garden-wall bond, also known as Sussex bond, with three stretchers to each header in each course and the headers placed one above the other, was generally confined to the South-east. Another bond similar to Flemish bond in that there are alternate headers and stretchers in the same course is rat-trap bond. It differs from Flemish bond in that the bricks are laid on their edge instead of on their bed, resulting in a wall with a three-inch cavity within the thickness of the wall, with the headers tying the wall together. Obviously there was an overall saving on bricks but the general appearance is somewhat disagreeable. It is, however, to be found on the occasional cottage in Kent, generally of nineteenth-century date, for instance at Cowden and Plaxtol. Sometimes its use was restricted to the side and rear walls, the walls to the front being in Flemish bond and constructed of better bricks.

Stretcher bond, widely used today in cavity walls, is formed with rows of stretchers, the only headers being at the quoins. Consequently walls constructed of stretcher bond are only a half-brick (four and a half inches) thick and are therefore not generally used as structural walls. The use of stretcher bond was confined therefore to the brick-nogging or cladding of timber-framed buildings. Occasionally one finds a house built entirely of headers – header bond. One example is the early eighteenth-century Streetend House at Ash.

One of the advantages of using brickwork was that it was relatively easy to incorporate decorative effects. Of these, surface patterns using different-coloured bricks were the most popular (*127*); they originated in northern France in the latter part of the fifteenth century and soon afterwards spread to England. Diapered work was a popular form, being used not only on larger buildings but also on some small houses. It can be seen at Badsell Manor Farm, Capel, a house which incorporates a fragment of a late fifteenth- or sixteenth-century house,

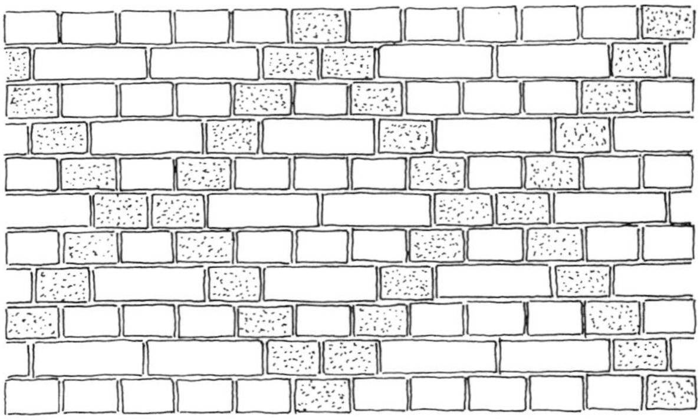

A

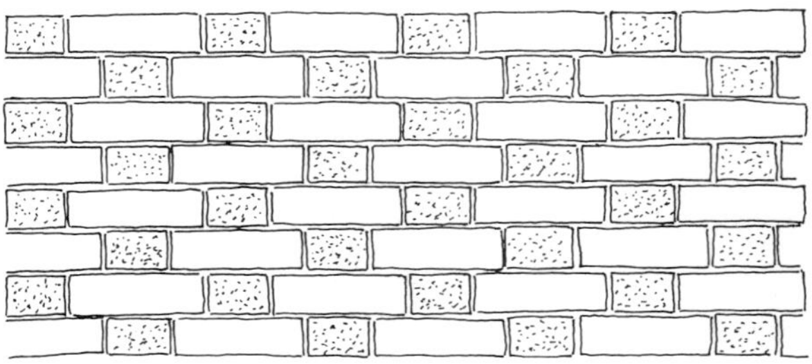

B

127. Brick patterns. A. diapered; B. chequered.

as well as at Bax Farm, Tonge, which also incorporates some diapering to the chimney stacks.

Diapered work declined after the reign of Henry VIII and with the introduction of Flemish bond an all-over chequer pattern could be easily produced; throughout the Georgian period this was the most common form of polychrome patterning. Red stretchers with purple-coloured headers were widely used in Kent, and in particular the Weald, where not only larger houses but small houses and cottages were frequently given this treatment. Bricks of different colours became a feature of eighteenth-century brick houses, especially recessed panels of contrasting bricks, perhaps below the windows as at Delbridge House, Wingham. The introduction of bricks of different colours to the main body of the work – quoins, jambs, arches or horizontal bands, two or three courses high at first-floor and on occasions at eaves level – are all features of Victorian houses.

Also a feature of Kentish brickwork, were raised decorations, which could in many cases be produced without the expense of special

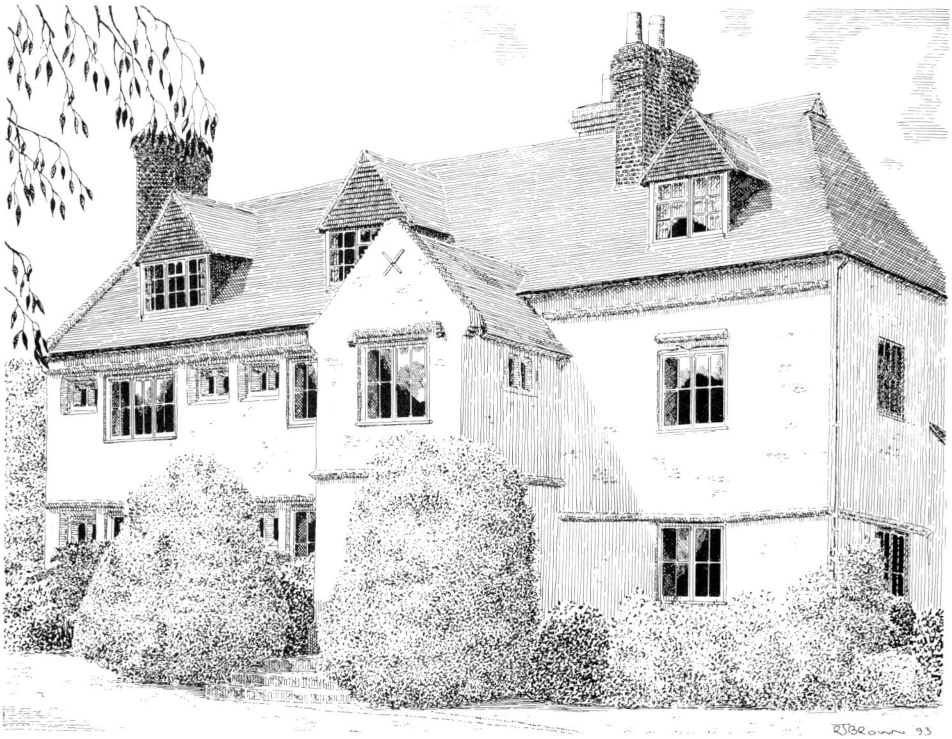

128. Snoad Street Manor, Throwley Forstal.

bricks. Projecting horizontal string courses, known as platbands, one, two or three courses high at first-floor level, are common enough from quite early times; Brunger Farm is one early example. Oversailing courses employed at the transition from wall to roof are less frequently found in Kent than in other parts of the country. These sometimes incorporated dentilations – a course of headers with alternate bricks projecting – or a dog-tooth pattern obtained by laying each brick diagonally so as to produce a serrated edge.

Decorations requiring special bricks obtained by moulding, cutting or rubbing and imitating classical forms are also a feature of Kent houses. Moulded-brick window mullions are to be found on occasions, though not generally of early date. The lucky 'Dering' window at Pluckley and Little Chart are of the nineteenth century. Some mullioned windows are older – as at Bax Farm, Tonge – and these together with the jambs are often rendered to represent stonework. One such example is Bicknor Court, Bicknor. Moulded hoodmoulds above the windows can also be found – Snoad Street

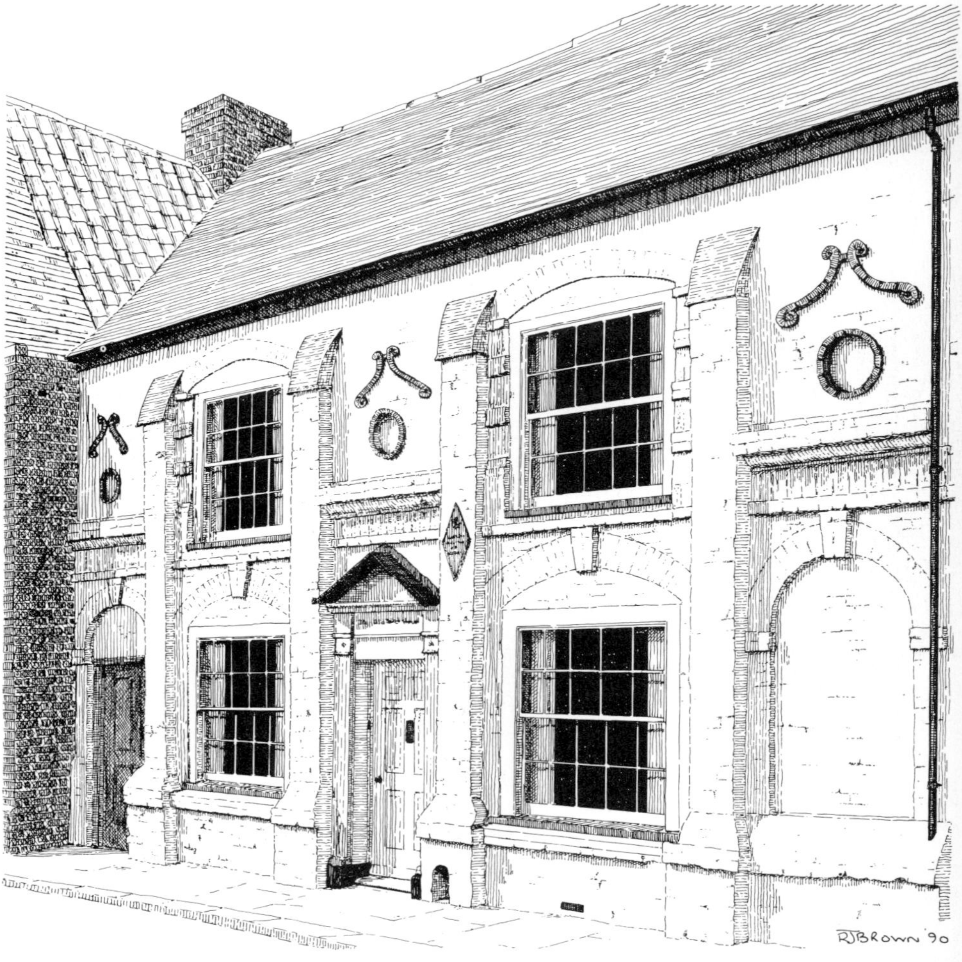

129. The Old Dutch House, Sandwich.

Manor, Throwley Forstal (*128*) and Vine Farm, Northbourne. Snoad Street Manor also has a moulded string-course as does Vicarage House, Wingham. This house (now a shop) bears a date-stone of 1698 and has many details characteristic of late seventeenth-century Kent brickwork. Above the string-course is a row of pilasters dividing the upper storey into nine bays – alternately wide and narrow with casements to the wider bays. The Old Dutch House, 5 King Street, Sandwich (*129*) is probably of similar date to Vicarage House. The house is built of so-called Dutch bricks which are much smaller than English bricks being only some 6–7 in. × 2¼–3 in × 1¼–1½ in.

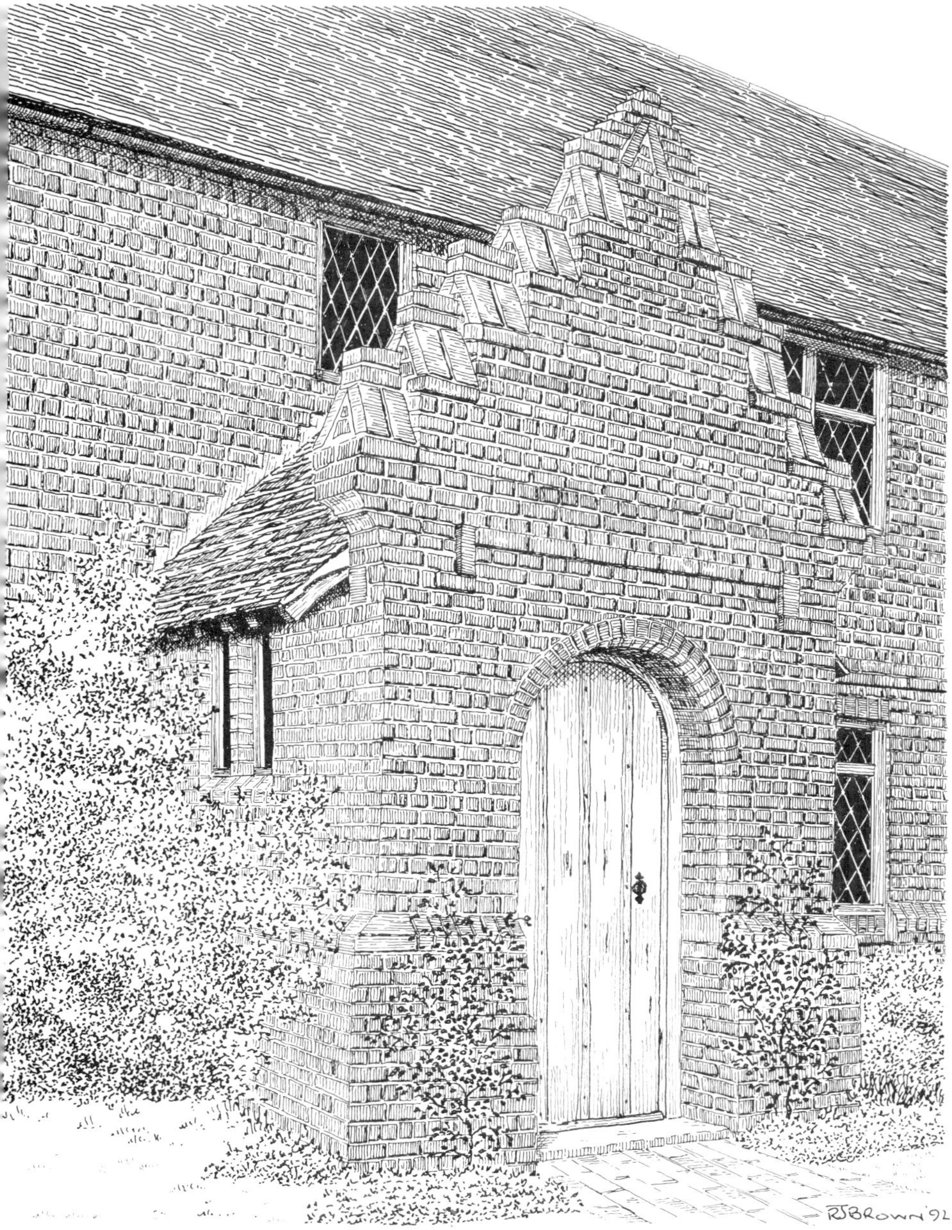

130. Porch, Brunger Farm, Tenterden.

Here, like Vicarage House, the elevation is divided into alternate narrow and wide panels by pilasters incorporating raised band courses, blank arches with key-bricks and circular panels. The use of these Dutch bricks can also be seen at 7 King Street.

Undoubtedly some of the most ornate brickwork can be seen at Swanton Farmhouse, Bredgar, built in 1719 and described by John Newman as a 'fabulous display of virtuoso brickwork on the front of what is hardly more than a cottage'. The front is of five bays built of brown brick with reddish brick enrichments; the parapet is shaped and curved to provide a third storey to the centre. The central bay projects and is curved at the top to meet the curve of the parapet. The windows to the ground and first floors have straight arches of rubbed bricks with projecting key-blocks, moulded projecting heads and projecting aprons below. The central window above the entrance door has a semicircular hood, the jambs and head rusticated. The window heads to the third storey are all semicircular.

Porches on brick houses became popular in the seventeenth century but unlike timber-framed ones which in the main were two-storey or more, brick-built ones were generally single-storey. Although many are plain with straight gables, some incorporated shaped gables of some sort. One very fine example is at Brunger Farm (*130*), with crow-stepped gables and a semicircular arch and two-light moulded-brick mullioned windows. The door is modern, for porches did not originally have doors. A similar porch can be seen at Snoad Street Manor, Throwley Forstal. The porch at Rushbourne Manor has a shaped gable while those at Old Farm House, St Peter's, Broadstairs and School Farm, Guilton, have Dutch gables. Sometimes one finds a brick porch attached to a timber-framed house; Tudor House at Chislet Forstal, a Wealden house, has a brick porch with a shaped gable.

Such was the quality of Kentish brickwork that it seldom needed painting. It was often painted in towns, especially to harmonize with the rendered timber-framed houses to be found in, say, Canterbury and Faversham; but outside towns painted brickwork is rare, the finest example being Snoad Street Manor.

Stone Houses

Stone does not play a significant part in the overall picture of post-medieval housing in Kent for although stone was plentiful enough in some areas, timber and then later brick were the two building materials preferred by most. Such was the social standing of brick that few of the country houses built in the county were built of stone. Boughton Place, Boughton Malherbe, was built of ragstone at the beginning of the post-medieval period, between 1520 and 1530, but only one wing remains of the original house which was extended in 1553 to the south; even here brick was preferred for the later extension to the north. Ragstone was again used for the construction of Boughton Monchelsea Place in 1567–75; all that now remains of this house is the east range, the south range having been largely rebuilt in around 1819. Boughton Quarries, the most prolific medieval source of ragstone, was situated at Boughton Monchelsea but even here timber was preferred for domestic housing. It was not until Victorian times that ragstone became popular again for country houses, for instance Preston Hall, Aylesford, built in around 1850. A few houses were constructed of Wealden sandstones, two of the finest being Somerhill, near Tonbridge, of early seventeenth-century date and Brasted Place, built in 1784–5. Flint, a major building material in medieval times, was regarded as too humble for use in anything other than cottages and houses. Despite its unpopularity during the eighteenth and nineteenth centuries stone, where readily available, was frequently used at the vernacular level, and of the stones used ragstone and flint were the most important.

The principal ragstone quarries were around Maidstone, at Allington and Boughton Monchelsea, but it was also quarried to the south and south-west of Wrotham at Basted and Offham and elsewhere to the east of the county at Hythe and Sandgate. It was in Maidstone and the surrounding villages, particularly westwards towards Sevenoaks, that it was most widely used in the construction of cottages and houses. Although ragstone was a hard, brittle stone it was frequently squared and laid in what is known as coursed square rubble-work, in which the walls were built in courses of varying heights but with the stones within any one course of the same height. Because of the nature of the stone, the houses are rather plain for it was not possible for such refinements as hood-moulds, mullioned windows and the like to be provided. Examples of eighteenth-century houses can be seen in a number of villages, particularly to the west of Maidstone, such as Plaxtol and St Mary's Platt. In Victorian times ragstone again became popular; now, instead of the stones being squared, they were shaped into irregular blocks bedded in position so as to show the face joint in all directions – a bond known as polygonal rubble or 'Kentish Rag'.

The use of flint in conjunction with brick quoins, jambs and lacing courses is far more widespread. It can be found in a number of villages along the edge of the North Downs from Shoreham in the West to Newnham and beyond to the east. Here the flints are often large, of irregular shape, with little attempt at coursing but along the coast where the chalk meets the sea the houses are built of 'sea-washed' flints picked no doubt from the beach and generally laid to some kind

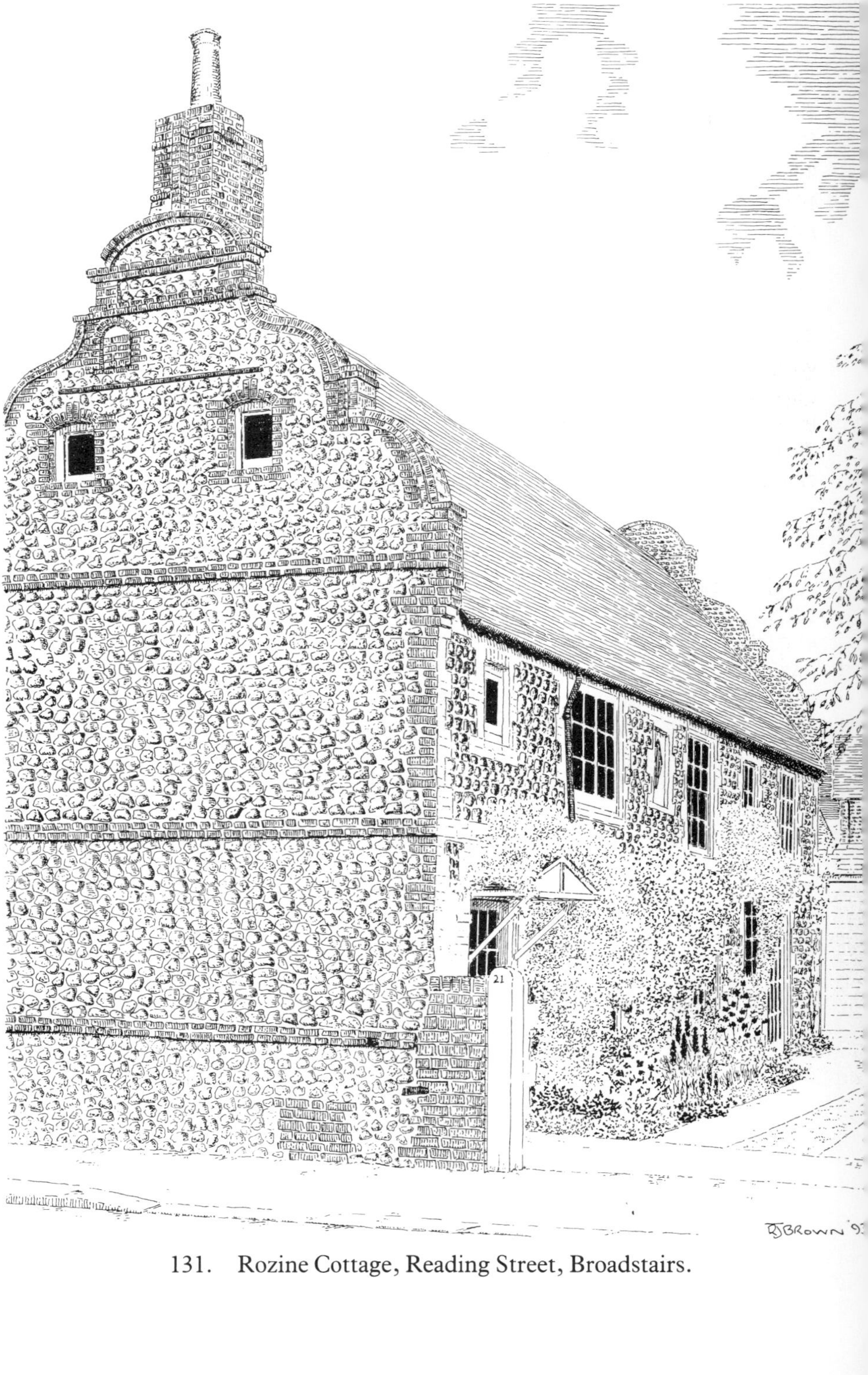

131. Rozine Cottage, Reading Street, Broadstairs.

of course. These flint-built houses can still be found in the older parts of the coastal towns of Margate, Ramsgate, Deal, Dover and Folkestone. Some of the finest can be seen at the former old villages of St Peter's and Reading Street, which still retain some of their former appearance. The most pleasing are at Reading Street, where there are three flint houses with Dutch gables all edged with brick, each with gables facing the road. Rozine Cottage (*131*) and White Swan Cottage are the best, for Stone Farm, which is dated 1710, is much extended and enlarged.

Houses of the two other building stones found in the county, Wealden sandstone and carstone, are not too common. Carstone generally consists of random rubble as can be seen at Trottiscliffe, although evidently it can be squared and 'brought to course' as in the eighteenth-century house, Stone Cottage, on the Maidstone Road at St Mary's Platt (*132*). Wealden sandstone was used by George Devey on the cottages at Penshurst and again by Lord Hardinge at Fordcombe.

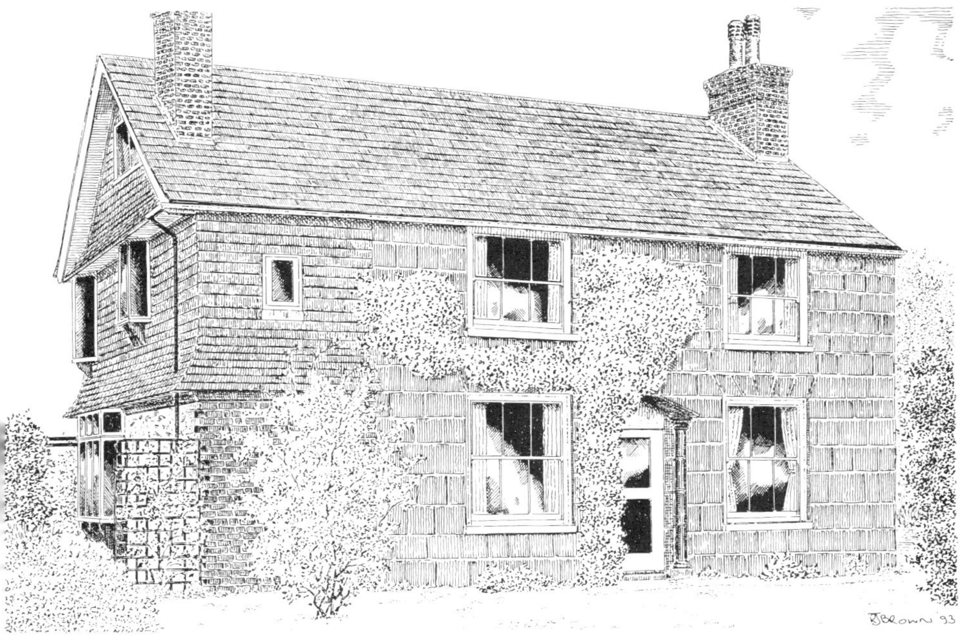

132. Stone Cottage, St Mary's Platt.

Bibliography

Archibald, J., *Kentish Architecture as Influenced by Geology* (Monastery Press, Ramsgate, 1934)
Ashenden-Bax, M., 'Copton Manor, Faversham' (*Traditional Kent Buildings*, no. 1, Kent County Council, 1980)
Ayres, James, *The Shell Book of The Home in Britain* (Faber & Faber, 1981)
Barley, M.W., *The English Farmhouse and Cottage* (Routledge & Kegan Paul, 1961)
Blomfield, R.T., 'Half-timbers in the Weald of Kent and Neighbourhood' (*The Portfolio* 18, 1887), pp. 1–7, 39–43, 45–52.
Clifton-Taylor, Alec, *The Pattern of English Building* (Batsford, 1962; new edn: Faber & Faber, 1972)
Cowper, H.S., 'Some Timber-framed Houses in the Kentish Weald' (*Archaeologia Cantiana*, 29, 1911), pp. 169–205
— 'Two Headcorn Cloth Halls' (ibid., 31, 1915) pp. 121–30
Davie, W.G., and Dawber, E.G., *Old Cottages and Farmhouses in Kent and Sussex* (Batsford, 1906)
Gravett, Kenneth, *Timber and Brick Building in Kent* (Phillimore, 1981)
Hayes, D., 'Some Hall-house Plans in East Kent' (*Traditional Kent Buildings*, no. 2, KCC, 1981)
Hewett, C.A., *English Historic Carpentry* (Phillimore, 1980)
Jessop, Frank W., *Kent History Illustrated* (KCC, 1966)
Johnston, P.M., Appendix VII – *Little Red Guide to Kent* (Methuen, 1935)
Leveson-Gower, G., 'Three Ancient Houses in the Parish of Cowden' (*Archaeologia Cantiana*, 21, 1895), pp. 103–8
Lloyd, N., *A History of the English House* (Architectural Press, 1931)
Mason, R.T., *Framed Buildings of the Weald* (Coach Publishing House Ltd., second edn 1971)
Mason, R.T., and Wood, R.H., 'Winkhurst Farm, Bough Beech' (*Archaeologia Cantiana*, 83, 1968) pp. 33–7
Melling, E., *Kentish Sources V: Some Kentish Houses* (KCC, 1965)

Mercer, E., *English Vernacular Houses* (Royal Commission on Historical Monuments, HMSO, 1975)
Mills, H.L., 'The Dating of Timber Framed Houses in the Weald' (*Archaeologia Cantiana*, 44, 1932), pp. 120–8
Newman, John, *The Buildings of England: North East and East Kent* (Penguin, 1983)
— *The Buildings of England: West Kent and the Weald* (Penguin, 1980)
Oswald, A., *Country Houses of Kent* (Country Life, 1933)
Parkin, E.W., 'The Vanishing Houses of Kent', no. 1 'Durlock Grange, Minster-in-Thanet' (*Archaeologia Cantiana*, 77, 1962), pp. 82–90; no. 8 'Lake House, Eastwell' (ibid. 83, 1968), pp. 151–62); 'Cogan House, St Peter's, Canterbury' (ibid. 85, 1970), pp. 123–38)
Quiney, Anthony, *The Traditional Buildings of England* (Thames & Hudson, 1990)
Rigold, S.E., *Temple Manor, Strood* (DOE guide book);
— 'Fourteenth-century Halls in the East Weald' (*Archaeologia Cantiana*, 82, 1967), pp. 246–56
— 'Timber-framed Buildings in Kent' (*Archaeological Journal*, 126, 1969), pp. 198–200
Scott-Robertson, W.A., 'Richard Tichbourne's House of Crippenden in Cowden' (*Archaeologia Cantiana*, 14, 1882), pp. 153–6
Swain, E.R., 'Divided and Galleried Hall-houses' (*Medieval Archaeology*, 12, 1968), pp. 127–45;
— 'A Wealden Type House in Cobham' (*Archaeologia Cantiana*, 78, 1963), pp. 173–9
— 'A Hall-house at Upper Bush, Cuxton' (ibid., 79, 1964), pp. 149–57
— 'Starkey Castle, Wouldham' (ibid., 81, 1966), pp.118–25
— 'A Timber-framed Building in Tonbridge High Street' (ibid., 78, 1963), pp. 169–73
— *William Twopeny in Kent* (Winston Publications, 1986)
Smith, J.T., 'Medieval Aisled Halls and their Derivatives' (*Archaeological Journal*, 112, 1955), pp. 76–94
— 'Timber-framed Building in England its Development and Regional Differences' (ibid., 122, 1965), pp. 133–58
Vallance, A., 'Note on an Old House in West Street, Faversham' (*Archaeologia Cantiana*, 30, 1914), pp. 215–17
— 'A Medieval Timber-framed House at Sundridge' (ibid., 37, 1925), pp. 167–75
West, T., *The Timber-framed House in England* (David & Charles, 1971)
Wood, M.E., *The English Medieval House* (Phoenix, 1965)

Place Index

Page numbers in *italics* refer to illustrations

General Index

Page numbers in *italics* refer to illustrations